Linking Architecture and Education

Sustainable Design for Learning Environments

Anne Taylor

with Katherine Enggass

Foreword by Andrew Pressman

UNIVERSITY OF NEW MEXICO PRESS | ALBUQUERQUE

14   13   12   11   10   09   1   2   3   4   5   6

LIBRARY OF CONGRESS CATALOGING-IN-PUBLICATION DATA

Taylor, Anne P.
    Linking architecture and education : sustainable design
    for learning environments / Anne Taylor with
    Katherine Enggass.
        p. cm.
    Includes bibliographical references and index.
        ISBN 978-0-8263-3407-7 (CLOTH : ALK. PAPER)
1. School facilities—Design and construction.
2. School buildings—Design and construction.
3. Sustainable design.
I. Enggass, Katherine. II. Title.
        LB3205.T39   2008
        727—dc22

                            2008021837

Book and jacket design and type
composition by Kathleen Sparkes.

This book was designed and typeset using the
Fontfont families Scala and Scala Sans OTF.

My design incorporates a Fibonacci relationship of
text size, leading, grid, column size, and page size,
in keeping with the philosophy of relationship,
harmony, and rhythm discussed in the text.

To Marion Parker, my mother,
who cultivated beauty
and filled my childhood home
with beautiful repas,
flowers, aesthetic order,
and love.

Contents

PART TWO:
USING AN ORGANIZING SYSTEM:
PLANNING FOR EDUCATIONAL ENVIRONMENTS
WITH THE KNOWING EYE

Foreword

Anne Taylor has produced the definitive guide to creating magical learning places. This book is the culmination of a lifetime of research, teaching, and design, elegantly packaged to inspire architects, teachers, school administrators, community members, and, most importantly, students of all ages.

The book is not merely a design primer. It provides readers with a logical—almost inevitable—framework for an inclusive programming and design process that has a strong philosophical underpinning. Moreover, Taylor suggests ways to translate philosophy and curriculum to an architectural program and then to actual physical design. Herein lies the brilliance of the book: Ideas about learning are given life in the buildings, furniture, and landscape architecture of school facilities. Substantive examples of innovative designs at a variety of scales are peppered throughout the volume.

Challenging the status quo—not accepting "standards" at face value—is a continuous theme in the book to promote critical thinking. This is especially salient during the early phases of a school facility project when the program is developed. The program is the design problem, the foundation for design decisions, and the tool that empowers stakeholders in helping shape the design. Taylor underscores the value of a deep and thorough examination of the issues at this predesign stage in order to produce the most responsive architecture possible. This is quite a compelling—and essential—way to launch the process of building a great facility.

Taylor identifies and describes the critical issues and features of what constitutes the best school facility design. All of these elements, including both the process and the final product, are viewed as learning opportunities for all participants. She reminds us to keep our minds open so we can actualize our full potential as contributors to the process. For seasoned school facility designers, this volume provides fresh insights and new tools. For those who are not design professionals, it provides ideas that would not have been imagined previously. For all, it underscores the big picture, which is a mandate to create a direct linkage of the physical environment with learning and curriculum.

The opportunity to be part of a team designing a school facility is a privilege. This book implores you to embrace a collaborative approach to produce the most responsive and highest-quality outcomes, especially in the context of aggressive schedules and limited budgets.

In their landmark report on the future of architecture education and practice, the late Ernest Boyer and Lee Mitgang of the Carnegie Foundation called for practitioners who are capable of creating beauty and who can communicate clearly and convincingly its value to the public. Boyer and Mitgang saw a need to elevate the importance of aesthetics in elementary and secondary education. Architects must become "more effective advocates for beauty in the structures that touch so permanently the lives of everyone in society." One of Anne Taylor's primary directives has been to develop ways to enhance public consciousness so people can become active and competent participants in helping shape a responsive built environment of genuine aesthetic quality. Taylor's concept of a building as a three-dimensional textbook speaks directly to facilitating such an aesthetic education in addition to learning and integrating subject matter across disciplines.

This book is intended to be not only a prescriptive guide for everyone involved—even tangentially—in school facility design but also to cultivate a very special kind of inquiry and discovery. Thinking outside of the box or classroom is what makes this work such a significant contribution to the literature.

Andrew Pressman,
Fellow of the American
Institute of Architects
Washington DC

Preface

The Knowing Eye

For the past forty years my mind has been on the topic of learning environments and how schools, classrooms, playgrounds, homes, museums, and parks affect children and their learning. As I look back, I see that each year of experience is layered one upon the next, much as an architect uses tracing paper during early planning to explore iterations and suggest solutions to design problems. Similar to architects, those of us trying to build new ideas move from the first quick sketch of thought to increasingly careful renderings, finally fleshing out our ideas and giving them dimension through design of models and construction of the final product. The meaning of our work is in the process as well as in the end result.

As a professor working in the University of New Mexico's School of Architecture and Planning, I have had the unique opportunity to act as a pioneer, merging the two disciplines of education and architecture in my daily thinking and experiences in the field. Architecture first impressed me as an applied learning and teaching tool through its studio design method and its interdisciplinary nature. Next, as I took students out into the world to develop their sense of perception and wonder, I saw how architecture and the physical environment were in themselves teaching tools. This, in turn, suggested a new path for the architect, who can become an educator of aesthetics, and for the teacher, who becomes a designer of the mind. This is the personal cycle of pragmatic learning that informs my book.

My colleagues and I have worked hard to link the disciplines of architecture and education through the investigation and development of architectural programming processes and the remediation of school design based on best educational practices. Our key contribution has been to help planners and their clients translate educational theory, academic goals, and developmental rights of children into architectural design criteria for schools. As a result of thoughtful and qualitative planning, educational concepts are built into the learning

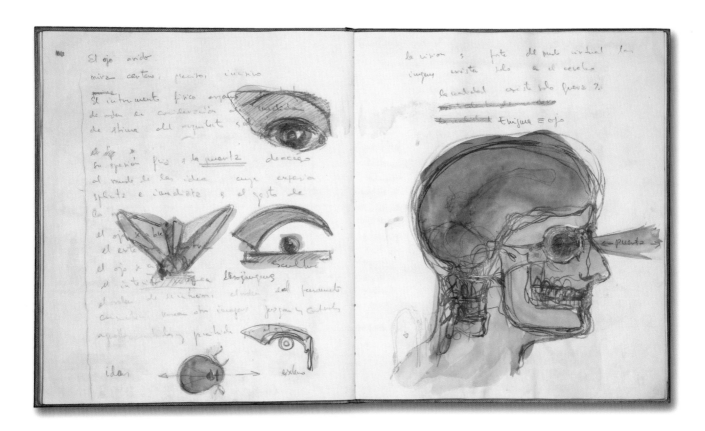

Above: The work of Santiago Calatrava fuses art, architecture, and engineering, linking the technical demands of structure with the freedom of transforming creation. These studies of the eye and eyelid are courtesy of the Santiago Calatrava Archive. © Santiago Calatrava. **Right: Cuidad de las Artes y de las Ciencias (City of Arts and Sciences), Valencia, Spain.** The design result of Calatrava's thought processes is manifested in the form of the planetarium with its elliptical, eye-shaped plan and hemispheric dome with movable ribbed covering. Similarly, our educational goals must be embedded in our learning environment designs. Santiago Calatrava, architect and engineer. Photograph © Barbara Burg and Oliver Schuh, Palladium Photodesign, http://www.palladium.de/.

environment. The environment itself and the objects within it become a teaching tool or "three-dimensional textbook."

Architects must integrate many aspects of design to create a whole and wholesome learning environment by not addressing merely a numerical program, however important the size and cost, but also a deeper program responding to the needs of the user, the community, and the Earth. Educators, in turn, must identify the current needs of the active, whole learner while expanding their own understanding of built, natural, and cultural environments as teaching and learning tools. Once we learn to "read" the environment, we become more aware. We open our eyes and minds to the wisdom and order in the universe, thus cultivating what I have come to call the "knowing eye."

Architect Robert Peters describes the knowing eye as a type of visual literacy that enables architects and artists to see and critically analyze the physical world. The special training architects receive sharpens perception, increases discernment, and helps individuals form an aesthetic sense of the environment. The knowing eye is not solely a sensory mechanism, but rather an organ of wisdom, a mind's eye that allows us to read the environment with deep understanding. I believe we are all inherently wired to seek meaning and that the knowing eye does not have to remain the province of a select few. Developing the knowing eye means temporarily suspending the past, opening ourselves to new possibilities, and choosing creativity over destructive or negative impulses. As we move beyond traditional images of schools so familiar to us that they have become essentially invisible to our critical judgment, we ultimately reach a thoughtful and deeply felt understanding of the harmonies, patterns, and underlying wholeness that could grace our learning environments.

Over the years I have been on many trips to give speeches and workshops about school facility planning across the country and overseas—from Alaska to Native American reservations in New Mexico and Arizona to sites from Connecticut to California, and on to Japan, Finland, and more. During my travels, I have not only advocated best practices for programming and design of schools, but I have also tried to listen to what children want in their schools. My colleagues and I have developed, refined, and used an Architecture and Children curriculum as a tool to encourage children and teachers to communicate their ideas effectively. Program participants express their ideas through the visual language of architecture and design during project-based studio workshops. In Stockton, California, students told us they wanted a farm and an environmental study center on the San Joaquin Delta, not just another ordinary high school. In Washington State, a fourth-grade student suggested that repetitive classrooms be converted to greenhouses, music and dance rooms, career centers, and art studios. At a summit of Native American Pueblo leaders, I learned that Pueblo communities deeply value children as the "caretakers of culture." Preservation of the culture subsequently was the primary educational goal that guided programming of spaces at the new Santa Fe Indian School (SFIS) in New Mexico. The deeper message behind these and many other stories is that children want us to make their learning real and relevant to their lives.

This book is about progressive, breakthrough thinking. It is intended to stimulate new ideas in the minds of architects, administrators, educators, school boards, and community members who want to make a positive and informed difference in the lives of all children. It presents a new model of learning for students and for professional development of educators and architects, and it illustrates how inspired design transforms and enriches our world. I am talking not only about constructing beautiful buildings for our children, but also setting those buildings in thoughtfully transformed playgrounds called "learning landscapes." Ultimately, our populations must understand, revere, and steward the environments in which they live, work, and play.

As my father, an educator, once said, one can learn how to earn a living in a very short time, but it takes a lifetime to learn how to live. My goal is to empower children to be the leaders of the future, to respect each other and the Earth, and to become happy people who have truly learned how to live. I want to give all children—including my seven grandchildren—an education that optimizes their talents, exposes them to what is real and true, gives them a sense of ethics and aesthetics, lifts their spirits, and prepares them to preserve our democratic society. I want them to become active global citizens and representatives of a culture that supports a more loving ambience than we have today. I want children to love learning, love themselves, and love each other.

A Note on the Book's Structure

The Nonlinear Approach

Though it appears to meander randomly, a stream has a logical proportional flow based on topography and mathematics. The natural geometry of a meandering river is a response to volume and silt load resulting in alternating shallows, deep pools, and cleansing currents. Tampering with these graceful bends can result in more frequent and extreme flooding.

My work has not taken a purely linear path, and I view my experiences as interconnected rather than isolated. It has been a challenge to convey this rich sense of fullness and complexity while providing an orderly narrative. I have opted for a multifaceted approach to impart my ideas and those of the many people who have enriched the journey.

The "spine" of the book is composed of a core narrative in four parts with ten chapters, a distillation of the main themes I have uncovered and the thinking that has evolved over the years. The narrative unfolds along the lines of the architectural planning and design process and concludes with a look to the future of learning environments. My work achieves continuity through the essential beliefs and thought processes in the core narrative.

To me, though, this is not enough, so I have saved space "in the margins" to share related ideas from colleagues—quotes, questions, anecdotes, sidebars, photographs, illustrations, and charts (Tools for Thought)—all designed to stimulate thinking about learning environments and to encourage an open, diversified approach to the problems school planners and designers face today. The ideas in this running visual and verbal commentary are identified and separated graphically into color coded sections.

A designer perspective section written by outside contributors appears at the end of each chapter. In addition, each major part of the book concludes with an open stewardship forum of case studies and commentary derived from many different contributors on selected topics vital to school planning. The idea of stewardship—the individual's responsibility to manage and care for life and property with proper regard for the rights of others—is at the heart of my thinking. The forum contributors provide examples of corroborating fieldwork for the ideas expressed in the book. Their writing is excerpted and consolidated from longer articles generously shared with me early in the book-writing process. I remain indebted to these contributors—colleagues, friends, and, of course, the children—who have been part of a collaborative life's work.

designer perspective

stewardship forum

tools for thought

sidebar

PART ONE

THE PHILOSOPHICAL FRAMEWORK BEHIND THE KNOWING EYE

Diamond Ranch High School, Pomona, California.
Thom Mayne, principal architect, Morphosis.
Thomas Blurock Architects. Photograph © Kim Zwarts

CHAPTER ONE

The Need for New Thinking

Overview

Architecture and education intersect when it comes time to plan, design, build, and use new learning environments. How can educators, architects, administrators, school boards, parents, and other interested community members make the most of this interaction? What can architects do to support education, and how can educators contribute to the design process? How can we create interactive environments that serve as three-dimensional textbooks for learning? What elements in the physical learning environment will compel students to be responsible for their own intellectual growth and whet their appetites for knowledge?

In discussing these questions, this book connects the two complex disciplines of architecture and education for their mutual benefit and the benefit of society. Architects and educators must understand each other and develop a shared vocabulary encompassing educational theories, developmental requirements of growing children, aesthetic theory, and practical issues of designing schools. Our children will reap the rewards of this integrated approach when they are able to occupy and use spaces designed expressly to stimulate their natural curiosity, where architecture is not a vacuous space but a learning tool.

Many valuable resources for school facility planning list educational specifications, cite codes and regulations, outline the planning process, show precedents, and give predetermined guidelines for design. Other publications written for educators explain educational philosophy, advocate current trends in instructional methods, or list content standards for schools. Rarely, however, do authors attempt to explore the connections between architectural design and learning theory. A goal of this book is to define the unique territory that can arise from a true interdisciplinary understanding of place. When architects are cognizant of educational concepts across subject matter areas, they can design spaces that support those concepts. When educators learn to view the environment as a source of meaning, they begin to use the world of physical objects as a teaching tool to help students understand the underlying laws and principles that govern our complex, precious universe.

This is a book about transcending narrow or limited views of both education and architecture. It is not merely a catalog of typical existing schools to be used as precedents for design. Instead, this book looks

Top: Architect Steven Bingler acts as an educator as he prepares schematic drawings for discussion with stakeholders during the planning process. Photograph courtesy of Anne Taylor. **Bottom:** Van Sanders, an educator not formally schooled in architecture, acts as a designer as he presents his portfolio as part of teacher professional development for teaching architecture in public schools. Note that the presentation shows the entire visual thinking process, not just the end product. Photograph courtesy of Architecture and Children and Anne Taylor.

forward and outward to design innovations that are not yet commonly found in our schools. My aim is to present examples of informed design to help people everywhere develop the knowing eye and attain a heightened state of awareness that allows them to see and "read" the interconnectedness of all things in the built, natural, and cultural environment.

The book introduces new ways of thinking about design of school facilities and encourages a deep sense of responsibility toward the betterment of society reflected in the choices educators, architects, parents, and other citizens make on behalf of children. Educators need to stop talking only to themselves and initiate a dialogue with the public about more successful ways to educate children and adults. The call for progressive leadership presents a special challenge to architects, too, not only to design effectively, but also to explicate the ideas that formulate their work.

This is an idealistic book that asks architects, educators, and parents to aim high and set new priorities. It is a book about entertaining possibilities, suspending disbelief and cynical thinking, and overcoming apathy and perceived barriers to high-quality educational environments. It is about choosing the path of creativity, generosity, and caring over that of distrust, fear, or destructiveness. An intelligently designed, attractive, ecologically responsive learning environment is not a waste of taxpayer money or an unrealistic dream, but rather a vital, concrete endorsement of our better nature and our professed concern for children and the future of the world.

Author Jonathan Kozol asserts that America can afford to pay for good schools for all children. Kozol's *The Shame of the Nation: The Restoration of Apartheid Schooling in America* (2005) documents inequities in our public schools. During a recent book tour stop in Portland, Oregon, Kozol expressed his frustration with the frequently asked question, "Can you really solve this kind of problem by throwing money at it?" Why is it, he wonders, that we "allocate funds" to the Pentagon, but we "throw money" at schools? And why, if money is not important to education, do so many affluent families pay huge sums for private education for their children?

In an interview taped for Alternative Radio in Boulder, Colorado, Kozol's response to the question of money for schools was: throw it! "I don't know a better way to put a new roof on a collapsing school. I don't know a better way to stock one of these sparse and barren libraries with a wonderful, rich, super-beautiful collection of all those lovely books . . . I don't know a better way than money to stock an inner city classroom with good computers and software. Strange as it seems, they actually make you pay money for those things."

Our Priorities

▸ In 2003, the U.S. public school average per-pupil spending for the year was $8,044. In 2008, the average education cost per child in New Mexico is $7,580, while the average U.S. cost is $8,701. New York spends $14,119 per pupil (Chan, 2008).

▸ In 2005 Kozol stated that New York City schools spent $11,700 per pupil, while in a mostly white suburb in Manhasset, expenditures per pupil were more than $22,000.

▸ The average cost of incarceration for one year in a federal prison was more than $25,000 per prisoner in 2003. According to a 2007 *Albuquerque Tribune* article, "New Mexico pays more for private prisons"—more than $70 per day per inmate ($25,550 per inmate per year) at the Guadalupe County Correctional Facility outside Santa Rosa (New Mexico Legislative Finance Committee, 2007).

▸ For the war in Iraq, the cost based on operations with some 138,000 soldiers deployed in Iraq works out to approximately $383,000 per soldier per year. A 2006 *Houston Chronicle* article stated that the cost of putting each soldier in the war zone neared $400,000 per service member (Hedges, 2006).

Beginning with Excellence and High Aspirations

Unfortunately, many architectural programs or plans for public school facilities begin with predetermined needs and minimal technical requirements such as square footage or standardized educational specifications. Programs can easily bog down with budgets or value engineering before achieving higher-order values such as support of curriculum, enduring usefulness, beauty, or sustainability. How do we create excellence and optimize tax dollars?

In my work as motivator, educator, and programming consultant, I begin the planning process for any learning environment with best practices in education so that every consequent design decision is informed by a vision of academic excellence. Similarly, I also stress the best architecture has to offer so that educators and administrators can begin to appreciate the physical learning environment as a rich resource for learning. I try to provide stakeholders in the different professions alternative thought processes that lead to new solutions about learning environments. I believe success is linked to how clearly and explicitly one can define ambitious academic and aesthetic goals early in the process. The economic bottom line is important, but it is just that: the bottom.

When we look beyond the immediate finances for individual schools, the big picture shows us that more investment in education, from preschool to college, spurs economic development. Adequate and effective funding of

Holistic Goals of Educational Facility Design	
Goal of Education: **Reaching the whole learner**	**Goal of Architecture (Vitruvius):** **Designing the whole building**
Body (physical learning)	Firmness (structure)
Mind (cognitive learning)	Commodity (function)
Spirit (emotional learning)	Delight (beauty)

education is the best way to achieve faster growth, more jobs, greater productivity, and more widely shared prosperity, thus meeting the competitive demands of our knowledge-based economy (Schweke, 2004).

Even so, tight constraints on budgets and time for school construction are commonly cited across the nation when planners try to break the "box store" mentality with high-quality design solutions for schools. A student of mine recently shared a report from a citizen school oversight committee submitted to Albuquerque Public Schools (Community Oversight Committee, 2004). The report stated that it was time to "rein in the designers" and start using prototype designs for new schools, following the speedy and cost-effective methods of Wal-Mart, Costco, McDonald's, and other economically viable institutions. The idea of a prototype has some merit, but the inspiration for that prototype reveals the poverty of our design understanding and our imaginations. This limited worldview can be frustrating for those trying to reform education and support that reform with innovative school designs and sustainable architecture. This is why it is so important that our designers share their expertise and enthusiasm with the general public.

What are our priorities? Rather than begin with narrow adequacy standards or school population ratios or projections (all important at later stages of programming), designers and planners might refer to the respective goals for excellence in the above chart. Developmental psychology gives us insight into the needs of learners across body, mind, and spirit. Vitruvius, a first-century Roman, offers us one of the enduring definitions of architecture. A parallel arises when we compare the two sets of goals.

The child is not fully educated and the building is not complete unless all goals are met, including high levels of aesthetic satisfaction and psychological comfort. From these humble parallels of body/structure, mind/function, and spirit/beauty, we begin to see the types of questions we must ask before we design educational facilities. In terms of the body, which building systems (lighting, ventilation) and spaces or forms (open, closed) will best support the physical well-being and kinesthetic learning of children? What environmental factors make children feel safe? To develop the mind, how can designed spaces best support learning about subject matter disciplines and related concepts? How does the design support the work of children of all ages and learning styles? How do spatial relationships affect instructional delivery systems or how teachers teach? And, finally, in light of spiritual learning, what is delight to a child?

Children wonder why schools can't be more like this. Students from nearby schools often visit Bart Prince's home and revel in its futuristic spaceship design. Photograph courtesy of Bart Prince, architect.

America, Wake Up!

I admit I have a difficult time understanding our complacency as a nation when it comes to the current state of our public school facilities. Perhaps many adults are in denial about or feel powerless to change the conditions in our schools. If so, consider this book a wake-up call about our need to think differently. Even in fairly wealthy suburban high schools—let alone the appalling state of many large inner-city schools—I have encountered armed police officers patrolling bleak and barren hallways, prisonlike lockable gates, chain link fences, and surveillance cameras. Are we preparing students for a democracy or a police state? I have witnessed children sitting on the cold floor like refugees and gulping their fast food lunches, then stuffing half-eaten leftovers and wrappers into overflowing garbage cans without a thought for recycling. What does this "health illiteracy" say about nutritional habits and lifelong wellness? I have seen children stuck in portables with no plumbing, a lack of storage and order, shades pulled against the natural light, students sitting at desks that are ergonomically inappropriate, possessions and clothing piled everywhere, mouse droppings among the computers, and trash, weeds, and abandoned furniture on playgrounds. In a discussion with my granddaughter about school bathrooms, she disclosed that she only goes to the bathroom at home in the morning and later in the afternoon because her school bathrooms are dark, scary, and dirty. At age ten she was knowledgeable enough to suggest windows or skylights, smart lights, smart faucets, and self-flushing toilets. "Put *that* in your book, Grandma," she said.

The obvious question is: what messages are we sending to our children?

The National Clearinghouse for Educational Facilities (NCEF) has compiled the world's largest and most widely used database about school facilities and how to create, renovate, and maintain safe, healthy, high-performance schools. A quick trip to the NCEF Web site reveals the latest evidence that the need for new or modernized school facilities in the United States is great. Statistics gathered in preparation for this book include a 1999 report by the National Center for Education Statistics (NCES, June 2000), which stated that the average public school building was forty years old. NCES estimated that it would take more than $112 billion to update U.S. school facilities, while the National Education Association (2000) estimated the full nationwide cost of modernization including new construction at about $322 billion. The American Society of Civil Engineers's 2005 report card on America's infrastructure gave schools a grade of D, citing aging, outdated, and overcrowded facilities, and estimated that 75 percent of the buildings were inadequate

Top: Hidden behind its chain link fence and isolated from the community, this school could be anywhere in the United States. Photograph courtesy of Anne Taylor.
Bottom: Gates and fences are not only for keeping strangers out; they are for locking students in. In a California junior high school (not pictured), students lobbied to keep their school unfenced, even though it is in a busy area. The argument is that openness is not just about aesthetics, but also the belief that freedom promotes responsibility in students (National Clearinghouse for Educational Facilities News, 2006). Photograph courtesy of Anne Taylor.

Top: The portable classroom is a temporary solution that all too often becomes a permanent part of a public school campus. An estimated 220,000 portables are used by U.S. public schools. They are springing up across the country due to poor urban planning, overcrowding, fast growth, and new laws governing small class size. Portables require more maintenance and upkeep than regular classrooms and are often associated with the health effects caused by indoor pollution (National Clearinghouse for Educational Facilities News, 2006). Photograph courtesy of Anne Taylor. **Bottom:** In a New Orleans classroom before the 2005 hurricanes, termites were consuming window shades and mullions. The teacher using this room told me termites were also eating the floors and that she fully expected to fall through to the basement someday. Photograph courtesy of Anne Taylor.

to meet student requirements. Making necessary repairs in these schools would cost an average of $3,800 per student. According to the Government Accounting Office (GAO), one-third of all schools should receive extensive repair or replacement, and 60 percent require repair or replacement of at least one major building feature. U.S. Department of Education figures indicate that enrollment increases are expected, too, with increases from 53 million students in 2000 to 94 million by the end of the twenty-first century.

To top it all off, a 2001 *IssueTrak* briefing online from the Council of Educational Facility Planners International (CEFPI) stated that students who attend schools in a good state of repair score five to seventeen percentile points higher on national tests than students who attend schools in poor repair. Teachers report that much of the infrastructure they work in is inadequate to meet the increasingly strict standards for academic achievement now in place at all levels of government (Schneider, 2002). It is vital to student achievement that our schools are in good repair and that money is escrowed to support ongoing maintenance.

Furthermore, these statistics do not even begin to address the urgent demand for school improvement, design, and construction worldwide in areas where war, terrorism, revolution, or natural disasters have destroyed the infrastructure of existing schools. The list of improvements for educational facilities is endless.

The call for new and renovated structures opens an opportunity for the innovative type of school facility programming and design outlined in this book. It would be a tragedy to compound the problem of inadequate facilities by repeating outmoded designs that are unsafe, do not apply the latest educational discoveries and learning theories, and fail to support sustainable, ecologically sound design. Our children deserve schools that give them a sense of dignity, worth, and freedom.

The difficulties outlined above can and must engender constructive responses rather than apathy or despair. Several valuable resources look positively on the relationship between educational planning and facility planning. CEFPI has an online design portfolio and publishes guides for sound practices in school design. *DesignShare* is an excellent online journal and library of innovative facility planning and award-winning learning environments from early childhood to university settings. It shares design research from a global forum of professional stakeholders. The George Lucas Educational Foundation (GLEF) tells stories of education through its publication, *Edutopia*, and through its Web site, with a special emphasis on creative uses of technology in education. The Academy of Neuroscience for Architecture (ANFA) has aimed recent efforts at building

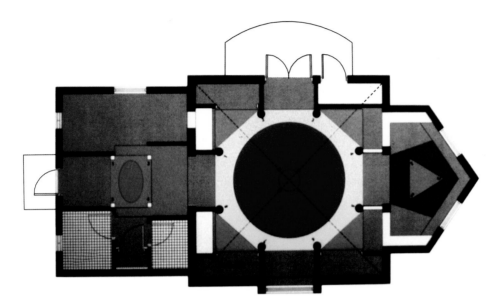

bridges between consciousness research and those who design places for human use. Among other tasks, researchers hope to uncover which architectural components trigger delight in the mind of the user and why those positive responses occur (Eberhard, 2002).

I offer as another encouraging example the reform efforts for education in New Orleans, Louisiana. Well before the storms Katrina and Rita, architect Steven Bingler of Concordia LLC and others had already begun work on a new grassroots community strategy and vision known as the New Orleans Community Trust, a partnership between schools, city government, and community dedicated to collaborative public facilities planning. Neighborhood Learning Center sites would ultimately serve for the coordination of community services as well as lifelong education (Bingler, personal communication, October 4, 2005). Another initiative from Global Green USA has advanced sustainable building design principles during rebuilding efforts in New Orleans and Louisiana (2008). It is too soon to tell what the outcome in New Orleans will be, and there are many struggles ahead, but it is important to remember that the difficulties we face are also opportunities for creating new systems that will better connect our efforts for reform.

I am encouraged that many groups now support the goals of stewardship and environmental responsibility in a movement galvanized in part by former vice president Al Gore and his urgent call for all citizens to face and respond to global warming. In terms of architecture, important contributions from Leadership in Energy and Environmental Design (LEED)

Top: The well-proportioned, two dimensional plan view for the New Orleans Prototype Pre-Kindergarten embodies primary concepts of shape, form, color, numbers, and cardinal directions. Image courtesy of Concordia LLC and Steven Bingler. **Bottom:** A well-designed floor plan at the New Orleans Prototype Pre-Kindergarten translates into three-dimensional forms that can be aesthetically pleasing without adding much cost. Neoclassical touches are seen in the graceful proportions, high ceiling, columns with capitals, and the symmetrical layout. Image courtesy of Concordia LLC and Steven Bingler. Photograph by Neil Alexander.

The Factory Model

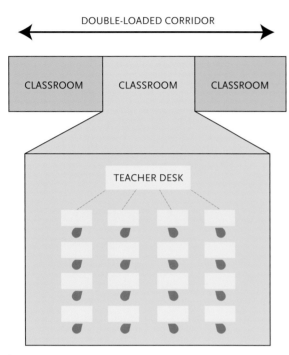

The industrial assembly line model for school design, sometimes known as the factory model, is still seen in schools being built today even though its repetitive identical classrooms and passive classroom configuration no longer provide support for learning in today's interdisciplinary, knowledge-based economy. Graphic by Atsuko Sakai.

include a "green architecture" rating system developed by the U.S. Green Building Council (2001). The LEED rating system defines standards for environmentally responsible, healthy, and profitable architecture. LEED criteria specifically for schools were launched in early 2007. The rating system offers a voluntary certification program that measures four levels of achievement in green building for schools based on the number of points awarded to a project across six categories:

- ▶ Sustainable sites
- ▶ Water efficiency
- ▶ Energy and atmosphere
- ▶ Material and resources
- ▶ Indoor environmental quality
- ▶ Innovation and design process

LEED awards a credit for using a school as a teaching tool for sustainable practice if designers provide curriculum based on the high-performance features of the building. The new LEED for Schools system (2007) must be used by those interested in certification for school projects. The LEED criteria specifically address the uniqueness of school spaces and children's health issues.

Also, in late 2005, the American Institute of Architects (AIA) Board of Directors issued a press release calling on architects to cut by 50 percent the fossil fuels used to construct and operate buildings by the year 2010 (Mazria, 2005). These important steps are intended to transform the architectural profession through a new emphasis on sustainability in building design, including schools.

EDUCATIONAL IMPLICATIONS FOR DESIGN

As education changes, so must design. Some commonly cited changes emphasize new models of teaching and learning and corresponding ways of planning for school facilities:

- ▶ Schools are moving from the old industrial factory model (the mode of education that relies on uniformity, memorization, and lecture learning) into the digital information age, with a consequent shift from the old style of "broadcast" learning to interactive learning (Tapscott, 1998, pp. 127–30).

- ▶ The old "assembly line" model no longer supports what we know about how the brain/mind learns (Caine & Caine, 1991, pp. 13–14). This means architects must provide different configurations for learning environments, more flexibility, adaptability, movable components, and future conversion to other uses (Locker & Olson, 2004).

▶ The industrial/factory model must be replaced by a model based on the way the mind develops (a process), recognizing the variety of children's developmental profiles (Greenspan, 1997, p. 314).

▶ Current educational best practices and learning theories indicate that environmentally based, project-based, hands-on, active, relevant, constructivist learning can close the achievement gap (Hoody & Lieberman, 1998). Project-based learning often requires more learning space and architectural support for different space usage and for changing student/teacher/community relationships.

▶ Students become responsible for their own learning (Brooks & Brooks, 1993, p. v), and teachers act as facilitators (Caine & Caine, 1991, p. 22).

▶ Classrooms will become more like studio workplaces (Second National Invitational Conference on Architecture and Education Report, 1992, p. 3).

▶ Special programs and individualization of the curriculum are on the rise and require a variety of specialized spaces and universal access (Preiser, 2001).

▶ Schools must become more community oriented through shared facilities, multiple use, and community participation in the planning process (Brubaker, 1998).

▶ School design changes must be driven by new technology requirements (Myers & Robertson, 2004).

▶ Budgeting must shift from short-term, up-front costs to include whole building life cycle costs and ongoing maintenance and operations (Perkins, 2001, pp. 89–90; Council of Educational Facility Planners International, 2004).

▶ Deferred maintenance harms our schools, resulting in health risks, increased cost of maintenance and replacement of equipment, and increased rates of deterioration of facilities (National Clearinghouse for Educational Statistics, 2000).

Top: Kiva form, Ray and Maria Stata Center, Massachusetts Institute of Technology. Variegated facades of brick, painted aluminum, and stainless steel lend visual interest. Vivid sculptural pieces are scattered throughout the site. Frank Gehry, architect. **Bottom: Walt Disney Concert Hall, Los Angeles.** The work of well-known architects can provide an antidote to the industrial model found in many schools. Frank Gehry, architect. Photographs courtesy of Gehry Partners, LLP.

Listening to Children

Schools I'd Like

In 1967 and again in 2001, British schoolchildren submitted their ideas to a competition titled "The School I'd Like." The ideas collected from children frequently emphasized circular schemes, suggesting a reaction against authoritarian and controlling "squareness," according to Burke and Grosvenor (2004), authors of an excerpted online article about the competition. "Within a circular school, with circular classrooms and spiral staircases, what becomes challenged is the institutional: the regulation and order of bodies in precise spaces, the processing of children as in a factory, the rehabilitation of individuals as in a prison" (p. 2). Other key design concepts participants called for included comfort, privacy, places for rest and socializing, colorful, softly textured, and inviting places—the same amenities many adults enjoy in their work and home environments (p. 3).

▶ *American School Board Journal* reports through several online articles that the business and financial approaches of education are changing. In "The New Finance," Verstegen (2002) writes that the financial system is "antiquated," designed to support a minimal education in an industrial era, and is in need of reinvention with quality for all. For example, some school districts receive eight times as much per-pupil spending as others. We must do more to equalize spending across school districts nationwide.

▶ A report from the Economic Policy Institute in Washington DC states that investment in education advances economic equality, helping poor, minority, and new immigrant learners avoid social problems stemming from poverty and inequality and become skilled, productive workers (Schweke, 2004).

▶ New thinking can lead to changes for school management. In his book *Crash Course*, Chris Whittle, CEO of Edison Schools, the largest private operator and designer of public schools, suggests that students assist in running schools, that teacher pay be doubled or tripled, that we build a "West Point" for principals, and that the U.S. government pay for research and development for schools (Whittle, 2005).

▶ Kats (2006) reports in "Greening America's Schools" that students in sustainable, high-performance school buildings experience health and learning benefits tied to green design and improved ventilation, temperature controls, good lighting, and better views. Teachers also benefit, which increases teacher retention.

▶ Global sustainability affects the entire construction market, including schools and portables. Buildings and their construction account for nearly half of all the greenhouse gas emissions and energy consumed in the United States each year (Mazria, 2004.) Students must become knowledgeable citizens who understand sustainability.

There is a call for more empirical data and corresponding medical research to support new findings in education. Researchers are slowly beginning to compile quantitative evidence about issues in school design that my colleagues and I have been researching and recommending for years. As long ago as 1969–1971, I conducted an experimental and replication study at Arizona State University on the effects of selected stimuli on the learning and behavior of four-year-olds who were placed in a learning environment that was carefully conceived based on developmental needs of children. The results demonstrated that environment does indeed affect learning and behavior (Taylor, 1971). How much more time will pass before educators and designers translate this information into positive action?

The research continues. School size, classroom size, and provision for secluded study areas (personal space) within classrooms are now shown to impact student performance (Moore & Lackney, 1992). Mark Schneider and others writing for NCEF have reviewed the emerging research on daylighting, acoustics, and other ambient quality issues that affect student achievement and learning outcomes (National Clearinghouse for Educational Facilities, 2002).

Bhutan and Gross National Happiness

Greenwald (2004) writes of the tiny country of Bhutan and its people who are trying to reconcile their Tibetan Buddhist beliefs with the materialism so rampant in the world today. Several years ago, the young monarch of the Himalayan nation stated his opinion that "gross national happiness" was more important than "gross national product" (p. 98).

I can't help but stop and reflect upon the phrase *gross national happiness*. What would America and its institutions be like if we were to adopt a similar attitude? What if we were to think more deeply about the impact our actions have on others? What kinds of school designs and curricula would encourage a shift from gross national product to gross national happiness?

The New Economics Foundation (NEF), a British think tank, has created a new measurement tool for more accurately rating nations beyond mere gross domestic product. The "happy planet index" measures the length and happiness of people's lives as well as the amount of the Earth's resources used. Under this measure, Bhutan scored thirteenth out of 178 nations ranked for the well-being of its citizens, and the United States scored 150th (New Economics Foundation, 2008).

Diamond Ranch High School, Pomona, California.
Top: The building and site are perceptually interchangeable, and there are no references to traditional typology. According to the architectural firm Morphosis, "The intention of the whole is to challenge the message sent by a society that routinely communicates its disregard for the young by educating them in cheap institutional boxes surrounded by impenetrable chain link fencing." Thom Mayne, principal architect, Morphosis. Thomas Blurock Architects. Photograph © Kim Zwarts. **Bottom:** Canyon for student interaction. Organizational cues come from the natural topography of the steeply sloped site in the jagged terrain of the Los Angeles foothills. Two rows of fragmented, interlocking forms are set tightly on either side of a long central "canyon," or street, which cuts through the face of the hillside as a geologic fault line might. Thom Mayne, principal architect, Morphosis. Thomas Blurock Architects. Photograph © Tim Hursley.

University of Virginia Professor Daniel L. Duke (1998), however, frames the problem of research in a way that resonates with the themes of this book. In *Does it Matter Where Our Children Learn?* Duke says that even though more research is needed to understand the subtleties of how environment influences learning, it is important to point out that research is not required to justify high-quality schools. "Where we choose to send our children for educational purposes ultimately is a matter of ethics and morality. . . . Even if no links between learning and facilities could be demonstrated scientifically, our society still would have a moral obligation to assign young people to safe and well-designed schools" (Duke, 1998, p. 4).

FIVE KEY POINTS

To summarize, this chapter identifies the need for new and renovated school facilities that support what we now know about how children learn. The problem is clear, but how do we tackle it? Here are the five key points I make during the course of this book, phrased as an action plan for strengthening the connection between architecture and education through school facility planning and design.

> **Point one:** Begin with aesthetics and a philosophical frame of reference.
>
> **Point two:** Develop and use a curricular organizing system to govern the school facility planning and development process.
>
> **Point three:** Design and learn from the environment as a three-dimensional textbook.
>
> **Point four:** Aim for the future.
>
> **Point five:** Foster ecological stewardship by nurturing the individual, the community, and the Earth.

The Three Qualities of an Effective School Facility

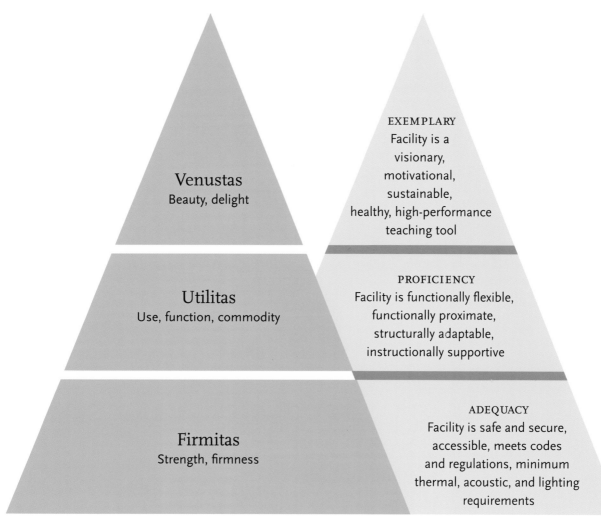

From Vitruvius to the modern school facility. Graphic courtesy of Jeffery Lackney.

The Need for New Thinking

Design themes for the 2006 DesignShare awards included small learning communities, many layers of community, sustainability and constant renewal, learning outcomes focused on the future, radical flexibility, movement and collaboration, evolving building projects, and openness and transparency.

Great Schools of the World
The Best of DesignShare

Randall Fielding, American Institute of Architects
Founder and editorial director of DesignShare.com

What do schools of the future look like? By analyzing *DesignShare*'s database of more than four hundred award-winning schools from around the world, we find many solutions already in place. Sharing these ideas is as important as inventing new ones—it is a philosophy that can sustain our planet. This essay includes an overview of key features of schools of the future, as well as summary case studies of three selected projects.

KEY FEATURES OF GREAT SCHOOLS

Schools of the future foster personalized learning, recognizing that every student is different, learns at her own schedule, and follows her own interest. They provide nooks, niches, and small spaces for individuals who need "cave" time for reflection.

Great schools organize into small learning communities, fostering collaboration, social interaction, and caring. More space is devoted to learning and less to nonacademic spaces. Corridors are often replaced with wider multiuse common areas. Common areas have flexible furnishings, allowing students and teachers to rearrange elements for different types of real-world, project-based learning.

Great schools rely on daylighting and use electric lighting artfully. They use water from the roof and showers to water the grounds and photovoltaic panels for entry canopies. They draw on thermal mass for heating and cooling. Walls are not limited to right angles, reducing reverberation and improving sound quality.

Great schools connect fluidly to the outside, recognizing nature and the city as extensions of the learning space. Schools of the future may involve less building but operate as larger entities because they are interdependent with community and business organizations and share facilities; this is an ecologically sustainable model at its broadest level, involving systems of relationships that expand the boundaries between living, learning, and working.

CASE STUDY

The Learning Street

Peel Education and Tertiary and Further Education Campus, Mandurah, Australia

HASSELL and Jones Coulter Young, Architects in Association

This project, built on the site of an existing Tertiary and Further Education (TAFE) campus, is unique because its master plan combines senior school students, TAFE, and university students on a single campus. The facility allows adult education and vocational training to occur within one facility, therefore helping boost student retention rates and promote the concept of lifelong learning.

A "learning street" consolidates display, exhibition, gathering, and learning spaces within one large covered area, offering easy access to learning and specialist facilities. Group discussion rooms are scattered throughout the campus in an effort to limit the "ownership" of individual curriculum areas. A "ubiquitous technology" approach to general, flexible, and group learning areas is designed to address short- and long-term needs as well as the future sharing of facilities, which is likely to occur as a result of the evolving relationship between the different educational providers.

An indigenous center within the TAFE facilities promotes cross-cultural interaction. The grounds include tracts of natural vegetation as part of an indigenous natural heritage zone within the horticultural studies area. Connection to the outside community is also part of the campus's master plan. Zones are set aside for development by businesses that want to partner with the school and create ties to the vocational study and workshop facilities.

Peel Education and TAFE Campus, Mandurah, Australia. Learning Street. HASSELL and Jones Coulter Young, Architects in Association. Photograph by the Architects.

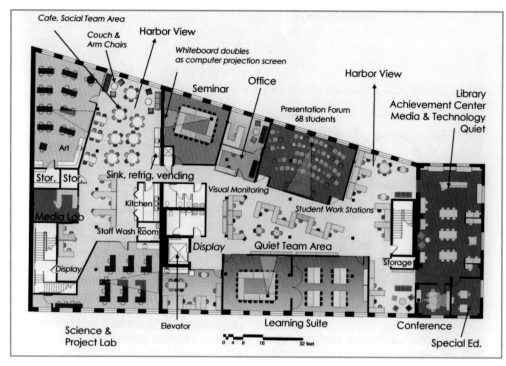

Harbor City International School, Duluth, Minnesota. Plan view. Randall Fielding, design architect. Fielding Nair International with Scalzo Architects.

CASE STUDY

The Death of the Classroom

Harbor City International School, Duluth, Minnesota

Fielding Nair International and Scalzo Architects

A handful of teachers with a passion for working with teenagers launched this school from their living rooms. The two-hundred-student public charter school occupies the third floor of an 1860 industrial building in Duluth's central business district. The school provides a small, learner-directed community that encourages investigative learning and global citizenship and nurtures a sense of belonging; its purpose is to graduate students who are knowledgeable, discerning, passionate, creative, and reflective.

The floor plan is notable in that there are no corridors and no conventional classrooms, yet it is a far cry from the warehouselike open classrooms of the 1970s. A wide variety of spaces of different sizes with varied finishes and furnishings supports a rhythm of daily activities personalized for each student. Individual student workstations allow for

reflective "cave" time, and clusters of couches support social interaction and collaboration. A wireless network allows students to work on laptops and access their personal portfolios anywhere in the school. A presentation forum supports both digital and oral faculty and student presentations.

Harbor City has developed programming at a variety of local businesses and community partners, including a nearby broadcasting station, newspaper office, YMCA, library, and aquarium. A lead student with a cell phone takes groups of students to the lakefront for soccer. The prescriptive limits of classrooms—rectilinear spaces where twenty-five students learn the same thing at the same time—are irrelevant at Harbor city. The design reflects the death of classrooms and the rise of learner-centered schools that respond to the needs of each individual student.

Earth Connections

Kvernhuset Junior High School, Fredrikstad, Norway

Pir II Arkitektkontor AS, Architect

Nature and learning are in love at Kvernhuset Junior High. The organic, varied furniture arrangements in the "home base" learning wings remind one of leaves on a forest floor—orderly and random at the same time. Isn't this how we live and learn? Inside and out, the rocky, forested site is expressed but never dominated.

To approach the site, you cross a bridge over a pond. Three individual learning wings/houses are cut into the natural rock on the ground floor, and forty-ton granite blocks that were removed during excavation were later built back into the main hall. Holes drilled directly into the rock provide geothermal energy. Students helped remove the bark from trees harvested on the site for use as columns in the main hall to hold up a concrete roof covered with living green sod. The same trees are part of the facade, juxtaposed with concrete to appear modern and primitive at the same time, like a pagan dance on a twenty-first-century stage.

Each of the learning houses has a different color and theme, all relating to the site: The yellow wing focuses on energy—active and passive use of solar energy, solar cells, and monitoring of energy use. The blue wing focuses on water, collecting water from the roof, water-saving utilities in toilets, and wash-basins. The green wing focuses on ecological cycles, including the growth and recycling of materials, vegetables, and plants inside and outside.

The "home base" learning areas offer a wide variety of furniture configurations supported by movable walls and a flexible structure. Workbenches with sinks and informal large and small meeting places enhanced by light filtered through the surrounding forest permit individual, group, and project-based learning to occur fluidly.

El Papalote Children's Museum, Mexico City.
Legorreta + Legorreta Architects. Photograph by Lourdes Legorreta.

CHAPTER TWO

The Learning Environment

The Order of the Universe

It is hard not to view our world as chaotic and random, especially because we often find ourselves removed from natural settings, surrounded by material proliferation, and living in discord with other people and our deepest personal wishes. It should be possible to establish a sense of harmony within ourselves and with the world, as there exists an order to the universe that we can capture and enjoy. Philosophers, mathematicians, physicists, ecologists, religious leaders, musicians, and Native people who have uncovered the interconnectedness of all things through their observations of natural phenomena have described this sense of pattern or underlying meaning in different ways. Perhaps architects, with their understanding of proportion and geometry, can help us discover our own interpretations of cosmic harmonies and balance.

Many authors and designers have used their visual acuity and design ability to reveal formal relationships and connections in the world around us through text and illustration. Three such authors who demonstrate the principle of the knowing eye are Gyorgy Doczi, an architect; Michael S. Schneider, an educator and author interested in nature's numerical language and the designed environment; and Fritjof Capra, author and founder of the Center for Ecoliteracy in California.

Doczi coined the word *dinergy* to describe the dynamic way in which all things grow or are made by a union of complementary opposites. Through a series of diagrams in *The Power of Limits*, his book on proportional harmonies and logarithmic principles in nature and art, he illustrates commonalities in form and proportion across disciplines. Doczi begins his book with the example of a daisy's center, which is formed by a pattern of spirals moving in opposite directions. The pattern is in turn analyzed and then related to the Fibonacci number series and the Golden Mean. The Golden Mean is a long-revered, aesthetically pleasing proportional relationship between two unequal parts of a whole. The small part stands in the same proportion to the large part as the large part stands to the whole. Similar proportions are found in musical harmonies, crafts, the physical proportions of species of all kinds, including humans, and—of course—in architecture (Doczi, 1981).

Michael S. Schneider's understanding of pattern and connection is equally intriguing. Schneider has authored several activity books and *A Beginner's Guide to Constructing the Universe: The Mathematical Archetypes of Nature, Art, and Science* (1995). With the use of a geometer's compass, straightedge, and pencil, Schneider takes the reader on an interdisciplinary journey of the numbers one through ten. He urges readers to create their own geometric constructions as they follow the text, to "construct the patterns that construct the universe" (p. xxxii). In his conclusion he suggests we have the opportunity to restructure education and teach children differently, "to expose them to harmony in all its forms, in nature, music, art, and

Using a compass to construct the Golden Rectangle. A Golden Rectangle is one whose sides are in phi ratio. Phi (Φ) expresses not a number so much as a relationship:

$$\frac{\text{Whole}}{\text{Large part}} = \frac{\text{Large part}}{\text{Small part}} = \Phi \text{ (phi)}$$

The small, newly added rectangle is itself a Golden Rectangle. Adapted from Michael S. Schneider's *A Beginner's Guide to Constructing the Universe* (1995). Used by permission of the author.

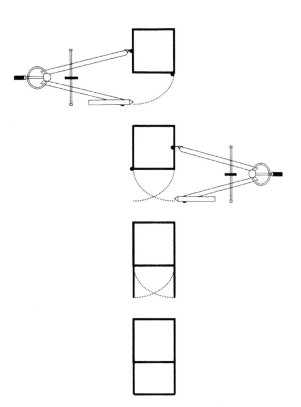

mathematical beauty. Perhaps children steeped in harmony will become generations of adults who will strive to achieve harmony in the world" (p. 350).

Fritjof Capra, physicist and systems theorist, is well known for his many lucid books translating a complex scientific understanding of living systems into an accessible philosophy of deep ecology that encompasses social systems and has direct applications to education. Capra identifies six principles of ecology, principles of organization common to all living systems:

- ▶ Networks
- ▶ Cycles
- ▶ Solar energy
- ▶ Partnership
- ▶ Diversity
- ▶ Dynamic balance (Capra, 2002, p. 231)

Capra writes that we must understand these principles and experience them in nature in order to develop a true sense of place. Consider for a moment that every school playground, if not covered in asphalt, could be designed instead to highlight these principles. Capra's Center for Ecoliteracy Web site describes the mental shift to systems thinking: from the parts to the whole, from objects to relationships, from quantity to quality, and from hierarchies to networks. This constitutes a movement from a linear to a nonlinear worldview, which could also be adopted for our designs of school spaces and their spatial relationships. For more insights, I urge everyone to read Capra's *The Web of Life*, in which he summarizes emerging understandings of life tied to complexity theory and nonlinear dynamics. In short, Capra shows that in order to sustain life, the design principles underlying our social institutions must be consistent with the defining characteristics of life and the organizational patterns in nature.

Capra further explores the implications of complexity in philosophical attempts to explain the mind/brain relationship. Although difficult to summarize in the space I have here, the Santiago Theory of Cognition Capra outlines in *The Hidden Connections* (2002) characterizes the mind not as a thing but as a process. The mind/process operates within the structure called the brain. Capra writes, "At all levels of life, beginning with the simplest cell, mind and matter, process and structure, are inseparably connected" (p. 38).

I build on the work of Doczi, Schneider, Capra, and others who have described the magnificent order in the universe through careful observations derived from merging aesthetics and philosophy. These writings demonstrate the great potential of environmental teaching and learning. Why not build harmonious connections, patterns, and ideas into the very structure of our educational facilities? Why not use Capra's principles of ecology as design criteria for the ambience of schools?

The Soul and Spirit of Our Schools

I remember the philosophy of a friend of mine, a Hopi jeweler. This magnificent artist would always inlay the inside of his rings with turquoise. I asked him why, because no one ever saw the inside of a ring, especially when someone was wearing it. He replied that his art is much like a person, with the beauty of the soul or spirit on the inside as well as the more visible external beauty. The jeweler's aesthetic philosophy expresses my hope for our schools: carefully crafted architecture throughout, revealing an inner, as well as an outer, beauty.

In my work in the Southwest I have often encountered and admired the belief systems and symbolism of Native American culture. It is not my intent to romanticize the experiences of ancient cultures—mere survival for these cultures has been difficult—but I do feel we have much to learn from people who are attuned to natural rhythms and a sense of the sacred in our world. We have lost a sense of awe, wonder, and connection to the Earth, which has caused many of us to lead impoverished lives. The story of the rings is about seeing holistically, and applied to education, it is about creating school designs that bring a multifaceted depth to the indoor and outdoor spaces in which we learn.

The Holistic Worldview

Shannon Horst of Holistic Management International writes that holism, a term coined by Jan Smuts in 1926, is the concept that all natural things, including humans, function in wholes and processes. There are no parts and the whole is not the same as the sum of its parts. As a simple example, there is nothing obvious in hydrogen or oxygen that, considered in parts, would lead you to know anything about a substance called water.

Horst (2006) explains that in the latter part of the twentieth century, Allan Savory, a wildlife biologist, determined that the challenges facing the human species are all—except the random earthquake or tornado—a result of a linear worldview and the decision-making and actions that follow from that worldview. In essence, Horst writes, the cumulative effect of millions

Creating a Golden Spiral from a Golden Rectangle. The coils of the Golden Spiral grow in a pattern often found in nature in seashells, rams' horns, some plants, human ears and fists, whirlpools, and galaxies. Perhaps our schools can be designed to reflect these and other archetypical forms that resonate with deep historical, mathematical, and natural meanings. Adapted from Michael S. Schneider's *A Beginner's Guide to Constructing the Universe* (1995). Used by permission of the author.

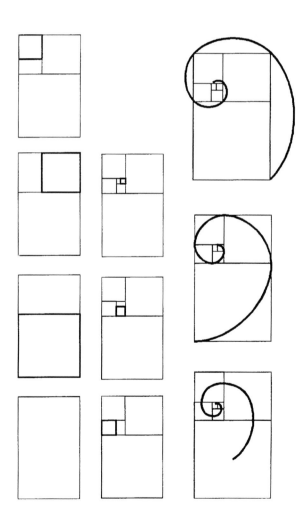

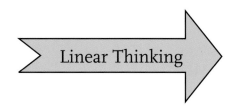

of decisions made without considering equally the social, financial, and biological ramifications is the destruction of the very "earth ship" that sustains human life. The same attitudes continue to affect how we plan and manage our educational facilities.

My own view of the environment begins with three basic principles tied to holistic thought:

The first principle is that people are a part of, not apart from, the environment. During our brief history on Earth, human beings have struggled to conquer nature and dominate the globe through our inventions and technology. We Western thinkers in particular have evolved the mistaken view that we are apart from or superior to our environment. The attitudes expressed in this book are in direct contrast to this dominating view of the universe. We are a part of, not apart from, the built, natural, and cultural environment. We must be aware of the consequences of our actions and act responsibly. Our actions come full circle and affect each of us.

The second principle is that the order of the universe is holistic and interdisciplinary. Seeking to make sense of a complex world, early Western thinkers artificially divided the principles and laws of the universe into distinct, discrete subject matter disciplines that are usually taught independently and in isolation (i.e., math, sciences, language arts, philosophy, social studies, the arts, and physical education). However, the true content of the universe is holistic, or, in educational terms, integrated and interdisciplinary.

The third principle is that the concept of a split in the body/mind/spirit continuum is in contrast to our natural capacities as whole learners. The human mind naturally functions in a holistic, integrated way, which influences how we learn. Western thought has created a false dichotomy between body and mind that favors and elevates the intellect at the expense of emotional, practical, or creative learning in schools. Instead, we learn as whole people across body, mind, and spirit. We learn in multiple ways through our bodily senses and movement, through the mind's problem solving and idea formation abilities, and through our spiritual respect for cultural plurality, emotions, and self-expression. Psychologist and educational theorist Howard Gardner's theory of multiple intelligences explores the many ways in which people process information. Gardner has identified eight intelligences or competencies ranging from verbal/linguistic to kinesthetic, musical, naturalistic, and more. (Please see chapter 5 and stewardship forum 2 for more on learning processes.)

How can architecture support the three main principles that for me define environment? We look for an architecture that

▶ Establishes a sense of belonging versus isolation from the world

▶ Supports an instructional delivery system that connects disciplines in real-world, holistic contexts

▶ Engages the whole learner by reaching highest levels of satisfaction in the users of schools, across levels of health and safety (body), functionality (mind), and psychological comfort and aesthetic satisfaction (spirit)

Defining the Learning Environment: A Silent Curriculum

The environment consists of one's physical surroundings—the natural, built, and cultural world and the objects within it. The learning environment traditionally refers to school facilities and settings within schools. Unfortunately, the physical environment of the school has become nearly invisible to teachers and families in part because it is so familiar; basic school design has not changed in one hundred years (Brubaker, 1998). There is also that convenient myth that a good teacher can teach anywhere or a willing student can learn anywhere. We avoid dealing with problems in school facilities by marveling at how adaptable humans are and by making do with poor conditions, but as architect Gaylaird Christopher asks, why shouldn't we design quality environments to enhance the performance of dedicated individuals? I add to Christopher's question: why are we ignoring the powerful effect of the physical learning environment on teaching? The environment is indeed a "silent curriculum" that can provide positive (or negative) learning experiences.

The key is to view the physical environment and its ambient quality as active and indispensable parts of the learning process. This is done in part by responding to the human experience of school facility users. The objects and buildings we design are not merely things to own, but also represent human ideas, actions, and beliefs. Good designs serve people well. Remember that we human beings exist as a part of—and not apart from—the environment. Regardless of what we are doing, we are always operating in a physical context in space (Caine & Caine, 1991, p. 40). Our natural ability to learn is directly linked to constant interaction with the environment. This integrated definition of learning and environment is crucial to educational facilities design. We cannot help but interact with our environment. Thus, the quality of the environment affects the quality of learning.

A general pattern emerges when we contrast architectural and educational views of environment. Architects are accustomed to assessing and evaluating physical spaces and gain considerable practice in spatial thinking. As designers, architects are well versed in the world of matter, of objects and things. They see and analyze the physical world and its relationships with the knowing eye. They know how to accurately translate percepts and concepts into functional objects and buildings that symbolize ideas and provide aesthetic ambiance.

Many educators, however, have little training in space planning. Educators often refer to "environment" in abstract, behavioral, psychological, or connotative terms while neglecting the implications of the physical condition of the space, which may be cluttered or overcrowded. The prevalent focus in teacher professional development is on how to establish and manage the emotional quality or mood of a place, rather than the actual physical form a space takes. Teacher textbooks provide advice on how to set an orderly tone through classroom management techniques, or they define strategies that create an atmosphere conducive to learning, a supportive atmosphere that encourages risk-taking, for example. Training implies to teachers that their management skills can overcome deficiencies in the physical learning environment. It also places teachers at the center of learning as managers and directors, rather than empowering

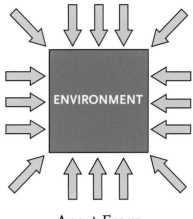

Apart From

A Part Of

students to interact with the physical environment to create their own meanings.

Educators and architects often operate as if in a vacuum, thereby failing to ensure that both the physical place and the interpretation of that place contribute to the creation of a complete learning environment. This is mirrored in many of the visual images I have collected over the years. I have beautiful photographs of children deeply engaged in project-based work, but often working in drab settings that are an impediment to their activities. I also have photographs gathered from architects of beautiful facilities devoid of children. It is my intent to somehow merge these images into a new aesthetic for schools. There is a relationship between the individual learner and the physical environment that cannot be ignored when we think about how to design high-quality learning environments.

In his classic book on urban design, *The Image of the City*, Kevin Lynch states that forming mental maps or images is the "strategic link" between the individual and his or her exterior environment. Although he is talking about cities, many of his observations apply naturally to schools and the learning process:

> Environmental images are the result of a two-way process between the observer and his environment. The environment suggests distinctions and relations, and the observer—with great adaptability and in the light of his own purposes—selects, organizes, and endows with meaning what he sees. The image so developed now limits and emphasizes what is seen, while the image itself is being tested against the filtered perceptual input in a constant interacting process (Lynch, 1993, p. 6).

For Lynch, the key to his urban study is the "imageability" or "legibility" of the built environment—a physical clarity that inspires clear and useful images or representations in the viewer (p. 9). A muddled setting creates a weak or confused image.

Lynch's description of the constant interaction of the individual with his or her environment is strikingly similar to descriptions of learning in cognitive neuroscience, and how learning actually alters the structure of the brain, the engine of the mind. In *The Growth of the Mind* (1997), Stanley Greenspan laments the long-held dichotomy of reason and emotion in our educational system. He states that new research into infant development, neuroscience, and clinical work reveals links between affects and intellect, and that early experiences influence the structure of the brain itself (p. 7). "In general, during the formative years there is a sensitive interaction between genetic proclivities and environmental experience. Experience

Cluttered Classroom. Although we may be accustomed to the visual cacophony of the typical American classroom (alternately known as the supermarket effect), such images can be confusing to young learners. Embedded figure and figure ground discrimination are visual perceptual skills essential to learning how to read. The careful use of negative space to offset positive forms can bring clarity and focus to the learning space. Photograph courtesy of Anne Taylor.

appears to adapt the infant's biology to his or her environment" (p. 8). How does it affect the development of a child's mind to spend years in dull, impersonal, poorly designed environments that support passive learning?

In *Making Connections: Teaching and the Human Brain*, Caine and Caine (1991) suggest that school reform be extrapolated from a growing scientific understanding of how the brain/mind works. The authors offer a metaphor of the brain as a city, a complex and busy place with its many physical structures, simultaneous functions, interconnections, and dependencies (p. 26). Learning does not occur in a vacuum or by rote memorization, but through a process of immersion in complex, rich environments (p. 5). Caine and Caine report that brain-based education involves orchestrated immersion, relaxed alertness, and active processing.

According to Caine and Caine, orchestrated immersion means providing rich opportunities for students to make connections between new material and what is already known. It is characterized by instructional methods such as theme teaching, reality-based project learning, multisensory learning, storytelling, teamwork, and using the physical and perceptual context as "packaging" for learning (pp. 107–15).

Relaxed alertness is the desired mental state for learning. Because children absorb the entire context when learning, if the atmosphere is intimidating, the brain/mind of the learner may downshift or basically shut down. The ideal learning state combines a sense of safety with student self-motivation and high challenge (pp. 126–33).

The third component identified by Caine and Caine is active processing, or the work of learning. Some methods of active processing are reflection, analysis, contemplation, questioning, using personal analogies, and performance assessment techniques (pp. 146–57).

Caine and Caine and other authors mentioned here provide a valuable description of the *qualities* of the optimal mental state and ideal academic situation for learning. Administrators and other educators may wish to refer to these same authors, or they may research, compile, and articulate their own approaches to education, which can then be translated into architectural forms during the process of planning educational facilities.

In terms of architecture, how might we characterize qualities of legibility, the importance of the thinking and feeling individual interacting within a rich environment, and the functioning of the brain/mind? How can our environments reflect the order in the universe? How can we build these concepts into the very structure of our schools?

Top: In contrast to the cluttered classroom, endless double-loaded corridors are often barren, dim, and prisonlike. Photograph courtesy of Anne Taylor.
Bottom: Curators link architecture and kinesthetic learning in Japan through clear, well-designed signage. Children learn how to experience firsthand the forces at work in a truss structure. Image courtesy of the Architecture and Children Network in Japan.

Children's Museums as Models
for Learning Environments

Educational theorist Howard Gardner has suggested that a good design model to keep in mind for the learning environment of the future is the children's museum, where teaching and learning are based on the ideas of apprenticeship and learning by doing. In a children's museum children are encouraged to touch and explore interesting objects in a carefully arranged setting scaled to young people. It is a highly legible place that embodies the attributes provided by Caine and Caine and celebrates childhood developmental rights as advocated by Greenspan. Effective museums are no longer storehouses of artifacts in display cases, but rather places where active participation abounds.

The legibility of museum-quality display, with negative space around signage, increases clarity and supports perceptual skills essential for learning how to read. Professional-quality display offers an alternative to the visual cacophony so prevalent in classrooms today—the "visual bombardment of images" Patricia Tarr (2001) described in her article about the aesthetics of the typical North American early childhood environment. Tarr accurately observes that the stereotypical and cartoonlike art, greeting card and crafts shop aesthetics, as well as skewed display and profusion of color talk down to young children.

Teens also benefit from legible, authentic learning environments that encourage autonomy and offer choice. In many hands-on museums such as Albuquerque's ¡explora!, which is featured later in this book, an open questioning strategy in museum signage and by docents facilitates learning without dictating answers.

Perhaps museum exhibit curators and designers could offer their expertise as part of teacher professional development or as part of the architectural programming workshop process. Every school should have a museum for realia (objects used to relate learning to real life) based on curricular themes and design related to science, math, local industry, arts, and culture. Older children can learn curatorial skills by designing settings with adequate display and storage. In any case, the larger goal is to encourage the development of learning environments with an overall aesthetic that respects and empowers children, is based on the real world, and reinforces the concept of hands-on problem solving.

El Papalote Children's Museum, Mexico City. Top: Interior. Open floor space and interactive displays enable self-selection and can be translated to school environments. Photograph by Lourdes Legorreta. **Center:** Toddler area. Playful climbing structures, portholes, and mirrored environments support early learning. Photograph by Luis Mendez, courtesy of AD Mexico. **Bottom:** External learning spaces. Multisensory environments extend to the outdoor learning environment, which is also an effective tool for school design. The playful exterior makes use of traditional Mexican glazed tiles, basic geometric forms, stone, and water. Photograph by Lourdes Legorreta. All designs by Legorreta + Legorreta Architects.

Anchorage Museum of History and Art. Top: Phantasmagoria Structure Gallery. Different capitals show the classical architectural orders, and signage is incorporated into the exhibit at the child's scale. Tensile structures in the foreground are operable by children. Suspended Nerf balls give the spatial feel of basic architectural spaces, such as domed interiors, and teach geometry concepts. A point becomes a line, a line becomes a shape, and a shape becomes a three-dimensional architectural form. **Bottom:** Exhibit entry. A vaulted hallway teaches architectural elements while acting as a children's art gallery in a major museum setting. You can teach anything to anybody if you bring it to the appropriate level of understanding. Anne Taylor, curator. George Vlastos, architect. Assistance from the Anchorage, Alaska, AIA chapter. Photographs © Paul Warchol.

Strong National Museum of Play

Rochester, New York

CHAINTREUIL JENSEN STARK ARCHITECTS

The cultural history of play illuminates the American experience, according to the mission statement of the Strong National Museum of Play. Play reveals our feelings, the way we construct our identities, and how we represent the world's challenges. Knowing how we play, what games we choose, and with whom we play traces connections between individual and group, group and culture, and self and society. Play has a critical role in learning, creativity, and discovery. In addition to offering a venue for playfulness, the museum collects, preserves, and researches historic objects, toys, artifacts, manuscripts, and other materials that reflect and document the importance of play, and it is also home to the National Toy Hall of Fame.

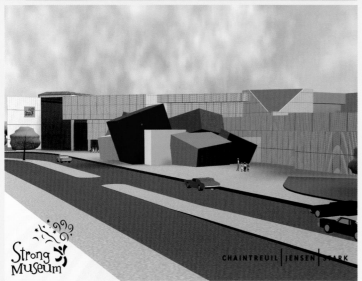

Top: Exterior rendering of the completed museum expansion. I implore school designers to take cues from imaginative museum designs. Here, the "caterpillar atrium" (in yellow) emerges from the center of the building. At right, perched like a giant butterfly, is the Dancing Wings Butterfly Garden, a rain forest environment with some eight hundred butterflies and a "chrysalis case" for viewing emerging butterflies. **Center:** Exterior rendering of the caterpillar atrium. **Bottom:** Exterior rendering of the brightly colored "Field of Play" exhibit, a hands-on lab with creative play stations. Courtesy of Strong National Museum of Play. Renderings by Chaintreuil Jensen Stark Architects.

The Informed Environment

An informed sense of environment merges learning goals with architectural design. My definition of the learning environment is this: **The ideal educational environment is a carefully designed physical location composed of natural, built, and cultural parts that work together to accommodate active learning across body, mind, and spirit.** The *qualities* of the environment must be clearly outlined by educators to provide a guideline or "academic blueprint" for architects and community members as they contemplate school facilities design. But what do these qualities mean in terms of walls, windows, doors, ceilings, and other physical design elements of schools? To define the physical manifestations of abstract concepts is the architect's province. Architects have a reciprocal responsibility to teach the public that the design of physical spaces matters, and that they can be read and translated by our minds into ideas for better understanding of our relationship with the environment.

Mutual understanding calls for a new model of professional development that blurs the boundaries between architecture and education by teaching educational theory to future school architects and teaching design and space planning to educators and their students. In cross-listed courses I have offered in school facility planning, I find that it takes all semester for students in different disciplines to begin to understand each other's language and vocabulary, but once they do, their capacity to communicate gains depth and sophistication.

Our Choices Have Meaning

The choices we make for our educational environments say something about our values as a nation.

> In the sense that design and construction involve many people, architecture is a collective pursuit. But buildings are also the product of society as a whole—of legislation, of wealth, of technology, of custom, and, above all, of cultural traditions. That is why buildings are so precious: they tell us who and what we are—or wish to be—not only as individuals but as a community (Rybczynski, 1992, p. 191).

Chapter 3 turns to philosophy as the discipline that helps us define who we wish to be and allows us to set a course for meaning in our endeavors. This meaning can be incorporated into the structures we build, including school facilities.

The Informed Learning Environment:
Combining Architecture and Education to
Create a Model for School Design

	Natural	Built	Cultural
Architecture	School playgrounds function as community parks, nature trails, fitness courses, gardens, zoos, habitats, weather stations, and places for experimentation.	Building systems teach through structural clarity, or "legibility" as described by Lynch (1993). The curriculum determines the design of the architecture.	Design ideas from cultural institutions are applied to school design: museums, galleries, plazas, health centers, local ethnicity and style, the workplace, families, and homes.
Education	Students perform site analysis as curriculum for understanding the life zone: climate, topography, plant and animal life, water, etc. Landscape architecture of the playground becomes a learning tool. Students collect data for the architect.	Behind every object is an idea or concept. Learners "read" physical objects and translate them into ideas. Thus, architecture is pedagogy. Physical elements or manifestations in the environment act as visual cues or prompts for learning.	The studio learning model, experiential learning, and design education are borrowed from architecture as teaching tools. The entire process of learning is visually and verbally documented. Performance is critiqued and assessed in more depth than testing alone can provide.
Summary of Unifying Concept	**The Learning Landscape**	**The Three-Dimensional Textbook**	**The Design Studio for Project-Based Learning**

It is never too soon to learn that we are a part of the global village. Gilbert Choy writes of a preschool program that combines a philosophy for the future with aesthetic sensibility by offering students bilingual, bicultural experiences in English and Chinese in a beautiful architectural setting that honors children.

Preparing Children for the Challenges of Global Citizenship

3e International Kindergarten

Gilbert Choy

CEO of SunWah Education Foundation

The story of 3e International Kindergarten begins at the legendary Skywalker Ranch in the countryside of Marin County, near San Francisco. On January 28, 2005, a group of top educators with backgrounds in human development and psychology, early childhood education, educational psychology, second language acquisition, gifted education and talent development, and school facility planning gathered at the ranch for a four-day closed-door session hosted by GLEF. Together they formed a dream team for the creation of a cutting-edge curriculum framework for a pilot preschool to be launched in Beijing, China.

The impetus for our preschool came from the following four realizations:

1. **Sociocultural influences:** Globalization has become a fact of life. Most of us have already become daily cultural travelers and cross-cultural workers. This trend will only continue. And by the time children entering school today enter the workforce in fifteen to twenty years, the world will be even more integrated, becoming a global village. For these children to live competently in such a society where multiple cultures interact all the time, they need to develop what we call sociocultural fluencies, which include the ability to move across cultures fluidly and the capacity for not only understanding and tolerating differences, but also participating and living productively in different cultures.

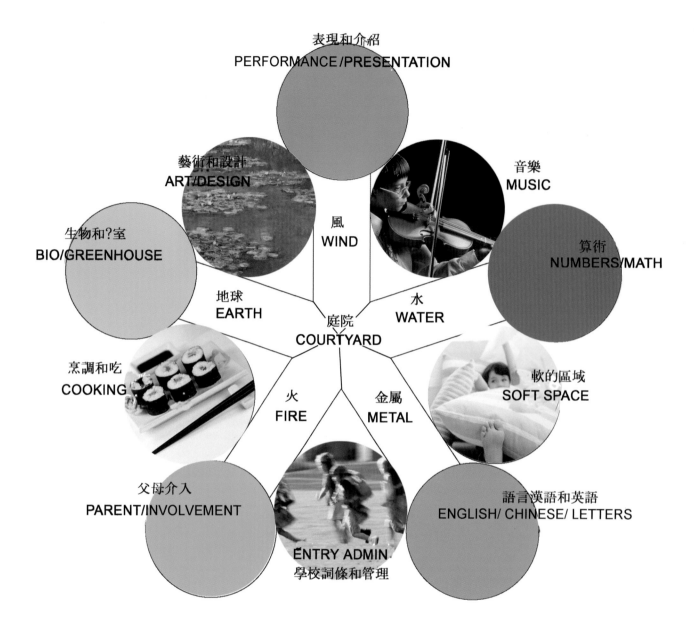

表現和介紹
PERFORMANCE/PRESENTATION

音樂
MUSIC

藝術和設計
ART/DESIGN

算術
NUMBERS/MATH

生物和?室
BIO/GREENHOUSE

風
WIND

地球
EARTH

水
WATER

庭院
COURTYARD

軟的區域
SOFT SPACE

烹調和吃
COOKING

火
FIRE

金屬
METAL

父母介入
PARENT/INVOLVEMENT

語言漢語和英語
ENGLISH/ CHINESE/ LETTERS

ENTRY ADMIN
學校詞條和管理

3e International Kindergarten, Beijing.
A Schematic image of the program for the
kindergarten features the interaction of spaces
converging on a central courtyard, with planning
elements based on Chinese symbolic elements
of earth, wind, water, metal, and fire. Courtesy
of University of New Mexico student program
participants Andrew Aulgur, Yoshi Blizman,
Jerod Bosey, Adrienne Horton, James Olsen,
Alyssa Shapkoff, Laine Sparks, Holly Spellman,
and Scott Stoll.

A.

The 3e International Kindergarten, Bejing.
Clockwise from top: A. The entry dome with waterfall (shown here) has curvilinear elements, with a view to landscaped greenery, an oasis in the city. The lobby also includes an aquarium (not pictured) and an echo ceiling. Photograph by Ken Dirkin. **B.** Dance studio. Elliptical windows in doors, operable windows reflected in mirrors. Photograph by Ken Dirkin. **C.** Hallway with seating, plants, curvilinear soffits, and semitransparent fenestration to classroom spaces. Photograph by Ken Dirkin. **D.** Designers make opportunities for aesthetic choices at all levels, from provisioning of the smallest manipulatives to the architecture of the entire school. Learning at 3e is recorded throughout the school year by a photo documentarian. Photograph by Rose Carbajal-Lemly. **E.** Cloud ceiling tile in entry. Photograph by Ken Dirkin. All © 3e International Kindergarten.

B.

C.

E.

D.

2. **East-West pedagogies:** Effective learning requires combining the best practices of Eastern and Western pedagogies. There are distinct advantages and disadvantages in the Western and Eastern philosophies of education. Both casual observations and serious empirical research have revealed that the Western educational approach, which celebrates individualism, has been effective in producing citizens who are more likely to be creative and critical thinkers, but loses on imparting to students a systematic understanding of knowledge. The Eastern educational approach, which is knowledge centered and group oriented, seems to be more effective in producing students who are cooperative and well disciplined with a firm grasp of systematic knowledge of subject matter, but fails in creativity and flexibility. These differences go deeper than curriculum or teaching styles and are the result of culture. Hence, the best way to combine them for maximum benefit is to give children both experiences in a comprehensive and holistic way.

3. **Importance of physical environment:** Physical design of schools and how content is delivered are keys for successful learning. Anne Taylor was instrumental in translating our revolutionary curriculum into a rich, new architectural design that supports optimal early learning. As soon as you step foot onto the grounds of 3e International Kindergarten, you'll notice its innovative learning environment. From the echo ceiling in the entrance foyer to our botanical garden behind the school, every aspect of the environment has been developed to stimulate and inspire inquiring minds. As Winston Churchill once said, "We shape our buildings and thereafter our buildings shape us."

4. **Bicultural fluency:** Authentic bilingual and bicultural experiences are the only effective way to help students develop not only cultural fluency, but also more sophisticated cognitive abilities. Many existing bilingual programs simply teach a second or foreign language in a vacuum without offering authentic cultural experiences. By being exposed to different cultures (i.e., different ways of doing things or thinking) a child becomes more likely to question, investigate, and explore culturally conventional beliefs. By being bicultural rather than simply bilingual, a person grows up with the advantage of becoming more reflective, broad-minded, and scientifically minded.

Although our school emphasizes two different cultures, the curriculum is united under seven universal themes that we believe all human beings need to understand. These themes—for example, **change** and **system**—are embedded in both sides of the school and are in essence the seeds of creative and scientific thinking.

The following were participants in the cooperative effort:

▶ Anne Taylor, professor, University of New Mexico

▶ Beijing Foreign Language University

▶ Beijing Normal University

▶ The Exploratorium Museum, San Francisco

▶ The George Lucas Educational Foundation

▶ George Vlastos, architect and illustrator

▶ Gilbert Choy, CEO of SunWah Education Foundation

▶ Michigan State University (MSU) College of Education

▶ Norman Crowe, visiting professor from
the University of Notre Dame

▶ Sesame Workshop, New York

▶ Simon Lee and David Lustick, critics and reviewers

▶ Students from the spring 2005 school facility planning
class at the University of New Mexico's School of
Architecture and Planning (Andrew Aulgur, Yoshi Blizman,
Jerod Bosey, Adrienne Horton, James Olsen, Alyssa
Shapkoff, Laine Sparks, Holly Spellman, Scott Stoll)

▶ SunWah Corporation

▶ Yong Zhao, MSU

George Pearl Hall,
School of Architecture and Planning,
University of New Mexico.
Antoine Predock Architect PC.
Photograph by Kirk Gittings.

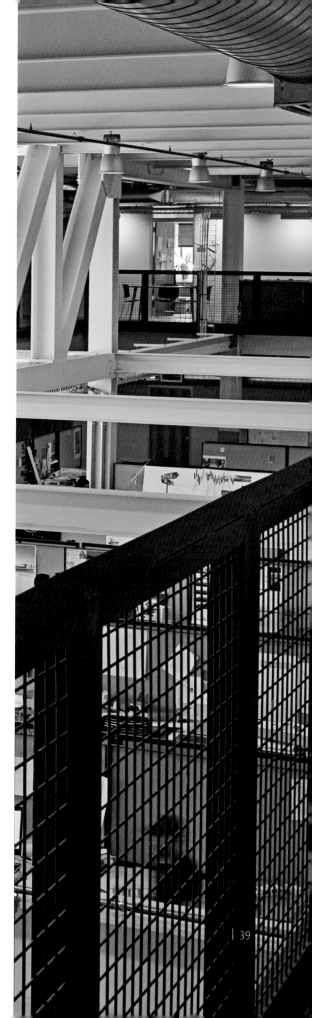

CHAPTER THREE

Philosophy 101

Introduction: Patterns for Operating in the World of Education and Design

Philosophies are logical patterns of human thought created to make sense of our world and uncover its large truths.

Entrenched beliefs do influence current practice. The study of philosophy helps us understand that there are multiple ways of viewing the world and that our long-held assumptions may not always define what we want for the future. The discussion here is designed to help all participants in the design and education process think deeply about the meaning behind educational facilities, their purpose, and how they can be better planned, built, and used to educate our children. My teaching of graduate architecture students always begins in this way, with philosophy and student articulation of their own belief systems for living, thinking, and designing. The goal is to base one's life work on a sound philosophical framework.

THE PURPOSE: BEGIN WITH VALUES

I have multiple reasons for including a chapter on philosophical approaches to education and architecture. The first is a concern that ethics and respect are sometimes left out of the equation when we assess our schools and student attitudes toward faculty, staff, and each other. Are schools places that nourish our values and encourage empathetic behaviors? As designers, examining our moral imperatives leaves an impression on the entire design process. Awareness of philosophy serves additional purposes:

▶ To provide a model for professional development that exposes architects and educators to different ways of thinking so they can understand and reflect on implications for current practices in both fields

▶ To define on what basis curriculum, instruction, and design decisions are made, and to make sure those decisions are made in the full light of consciousness and awareness

- To help architects and educators identify their own philosophical leanings and motivations so they can formulate clear goals when designing schools and curriculum, and in doing so provide leadership for optimizing expenditures on schools

- To provide a link between the professions in different categories of thought

- To help educators promote ecological literacy (ecoliteracy) by suggesting an overarching philosophy that merges the strengths of each major philosophy with a new attitude toward sustainability or ecologically responsive green design, a philosophy for our time and the future

Spirituality and Schools

Largely missing from the upcoming discussion are religious philosophies in America and a deeper discussion of Eastern philosophy, Islamic values, Native American religious practices, and much more. Religious doctrine does not have a place in American public schools, but this does not mean that student spirituality should be left out of the curriculum. In *The Soul of Education*, Rachael Kessler (2000) cites her desire to reduce violence and honor spiritual yearnings in young people as motivations for examining the spiritual dimension in the classroom (p. xiii). She describes seven "gateways to the soul" in education, including the needs for connection, meaning, creativity, solitude, and more (p. 17). Architects could respond with designs exploring the metaphorical implications of gateways based on Kessler's categories. Perhaps architects can provide for an ecumenical place on a school campus where the outward din of group behavior can be silenced in exchange for inward inspiration.

My point is that good schools cannot be designed and operated in a conceptual vacuum, and that the environmental learning I advocate demands a new, integrated philosophy or curriculum for professionals. Knowing where ideas originate and on what basis creative decisions are made requires the deep understanding of the philosophy from which one's life springs.

The Big Questions

All philosophies address fundamental questions:

- What is real? (Ontology)

- What is true? (Epistemology)

- What is moral or good? (Axiology, ethics)

- What is beautiful? (Axiology, aesthetics)

Different philosophical beliefs respond to these core questions in different ways (Morris, 1961; Ornstein & Levine, 2003).

Four Philosophies or Ways of Thinking

We begin with a simplified look at four major schools of Western thought:

▶ Idealism: The world of mind and ideas

▶ Realism: The world of matter

▶ Experimentalism: The world of human experience

▶ Existentialism: The world of the self, choice, and responsibility

Is truth universal, or does it change with circumstances? Idealists and realists in education share a belief in a preexisting, absolute, or universal realm of knowledge. They differ on the exact content of that realm, but they agree it exists objectively, independent of the learner. This is a subject matter or *content-centered* approach to truth in education. Experimentalist and existentialist educators, on the other hand, take a *student-centered* view based on subjective experience, self-discovery, problem solving, and choice. They agree that meaning is relative, constructed by people, and characterized by change and growth. Education for experimentalists and existentialists is open-ended and interpreted, rather than predetermined and set, as idealists and realists suggest.

These two camps—content-centered and student-centered—still provoke debate. Some educators believe that there is a core body of knowledge that all students must know and that the skills and heritage of a culture must be transmitted directly to students. Other theorists argue that students learn best when they are engaged in learning through their own interests while solving problems through a hands-on process of interacting with the environment. Many current educational discussions and theories can be distilled to this basic philosophical split in defining the true purpose of education (Ornstein & Levine, 2003, p. 122).

How does each philosophy regard the physical learning environment? Briefly, idealists seek to transcend environment to reveal absolute ideas behind objects. Realists discover the essence of environment and its patterns through nature, the senses, and reason. Experimentalists experience the environment, testing and retesting phenomena through problem solving and the scientific method, while individual existentialists choose which meanings to attribute to the world through intuition, self-awareness, choice, and responsibility.

In the following section, I examine each philosophy across the basic questions of reality, truth, ethics, and aesthetics, concluding with my own thoughts on the future direction of philosophy in making choices about school facilities design. A final chart at the end of the chapter (see pg. 51) brings all the philosophies together for a comprehensive picture of belief systems in education and architecture. The chart is intended as a take-off point for discussions about philosophy and the meaning we bring to our endeavors. The designer perspective for chapter 3 complements the philosophical discussion by outlining differing beliefs and motivations of architects, with examples of famous structures that embody the various approaches.

IDEALISM

Plato's *Republic* introduced us to the genuinely real world as the intangible realm of absolute, perfect, unchanging ideas. Reality is mental, psychical or spiritual, universal, and eternal. The world we perceive through our senses is but an imperfect impression of the ultimate reality, as in Plato's *Allegory of the Cave*, a narrative in which prisoners chained in a cave see only shadows and hear only echoes of the true reality that exists outside the cave. Some idealists use the idea of macrocosm and microcosm to explain the relationship of the ultimate mind to the human mind.

Implications for education today include an emphasis on the Western world's great thinkers in history and literature, traditional curriculum, and the great questions of humanity and the liberal arts. The ideal learner is the well-rounded academic "student of letters."

Architects might reveal idealistic thinking in their use of classic precedents and an interest in architectural continuity, historical preservation, or reapplication of classic notions of form, proportion, scale, and balance. Idealist architects embrace our heritage, as reflected in the work of architect Benjamin Latrobe, who designed the U.S. Capitol in the Greek Revival style.

REALISM

Aristotle gave us the philosophy of realism. Reality is fixed and regular, based on natural law, and composed of matter and form. The world is a mechanism; it is a world of things in motion. Meaning is located right here in the physical world we inhabit, not in other worlds of abstract ideas. Reality is objective. There is a pervasive order in the universe, a cosmic pattern that operates independently of man but can be perceived and known through the senses and rationality. Natural law can by extension imply social orders, economic laws, and inalienable human rights. Balance in nature sets a precedent for balance in behavior.

The study of science and nature helps us uncover the operation of the universe, just as study of social systems and laws helps us understand and analyze society.

The realist architect prizes nature and rationality. Organic systems, physics, structure, mechanical systems, construction, and materials and their properties are all part of the realist's focus. Because all architecture deals with matter, all architects employ realistic philosophy in some manner if they want their structures to remain standing. This does not mean, however, that the philosophy behind all architecture must be realistic or the aim purely rational.

EXPERIMENTALISM

Immediate, concrete experience is the true source of knowledge, as educator John Dewey postulated. Experimentalists or pragmatists believe education's purpose is to "promote optimum human growth" (Ornstein & Levine, 2003, p. 105). Reality is a changing, moving process. Humans are part of the world, and their knowing is a transaction and interaction with that world.

Renovating and Retrofitting Buffalo Public Schools

The Buffalo School District and LPCiminelli, Inc. are involved in a $1 billion capital project to reconstruct Buffalo's aging schools. Paul McDonnell, AIA, associate architect for Buffalo Public Schools, writes of the obvious deficiencies found in the older school buildings such as inadequate power for computers and electronics, old plumbing, drafty windows, leaky roofs, inefficient heating systems, and worn finishes. Even so, the inherent quality, durability, and classic beauty of the architecture shone through. Masonry construction, large windows, terrazzo floors, rich woodwork, and in some cases, elaborate auditoriums, made the structures ideal candidates for renovation (McDonnell, 2006).

Above: PS 97 Harvey Austin School, Buffalo, New York. Adaptive reuse. The building was reconfigured by Cannon Design while maintaining the full height of the renovated factory windows and the north-facing sawtooth skylights. From the outside one can't tell that the function has changed. This is a good example of contemporary historic conservation. Photograph by Biff Henrich/ Keystone Film Productions, Inc. Photograph courtesy of Cannon Design.

PS 67 Discovery Elementary School in Buffalo, New York.
Above: The school maintains its historic exterior integrity while housing a fabric tensile roof over the former central open space. A glass elevator with four red columns is housed under the structure, and all conduit, plumbing, wiring, and sprinkler systems are left exposed so children can learn about building systems.
Right: Interior fenestration. Functions of the central courtyard include the library, cafeteria, technology shop, and a central circulation path. Hamilton Houston Lownie Architects, LLC. Photographs by James Lai.

George Pearl Hall, School of Architecture and Planning, University of New Mexico.
The learning environment exemplifies the experimentalist's emphasis on inquiry, problem solving, and students in charge of their own learning. Antoine Predock Architect PC. Photograph by Kirk Gittings.

Experimentalism's emphasis is on connectedness and relativity rather than inherent truths or essences. No truth lasts forever. The chief means of knowing is through critical inquiry, problem solving, experimentation, and the scientific method, which has five basic steps:

- Perceiving a felt difficulty

- Forming the hypothesis

- Collecting data

- Synthesizing and analyzing information

- Testing solutions to refute or accept the hypothesis

This spirit of inquiry is central to the experimentalist's concept of education. The freedom to think and question encourages democratic outlook, participation, and shared experience (Ornstein & Levine, 2003, p. 149).

Architects also value and use this problem-solving process. The design process is similar to the scientific method but has been adapted to relate visual language, creative design, and human need into the art of architecture. A pattern of testing ideas, responding to criticism, and then retesting is inherent in the design studio method by which architects are trained. In a way, most architects are experimentalists. Experimentalists value what works—what supports the hypothesis—in education and architecture.

EXISTENTIALISM

The phrase "existence precedes essence" is often associated with existentialism (Angeles, 1992, p. 99). This means that humans are born into existence before they know what their essential nature is. They are alienated and on their own. Existential freedom lies in individual choice and commitment, and the individual determines what is true. Truth is therefore subjective. The existentialist operates with a dual awareness of perception and consciousness, with the primary interest being the authentic self. Moral values do not exist outside of human consciousness.

The Philosophical Framework

Philosophers Soren Kierkegaard and Martin Heidegger, as well as authors Jean-Paul Sartre and Albert Camus, are pioneers in this system of thought. Humanistic psychologist Abraham Maslow (1968) describes the fully functioning adult in existential terms as attaining the highest levels of full humanness or "self-actualization." People experiencing peak moments are closest to their real selves (p. 103). Maslow states that education's goal is to encourage learners to develop a profound awareness in which polarities, dichotomies, and conflicts are fused, transcended, or resolved (Maslow, 1968, pp. 91–95, 211).

The arts, self-expression, and discussion of the big ideas that make up the human condition—life, death, and love—dominate existentialist curricula.

In architecture, the deconstructivist movement (think of the work of architect Frank Gehry, among others) has much in common with existentialism in that it follows no precedent and dismantles contemporary and traditional design to create something entirely individual and new. Aesthetics, emergent creativity, and responsible personal choice influence the existential architect.

PHILOSOPHY AS A KEY TO SELF-ASSESSMENT

How does one use philosophy to evaluate oneself? A Native American friend of mine once told me about the Aztec definition of a teacher. They felt that a good teacher was one who held up a mirror to the student. This mirror had a small hole through which the teacher could view the student's visage, and as the student grew and achieved selected goals, the teacher would adjust, coach the student, and have the student see his or her reflection. It seems that this technique was a forerunner of what we now call self-assessment. I love the idea of giving all the power of learning to the student. More schools should adopt these higher-level living skills and the process of self-reflection.

In a recent review of the mission statement of Wells College (from which I graduated and on whose board of trustees I am a member), I noted that the goals for students include high-level values. Students can certainly major in any subject matter discipline, but the main mission of the college is to produce graduates who possess qualities so needed in today's world with its global challenges. This taxonomy includes the ability to

▶ Think critically

▶ Reason wisely

▶ Act humanely

▶ Cultivate meaningful lives

▶ Appreciate complexity

▶ Embrace new ways of knowing

▶ Be creative

▶ Respond ethically

▶ Pursue lifelong learning, and

▶ Share privileges of education with others.

Evaluating the achievement of those higher-order skills would have to be an ongoing, individual process of self-reflection (with help from the faculty) for the formation of a compassionate adult who is fully functioning and self-actualized. (Wells College, 2007–2008).

SUMMARY: PHILOSOPHY AND IMPLICATIONS FOR THE LEARNER

To summarize, how do the four philosophies we have examined define a successful learner? Idealists perceive learners to be receptors of all the best culture and history have to offer. Learners are expected to be coherent thinkers across a broad range of topics. The realist learner is a good observer and analyst. He or she understands and can rationally explain patterns in nature and society by distilling sensory information into facts and formulas. Experimentalists consider

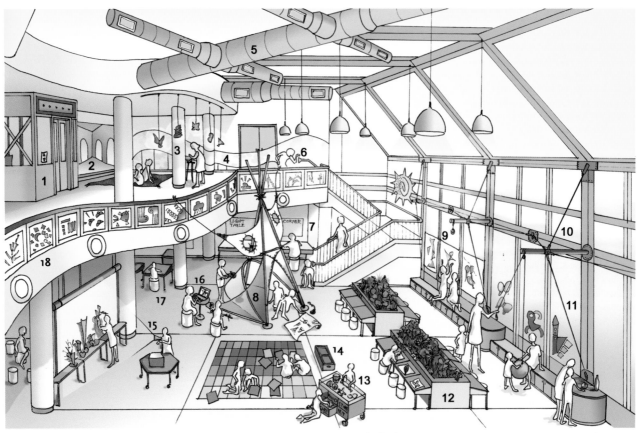

1. See-through elevator
2. Presentation area
3. Lighting design exhibit
4. Materials & textures exhibit
5. HVAC exhibit
6. Walkie-talkie handrail
7. Light table area
8. Large model area
9. Tracing area
10. Structure exhibit
11. Light & shadow area
12. Nature observation area
13. Mobile interactive cart
14. Pattern design area
15. Shadow theater
16. Laptops everywhere
17. Design studio area
18. Exhibition wall

Design of the learning environment supports multiple learning styles, philosophies, and student-centered learning. Meaning resides in student interaction with rich multisensory stimuli in spaces designed for individual, small group, and large group learning. The responsibility for learning is on the student, with facilitation by the teacher or coach. Illustration by Atsuko Sakai.

students to be successful problem solvers interacting with the environment and testing solutions. They are participants in the democratic process. The existentialist student takes responsibility for and thinks deeply about his or her choices and fully develops a creative sense of self. He or she is concerned with identity.

There are useful contributions to be found in each of these philosophies, especially when they are viewed as generalized approaches to life rather than precise doctrines. We need them all. I would include in my eclectic philosophy for schools of tomorrow:

- ▸ Appreciating the richness of the world of ideas and symbols (idealism)

- ▸ Taking a delight in the workings of the natural world and its interdisciplinary patterns, and using nature as a designer (realism)

- ▸ Constructing meaning through hands-on experimentation (experimentalism)

- ▸ Accepting responsibility for ourselves and the consequences of our actions in an increasingly chaotic and endangered world (existentialism)

The Question of Ambiguity and Change

There is, however, a territory we have not covered in our discussion of past philosophies, especially when we consider what schools of the future should be and what future citizenship might entail. How do we live with paradox and ambiguity? How do we make better connections and see the big picture? In readings about global and ecological patterns—networks, cycles, flow, and sustainability—we begin to see implications for a new, dynamic, "living," and ecologically responsive approach to the design of schools and the educational systems they house.

Taking a Step into the Future:
Ecoism, Ecosophy, or Ecologically Responsive Philosophy

As David Orr says in *Earth in Mind* (1994), all education is environmental education. Lacking in the philosophies just examined is the primacy of the physical environment to learning and the importance of ecological literacy to human survival. We must weigh the linear choices we have made in the past and determine whether they have done us harm by isolating us from the patterns of life. After all, if we cannot breathe the air or drink the water or if we develop "sick building syndrome" due to poor interior building conditions, not much learning is going to occur.

Our reality is the holistic environment and how it works. The real world consists of a network of systems within systems often studied through the science of ecology, which explores the interrelationship of organisms and their environments. A philosophy of ecologically responsive design addresses

The University Child Development School

Seattle, Washington

The architecture of the University Child Development School, a progressive pre-elementary and elementary school, captures the spirit of childhood through design and philosophy. The school takes an experiential approach to learning. Carlson Architects designed the facility to encourage exploration and create random opportunities for intellectual development. The new school building, with its distinctive and playful forms, was constructed adjacent to the existing facility and is organized on three levels with a "hilltown" function on the steeply sloping site. Stairs, bridges, ramps, and a variety of paths up and down contribute to the sense of discovery and creativity inside and outside the building.

Sustainability features include:

► **Rainwater collection:** holding tanks for garden watering, runoff watercourses for creative experiments and play

► **Natural ventilation:** large operable windows in every room, rooftop ventilation chimneys, and segmented building form maximizes potential for light and air

► **Daylighting:** Natural light for interior spaces from skylights and clerestory windows, light shelves reflect daylight to interior

► **Sun shading:** large overhangs on south-facing windows, sun screens on individual windows

► **Lighting:** efficient indirect fluorescent lighting in common areas

► **Impervious surfaces:** exterior hard surfaces confined to minimum playground needs; usable pervious surfaces include children's gardens, soft play areas, and green outdoor class areas

University Child Development School, Seattle. Conceptual sketch of early elementary classrooms. The plan pinwheels around the existing building, creating outdoor play areas. Sketch courtesy of Carlson Architects.

University Child Development School, Seattle.
Top left: Exterior built into a steep slope.
Top right: South roofline with cistern for
runoff. **Center:** Semicircular mouse door.
Bottom right: Second level. Levels are
functionally and visually tied together by a
variety of custom-designed open stairways,
ramps, and bridges. Carlson Architects.
Photographs by Gregg Krogstad.

questions about the habitability of the planet and how we can support the Earth's sustainable processes through education and design. Norwegian philosopher and professor Arne Næss coined the term *ecosophy* to describe a deep ecology grassroots movement, a philosophy of ecological harmony or equilibrium that encompasses not only facts about pollution, but also value priorities of well-being and diversity of life. Psychoanalyst and militant Pierre-Félix Guattari uses the term to address the limitations he sees in the science of ecology. His definition of ecosophy would define a new holistic field that would make clear the full complexity of the relationship between humans and their environment.

My initial philosophical discussion focused on traditional attitudes toward what is real and what is true. Sim Van der Ryn, in his work for the Ecological Design Institute in California, called for a new design epistemology in which ecological concerns play a central role. "In many ways, the environmental crisis is a design crisis," he states. "It is a consequence of how things are made, buildings are constructed, and landscapes are used. Design manifests culture, and culture rests firmly on the foundation of what we believe to be true about the world" (Van der Ryn & Cowan, 1996, p. 9–11). We now must look to the future and what it will require of school facility designers and educators.

A New Philosophy of Ecologically Responsive Design

Many of our best current thinkers are warning us about our treatment of the planet. Pulitzer Prize winner Edward O. Wilson warns us of a "bottleneck" effect in which the Earth's carrying capacity to support humans is approaching its limit. He reminds us that for every person in the world to reach present U.S. levels of consumption with existing technology would require four more Earths (Wilson, 2002, p. 23). Former vice president Al Gore's movie and book of the same title, *An Inconvenient Truth* (2006), both awaken the American public to the dangers of global warming and offer suggestions for individuals to "act affirmatively" (p. 161) to stop the harm. Architecture itself is a big part of the energy picture, and the potential for reducing energy consumption and carbon dioxide emissions with new sustainable design practices is enormous (Mazria, 2004).

Today's learners must come of age immersed in ways to incorporate green design into our communities. There is no better place to demonstrate examples of sustainability than in the schools we build, for it is the student who will become the enlightened citizen of tomorrow. Without a connection to the natural world and its patterns early on, children have little chance of developing a love for the Earth and all its inhabitants. It is my hope that over time, students will translate knowledge of their immediate world into a sense of global stewardship that will influence their adult decisions. Beyond simple stewardship lies a deep sense of kinship with the planet and with other people. Taking care of the planet becomes taking care of oneself and others.

Philosophies of Education and Architecture

Philosophy	Ontology: What Is Real?		Epistemology: What Is True?	
	Educator	Architect	Educator	Architect
Idealism	The world of mind and ideas	The world of design ideals	Absolute ideas are the truth behind physical reality	Absolute, ideal form
Realism	The world of matter	Designs distilled from the laws and principles of the universe	Truth is order inherent in the universe to be uncovered through the senses	Rational patterns, multisensory elements, and functions are reflected in design
Experimentalism	The world of human experience	The process of creating and problem solving	Truth is relative, changing, ongoing, in accordance with human experience	Truth depends on the user and form follows function (functional architecture)
Existentialism	A world of self and personal choice	Architecture of innovation and becoming	Truth is subjective	Truth is intuitive design
Ecoism (Ecosophy, sustainability)	A complex world of interdependencies, networks, and belonging	Holistic or systemic design for sustainability	Truth is deep connection as exemplified by ecosystems operating on the planet	Truth is architecture that works for the future of the planet

Philosophy	Axiology/Ethics: What Is Moral?		Axiology/Aesthetics: What Is Beauty?	
	Educator	Architect	Educator	Architect
Idealism	One must be faithful to the great, eternal ideas and the ideal self	Architecture should reflect and reapply the great, enduring design ideas in history	Beauty increases with proximity to the ideal	Beauty is timeless and classic
Realism	Morality is embodied in the laws of nature	Good design ought to embody the natural processes of the universe	Beauty is essence and order	Beauty is found in nature and logical design
Experimentalism	Education should encourage democratic participation and experimentation	Architecture should encourage problem solving and participation in design	Beauty evolves with the quality of experience	Beauty is in the quality of the design process and the appropriateness of the end product
Existentialism	The individual must decide for him/herself and be true to the authentic self	There is no moral imperative for design beyond personal responsibility	Beauty is authenticity	Beauty is architecture that challenges the public norm
Ecoism (Ecosophy, sustainability)	Education should create caretakers of the Earth and culture, and inspire kinship with all things on the planet	Architecture should give back to the Earth rather than deplete it	Beauty lies in relationships and stewardship	Beautiful design is responsive to and enhances the environment

This chart brings philosophies together for a comprehensive picture of belief systems.
It is a take-off point for discussions about what is real, true, good, and beautiful.

Roger Lewis, in his 2001 guide to the profession of architecture, states that a designer cannot make good architecture without taking a theoretical or philosophical position about architecture (p. 95). His description of differing architectural design philosophies has many parallels to our discussion of philosophy in education. The chart below summarizes Lewis's philosophical taxonomy for architects and adds some examples to illustrate the implications for built forms. Adapted from Architect? A Candid Guide to the Profession *by the MIT Press, revised and republished in 1998, with subsequent printings in 2001.*

Philosophy in Architecture
Roger Lewis

Fellow of the American Institute of Architects

Architect, urban designer, author, journalist, and professor at the University of Maryland School of Architecture, Planning, and Preservation

Schools of Thought in Architecture (ADAPTED FROM LEWIS, 2001)

Philosophy	Motivation for Design	Examples
Morphology	The study of form and shape; using systems, geometries, and patterns to create a sense of order; aesthetics	▶ Italian architect Andrea Palladio and his graceful ratios ▶ Floor plan grids ▶ Axis-based design ▶ Symmetry and asymmetry ▶ Ideal or Platonic building blocks and volumes (pyramids)
Historicism	Reacting in different ways to history: Extracting concepts; copying and updating; adopting and adapting; adding motifs	▶ Classicism in Washington DC ▶ Preserving and restoring buildings ▶ Santa Fe's adobe look ▶ California Spanish Mission style
Technology	Many systems are exposed or hidden. Overall form reflects the method of construction.	▶ Systems: structural, thermal, solar, illumination, acoustics, conveyance, plumbing, electrical, digital, furnishing ▶ Skyscraper ▶ Centre Pompidou, Paris

Philosophy	Motivation for Design	Examples
Deconstructivism	There are no rules, only possibility. Highly personal design interests are unfettered by tradition. Architects take apart and reassemble conventional building elements. A work of art depends as much on the observer as the artist.	▶ See Frank Gehry's Vitra Design Museum, Germany, and his Guggenheim Museum, Bilbao, Spain ▶ Daniel Libeskind's Jewish Museum in Berlin, and his design for the Victoria and Albert Museum, London ▶ Architecture that appears to be exploding, imploding, warping
Sociology and Psychology	The psychological response to place, and architecture for specific population groups	▶ A nursing home design takes into account that elderly like their own décor, like to watch life outside the window, and are sensitive to temperature. ▶ Perception and stimulus response (use of color, light, thermal, privacy) ▶ A school uses developmental rights for learning as design determinants.
Functionalism	Begins with what works; pragmatic. Uses the client's program to determine architectural form. Easy to apply; logical, problem-solving architecture	▶ Modernism ▶ Mies van der Rohe ▶ Le Corbusier
Methodology	Process versus product; how one produces versus what one produces	▶ Management theories ▶ Decision theory ▶ Computer formats ▶ Value engineering ▶ Marketing, efficiency, cost ▶ Diagrams, schedules, charts, data
Ecology	Green architecture; minimum consumption of natural resources and energy; understanding of ecosystems	▶ Jean-Marie Tjibaou Centre, New Caledonia ▶ Designs that take formal cues from the site, such as Frank Lloyd Wright's Fallingwater ▶ Vertiscapes: the skyscraper as garden ▶ Roof gardens and garden balconies; living walls ▶ New use of materials ▶ Eco-corridors or landscape bridges in cities ▶ Solar orientation and siting
Urbanism	Looks at civic space, community, settlement patterns, context, and restoration; seeks to facilitate the interaction of people; acts counter to sprawl, suburbs	▶ Designs that are pedestrian friendly, piazzas, public gardens, landmarks, courtyards, colonnades, greenbelts ▶ Transformed cities: Barcelona, Antwerp, Lyon, Berlin, parts of New York ▶ Multiple use and reuse ▶ Public transportation and access
Symbology	Architecture is a medium for the transfer of messages; it represents ideas, has rhetorical or metaphoric significance, and teaches through association.	▶ Church, temple, mosque, etc. ▶ Home ▶ Historical allusion ▶ Security might be suggested by nestlike, womblike, soft, cozy, human scale ▶ Power through huge, heavy, giant, hard facades

Cloud Gate, AT&T Plaza, Chicago. Anish Kapoor, sculptor. Photograph by Karina Wang.

CHAPTER FOUR

Philosophy Applied to the Physical Learning Environment

Introduction:
Five Images of the Learning Environment

In *Foundations of Education*, a textbook for educators, Ornstein and Levine (2003) examine the philosophical roots of education by examining the educational implications of different philosophies (pp. 95–129). The authors ask education students to identify and respond personally to elements of each philosophy by relating philosophies to their own classroom experiences. I am borrowing this general approach, but unlike Ornstein and Levine, the response to the classroom examined here is couched in terms of the physical environment and architecture. What objects in the environment offer clues to philosophy? How do ideas manifest themselves in the learning environment? How do we learn to "read" the environment with the knowing eye so that it reveals its meanings to us?

A MODEL FOR INVESTIGATING
THE LEARNING ENVIRONMENT

I have adopted and expanded an educational model of examination conceived by Van Cleve Morris (1961) in *Philosophy and the American School* to include architecture in the conception of learning environments. For each of the five philosophies introduced earlier (idealism, realism, experimentalism, existentialism, and ecosophy, or ecologically responsive design) I examine five "images" from Morris's book that when put together give an encapsulated summary of an educational environment.

▸ The image of the learner

▸ The image of the professional

▸ The image of the content to be learned

▸ The image of the process

▸ The image of the philosophy in society

Parallel Learning Environment Images in Education and Architecture

Image (from Morris)	Education	Architecture
The image of the student	Learner	Client/user
The image of the professional	Teacher	Designer/architect
The image of the content to be learned	Curriculum	Program for design
The image of the process	Instructional delivery system/ teaching strategies	Architectural design process
The image of the role in society	Role of education	Role of architecture

The image of the physical learning environment

The above table can be expanded and used as an organizational tool or worksheet for note-taking and sharing views about learning environments early in the planning process for new school facilities.

I extend the five images beyond Morris and his educational viewpoint to include architecture in order to examine the two fields simultaneously as we work our way toward a closer alignment of both disciplines. This process of alignment culminates in a combined image of the physical learning environment.

The Parallel Learning Environment Images in Education and Architecture chart shows us that in terms of educational facilities planning and design, it is important to see the complete picture: the child is viewed as a learner and also as an active client/user of the architectural space. Similarly, the educational curriculum equates with an architectural program for design, and the architectural design process can also be used as a teaching strategy. Each image gains dimension when we view it through the lenses of philosophy, education, and architecture.

WHERE DO YOU STAND?

Ask yourself what your five images of the learning environment are. Do they relate to a certain philosophy we've already discussed?

Image of the child
What is your general image of the child learner? What kind of learner were you when you were a child? Do you remember what it was like to be a child? What were your favorite spaces as a child? Did you ever learn anything from a specific place?

Image of the profession

What kind of teacher or administrator are you now? Or what kind of architect? Do you adhere to a certain philosophy of education or design? What is your view of the professions? Who was your favorite teacher, and why? Who are some of your favorite architects, and why? What makes a great teacher or architect?

Image of the content

What content should go into a curriculum? What early content did you retain from school and use as an adult? What should children learn? What information and spaces should be included in a program for a school design? If you are a parent, what do you want for your children in terms of education and facilities? As an architect, do you see yourself as an educator offering design alternatives to your clients?

Image of the process

What theories and instructional methods does your school employ to reach children? Should children be responsible for their own learning, and to what degree? What is your personal design process? How do you begin a project? Do you take certain steps every time you teach or design, or is the process more intuitive?

Image of the role in society

What are some examples of excellent schools in your area? Why do we have schools? What purposes do public schools serve? How do they differ from private schools or home schooling? Should schools be centers of communities? Describe a school building or other structure you like and why. What does architecture provide, beyond mere shelter?

Once we begin to look at the learning environment philosophically, we can begin to use the beliefs uncovered to suggest design solutions. Converting attitudes into concrete design elements is a process of *translation* governed by both philosophy and architectural planning, and is discussed further in chapters 5 and 6.

Philosophical Site Visit Scenarios

In this section I present short narratives that relate philosophy to learning activity settings. The following scenarios are creative and suggestive rather than comprehensive. This section is aimed at architects but also informs educators about the potential of the physical environment to support teaching. The point is to start looking at environments as places and spaces people can "read" for meaning at many different levels. Narratives are often used during planning stages for facilities to help architects envision the learning that might occur in certain activity zones, and to help educators see how the finished environment will work. I have often used a storytelling method of "day-in-the-life" scenarios to illustrate how students might operate in the newly designed classroom of the future.

The Language of School Design

Design Patterns for Twenty-First-Century Schools

Randall Fielding and Prakash Nair are architects specializing in modern school planning and innovative school design. In 2005, they published *The Language of School Design*, which identifies twenty-five "starter" design patterns for schools. These patterns range from activity settings (classrooms, labs, entries, eating areas) to ambient features (daylighting, natural ventilation, full-spectrum lighting), to sustainable elements and community connections.

Of special interest is how the list of patterns varies from the standard neutral list of learning settings so often seen in educational facilities programs. Values and quality are built into the language of the list. A main entry for a school is not merely an entry, for example; it is a "welcoming entry," which has implications for entry design as a "signature element" reflecting local culture and the school's uniqueness, as community space, as office space with security functions, and as space for student display (pp. 31–32). The entry space as a physical entity and its inviting attributes are addressed simultaneously for maximum quality.

IDEALISM—A WORLD OF MIND AND IDEAS— THE TRADITIONAL INTELLECTUAL ENVIRONMENT

As we enter the workplace of the idealist teacher we immediately recognize the familiar and traditional. We note the chalkboard with its list of math problems, the bulletin boards (one devoted to the classic proportions of the Parthenon and the Golden Mean), the teacher's desk in a dominant location, and student seating arranged in rows and oriented toward the teacher as presenter of information and imparter of knowledge. A dusty bust of Plato stands next to a globe on a shelf loaded with well-thumbed books. The teacher perches on a stool and reads aloud and with animation to the class, pausing every so often to ask a question about the text, or to ask a student to locate where the story's action is occurring on a map of the United States.

The children are listening, taking notes, responding in writing, or raising their hands to be called upon. The first impression: this is a quiet, studious, focused place directed by a teacher who loves ideas.

How Might the Architect Best Support Idealism in Education?

The architect wishing to support the idealist environment remembers that the focus is on great ideas and minds of the culture.

Idealist precedent

Turn to inspiring secular and religious precedents such as museums, libraries, university campuses, and churches; to historic style and classic architectural proportions; and to the ideas and ideals of famous architects.

Guiding design concept for the idealist environment

Convert the book-oriented atmosphere into an aesthetically pleasing three-dimensional textbook for teaching and learning.

Idealist process of translation

Movement is from physical object to the idea or concept behind the object, from the concrete to the abstract, from the microcosm to the macrocosm. Objects in the environment are therefore chosen for their rich, evocative qualities and for their classic beauty.

Idealist design potential

Incorporate or uncover Platonic and classic geometric shapes (circle, square, triangle) and forms (sphere, cube, pyramid) in the design—an exposed triangular truss could be used to teach principles of triangles and the concepts of angle, measurement, and physics of structure.

▶ Create a learning environment that is a microcosm of the larger historical world, a child-scaled temple for learning or replica of a famous location.

▶ Employ the Golden Mean, symmetry, or other classic proportions.

▶ Use graphics and arrangement of spaces to suggest a storyline or timeline: beginning, middle, and end. Refer to literature and culture in graphics and design.

▶ Develop an all-encompassing theme to organize individual design elements.

▶ Include adequate storage for classical props to "set the stage" for various idealist scenarios.

Entryways:
Philosophical First Impressions through Architecture
The images that follow throughout the chapter depict entryways and how they connect to the various philosophies.

Monte Vista Elementary School, Albuquerque, New Mexico.
Classic columns, arch, and symmetrical decoration combined with typical architecture of the Southwest and California Mission styles. Courtesy of Anne Taylor.

REALISM—A WORLD OF MATTER— THE MULTISENSORY, LOGICAL ENVIRONMENT

We enter the orderly world of the realist. The room resembles a small naturalist's museum, a revolving collection of objects for scientific study and the tools needed to study them, including magnifiers, balance scales, and many reference books and field guides, all arranged in alphabetical order. Items in the room are selected for their factual use, connections to nature, and contributions to order. Bulletin boards display rules, procedures, lunch count, and student jobs.

Students are on task observing, counting, classifying, and organizing different kinds of leaves collected from the neighborhood, led by the teacher, who is using a stopwatch to help children share the microscope. The first impression is that the room operates like a well-oiled machine, with little time devoted to emotions or ambiguous topics best left to a social worker or a parent (or so the realist believes).

Nome Elementary School, Nome, Alaska. This interior space for transition from the tough Alaskan winters, also known as the mud pod, is not only practical but also contains opportunities for science and math learning and stewardship of floors, personal items, and plant life. Illustration by George Vlastos.

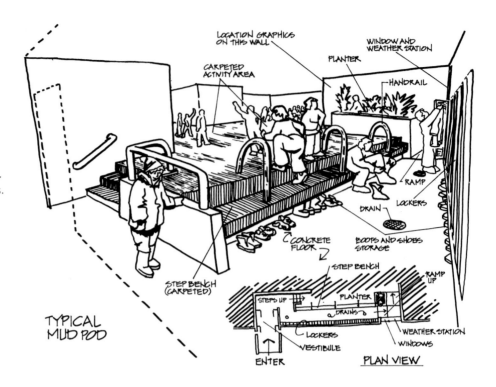

TYPICAL MUD POD

PLAN VIEW

Arroyo del Oso Elementary School, Albuquerque, New Mexico. Native fetish imagery of a bear (*oso* in Spanish) provides a welcoming entry that celebrates local culture and encourages community involvement. Garrett Smith Ltd.

How Might the Architect Support Realism in Education?

In this scenario, the architect remembers that design reflects the universal order of the natural world.

Realist precedent

The architect turns to the natural history museum, the natural world and its patterns, understanding of building materials, and empirical evidence for design determinants.

Guiding design concept for the realist environment

The architect incorporates *multisensory environments* into the design.

Realist process of translation

Multisensory perception is translated into logical ordering and pattern making, the movement being from perception to reason. Objects in the environment are selected for their tangible, sensory qualities and for their incorporation of natural patterns.

Realist design potential

Use a variety of building materials for approximations in wall, floor, and ceiling textures, and for revealing structural properties of matter.

- ▶ Create "soft" and "hard" play areas, i.e., a cushioned area for reading or a geometric climbing area.

- ▶ Provide museum-quality vertical and horizontal display for collections of natural artifacts.

- ▶ Develop the playground and/or outdoor courtyard to include sensory experiences: a wind chime garden for sound; herb and vegetable garden for taste and smell; plant variety for exploration of the visual distinctions in leaf patterns; a rock garden, woodchip paths, grass, pond, and sand areas for discovery of textures.

- ▶ Incorporate plants for student study and care.

- ▶ Make building systems visible and relate them to body systems (plumbing/digestive; electrical/neurological; heating, ventilation, and air-conditioning [HVAC]/circulatory) through graphics, explanatory signage, and color coding.

EXPERIMENTALISM—A WORLD OF HUMAN EXPERIENCE— THE ACTIVE LEARNING COMMUNITY ENVIRONMENT

The ideal experimentalist classroom is not a classroom at all but a fully functional workplace studio, laboratory, kitchen, office, construction site, park, ranger station, or community setting. At first glance it can seem disorganized, cluttered, and definitely noisier than the classrooms we've visited so far. It is a busy place, full of projects in various states of development, where children are purposeful. Space planning and use is flexible, improvised, multipurpose, and determined by the students rather than the teacher, who acts as a facilitator.

Students in this environment are clustered in shifting groups of various sizes from small to large, depending on the specific tasks of the day. They have appropriated the bulletin boards for planning and displaying their ideas while actively participating in designing a "geometrical village," which requires them to discuss, negotiate, and compromise as they assemble their individual ideas for a group presentation. Process appears to be at least as important as the end result. We are reminded of John Dewey, who said that democracy is a process of shared decision-making, growth, and renewal, not an end in itself (Dewey, 1916).

Gary Jewel Middle School, North Aurora, Illinois. Two interior entries with distinct architecture, floor graphics, and display give a sense of identity to different pods within the school. Perkins + Will Architects. Steven Turckes and Gaylaird Christopher, architects. Photographs courtesy of Lambros Photography, Inc.

How Might the Architect Support Experimentalism in Education?

Supporting experimentalism means remembering that design is pragmatic and useful, and the process is at least as important as the end result. (Architects may wish to recall the studio design model of learning by which they were educated.) The classroom is a microcosm of democracy in action.

Experimentalist precedent

For inspiration, designers look to the studio, workplace, and office designs, community centers, democratic institutions, multiple-use facilities, parks, and urban settings.

Guiding design concept for the experimentalist environment

The architect is guided by the importance of *participatory design* in a democratic society.

Jay Pritzker Pavilion, Millennium Park, Chicago. The Gehry band shell for outdoor concerts opens to a great lawn. Space is delineated by a trellis of curving steel beams that also serves as a mount for loudspeakers. Designers of school entries can borrow this concept of an implied transitional zone between indoors and outdoors. Frank Gehry, architect. Photograph courtesy of Gehry Partners, LLP.

Cloud Gate, AT&T Plaza, Chicago. Left: Visitors enter an arched opening to marvel at their own reflections from multiple perspectives. Anish Kapoor, sculptor. Photograph by Anne Taylor. **Right:** What if this sculpture were the gateway to your neighborhood school? Kapoor designed the 110-ton, thirty-three-foot-high sculpture of polished, seamless, stainless steel plates to reflect the surrounding cityscape and sky. Anish Kapoor, sculptor. Photograph by Karina Wang.

Experimentalist process of translation

Interaction leads to experience, a process revisited in an endless spiral of investigation and change. Objects in the environment are chosen for their potential to be manipulated in a variety of open-ended ways, for their usefulness to applied learning, and for their functional connections to the real world.

Experimentalist design potential

Design learning environments to accommodate multiple ongoing activities, with different activity settings for creation, teamwork, and whole-group presentation and display of work.

▶ Open up learning zones to reduce isolation and encourage interdisciplinary learning.

▶ Use the total volume of the space. Provide wallboard or fabric-covered board for floor-to-ceiling pinup space, critiques, and gallery-like display.

▶ Revisit the idea of storage to facilitate constructivist learning—wall units with large shelves, areas within reach of students and teachers, deployable storage and bookshelves, and adequate display space for three-dimensional projects.

▶ Pay special attention to multiple forms of lighting and task lighting to support different learning functions.

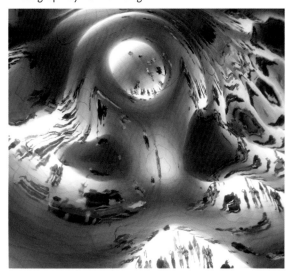

▶ Use a theme of change in design (think of theatrical set design, configurable by students): adaptability, transformation, flexibility, multiple use, variety, universal designs, and multiple access for spaces and furniture. Everything should be on wheels and movable by students.

EXISTENTIALISM—A WORLD OF SELF AND CHOICE— THE OPEN, SELF-DIRECTED ENVIRONMENT

There is no prototypical environment for the individual existentialist learner. We find existentialist spaces in private areas for reflection and introspection, art studios or theatrical dress-up areas for self-expression, or small group settings for serious discussion of profound issues. Spaces embody the idea of a journey or movement toward self, with display of personal artifacts and individual workstations that reveal the distinct personalities of their users. (The bulletin boards were removed when the students repainted the room.) Teacher expression takes a backseat to student expression.

In one classroom several activities are taking place as students work on their autobiographies, which can take any number of forms, from theatrical sketches to paintings, sculptures, manuscripts, poetry, or PowerPoint presentations. The existentialist teacher engages one group of students by asking them to visualize their first memories. The first impression is one of introspection combined with self-expression. Students are taking life seriously and spending time seeking answers to the mysteries of self, awareness, and choice.

How Might the Architect Support Existentialism in Education?

Existentialist quality is achieved by remembering that students have freedom of individual choice, which is tempered by responsibility.

Existentialist precedent
The architect looks to the modern art gallery, theater, influential designers, places that challenge tradition and authority, and deconstructivist architecture.

Guiding design concept for the existentialist environment
The child or client is a powerful chooser.

Existentialist process of translation
The process is entirely subjective and constantly evolving through a process of personal choice. Objects in the environment support individual choice, creativity, and are chosen for their expressive qualities.

Existentialist design potential
Build multiple levels into the classroom space (retractable platforms, steps, amphitheaters, pit areas). These emphasize personal autonomy, young student eye contact with adults, and self-selection of preferred spaces.

Lois and Richard Rosenthal Center for Contemporary Art, Cincinnati, Ohio. This urban center houses temporary exhibit space, performance space, an educational facility, offices, art prep areas, and a museum store. Note the transition from the external sidewalk to the vertical wall. The entrance and lobby lead into the circulation system and are organized as an "urban carpet." The ground level curves upward, rising to become the back wall. **Top:** Exterior. **Bottom:** Interior. Zaha Hadid Architects. Photographs © Helene Binet.

St. Bede's College, Mentone, Victoria, Australia. The passive recreational area at St. Bede's College replaced a muddy trail between buildings with a quiet outdoor retreat. Features include water recycling, planters, outdoor seating, colors reminiscent of the natural terrain, a memorial, and shade canopies inspired by foliage. Kneeler Design Pty Ltd. Architects. Robert Bienvenu and Penelope Mulholland, directors. Photograph by Silvi Glattauer, and courtesy of SchoolDesigner president Joel K. Sims, AIA.

▶ Create displays/galleries for student work.

▶ Scatter quiet areas for privacy, meditation, and reflection throughout the campus.

▶ Include mirror environments.

▶ Design personal areas for each individual, including storage space, student mailboxes, message boards, and display pinup.

▶ Use cubby areas or personal storage as buffer zones between busy hallways and quieter learning spaces.

▶ Provide an elongated group gathering space or media center that can support multiple simultaneous activities while maintaining an open feel.

▶ Provide individual workspaces with laptops for all.

ECOLOGICALLY RESPONSIVE PHILOSOPHY—
A WORLD OF INTERDEPENDENCIES AND BELONGING—
THE SUSTAINABLE, LIVING ENVIRONMENT

The first impression is that it is impossible to separate the ecological classroom from the rest of its environment. Sustainable schools exist in harmony with community, culture, and the local life zone. "Ecodesign" is apparent not only in building siting, solar orientation, natural lighting, recycling of materials, access to the outdoors, and places for agriculture, but also in how the students use the spaces. Groups move freely from indoor learning to outdoor locations and back again, using the school grounds as an agricultural laboratory. Some students

Francis Parker School, San Diego, California. Canopy entry. Recycled glass in the canopy is one of several green features at the school, including the use of sustainable and durable Brazilian redwood, clerestory lights for maximum daylighting, overhangs for shade and solar control, operable fenestration for cross ventilation, and water wise vegetation. Large sliding doors for indoor/outdoor teaching take advantage of the San Diego climate, and local stone pavers are part of a teaching exhibit on geology. Lake/Flato Architects. Photograph by Hewitt Garrison Architectural Photography. ©David Hewitt/Anne Garrison. Image courtesy of SchoolDesigner president Joel K. Sims, AIA.

are setting up a vegetable stand to sell produce they have grown, while others are researching how to build the wetlands habitat that will be funded in part by vegetable sales. An illustrated poster adorns the sliding glass door leading to the learning patio. The poster quotes architect William McDonough from a 2004 interview in *New Scientist Magazine*, in which McDonough describes his vision for ecologically intelligent buildings and products that would function like trees, putting more energy back into the system than they consume (as quoted in Bond, 2004, p. 46).

How Might the Architect Support Ecologically Sensitive Design in Education?

Ecological sensitivity means remembering the appropriateness of design for a sustainable future. All things are in harmony with nature and act according to the principles of ecological systems.

Sustainability precedent

The Earth, habitats, ecosystems, cycles, networks, and green architecture all offer precedents for ecologically responsive design.

Guiding design concept for the sustainable environment

Developing a sense of place leads to love and stewardship of the planet and each other.

Sustainability process of translation

We make connections between objects and the self, and we build networks, systems, and interdependencies. No object is viewed in isolation, but instead is seen in its larger context.

Sustainability design potential

Investigate siting, wind power, and solar orientation of school for maximum energy benefit.

▶ Provide systems for water harvesting and recycling.

▶ Design transitional spaces for learning, extensions to classroom areas, or links to the outdoors such as porches, patios, courtyards, decks, attached greenhouses, animal pens, shade structures, weather stations, planters, and water or sand areas.

▶ Design for agriculture and associated life skills.

▶ Create habitats for students to observe and maintain, such as a wetlands area on the playground, or preserve existing habitats.

▶ Design for student care and stewardship, not just janitor employment.

▶ Use local materials and vernacular building and landscaping (xeriscape) techniques.

▶ Follow LEED green design criteria to achieve certification.

Rio Grande Nature Center and Preserve, Albuquerque, New Mexico. An eight-foot-diameter corrugated drainpipe forms and frames the entry tunnel to the nature center. The interpretive exhibition building acts as an unobtrusive bird "blind," affording visitors discrete panoramic views of the wildfowl areas, and the center as a whole preserves the important connections between the city and the river. Antoine Predock Architect PC. Photograph © Robert Reck.

Conclusion

Five images of the learning environment combine to give us a model for examining and understanding learning facilities. All stakeholders in the planning and design process can benefit from identifying their own philosophies and attitudes toward the five images of the learning environment and their implications for design. We have seen in this discussion of philosophy, education, and architecture that a school can be a hallowed hall of learning, a fascinating repository for the variety in nature, a fully functioning workplace, and a center for self-development. It can be tied to the Earth as a living example of sustainability and stewardship. It may be that different places within a school support these differing philosophical functions.

As in the previous chapter, I have summarized the discussion in a chart that examines each philosophy in terms of the five images. The chart is a simple visual tool that helps organize complex information. Read the chart horizontally (in rows) to gain a complete picture of a given philosophy from both the educational and the architectural viewpoints. Read vertically (in columns) to compare images across philosophies. A final column distills the key educational design concept that emerges from each philosophy. This is the image of the physical learning environment that arises as the end result of the examination of philosophy. These five statements become our first planning goals, forming the foundation for future programming of a new type of school facility that will satisfy multiple approaches to education and philosophy.

Components of the Learning Environment across Philosophies

Philosophy	Image of the Child		Image of the Professional	
	Learner	Client	Teacher	Architect
Idealism	A vessel to be filled with knowledge; potential to become a thinker	Seeker of meaning; influenced by exposure to great design	Educational authority and center of knowledge	Expert using the highest ideals of the profession
Realism	Multisensory, rational explorer; potential to become an analyst, to discover new patterns	Multisensory being in need of functional structure and order	Subject matter expert and organizer of information	Rational being who understands the science and engineering of design as well as the inspiration of natural order
Experimentalism	One who experiences; potential to become a problem solver	Constructor of meaning and active user of spaces	Facilitator or project director	Generator of multiple solutions and options to support multiple experiences
Existentialism	An evolving identity; potential to reach self-actualization	Individual choosers needing diverse spaces and materials	Provocateur of the self (special thanks to Morris, 1961, p. 467)	Aesthetic director and innovator
Ecoism (Ecosophy, sustainability)	Has deep knowledge of and love for the order in the universe; potential to become a caretaker of the planet	User of a designed environment as a three-dimensional textbook	Interpreter and co-learner of built, natural and cultural environment; designer of the mind	Architect as educator and orchestrator of environment

This three-page chart examines philosophies across five images of the learning environment.
Use it to contrast and compare philosophies and to develop educational concepts.
These concepts can inform planning and design of the physical learning environment.

Components of the Learning Environment across Philosophies *(continued)*

Philosophy	Image of the Content		Image of the Process	
	Curriculum	**Program**	**Instructional Strategy**	**Architectural Design Process**
Idealism	Great ideas of traditional Western history; literature, math, and the arts	Consistent with enduring values of architecture; firmness, commodity, and delight	Lecturing, demonstrating, Socratic method, reading, giving examples, creating symbols	Looks at precedents, great institutions of learning, and classic and borrowed forms
Realism	Patterns and pervasive order of the physical universe; math, science, laws; core subject matter vs. social	Analytical assessment of materials, systems, and functions indoors and out	Demonstrating, lecturing, explaining, field trips; observing, collecting data, recording, and classifying	Examines nature, conducts site analysis, studies behavior and patterns, designs with natural law
Experimentalism	Interdisciplinary, project-based, community and real world problems to solve	Content reflects the participatory planning process	Using scientific method, constructing, experimenting, applied problem solving; interacting	Looks to users, community, and workplace for inspiration; cultural study
Existentialism	Self-awareness, self-expression, dialogue of big questions of life, death, and love; art, literature, biography, drama, ethics	Defies convention, open-ended, allows choice, deployable; looks to theater, art galleries	Discussing, reflecting, offering choices, making decisions, using intuition	Looks inward for ideas, turns away from tradition, out of the box; refers to expressive locations
Ecoism (Ecosophy, sustainability)	Interdisciplinary and integrated, ecology, systems, environmental study, technology, ecoliteracy	Site analysis, sustainable patterns and technology, principles and materials of green architecture	Engaging the real world to teach, studio design work, systems thinking, stewardship, and networking	Looks to field of deep ecology for ethical guidance, advocacy research, uses nature's patterns of sustainability

Components of the Learning Environment across Philosophies *(continued)*

Philosophy	Image of the Role in Society		Image of the Physical Learning Environment
	Education	Architecture	Key Educational Design Concept
Idealism	Enculturation; preserves the heritage; great ideas; and values	Preservation, history; upholds tradition; maintains standards of taste; symbolic	Converts the book-oriented atmosphere into a three-dimensional textbook
Realism	Transmits a fixed and rational core knowledge of natural and social law	Reinvents and interprets nature; demonstrates observable fact; engineering	Incorporates multisensory cues or manifestations into the design
Experimentalism	Helps to construct the social order, manage change, and create democratic citizens	Public design fosters democratic and pragmatic values	Supports the process of participatory design and learning in a studio setting
Existentialism	The examined, humanist; fully functioning life serves as a model for society	Sets trends and tastes, champions artistry, comments on society, includes celebrity buildings, sets no rules	Provides spatial options and variety for choice and self-expression
Ecoism (Ecosophy, sustainability)	Promotes stewardship, creates citizens responsible to each other and to the goals of sustainability	Architecture that teaches and embodies the principles of sustainability and uses the language of ecology	Promotes stewardship and sense of place through learning landscapes (people are a part of, not apart from, the environment)

The Met

Letting the Outside In and the Inside Out

Elliot Washor

*Cofounder of the Big Picture Company and the
Met School, Providence, Rhode Island*

Our facilities work at the Met and the Big Picture Company has given us a rare opportunity to design and build a new iteration of high school. Our work is touted as one of the most innovative school designs, and, as a result, we have been asked by the Bill and Melinda Gates Foundation to start up our systems of small schools in cities around the country.

Aside from creating small neighborhood schools of 120 students apiece, we also have remained true to the connectedness of the entire community environment. The dreams of many are now real parts of our school designs. For our Met Public Street Campus, which opened in 2002, we designed the elevations of our buildings to reflect the elevations of the surrounding homes and businesses. We maintained the street grid through the site, making it completely open to the community. Our students were active, too. They led the design work on a rock wall they wanted, started and led a board that developed our school health center, and designed beautiful porches as libraries that reflected the porches of the homes in the community.

Through all of this work our original ideas and vision have remained consistent. We educate one student at a time in a community of learners. To this end, our work at Big Picture schools with each student is highly personalized. We support the "personalization of relationships" in which people know each other intimately and use those relationships to advance learning and growth. We also encourage the "personalization of place" in which a school setting allows each student to craft his own experience. You can look at the feasibility study of the Met/Big Picture design done in 1996 and still clearly see our original learning signatures:

▶ A community school

▶ A school built on relationships in which there is space to accommodate all types of learning styles and sizes of groups— advisories, design studios, individual student space, flexible space

▶ A place that lets the outside in and the inside out, where learning is real and done in the world beyond the school's walls

▶ A welcoming space

▶ A school built for human scale—a network of small schools

▶ A quality school with high-quality student work

▶ A school where the space is flexible to change with the program

THE LEARNINGSCAPE

The Met School was built on our learning signatures. Our innovative practices pushed the design of our facilities, but now that our efforts are reaching a broader audience, how do we inform other school communities about the thought process for generating their own school environments? What is the simplest way to describe the space at any school that reflects both the outside and the inside? The answer for me is drawn from my past.

I grew up in Brooklyn, right next to Prospect Park, one of Frederick Olmsted's greatest works. Many years later, I found out that I was completely influenced by Olmsted but until I read Tony Hiss's *The Experience of Place*, I never realized the extent of that influence on me and on the Met facility.

My first recollection of Prospect Park is the color, the smell, and the playful sensation of the park experience. My uncle Gabby took me through that park every weekend and I knew every inch of it. He was a man with a third grade education but a man who was educated in the truest sense in and by the public domain. It was through him that I personally understood the meaning of Olmsted's term "the park experience." Parks were not to be taken in isolation but rather as part of a greater whole. That is why parkways were developed—to link greenways to other green spaces. In Brooklyn, Ocean Parkway takes you to Coney Island, and Eastern Parkway takes you to the farms of Eastern Long Island. Ocean Avenue, Coney Island Avenue, Prospect Park West, Parkside Avenue, and Park Circle all create a sense of place.

Similarly, schools should not be taken in isolation but rather as an educational experience generating a "learningscape" that extends learning out to the community. To boil it down to the simplest terms, Olmsted's principles work for a school experience. We should imitate these outside environments to feel more comfortable inside and then move our insides out and let the outside in.

At the Met, Olmsted's principles definitely play out. There is "**prospect**— a long sweeping vista where we can take in information for miles around. A place where viewing is unhindered." This is our Met commons, Olmsted's

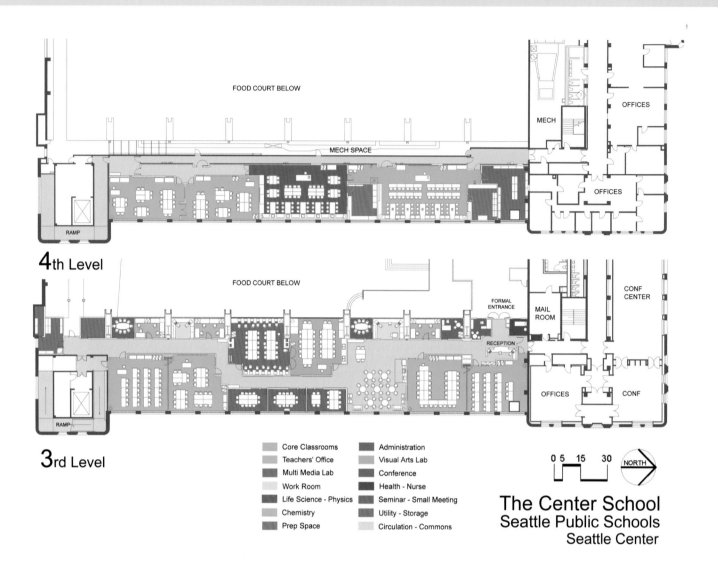

4th Level

3rd Level

Core Classrooms
Teachers' Office
Multi Media Lab
Work Room
Life Science - Physics
Chemistry
Prep Space

Administration
Visual Arts Lab
Conference
Health - Nurse
Seminar - Small Meeting
Utility - Storage
Circulation - Commons

0 5 15   30   NORTH

The Center School
Seattle Public Schools
Seattle Center

The Center School, Seattle. Plan view. The Center School embodies many of the attributes described by Elliot Washor. It is located at the heart of Seattle Center near the Seattle Repertory Theatre, Pacific Northwest Ballet, Theatre Puget Sound, Experience Music Project, Pacific Science Center, Seattle Children's Theatre, McCaw Hall Opera House, Key Arena, and the Space Needle, all of which can be used as learning destinations. The school occupies leased space in an existing active commercial building, and has a population of three hundred students, seventy-five in each grade level. Image used with permission of Dale Lang and Lorne McConachie of Bassetti Architects, Seattle.

sheep meadows, where students and adults gather in the morning for all sorts of daybreak events. It is the first place you see at the school and it calms you down.

Next, we find "**refuge**—a hiding place where, from concealment, we can see without being seen, and gain information without giving away information about ourselves." We have plenty of nooks at the Met where a single student or a small group of students can work. Here students can escape into their own work.

Finally, there is "**mystery**. Mystery gives the impression that one could acquire new information if one were to travel deeper into the scene." Winding paths are a good example. At the Met both inside and outside there are meandering paths, places where you have to keep going to see everything. The typical school facility's double-barreled corridor is *not* present in this environment.

Hiss talks about how all of these principles are legible to the participant. **Legibility** is the characteristic of an environment that gives the feeling one could explore extensively without getting lost. Environments high in legibility are those that look as if they would be easy to make sense of as one wanders farther and farther into them, with enough openness to see where one is going, as well as elements distinctive enough to serve as landmarks. In other words, when you enter a Met space (an advisory, a design studio, a student's workspace) you can "read it." It is legible; you know what you are expected to do there.

Olmsted's principles work well for thinking differently about the future of small schools built on a human scale. His ideas allow us to see how a twenty-first-century school space can be continued inside and outside the actual building to connect learning to the community. What Olmsted applied to the outside for parks and community can also work inside for schools reaching out to community. It worked for Olmsted, and it worked for us.

Pueblo of Isleta Head Start and Child Care Center. Janet Carpio, architect formerly with Cherry/See Architects. Photograph by Kirk Gittings.

Philosophy and Aesthetics for the Learner

INTRODUCTION

Years ago while walking along a beach in Mexico with a group of children, I received a gift or insight that helped set the course for my professional life. The children were collecting shells, discarding some and stuffing others in their T-shirts. I asked them why they kept some of the shells. They said, "Because they are beautiful and different." The children demonstrated an intuitive sense of beauty, an innate ability to read and respond to the environment. This love of beauty made me start to wonder how these children and others must feel, sitting shut away from the world for eighteen or more years in dull, cluttered, and featureless nine-hundred-square-foot classrooms learning mostly from textbooks.

That stroll on the beach thirty-five years ago spawned an experimental and replication study to test and later confirm the hypothesis that the physical environment did affect learning and behavior of young children. I worked with ten architecture students from Arizona State University to use the developmental needs of children and the curriculum to be taught as design criteria to determine the experimental setting, which, during selected dependent-variable testing, differed significantly from the control group. In subsequent projects inspired by the Arizona experimental study, I began designing the learning environment to be a teaching tool in and of itself to support concept development, language and literacy, creativity, and the ability to make critical aesthetic judgments. I was thinking holistically, combining education with architecture. In a sense, since that day on the beach I have been giving back to children the gift of understanding I had received from them years before.

REGGIO EMILIA PRESCHOOLS, ITALY

As a person who has had the opportunity to visit schools all over the world, I can say that the preschools in Reggio Emilia are the most impressive that I have seen.
—Howard Gardner, research psychologist (2003)

There's a difference between the environment that you are able to build based on a preconceived image of the child and the environment that you can build that is based on the child you see in front of you—the relationship you build with the child, the games you play. An environment that grows out of your relationship with the child is unique and fluid.
—Professor Loris Malaguzzi, founder of the Reggio Emilia approach (1993)

The Reggio schools constitute an international gift to the world of excellence in early childhood education. The schools were conceived as one answer to the devastation of World War II, wherein Loris Malaguzzi, inspired by the determination of local villagers, decided to build and run schools for a new generation of highly creative, rather than destructive, people. The environment of each school is not only beautiful and functional, but children are also given the power of choice, creativity, and support from teachers who document the process of their visual, verbal, and kinesthetic self-expression. Everything in the environment is carefully planned, organized, and scaled to the child. I believe the respect for children demonstrated by the Reggio schools and the Reggio approach should be adapted as needed and used as a model for all age levels worldwide, and I encourage all architects of schools to visit Reggio Emilia to see firsthand the fusion of aesthetics and learning.

Images of a Visit to Reggio Emilia

When I visited Reggio Emilia Preschools in Italy, it was with a sense of recognition and delight. Here was the embodiment of the aesthetic and philosophical learning environment my colleagues and I had been advocating through our design work for children. I was excited to see the idea of the strong, powerful learner in action. I witnessed several children designing with an overhead projector and found objects. They were creating a work of art, a composition, and a design as they investigated concepts of shape, shadow, light, texture, transparency, and opacity. The teacher documented their conversation as they designed. This was an investigation on multiple levels, led by students and studied by the teacher, who demonstrated an interest in process over product. Reggio teachers follow the children's ideas and natural interests when structuring curriculum projects.

The architecture of the schools I visited varied from remodeled houses to modern, high-tech centers. The interiors of all the schools were immaculate, full of light and order, and rich with greenery from interior gardens and potted plants. The architecture functionally supported the program and the schools were magical. Displays were student-centered. The walls of all the rooms displayed the artwork and communications of children and the teachers executed the displays with the expertise of exhibit curators. I did not see any cartoons or overloaded visual clutter as one might see in the classrooms of America.

Top: **Nilde Iotti Municipal Infant-Toddler Center, Reggio Emilia, Italy.** The Piazza. The bright, open plaza with mirrored triangle and curved coat storage/dress-up areas. **Bottom: Diana Municipal Preschool, Reggio Emilia, Italy.** Landscapes in light. Students experiment with patterns, opacity, translucency, light, and shadow using overhead projectors and screens. Photographs courtesy of Reggio Emilia Preschools and Infant-Toddler Centers. Reggio Children.

Even small details contributed to the overall aesthetic impression and reinforced the order of place. I was impressed with coat storage, which is usually located in the hallway. Coats were put on hangers, sometimes in a closet, not hung on hooks or left on the floor in a heap. The dress-up area in one school was tucked behind two blue laminate half circles. A clothes tree stood in the middle, with hooks placed around the inside of the circles. This contained the clothes well, kept them orderly yet accessible, and screened them from outside view.

Free choice is a function of the Reggio schools. Even the infants' sleeping rooms demonstrated this principle. Young toddlers or crawling babies could crawl in and out of basket beds placed on the floor and could access an adjacent playroom on their own. This ability to choose fosters great independence in young children. In America, young children are often adult-dependent. We put them in cribs, and when they wake up, they have to cry or call to be taken out of their cribs. There is a need for a redesign of protective sleeping furniture for young children that corresponds to our greater need to rethink our attitudes toward children and their capacity for independence.

Sensory Atmosphere

A great sense of light and an ambience of transparency exist in all the Reggio schools. One can see through fenestration into other rooms sometimes placed off a piazza or a courtyard. There were mirrors everywhere. Every room had light tables for designing, tracing, color mixing with tissue paper, and even displaying children's work. When the light tables were hung vertically on the wall they gave a backlighting effect to the children's work.

In one school the cooks were in the kitchen preparing wonderful minestrone soup, and of course our sense of smell was treated to a delicious wafting of scents. At Reggio, eating is a social event and a part of learning. Children dine family style at small tables with tablecloths and silverware. They converse. This is in direct contrast to the American cafeteria where time is of the essence, and children line up like prisoners and gulp their meals according to a tight schedule while the janitor waits by the door with a large garbage can for uneaten food that could be recycled or composted but is not.

Architectural Concepts from Reggio Emilia Preschools:
Key Words for the Designer

Reggio Children and Domus Academy Research and Consulting (DARC), the research center of the Domus Academy in Milan, have been conducting research with architects, designers, teachers, and *pedagogistas* to develop a metaproject and document

Top: Interior fenestration and plants everywhere. Image from "Open Window" (1994), a slide series produced by Reggio Emilia. **Bottom:** Family-style dining is a social event. Image from "Open Window" (1994). Photographs © Reggio Emilia Preschools and Infant-Toddler Centers, Reggio Emilia, Italy.

titled *Children, Spaces, Relations: Metaproject for an Environment for Young Children*. The project examines the physical characteristics and "soft qualities" of the learning environment for young children.

The designers and educators involved in the research use key phrases to describe the ambience of spaces they have developed for early childhood learning. Other schools may want to follow this example as a planning exercise, distilling long lists of educational objectives or learning concepts into a short list of evocative, qualitative characteristics that guide decision making about design. The metaproject's environmental concepts include:

Overall softness: Spaces that are complex, made of many languages, and at the same time plain, livable, and welcoming

Relational space: Integrated spaces and connections linking other fields of knowledge, identities, and ways of thinking

Osmosis: Schools reflecting community and culture, rejecting isolation of schools, and allowing real-world learning to permeate the school

Multisensoriality: Students using the whole body to explore and investigate, emphasizing perception, interpretation, and synthesis

Epigenesis: Children acting on and modifying the environment through deployability, flexibility, and evolving spaces

Community: Piazza spaces or collective environments valuing participation and shared values

Constructiveness: Workshops, studios, and spaces supporting students as they construct knowledge (Ceppi & Zini, 1999)

These concepts guide planning and design at Reggio Emilia infant centers and preschools. I believe they also form excellent starting points for the aesthetics of all school design.

The following stewardship forum contributions embody the same qualitative attitude toward synthesis of architecture and education. The writers take children seriously by believing in and respecting the aesthetic capabilities and sensibilities of young people.

Top: Outdoor constructive play. Image from "Open Window" (1994). **Bottom:** The atelier, or art room. Image from "Open Window" (1994). Photographs © Reggio Emilia Preschools and Infant-Toddler Centers, Reggio Emilia, Italy.

The title of this piece has stuck with me as a succinct guiding principle for school reform and future design.

Can't Learn in Ugly

Eeva Reeder

Instructional coach in Seattle middle and high schools, and former math teacher

New principal Gloria Mitchell, on her first site visit after being hired to help turn around a very low-performing elementary school in inner-city Seattle, took one look at the hallway floors—a sorry patchwork of peeling linoleum tiles—and decided they had to go. "They were *ugly*," she said. "I don't think you can learn in ugly." When students returned to school in the fall, shiny new tiles lined the floors, the building trim sported five different color patterns, and the asphalt playground had been turned into a park and garden (Shaw, 2002).

Students who had not yet learned to read were nonetheless able to read the messages even those modest renovations communicated to them every day they came to school: Someone values me and values the work we do in this building. Someone wants me to succeed. The buildings in which we ask our children to learn are themselves teachers. Without question, our design and construction decisions speak volumes to students about what adults believe and honor.

The eloquence of chairs. Three images from recent visits to American schools. For those who would like a more positive look at the language of chairs and design diversity, look for *1000 Chairs* by Charlotte and Peter Fiell (2005). Chairs shown in the book encapsulate the history of chair design through function, symbolic intent, culture, and fashion. Photographs courtesy of Anne Taylor and Murray Enggass.

  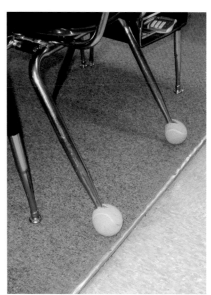

A Native American Head Start School
Isleta Pueblo, New Mexico

Janet Carpio

Formerly with Cherry/See Architects in Albuquerque, Carpio now works at Ronnette Riley Architects in New York City.

In 2004, Janet Carpio designed as her master's thesis a new Head Start building for Isleta Pueblo. She traced Isleta's history back to Chaco Canyon and tracked the migration of the Tiwa people in order to establish a cultural precedent for the design. The resulting facility reveals an understanding and appreciation of the interrelationships between terrestrial, celestial, cosmic, and human worlds. Carpio integrated solstice points into the site plan, construction, materials, and floor plan to allow people to observe and connect with the much larger landscape that is integral to indigenous architecture.

Head Start students enter their homerooms from the playground to the east, in Pueblo Indian tradition. A masonry wall mimics mountains to the east. The floor plan integrates creation and the path of Tiwa life through room arrangement—infants in the center with other children's rooms spiraling out counterclockwise with age. The floor pattern reflects Isleta life with blue representing water, brown for the Earth, and green signifying crops. The sacred colors of the cardinal directions appear in the multipurpose room, a circular space with a dome that gives the room natural light. Pathways lie in the direction of solstice and cardinal directions, while a hallway that descends as it curves out toward the southeast playfully symbolizes a return to Earth. The school is not just another building, but also a journey of myth and traditions for the Native Americans who live at Isleta (Gonzales, 2004).

Pueblo of Isleta Head Start and Child Care Center. Top left: Entry.
Bottom left: Hallway with floor graphics indicating student pathways sometimes used by children as an organizational tool for lining up. **Center:** Circular multipurpose space with dome skylight, cardinal directions embedded in ceiling skylights, and cultural pathways in the floor. **Right:** Curvilinear hallway with multiple light sources, including child-height windows. Janet Carpio, architect formerly with Cherry/See Architects. Photographs by Kirk Gittings.

Richard Fleischman writes that the culture in his studio constantly tells the client that "from many minds come singular results."

Innovation in School Design
The Mosaic of Diversified Space

Richard Fleischman
Richard Fleischman + Partners Architects, Inc., Cleveland, Ohio

It is critical that we all put aside preconceived notions of where "best ideas" come from. Once we do that, innovation will flourish.

I remain faithful to the notion of architecture as incessant research in which innovation is counterbalanced by powerful bonds with the physical and historical environment. Designing a school means creating a vibrant facility that has the great dignity and visual appeal all communities need. I feel that any specific community is a statement of social progress, and the quality of design reflects the success of the community's values.

As the crossroads of our cultural, social, and commercial activity, schools must reflect our civic values, sense of place, and commitment to the quality of life we have promised our youth. In an effort to discover this richness for education, we must create spaces that reflect the celebration of learning. We must refuse to yield to the temptation of form as pure image or technology as pure language. Ideas can emerge from the crisis of rationalism but without the characteristic overindulgence of personal poetics. Architecture should introduce each school project as an experience in itself and as the embodiment of a significant abstract design theory.

The image of my thought process is that of a mosaic of diversified space in which I am constantly searching for the intangible and unidentified functions that help bind individual spaces to create an art form: a place for learning.

Below, fom left:
A. Windermere, East Cleveland, Ohio. Head Start circulation spaces. Engaging forms, patterns of color, light, and shadow.
B. Cleveland Music School Settlement. Preschool classroom. A 1910 house was renovated for music education, forming a single, efficient complex for all music and performing arts. Note the fenestration open to the street view.
C. Cleveland Public Library, Villa Angela branch, Cleveland, Ohio. Entrance. Transparency, color, and dramatic structure direct the user to the entry.
D. Cleveland Public Library, Villa Angela branch, Cleveland, Ohio. Clock tower. An existing high school facility was transformed into a renovated public library with casual and well-designed seating.
E. Cleveland Public Library, Villa Angela branch, Cleveland, Ohio. The commons area provides overlooks and interior views. Photographs by Eric Hanson, and courtesy of Richard Fleischman + Partners Architects, Inc.

A. B. C. D. E.

Top: Kasahara Elementary School, Miyashiro, Japan. Attention to culturally significant aesthetics in the rhythm and angles of roof planes, patterns of shingles, and the carefully tended flower boxes lining the broad steps. **Center: Kasahara Elementary School, Miyashiro, Japan.** Interior spaces expand into hallways. **Bottom: Salesio Elementary and Secondary School, Tokyo, Japan.** Classrooms are in individual round, house-shaped buildings. Photographs courtesy of Kumi Tashiro.

Kumi Tashiro writes that in seventeenth-century Japan, Terakoya was a place where children who were gathered from the surrounding neighborhoods learned reading, writing, and arithmetic. Temples, shrines, and houses were used as schools. Today, a new style of school is being built in Japan. This style aims to break from the square buildings and box-shaped classrooms exemplified by the Basic School Building Plan and Description of 1895, and now primarily consists of classrooms without walls and with wide corridors. The alternative workspace and combined hall space form multipurpose rooms that define the current Japanese-style open school.

School and Learning Space Design in Japan

Kumi Tashiro, PhD

Miyagi University

CASE STUDIES AND EXAMPLES

Case 1. Kasahara Elementary School (Miyashiro, Japan, 1982)
This was one of first schools the Ministry of Education built to incorporate the open-school ideal.

The school's designers demonstrated attention to detail by using various motifs and themes such as animals/creatures, stars/constellations, poetry, and friendship between children. For the lower grades, the bathroom was built as part of the classroom. The reading corner was made to resemble a Japanese-style living room with tatami mats. Areas such as space in the hallways for chatting were a wonderful innovation.

Case 2. Salesio Elementary and Secondary School (Tokyo, Japan, 1993)
This is a small-scale private school founded on Italian Christianity. The design of space supports individualized learning and the close interaction of child and teacher. Although designed by architects, teachers employed at Salesio participated in designing the basic plan after inspecting many schools in the local area and throughout Italy. Each grade has only one class, and the maximum number of pupils in a class is twenty. Every single class has an individual house-shaped building containing a classroom area and semicircular workspace. Wooden decks connect the classrooms. The school looks like a small, friendly village in contrast to the very urbanized secondary school that stands on the same site.

Case 3. Utase Elementary School (Chiba, Japan, 1995)
This pilot school challenged the definition of environment, as it was built in a completely new town on reclaimed land near the sea. Even though this is a public school, interested parties invested twice the normal construction cost of a regular school. Features of the school building are unit-based classrooms and an elliptic gymnasium placed in the center. Each classroom is composed of units representing five categories—classroom, workspace, alcove, inner court, and entranceway. Providing these elements has given the children the opportunity to exercise decision-making skills. By using various pieces of uniquely shaped furniture, the children are able to create their own comfortable places.

Case 4. Sendai Science Museum (Sendai, Japan, 1990)
The exhibitions inside the Sendai Science Museum are intriguing, but it is also possible to learn from the building's structure, as the appearance of the building imitates a bridge, and the mechanisms of the elevator, escalator, and some exhibits are open to view. The museum is highly regarded nationwide as a social education facility. All junior high school students in the city receive the opportunity to participate in a special science class there at least once a year. During summer vacation, students may bring their own projects to the museum for advice and input from museum staff. On weekends, national holidays, and during school vacations, elementary pupils and junior high students of the city enjoy free admission.

Utase Elementary School, Chiba, Japan.
Top: Deployable display panels on wheels and easily reconfigured furnishings support student independence and flexibility. **Bottom:** Tiered break-out assembly space. Photographs courtesy of Kumi Tashiro.

Sendai Science Museum, Sendai, Japan. Left: Exterior. **Center**: Interior. **Right**: Accessible archive for natural objects drawer and wall display systems. Photographs courtesy of Kumi Tashiro.

Minamikoizumi Elementary School, Sendai, Japan.
Left: Students learn about civics and geography as they research and develop an urban plan for their community.
Right: Students use knowledge gained during architectural workshops to present a model they have made of the future community. Photographs courtesy of Kumi Tashiro.

Case 5. Minamikoizumi Elementary School
(Sendai, Japan, 1990)

Students participated in community planning as part of integrated learning about civics, geography, and design. The process began when students discovered that a new subway station was to be built near the school within ten years. They set out to learn from the real world by interviewing local residents and taking design workshops with architects. The students then developed a plan and constructed a model of the future community. At the end of the project, they invited all relevant parties as guests and made a detailed presentation. They also handed a report of their findings and their future plan to the mayor. As a result, the link between the real world and the world of education has been strengthened.

Howard Kaplan would like to see criteria for green architecture such as the LEED accreditation requirements for ecologically responsive design included in building codes. Building assessments should incorporate data about the structure's ecological footprint. He makes the point that cannot be made too often: thinking green is the new aesthetic.

The Time Is Now

Howard Kaplan

Registered Architect, American Institute of Architects
LEED accredited professional

There is no greater challenge facing us today than the issues of global warming, climate change, and the depletion of energy and material resources. It is now known that buildings are far and away the greatest consumers of energy and materials and are direct contributors to greenhouse gas emissions through the combustion of natural gas and oil in heating and cooling. These two factors taken together amount to about 50 to 55 percent of all energy consumed in this country. Because school buildings are the largest building sector in the nonresidential construction industry, changing the way we design schools will have a profound effect on the environment.

Green or sustainable schools are energy, material, and resource efficient and optimize student health and productivity. Additionally, they can provide a unique educational opportunity to link building design to environmental issues and their solutions. Several studies have already shown that students perform at a higher level when they have natural light in their classrooms.

Despite the obvious advantages of green school design and the growing number of facilities being designed as green schools, the total represents a very small percentage of schools currently on the drawing boards. We need a new, sustainable accounting of what constitutes success in design.

It is now time for architects to step up and take control of the process and realize that the actions we take in our day-to-day practice have a profound influence. Design must lead the way. Integrating sustainable principles at all levels should be the norm, and technology must support that effort rather than vice versa. The future of education is linked to what is happening to our planet and is in turn linked to the design of our schools. Today is not too early to begin—tomorrow may be too late.

Loma Colorado Public Library, Rio Rancho, New Mexico.
The library is a thirty-three-thousand-square-foot LEED-registered building located on a site adjacent to the local high school. Designs for water efficiency, task lighting at study tables, recycled carpets, and bamboo flooring contribute to green goals for the library, which received the 2007 Citation Award from the Albuquerque chapter of the AIA. Hidell-Wilson Architects. Howard Kaplan, RA, AIA, operations manager.

The distinctive work of Legorreta + Legorreta is known for an architectural vocabulary that celebrates Mexico's timeless forms: attention to the changing quality of light, color, wall planes, and platonic shapes that link elements of earth, water, and sun. **Above left: Business Administration Graduate School, Monterrey, Nuevo León, Mexico, 2001.** Exterior. **Above Right: National Center of the Arts, Mexico City.** Interior, painting studio. **Left:** National Center of the Arts (NCA) Administration and Research Building, National School of Arts, Mexico City, 1994. Exterior. Aerial view of the NCA, where several art schools were brought together into one complex.

Visual Arts Center, College of Santa Fe, New Mexico, 1999. Above: Geometric Volumes. **Right:** Corner window. Use of color and purity of form.

All Photographs by Lourdes Legorreta, courtesy of Legorreta + Legorreta Architects.

*Every university is an oasis for knowledge in a world that is each
day more dominated by economic interests.*
        —Legorreta + Legorreta Architects

Legorreta + Legorreta on Educational Facilities

A Personality of One's Own

*Legorreta + Legorreta, father and son architects, have
worked extensively in the area of educational design.*

In each educational project our main objective is to create
a series of spaces where informal communication can take
place; the design of corridors, stairs, halls, and patios becomes
a unique opportunity to augment the exchange of ideas. We
are convinced that new information technologies are wonderful tools for education, reaching more people and places, but
the experience of attending a university will always be unique
because of this personalized contact.

Our philosophy has always been to design buildings where
students can feel stimulated to reach new levels of creativity and
to be able to think in terms of great ideals, and yet do this without
big budgets or fancy materials. We believe that architecture for
universities should have the same dignity as the institutions they
house, and at the same time should be an example for the student
in the correct use of resources, be logically aligned to the society
in which they are placed, and be environmentally efficient.

Universities today are resisting homogenizing their designs
and characteristics, searching harder than ever before to have a
personality of their own. We seek to relate individual schools culturally to their local environments and return them to their former status as vital centers of community while developing a clear
identity designed to distinguish each campus from the rest.

PART TWO

USING AN
ORGANIZING SYSTEM

*Planning for Educational Environments
with the Knowing Eye*

Albuquerque Aquarium and BioPark, New Mexico.
Photograph courtesy of Van H. Gilbert Architect PC.

CHAPTER FIVE

Using a Curricular Organizing System for School Facility Planning

A Learner-Centered Basis for Planning Facilities

The early stages of school facility planning require returning to ground zero and asking, "What is best for the learner?" When I visit schools, I see in the children's eyes that they are desperate for an active role in their own learning. When they encounter opportunities for problem solving and creativity their eyes light up. Learning facilities must be designed to bring out this enthusiasm.

Because effective lifelong learning is the focus for all we are doing, we must pause here and review educational theory, instructional strategies, and qualities of learners. My experience has shown that time spent developing an organizing system of thought about education is truly essential to excellence in school facilities design. Every organizing system should articulate an educational philosophy, create a taxonomy of learning experiences and activity goals, identify developmental rights of children, and create valid forms of assessment and evaluation. These academic goals are then addressed and enhanced through design by the architect, who needs to take the time to deeply understand the instructional delivery system for which he or she is designing.

In this chapter, I offer best practices for educational excellence that my colleagues and I have researched and shared with many stakeholders early in the school planning process. This system represents what I believe is the strongest approach to education and making learning real. It may be used as is or modified to fit the particular needs of your school district. In any case, it is imperative that designers and planners (as well as educators, parents, and politicians) understand and respect the true client—the student. Of equal importance is the goal of architectural excellence through thoughtful programming (architectural planning), which is explored in chapter 6.

The Curricular Organizing System

My organizing system for curriculum development makes a distinction between what we learn (content) and how we learn it (learning process), while at the same time locating and using learning in a physical and thematic setting (context).

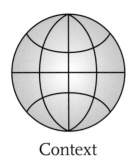

Context

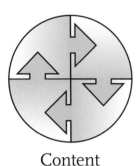

Content

Learning processes

No educational space can functionally and aesthetically support what goes on in a learning environment if planners fail to investigate:

The context
The whole setting for learning indoors and out, including school grounds and moving beyond school walls to community and the world—the entire built, natural, and cultural environment

The content
What is to be learned, including subject matter disciplines and related interdisciplinary concepts (ideas)

The learning processes of children
How developmental learning occurs in multiple ways across body, mind, and spirit; and how to set the groundwork for lifelong learning (skills, retrieving information, and problem-solving processes)

Context, content, and learning processes work together to provide a simple framework for organizing design ideas that can be applied to any school planning project or programming format.

MORE ABOUT CONTEXT, CONTENT, AND LEARNING PROCESSES

Context is the physical setting where learning occurs: the built, natural, and cultural environment. This means that the entire school site, grounds included, is part of the planning and the learning. Context implies community, culture, and the connections to be found in the real world. Context is also the big picture or the abstract, thematic setting for learning. The research phase of architectural programming should uncover the underlying organizing educational principles at each site, as well as the unique parameters of the physical environment. Architects must investigate ethnicity, culture, and the vernacular as part of their understanding of context.

As landscape architect Paul Friedberg says, "The site is an attitude as well as a physical presence" (as quoted in Pressman, 2001, p. 180).

Content is what is being learned. In schools, content usually takes the form of subject matter disciplines: math, science, language arts, social studies, technology, health and physical education, and the arts. It should be noted that even though subject matter disciplines are often taught in a discrete manner, we know from learning theory that this separation is artificial and does not represent the way the mind works. The mind learns in an integrated and holistic way by making connections. Interdisciplinary thinking is the goal.

The content contained in each subject matter area is related to certain **concepts** (ideas) that we want children to master. A concept is an idea or understanding, from the concrete to the abstract, formed in the mind of the learner. Concepts are usually expressed as nouns (see the "Interdisciplinary Concepts" chart at the end of the chapter in Tools for Thought for a representative list).

We make important connections *across* disciplines when we think of learning in terms of concepts or ideas that have broad meanings applicable to a variety of learning situations. Take the concept of balance, for example. In physical education or dance, a child can experience the concept of balance in a direct, concrete way through movement. The concept of balance in physics and engineering can be demonstrated through experiments with equilibrium of force and structure. Ecological balance is studied in Earth science. In math, balance is related to scale and weight, or balancing a checkbook, or symmetry, while in social studies discussion might lead to an abstract examination of the balance of power. Balance also has philosophical overtones suggesting fairness or evenness of approach to life's challenges, or a sense of justice, as in the abstract meaning of the scales of justice. The essential meaning of balance moves from concrete to abstract and is reinforced with increasing subtlety as students explore its many meanings. Once architects are aware of this continuum of meaning, they can build inventive encounters with the concept of balance (or any other concept educators wish to emphasize) into the physical environment. Architects and educators should study state and national educational content standards and benchmarks to choose cross-disciplinary concepts or themes to build into school designs.

Learning processes are how we learn, or different ways of learning. I make a clear distinction between curriculum content and learning processes, which are sometimes blurred in state and national school standards. The distinction has important implications for how we teach and how we design to include individual learning styles and the developmental needs of children. We know that not everyone learns in the same way or at the same rate. Many learning theorists have provided insight into how people build perception and process information, from Jean Piaget's explorations of developmental stages of learning to Howard Gardner's multiple intelligences theory (please see the Influential Educational Theorists chart at the end of this chapter). Learning processes are fundamental to public school facilities design in that they provide an active (rather than the traditional passive) view of the learner while also requiring a personalized understanding of the learner. Students are not identical products turned out by a factory!

Several instructional strategies based on learning processes are worthy of further discussion here, including the design studio model used by artists and architects, constructivism theory, environment-based learning, new models for assessment of student work, a six-step strategy or taxonomy for building wisdom, and the developmental rights (needs) of all children. These instructional models and practices cannot operate effectively in the traditional classroom as it is presently designed and furnished.

LEARNING PROCESSES AND THE DESIGN STUDIO MODEL

Design studios and their counterparts—science laboratories or art studios—can serve as models for applied learning in the classroom. My goal for education goes beyond merely imparting facts to teaching children how to think. To do this involves a shift in emphasis from product to process, to an inquiry-based methodology that motivates children to see connections between their own learning and the real world.

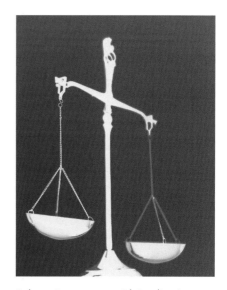

Balance is a concept with implications across disciplines, from balance experienced in dance, to balance demonstrated by a symmetrical building or by weights and counterweights, to our historic understanding of justice, as represented in images of scales, often held aloft by the blindfolded and impartial statue of Lady Justice. Illustration © Veer, Incorporated.

Context, Content, and Learning Processes
Translated into Effective Design

Albuquerque Aquarium and BioPark

The Albuquerque Aquarium is part of a comprehensive environmental biopark and urban learning environment (context) that includes an adjacent aquatic park, botanical garden, bosque, river, and nearby zoo. The aquarium has become a unique educational tool for environmental awareness, understanding, and stewardship through application of the Taylor method of programming and the philosophy of Van H. Gilbert Architect.

Criteria for designs are based on concepts and principles to be learned (content) through discovery by the visitor. Water is life's beginning and the lifeblood of New Mexico, beginning with a drop of water in the mountains. The aquarium is not just about seeing fish in a big tank but also about more deeply understanding aquatic life in terms of interdependencies such as cycles, ecosystems, and symbiosis; biodiversity of niche, form, and function; and stewardship of empathy, action, and reaction. An emphasis on multisensory access and types of exhibits (living, nonliving, and technological) address how people learn (learning processes).

Albuquerque Aquarium and BioPark, New Mexico. Local physical context. View of the aquarium and surrounding biological park. Photograph courtesy of Van H. Gilbert Architect PC.

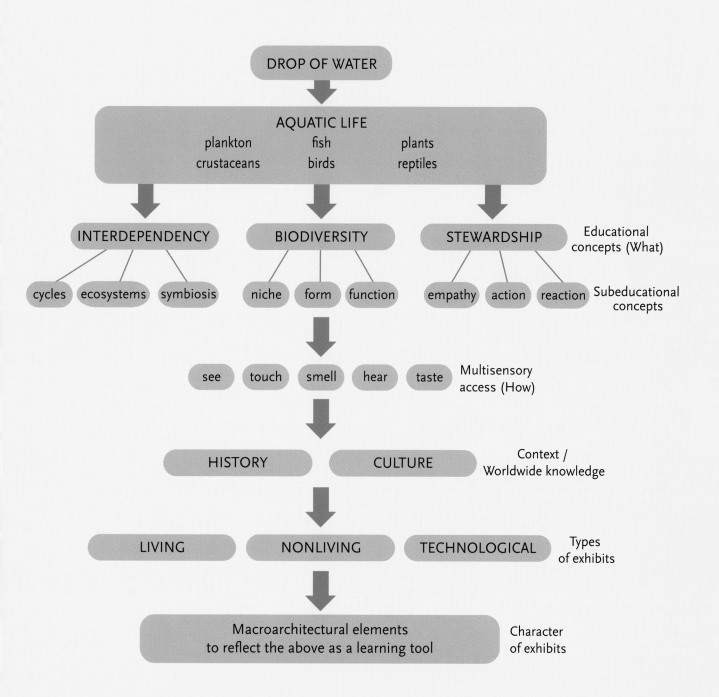

The Aquarium Exhibit Programming System. Designers used this format during programming and beyond as a tool for planning and coordinating visitor guides, signage, educational materials, and curriculum. Van H. Gilbert Architect PC. Anne Taylor Associates.

My last year in the classroom (2001) I had use of a set of three adjoining spaces in the technology department that allowed me to teach in a manner consistent with my highest understanding of how learning happens. The main classroom was connected to a huge, high-ceilinged, well-lit workroom furnished with extra large, sturdy tables. Students could spread out their projects and had safe places to stash their works in progress. There were ample storage cabinets for tools and supplies. The room next door housed computers loaded with design software. Although in good repair, it wasn't the most aesthetically pleasing space, but it was so perfectly *functional* that it was a thing of beauty to me.

—Eeva Reeder, consultant and former teacher

Design studio workshop students are not sitting passively in their seats awaiting instruction but are instead actively engaged in their learning, which invigorates the classroom atmosphere. Photograph courtesy of Anne Taylor.

The design studio model is at the heart of the Architecture and Children program, an interdisciplinary curriculum my colleagues and I have developed, refined, and used in the United States and abroad for nearly twenty years. This curriculum has consistently demonstrated the success of the design studio model to bring forth high-level thinking in students. Architecture, design, and the environment become the vehicle for studying the basic subject matter areas that are usually taught in schools.

The program, used as a teaching strategy, begins by increasing students' visual awareness and stimulating their curiosity about the world. Students of all ages, including teachers, learn visual-spatial tools of schematic drawing, diagramming, scale and enlargement, and architectural conventions (plan view, elevation drawings, perspective drawing, and model building). After gaining fluency in this design vocabulary, learners follow a series of specific, carefully developed interdisciplinary problems to resolve through design. There are no right or wrong answers to these problems. Creative problem solving encourages students to participate actively, design their own approaches and come up with new ideas, build on what they do know, investigate multiple solutions to a given difficulty, and organize and present their findings. The entire process requires teamwork, a skill vital to today's workplace.

The school environments we design can either help or hinder the studio workshop process of discovery and the development of lifelong learning skills. The following are some requirements for the architecture and interior design of a studio model:

- Large, horizontal work surfaces for individuals and groups (workstations and large tables)

- Adequate spaces for model building and storage of works in progress

- Vertical surfaces for personal pinup

- Tackable walls for student critiques of design solutions

- Presentation space

- Task lighting

- Windows and natural lighting

- Storage for supplies and personal belongings

- Light tables

- Movable furniture (see more in chapter 9)

- Erasable and smart walls for brainstorming, discussion, and presentation

- Connections to the outdoors: plants, patios, and courtyard access

LEARNING PROCESSES AND CONSTRUCTIVISM

The organizing system stresses learning through interaction with the environment or the constructivist approach to learning advocated by many educators interested in education reform. Constructivism involves the shift from teacher-centric to student-centric learning. Constructivists assert that students learn through a process of constructing and reconstructing their own meanings and understandings of the world. The student is valued as a thinker and doer, while the teacher functions primarily as a facilitator. This approach also benefits from the architectural format of the design studio.

In *The Case for Constructivist Classrooms*, Brooks and Brooks (1993) describe five overarching principles of constructivist pedagogy:

- Posing problems of relevance to learners

- Organizing learning around big ideas or primary concepts

- Seeking and valuing students' points of view

- Adapting curriculum to address students' hypotheses and assumptions

- Assessing student learning in the context of teaching (p. viii)

Learning environments that support constructivism are linked to the real world, employ thematic learning strategies, and encourage children to take responsibility for their own learning. They also support teachers as facilitators and colearners.

Every learning environment should have light tables for tracing, designing, or experimenting with concepts of transparency, opacity, and color. Photograph courtesy of Anne Taylor.

Robert Fitzgerald Kennedy Charter School

Albuquerque, New Mexico

Students at Robert Fitzgerald Kennedy took charge of programming, analysis, and design to create their own learning environment in a former post office building. Teacher facilitators, architects, architecture students, construction workers, and volunteers all contributed to the students' efforts to clean up the exterior site as well as to collaborate on the interior design. The process soon became a curriculum to learn basic subject matter disciplines, responsibility, stewardship, and cultural pride through service learning in design, construction, urban renewal, landscaping, and architecture.

Robert Fitzgerald Kennedy (RFK) Charter School, Albuquerque, New Mexico. A. Preliminary design process and design development at RFK with help from Matt Pacheco, architectural educator and construction company president. **B.** Moving through the architectural conventions, from early sketches to floor plan to clay model, and the transformation from two- to three-dimensional design for RFK. **C.** Teamwork and cooperation during model building. **D.** Clay and wood used for three-dimensional models. **E.** Student teamwork as construction begins at RFK. **F.** Preparations for an adobe wall. **G.** RFK students build the forms for an adobe wall while learning an important historic skill. **H.** The final result is an informal, culturally valid space and a sense of ownership made tangible through hard work. RFK students gained valuable knowledge through researching, developing, and completing a project of their own from beginning to end. They used math, science, and art in a real-world situation from which they could see results. Images courtesy of RFK Charter School and RFK students. Robert Baade, founder. Rhonda Stanfield, Irwin Miller, and Evelyn Fernandez, teachers.

LEARNING PROCESSES AND ENVIRONMENTALLY BASED LEARNING PROGRAMS

School facility planners should also be aware of the extensions of constructivist ideas into the community, known as environment-based learning, which uses real-world natural and sociocultural settings as curricula. Think of the school year as one long field trip or service-based study, with school as a home base but most learning occurring in the community. Planners can support these excursions through a wider view of the uses of school grounds, location and siting of schools, and community access. A summary report by the State Education and Environment Roundtable (1998) of forty environmental learning schools revealed the benefits of this approach:

- ▶ Better performance on standardized measures of academic achievement in reading, writing, math, science, and social studies

- ▶ Reduced discipline and classroom management problems

- ▶ Increased engagement and enthusiasm for learning

- ▶ Greater pride and ownership in accomplishments (Hoody & Lieberman, 1998, p. 4)

LEARNING PROCESSES AND NEW EVALUATION TOOLS FOR ASSESSING STUDENT PERFORMANCE

Modern teaching styles, active and project-based learning, experiential learning, and constructivism call for new methods of assessing student performance. Rubrics (matrices or lists with performance criteria ranked by levels of competence) and portfolios help answer the call for meaningful evaluation beyond mere testing. A good exercise for educators is to work with children to develop their own performance criteria. The objective is to have clear expectations for the quality of student work so that every child can succeed, rather than to fool learners with trick test questions.

To evaluate design projects, the Architecture and Children program uses a rubric that covers five categories of student performance across a rating scale of five levels of achievement, from one (lowest) to five (highest):

- ▶ Fluency and clarity of communication

- ▶ Imagination, innovation, and creativity

- ▶ Understanding the process

- ▶ Detail and overall aesthetics

- ▶ Technical competence

Students may be evaluated over time across these five levels upon completing many projects. This instrument is helpful for performing a trend analysis on students in which each student acts as his or her own control (please see the rubric in appendix A).

Summer Architectural and Children's Program at the Albuquerque Academy. Performance-based assessment allows students and teachers to discuss and more deeply evaluate their work. Photograph by Atsuko Sakai.

Summer Architectural and Children's Program at the Albuquerque Academy.
Children who engage in active learning interact with the environment on many levels of understanding, from observation to creative problem solving to valuing and stewardship. Photograph by Atsuko Sakai.

Portfolios provide another means for measuring student performance over time. For the Keystone Early Learning Center in Alabama, Anne Taylor Associates developed a "portfolio for the child's creative self-expression." This served dual purposes as a checklist of items to include in a student portfolio and a review/assessment tool. Work collected in portfolios shows the process of a student's thinking over time and is a source for reflection and evaluation (Concordia LLC, 1999). Portfolios are often bulky and require the architectural support of wide or deep storage shelves or drawers and increased space for personal storage.

Even as our current political system advocates standardized testing as the most effective method for measuring student performance, our nation's top educational researchers are looking into ways to augment this view with alternative formats that are better indicators of future student performance. Psychology professor Robert Sternberg's Rainbow Project Test aims for "right brain" aptitudes often missed by the traditional SAT, such as humor and response to real-life challenges (Pink, 2005, pp. 58–59).

LEARNING PROCESSES AND TAXONOMY

Over years of observing children as they interact with the environment, I have developed a taxonomy or pattern that shows how children can engage in deeper levels of thought. Taxonomy is a process of classification, in the case of education identifying levels of cognition or thinking that can be invoked in learners' minds. The taxonomy that has emerged through my work at School Zone Institute, a nonprofit consulting organization I founded with George Vlastos, is an informal tool that helps facilitators engage children as they reach beyond superficial knowledge of facts to higher levels of thinking, including synthesis, evaluation, and stewardship. As students move through the steps, they achieve new, complex understandings of the environment and its embedded concepts. Learning shifts from perception to concepts and problem solving to an often neglected ethical/spiritual dimension, not always in purely linear progression. In other words, the whole learner is actively engaged across body, mind, and spirit.

Once children evaluate their discoveries, they begin the process again with new hypotheses and fresh observations. In this way, learning evolves from the simple to the complex in spiral fashion, as students return to concepts at ever more sophisticated levels of understanding.

The Anne Taylor Associates (ATA) Taxonomy can be used to teach any subject or concept in any learning situation and at all age levels. Even very young children, whose abilities are often underestimated by adults, can benefit from its active, experiential approach. Teachers can memorize the taxonomy as a system, thought pattern, or instructional strategy for use over and over again. Architects can use the taxonomy to define the types of activities children must experience in the learning settings, and to plan spaces that support those activities.

The Experiential Approach to Learning:
A Six-Step Process or Taxonomy

1. Observation and multisensory discovery

- ▶ Using the senses (seeing, hearing, smelling, tasting, touching)
- ▶ Recording what is observed using a variety of media (drawing, writing, videotaping, entering data on a computer)

2. Data collection
- ▶ Counting
- ▶ Measuring
- ▶ Mapping
- ▶ Questioning and interviewing
- ▶ Sorting, classifying, and comparing

3. Concept formation and literacy in all disciplines
- ▶ Visual-spatial and verbal thinking, literacy, and language (concrete to abstract)
- ▶ Labeling and literacy across all disciplines (math, science, the arts, language, foreign language, social studies, ecology, technology/digital literacy, health, and physical education)
- ▶ Family literacy, emergent literacy, multilingualism to empower global citizenry
- ▶ Researching, reading, and understanding ideas

4. Creative problem solving (based on scientific method but applied to all disciplines)
- ▶ Defining the problem or felt difficulty
- ▶ Forming the hypothesis
- ▶ Testing the hypothesis through action on objects
- ▶ Synthesizing and analyzing data collected
- ▶ Using inductive and deductive reasoning
- ▶ Verifying or rejecting the hypothesis
- ▶ Starting over or building on what has been learned

5. Valuing
- ▶ Making critical aesthetic judgments
- ▶ Decision making
- ▶ Self-identifying and self-motivating
- ▶ Working with others, understanding multiple points of view, and working in teams
- ▶ Cultural pluralism
- ▶ Evaluation

6. Stewardship
- ▶ Ecoliteracy, environmental wisdom, nonlinear thinking, and systems thinking
- ▶ Respecting and taking care of the built, natural, and cultural environment

The taxonomy in action. Students creating birdhouses in different architectural styles experience a six-step approach to learning, from data collection on birds and architecture to synthesis represented in the built model to stewardship of birds in the environment. Illustration by Pat Lange.

▶ Cultivating a symbiotic relationship with the environment and a sense of belonging
▶ Employing global ethics (sustainability as a moral issue)
▶ Taking responsibility for the consequences of one's actions (freedom, not license)
▶ Thinking beyond the self

The taxonomy can help determine questioning strategies for learning and curriculum development. Educators and architects might also use the taxonomy during the planning phases for school facilities. To solicit feedback, planners can begin with simple questions aimed at observation skills, eventually progressing to questions that require students or stakeholders to define their decision-making process. Opportunities for higher levels of learning can be programmed into the school facilities design, and architects and educators eventually can use the taxonomy for evaluating learning environments once they are in use. Are there places for multisensory learning, creative problem solving, and stewardship in the finished environment? Does the environment promote imaginative thinking? Do users demonstrate higher levels of cognition while using the environment? Is vandalism nonexistent, and do students take care of their environment? Is the school clean and orderly? These questions and more apply to all learning environment design, from pre-kindergarten to higher education.

LEARNING PROCESSES AND THE DEVELOPMENTAL NEEDS OR RIGHTS OF ALL CHILDREN

The taxonomy outlined earlier is based on an understanding of the developmental needs of all children. Ways of learning take the whole learner into account. I often refer to these important developmental needs as "rights." Children deserve to learn in multiple ways, and educators must expand their repertoire of instructional strategies to include learning tools not regularly available to students.

I have included the summary below as a reminder to educators and architects of the variety of learning experiences that children enjoy and yet are sometimes omitted from daily learning, often due to a lack of flexible facilities. The richest learning experiences allow body, mind, and spirit to be engaged simultaneously. I am more concerned with the wholeness of experience than hierarchies.

Using an Organizing System

DEVELOPMENTAL RIGHTS SUMMARY

Body

▶ Multisensory perception

Seeing, hearing, smelling, tasting, touching

▶ Gross motor development

Using large muscles for crawling, walking, running, jumping, playing sports, dancing, coordinating movement (from simple to complex)

▶ Fine motor development

Using small muscles for manipulating objects, gripping, touching, drawing, lettering, painting, cutting, measuring, etc., with accuracy and control; hand-eye motor coordination

▶ Wellness

Health, safety, body systems, nutrition, exercising, fitness, taking responsibility for personal and family health, growing, emotional health

Mind

▶ Concept development

Experimenting, discovering, developing ideas across all disciplines, building knowledge and understanding in an interdisciplinary way

▶ Labeling, language, literacy, and technical literacy

Communicating verbally, reading, listening, writing, multimedia researching, analyzing literature across genres (developing a multifaceted form of literacy that incorporates Gardner's intelligences and is not confined to verbal-linguistic skills)

▶ Cognition and creative problem solving

Transferring and applying knowledge, sorting information, constructing, sequencing, thinking logically, employing the scientific method, making connections, using technology, and developing the spirit of inquiry

▶ Ecoliteracy

Understanding ecological principles and natural patterns, networking, relationships, global and systems thinking

Spirit

▶ Creative self-expression

Dancing, drama/acting, performing, music, visual arts, imagining, creative storytelling, self-identifying and motivation

▶ Cultural pluralism

Valuing other cultures, understanding diversity, developing a sense of community, participating

▶ Valuing and stewardship

Respecting all life forms, articulating likes and dislikes, forming aesthetic judgments, reflecting, examining ethics, caring for the Earth and each other

▶ Self and social development

Healthy interaction, cooperating, sharing, teamwork, taking pride in accomplishments, learning about emotions, developing a sense of self

All learners deserve the right to engage the world in multiple ways and with multiple literacies. It is the duty of instructors and designers to reach and motivate the whole learner in every student.

A RETURN TO PROGRAMMING

The educational theories expressed above remain in the mind as motivators for future programming and design decisions. Learning processes across body, mind, and spirit apply to architectural quality, too. The categories translate easily into architectural criteria for habitability, or the satisfaction the occupant has with a building's safety, functionality, psychological comfort, and aesthetic appeal. A discussion of habitability as it applies to developmental needs and the programming process comes in chapter 6.

The Anne Taylor Organizing System for School Facility Planning

Context
Where we learn

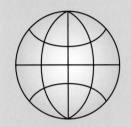

- ▶ The local geophysical setting: the built, natural and cultural environment
- ▶ Thematic learning
- ▶ Systems thinking
- ▶ Sustainable worldview
- ▶ Cultural environment as a learning tool

Content
What we learn

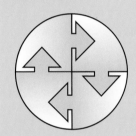

- ▶ Subject matter disciplines
- ▶ Interdisciplinary concepts
- ▶ Elements of architecture
- ▶ Manifestations for learning
- ▶ Art and design
- ▶ Project based portfolio assessment

Learning Processes
How we learn

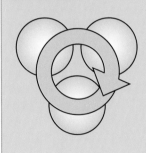

- ▶ Developmental rights of all children (body, mind, spirit)
- ▶ Multiple intelligences theory
- ▶ ATA Taxonomy, including stewardship
- ▶ Hands-on, constructivist learning
- ▶ Applied technology
- ▶ Project-based assessment

Example of Interdisciplinary Curriculum Content
Taught across the Disciplines by Common Concepts

ENVIRONMENT
Represents Laws and Principles in the Universe

Math	Life Science	Physical Science	Social Studies	Language	Art	Music	Dance & Phys Ed	Philosophy
Numbers Numerals Sets and logic Time Measurement Geometry	Cycle Change Metamorphosis Effect Rhythm	Motion Energy Matter	Culture Race Change	Syntax Grammar Description Comparison	Color Line Form Space Texture Rhythm	Harmony Scale Rhythm Interval	Body Time Space Form Force	What is real? What is true? What is good?
Balance as Symmetry/ Asymmetry	Balance in Nature	Physics of Structure	Balance of Power	Reason/ Logic Balanced Argument	Compositional Balance	Tonal/ Atonal Balance	Physical Balance	Balance as Equilibrium

Curriculum content represents the laws and principles which govern the material universe. Through architecture and design, educators can begin to show students the interdependencies of all things and the meanings concepts create from simple to complex. See "balance" above.

Interdisciplinary Concepts

Subject Matter Area	Concepts
Sciences	Ecology • Cycle • Change • Network • Plant • Animal • Interdependency • Habitat • System • Recycling • Earth • Physics • States of matter • Sound • Temperature • Electricity • Magnetism • Light • Motion • Forces • Balance • Energy • Machines • Weather • Space • Universe • Chemical • Element • Diagram • Inquiry
Mathematics	Numbers • Numerals • Counting • Repetition • Addition • Subtraction • Multiplication • Division • Equality • Calculation • Quantity • Symmetry • Time • Measurement • Geometry (point, line, shape, form, angle, proof) • Pattern • Sets and logic • Money • Scale/proportion • Fractions • Probability • Statistics • Data analysis • Graph
Language Arts	Alphabet/letters • Labeling • Word • Sentence • Paragraph • Writing • Reading • Editorial process • Communication • Comprehension • Text/publications • Description • Analogy/metaphor • Poetry • Story/narrative • Book • Philosophy • Research • Illustration • Languages (foreign, signing, Braille) • Listening • Symbolism
Social Studies	History • Geography • Map/globe • World • Place • Culture • Ethnicity/race • Religions • Limits/laws/rules • Location • Government • Civics • Separation • Inclusion • Conflict • Socialization • Citizenship • Service • Volunteer • Participation• Leaders/leadership • Urban planning • Transportation • Customs/manners • Economics • Jobs
Technology	Computer • Data/database • Systems thinking • Internet/World Wide Web • E-mail • Interaction • Software • Information management • Search engine • Equipment • Virtual learning • Digital age• Word processing • Disc • Connection • Blog • Simulation • Remote immersion • Biofeedback • Global communication • Game
Visual Arts	Architecture • Design • Painting • Drawing • Sculpture • Mixed media • Organizing elements of art and design (point, line, shape, form, space, color, texture, rhythm, balance, proportion, variety, emphasis, unity) • Spatial Organization • Photography • Self-expression • Perception • Appreciation • Gallery • Aesthetics • Symbol • Graphics • Creativity
Performance Arts	Dance • Music • Song • Element of music (harmony, tone, scale, pattern, interval, pitch, beat) • Instrument • Drama• Plays • Role • Speech• Presentation • Movement • Rhythm • Kinesthetic Expression • Improvisation • Composition • Audience • Plot • Action • Stage • Practice/rehearsal • Fantasy • Imagination
Physical Education and Health	Gross motor (large muscle usage) • Fine motor (manipulation of objects) • Muscle • Torso • Body parts (arm, leg) • Exercise • Sports • Sportsmanship • Fitness • Nutrition/diet/foods • Calorie/caloric balance • Hygiene • Relationships • Family • Body systems (neurological, skeletal, digestive, circulatory, pulmonary) • Growth • Development • Conflict management • Safety • Choice

The objects we see are representative of the underlying concepts, ideas, laws, and principles of the universe. Learning facility design can be executed to reflect interdisciplinary concepts such as the ones listed above.

Influential Educational Theorists

John Dewey **Experimentation**	▶ Children are intensely active and curriculum should reflect their active interests. ▶ Learning is a continual process of reorganization, reconstruction, transformation, experimentation, and reflection. ▶ Education should promote participatory democracy (Dewey, 1916).
Jean Piaget **Developmental Psychology**	▶ Children learn through concrete action, research, discovery, and construction in identifiable developmental stages. ▶ Children construct and reconstruct meaning through experimentation and error (Piaget, 1972).
Maria Montessori **The Prepared Environment**	▶ The curriculum is embedded in selected manipulatives in the environment. ▶ The well-provisioned environment supports learning in practical, sensory and formal ways. ▶ Early childhood learning requires methods that are intellectually and developmentally stimulating. ▶ Children are capable of sustained concentration and work (Ornstein & Levine, 2003).
Viktor Lowenfeld **Art Education**	▶ Children are motivated when they identify deeply with what is being learned (self-identification). ▶ There are many ways to motivate creativity in children, and teachers need to learn such techniques. ▶ Children pass through identifiable developmental stages of visual self-expression (Lowenfeld & Brittain, 1970).
Lev Vygotsky **Social Psychology**	▶ Learning occurs in social and cultural settings. ▶ Learning occurs through the adaptive process of internalization (Vygotsky, 1978).
Benjamin Bloom **Taxonomy of Thinking**	▶ Higher-level thinking extends beyond factual knowledge. ▶ A hierarchy of learning or cognitive categories outlined by Bloom includes Knowledge, Comprehension, Application, Analysis, Synthesis, and Evaluation. ▶ The goal of education is to reach the levels of higher order thinking (Bloom et al., 1956). ▶ For a recent revision of Bloom's taxonomy that helps teachers understand and implement a standards-based curriculum, see Anderson and Krathwohl, *A Taxonomy for Learning, Teaching, and Assessing: A Revision of Bloom's Taxonomy of Educational Objectives.*

During the programming process, I take time to examine and share the ideas of educators who have inspired and influenced my evolving view of the learning environment. A long tradition of research and theory supports my view of best practices in education. My philosophy builds on the contributions of the above.

Influential Educational Theorists *(continued)*

Howard Gardner **Multiple Intelligences**	▶ The theory of multiple intelligences has many applications in the classroom as educators seek strategies to reach all learners and to expand beyond traditional verbal/logical modes of teaching and learning. Gardner identified the following intelligences: Verbal/linguistic, Logical/mathematical, Musical/rhythmic, Visual/spatial, Interpersonal, Intrapersonal, Bodily/kinesthetic, Naturalistic (Gardner, 1983, 1990).
Sandra N. Kaplan and Bette Gould **Interdisciplinarity**	▶ Thematic interdisciplinary units of study allow for in-depth learning. ▶ Systems thinking is a valuable tool for curriculum planning (Kaplan & Gould, 1996).
Robert J. Sternberg **Triarchic Theory of Successful Intelligence**	▶ The Triarchic Theory of human intelligence helps teachers design curriculum to meet analytic, creative, and practical abilities in students (Sternberg, 1984). ▶ There are patterns learners follow to solve problems. The steps of the problem-solving cycle move from recognizing and defining problems to devising strategies, collecting data, and evaluating results (Sternberg, 1998).
Spencer Kagan **Cooperative Strategies for Learning**	▶ Kagan's *Cooperative Learning* is a practical guidebook to key concepts behind cooperative learning: Teams and team building, Class building, Cooperative management, Will to cooperate, Skill to cooperate, Structures for cooperation (Kagan, 1992).
Anne Taylor and George Vlastos **Design and Environment**	▶ The physical environment is a silent curriculum. ▶ The physical environment *is* pedagogy. ▶ Physical surroundings deeply affect the learning and behavior of teachers and students. ▶ Design education provides a dynamic system for integrating curriculum. ▶ Architecture and design studio workshops form a model for applied learning for all subject matter areas through visual-spatial thinking, facility and landscape architecture, and urban planning (civics). ▶ Educators are trained to use the environment as a teaching and learning tool. ▶ Collaboration with other professions is encouraged. Engineers, doctors, architects, economists, and attorneys could all be teachers, even without a teaching license. ▶ Essential to education of the future is environmental knowing, i.e., reading environmental messages and acting responsibly (stewardship).

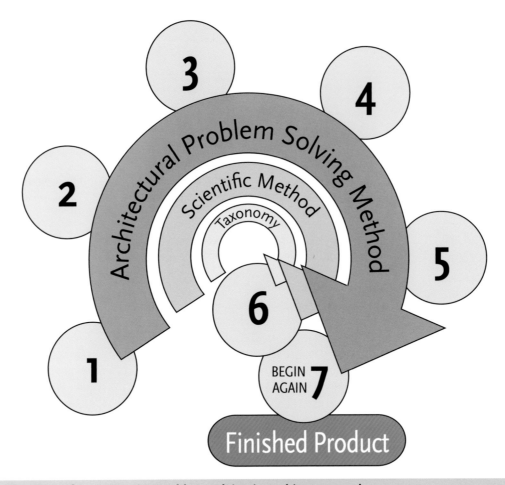

	The scientific method	Creative problem solving in architecture and design	Taxonomy for learning	
1	Felt difficulty, a problem to solve	A client has a need or problem to be solved	Observation and multisensory discovery	1
2	Hypothesis	Designer has an idea; sketches in a sketchbook	Data collection	2
3	Data collection	Collects data, studies precedents, conducts site analysis, analyzes spatial relationships, writes architectural program	Concept formation/ literacy	3
4	Analysis, synthesis	Begins design process in detail; pervasive quality of product emerges	Creative problem solving	4
5	Accept or reject hypothesis	Client and architect accept or reject final design or modify to meet selected criteria	Valuing	5
6	Replicate	Project is complete or building is built	Stewardship	6
7	Evaluate and begin again	User's guide and Post-occupancy Evaluation (POE) and begin again	Reflection and begin again	7

A Case Study in Collaborative School Design

McWillie School, Jackson, Mississippi

Jeffery Lackney, PhD

*Assistant professor, Department of Engineering Professional Development
at the University of Wisconsin–Madison*

Jackson Public School District's objective in the McWillie School project was to develop a K–2 elementary school facility program for approximately five hundred learners. A secondary objective was to use this project planning process to develop a model educational facility design guide for use in future projects. Initial project issues included the following:

- ▶ Creating a model school dedicated to early childhood education
- ▶ K–2 grade configuration
- ▶ A model Montessori program

THE WORKSHOP PROCESS

The planning team consisted of administrators, teachers, and parents invited from across the district as well as the architect chosen for the building design and construction. Members from the Educational Design Institute at Mississippi State University were asked to design and facilitate a total of five workshops aimed at creating a coherent set of design guidelines for a K–2 learning environment.

In the first workshop the planning team took a few moments to recall positive attributes and qualities of their early experiences in school. The team members then shared their personal visions, eventually forming a shared vision of ten learning goals for McWillie School. In subsequent workshops, the planning team brainstormed and edited down all the learning activities that might be expected to take place at McWillie School, and then identified the learning goals met by each learning activity. The team clarified learning group size and other physical descriptors and organized learning activities into their spatial and/or temporal relationships. Finally, the planning team conducted an exercise in which members identified physical design patterns that were needed to support the learning activities.

EDUCATIONAL DESIGN PATTERNS FOR MCWILLIE SCHOOL

The planning team successfully grouped patterns of activity into twenty-one learning setting patterns that were eventually combined to form six broad educational design patterns for McWillie School. The educational design patterns formed the basis for the final planning team exercise in which the layout of the school could be accomplished. The following are the six educational design patterns:

1. Welcoming center

2. Discovery center

3. Dining facilities

4. Family room

5. Learning room

6. Outdoor learning environments

What follows are the diagrams that form one of the core educational design patterns: the learning room. The learning room is at the heart of McWillie School and is intended as an area that is "owned" by learners. The learning activities matrix organizes the information generated in the planning team's workshops. A second table details the types of learning setting patterns for the learning room and the activities expected in those areas. Five learning rooms are grouped to form "houses," and the shared educational concept informed the eventual design of the school.

The Learning Room

Learning Activities Matrix

Learning Activity	Learning Goals	Learning Environment					Interpretation of Concepts
		Group	Location	Physical Attributes/ Qualities	Spatial Patterns		
Learning about growing food: gardens, cultivating, nurturing, "house" scale (planting tomatoes)	Developmental-appropriate, love of lifelong learning	10–15	Inside and outside	Flexible, everyday, adaptable, visible, colorful, vertical, spacious, oriented to views, active, shaded, natural, exposed, open	Natural light, door to the outside, learning garden, view of the outdoors, wet area, project work area, animal habitat		Group projects area: a central shared workspace for 10–15 students with display walls surrounded by various types of learning alcoves such as personal workspaces, technology alcoves, learning centers, and storage
Read aloud, whole group teaching, literature strategies/skills: peers, individual	Love of lifelong learning, Respect for one another, Developmental-appropriate, Early childhood education, Individual needs	10–15	Inside	Flexible, casual, large, everyday, cheerful, open, active	Stair seating, collection of books, sitting circle		Gathering space: open space with enough area for 10–15 to sit on the floor. Space is near windows and a door to the outside, with shelving. Stair seating in corner
Kinesthetic activities: building, sequencing, comparing, pretending, discovering	Developmental-appropriate, Early childhood education, Individual needs	10–15	Inside	Busy, child-sized, active	Performance platform, work surface, shared workspace, view of the outdoors, table with a place for everyone, quiet corner, open storage, closed storage, observation room, personal workspace		See group projects area
Learning about math: sorting, counting, classifying, adding, subtracting, grouping, taking apart, using hands-on materials	Love of lifelong learning, Developmental-appropriate, Early childhood education, Individual needs	3–4	Inside	Fixed, everyday, permanent, child-sized, cheerful, cozy, busy, loose fit, adaptable	Open storage, display wall, natural light, door to the outside, shared workspace, interactive work with the environment, work surface, learning centers, view of the outdoors, technology alcove, meeting space		See group projects area
Learning refined motor skills: "punching" works, sorting, puzzles, penmanship, block building	Innovative educational methods, Love of lifelong learning, Early childhood education, Reading/early literacy	1–2	Inside	Ordered, hands-on, unique, quiet, concentrative, repetitive	Personal workspace, view of the outdoors, project work area, table with a place for everyone, open storage, shared work space		See group projects area

The Learning Room

Design Patterns and Learning Activities that Make up the Learning Room

Learning Setting Patterns	Learning Activities
Gathering Space	
An open space with enough area for 10–15 to sit on the floor. Space is near windows and a door to the outside, with shelving. Stair seating in corner	Learning to listen: storytelling • Read aloud, whole group teaching, literature strategies/skills: peers, individual
Group Projects Area	
A central shared workspace for 10–15 students with display walls surrounded by various types of learning alcoves such as personal workspaces, technology alcoves, learning centers, and storage. Provide natural daylight	Learning about growing food: gardens, cultivating, nurturing, "house" scale (planting tomatoes) • Kinesthetic activities: building, sequencing, comparing, pretending, discovering • Learning about math: sorting, counting, classifying, adding, subtracting, grouping, taking apart, using hands-on materials • Learning refined motor skills: "punching" works, sorting, puzzles, penmanship, block building • Learning about art: Painting, drawing, cutting, gluing, displaying, printing, clay, color wheel, sculpting • Sociocultural learning: "traveling" to other places and times, experiencing other cultures and countries, designing communities • Learning social skills: diversity—sensitivity, training, respect for self and others, following authority • Scientific learning: exploring, discovering, investigating, inquiring, wondering
Learning Alcove	
A well-defined, out-of-the-way workspace for 1–4 learners with readily available book and resource storage. Directly adjacent to the group projects area	Independent reading • Independent computer activity • Learning to write: journalizing, independent writing, poetry, penmanship, conceptual writing • Individual tutoring
Porch for Learning	
A covered outdoor platform with a door to inside instructional areas. Offers a minimum of six-foot width along the face of the building for sitting circles, furniture, displays, and presentations. Accommodates 3–4 learners	Learning to write: journalizing, independent writing, poetry, penmanship, conceptual writing • Individual tutoring • Learning refined motor skills: "punching" works, sorting, puzzles, penmanship, block building
Learning Garden	
A garden that encourages active learning. Contains a place for 10–15 children and adults to sit with a fountain overlooked by a porch. Garden used for planting experiments, plant identification, and other learning experiences	Students met by adults, greeted in a kind way • Welcoming parents and community into school • Demonstrative learning: show and tell in a special environment • Learning about growing food: gardens, cultivating, nurturing, "house" scale (planting tomatoes) • Garden, planting, growing, weeding (outdoor classroom) • Scientific learning: exploring, discovering, investigating, inquiring, wondering • Individual tutoring • Learning refined motor skills: "punching" works, sorting, puzzles, penmanship, block building

Kuoppanummi School,
Finland. Interior design
and furniture by Architects
Meskanen & Pursiainen.
Photo by Jussi Tiainen.

CHAPTER SIX

Habitability of Learning Environments

Introduction: Before Design Begins

Moving from philosophy toward design of built facilities begins with programming. Programming is the architectural planning process that precedes design. Methods of programming vary widely in format, approach, and degree of participant involvement, but the key point to remember is that qualitative thinking and planning must come *before* design begins. Many school district planners are under pressure to save time and money, and are tempted to skim past this important step by relying heavily on replicated prototypes, non–site specific school designs, or predetermined square footage needs for design. Every request for a new building, however, should be viewed as a new problem to be solved. When we approach design problems with predetermined spatial solutions already in mind, we limit creative possibilities for new design, and we shut out student, teacher, and community input as well. Many of the strongest architectural designs for schools arise from a deep understanding of the particular client, place, and usage, and are site specific.

There are two main components to antecedent thinking about school design. As we saw in chapter 5, one concern is how well versed all members of the school planning process are in terms of educational best practices and how those practices can be articulated to help guide designers. A second determining factor in a program's effectiveness is that many stakeholders simply are not trained in aesthetics and the visual-spatial thinking that informs the programming process. Before actual programming begins, introductory sessions can provide an opportunity to educate the public in visual thinking and the principles of the knowing eye. It is rare that the educational potential of the school design process is fully exploited during programming.

Creative Circulation Solutions
The photographs that follow in this chapter reveal many solutions to circulation design and treatments for connective, transitional spaces.

Kuoppanummi Day Care Center, Finland.
Top: Concepts are built into what could have been wasted space. Homerooms connected by a kiosk/theater with stairs, a peek element, mirrors, and wood contribute to the overall aesthetic. Photograph by Jussi Tiainen. **Bottom:** Places for interaction and play. Perko Architects. Interior design and pedagogical furniture by Architects Meskanen & Pursiainen. Photograph by Pihla Meskanen.

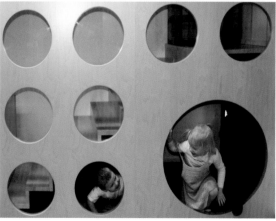

The Value of Preprogramming

Understandably, many do not know how to read architectural visual symbols and have little experience in the facility planning process. It has been my experience that many administrators, for example, relinquish their decision making to boards or architects who rely heavily on predetermined educational specifications. Since administrators and teachers should play a key role in planning and should work closely with architects, they must be properly educated in architectural processes and visual language so that their educationally valid ideas are included in the design. Preprogramming can help fill this gap through design studio workshops as introduced in chapter 5, and through presentations and walking tours that introduce stakeholders to exciting architecture. Ideally, however, I would like to see visual thinking skills and school facility planning and design courses included in certification programs for administrators and teachers. Architects, too, should be fully prepared through their university professional development programs to adopt the role of educator as they offer design alternatives for the future. We must take advantage of new technologies and opportunities to create and use virtual models, building energy simulations, global mapping systems for enrollment projections, and other assistive programs as tools for visualizing future learning conditions and environments.

Commissioning and Educational Commissioning

The holistic planning process known as "commissioning" has special import for planning efficiently and for implementing sustainable design. Commissioning begins with the first stages of planning and extends through the entire process of design and construction to post-occupancy use of the building. It goes beyond the heavy focus on initial costs that often limits design or results in value engineering, to include full life-cycle costs and costs of building maintenance and long-term operation. A recent study by Kats et al. at Capital E (2003) reveals that the up-front increase for green design is estimated at 2 percent, with life-cycle savings of 20 percent of the total construction costs.

Schools are assets to the community that are worthy of long-term investment. Planners can also overcome perceived barriers to spending by using a new educational component to commissioning. Educational Commissioning is a process of informing community partners and users of schools about the design intent of a new facility. The benefit is that educators and students know how to use the building to its maximum potential. Community partners understand why additional resources may need to be invested in schools to ensure that facilities are supportive of the educational process long into the future (Lackney, 2005).

Thirty-three Principles for School Facilities Design

From the School Design Research Studio

The intent of this document available online from architect and educator Jeffery Lackney (2003) is to provide a framework of educational design principles that can be used from the earliest planning strategy sessions through school occupancy. A shared premise or baseline links the design principles: learner-centered, development and age appropriate, safe, comfortable, accessible, flexible, equitable, and cost effective. Principles are grouped as follows:

▶ Planning and design of educational facilities

▶ Site and building organization

▶ Primary education space

▶ Shared school and community facilities

▶ Community spaces

▶ Character of all spaces

▶ Site design and outdoor learning spaces

The thirty-three principles are derived from a variety of sources, all cited for further reference.

Steps in the Taylor/Vlastos Programming and Design Process

The following list provides a simple overview of the programming and design process that architect George Vlastos and I have used when working with schools. The steps define the general scope of work for a typical school facilities project, but with a new focus on student/teacher learning and inclusion in the design process. A much more detailed summary table of the entire Taylor/Vlastos planning and design process with corresponding educational implications appears at the end of chapter 8.

INCLUSION OF THE LEARNER IN THE PROGRAMMING AND DESIGN PROCESS: INTRODUCTION TO THE SCOPE OF WORK

Client Orientation
Establish ties of communication and a common language, determine who will participate (select a representative stakeholder group from staff, students, and community), introduce the entire architectural team, and schedule the process.

Preprogramming

Begin with values and philosophy, review alternative educational practices, teach visual-spatial thinking, introduce architectural ideas for the future, review the budget and the project delivery method, create a general list of anticipated expenditures, and conduct master-planning research, including siting and ecological criteria and green certification standards.

Site Analysis

With student help, collect data on geophysical, biological, ecological, cultural, and regulatory aspects of the site, keeping in mind that the site can be used as a learning tool; identify community resources near the site (see more in chapter 10).

Programming

Examine needs and wants (with student, teacher, and parent input, using the visual thinking skills they have been taught earlier), review architectural adequacy standards, translate developmental goals into activity settings, perform a trial run of the cost estimate analysis and compare to budget; and review, seek feedback, edit, and write the program.

Schematic Design

Uncover preliminary design relationships and adjacencies; make schematic drawings, sketches and diagrams, and get feedback; refine cost estimates.

Design Development

Using architectural conventions of plan view, elevations, perspective drawings, and models, translate activity settings into physical design determinants, offer increasingly detailed design solutions and budgeting, and obtain stakeholder approvals. Make modifications based on feedback from students, educators, and community.

Construction Documents

Create large construction documents that contractors can use to build the structure. Coordinate technological/computer communication and programs for sharing information, including student access.

Construction

Bid contracts, and build and equip the structure.

User's Guide

Work with teachers and students to write and illustrate a document that can be used as a curriculum or as a tool for professional development. The user's guide describes the learning potential of the school based on the ideas uncovered during programming, educational standards of the school district, and objects built into the school environment. Include ideas for facility management, care, and stewardship. The user's guide can prompt professional development of staff or the use of the learning environment as a teaching and learning tool.

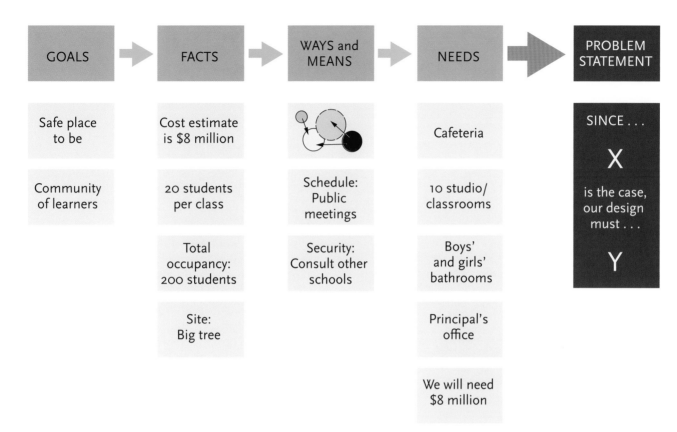

GOALS	FACTS	WAYS and MEANS	NEEDS	PROBLEM STATEMENT
Safe place to be	Cost estimate is $8 million		Cafeteria	SINCE . . . X is the case, our design must . . . Y
Community of learners	20 students per class	Schedule: Public meetings	10 studio/ classrooms	
	Total occupancy: 200 students	Security: Consult other schools	Boys' and girls' bathrooms	
	Site: Big tree		Principal's office	
			We will need $8 million	

This simple matrix system of display is adapted from the programming and problem-seeking methods of Peña and Parshall (2001). The schematic drawing illustrates a means of sorting and collecting concepts during a programming workshop. The method, easily understood and used by children and adults, usually involves using five-by-eight-inch index cards with one visual or printed verbal idea per card, displayed and organized on a wall for clear visibility up to fifteen feet away. Schematic by Atsuko Sakai. Adapted from Peña and Parshall, *Problem Seeking*.

Post-occupancy Evaluation

Conduct a Post-occupancy Evaluation (POE) linked to educational needs and programming criteria to determine the success of the design as perceived by users, architects, and evaluators representing groups such as the LEED program. Be sure the POE addresses the effects of the building on learning.

Specific procedures during planning will vary depending on the many options for project delivery that are now used by school planners and sometimes required by school districts. Some methods follow a linear design-bid-build route, while others consolidate the process. CEFPI and NCEF are excellent sources for understanding options and their pros and cons and directing planners to additional programming resources. *Problem Seeking*, the programming primer by William Peña and Steven Parshall (2001), also provides principles, definitions, examples, activities, and techniques of programming. This respected guide represents a tradition of involving and interacting with clients as the first step in the design process.

Top: Kuoppanummi School, Finland.
Gathering space. Built-in tiered seating for
informal gatherings outside classrooms.
Photograph by Pihla Meskanen.
**Bottom: Kuoppanummi Day Care Center,
Finland.** Storage space in corridors.
Circular child-scaled seating also serves as
storage, and vertical storage units divide
and define space. Photograph by Jussi
Tiainen. Perko Architects. Interior design
and pedagogical furniture by Architects
Meskanen & Pursiainen.

Inclusion of stakeholders in the programming process from
the beginning helps participants see the planning and design
process as an organic whole. Discoveries made in early programming later form the basis for the design, usage, and assessment
of the learning facility upon completion. Linking architecture
and education at each stage of the planning and design process
also provides a new value system for determining the worth
of different elements of the project, especially in light of budget constraints. For example, value engineering, in theory, is a
systematic method to improve value by examining function and
cost without losing quality. Value is defined as the ratio of function to cost. To create a higher value one can either improve the
function or reduce the cost. In practice, however, I have found
that value engineers cut design elements from the plan with
little concern for or understanding of the long-term learning
potential and developmental benefits to students. School quality
is sacrificed to low cost because budget writers are unaware that
the physical environment itself influences student performance
not only at health and safety levels but also by functioning as a
learning and teaching tool. Professionals make decisions that are
vital to the quality of education without fully understanding what
constitutes "value" for students. The programming process can
educate all stakeholders about the true educational value of well-
constructed schools.

Architectural Habitability and the Developmental Rights of Learners

The Taylor system for preprogramming identifies and defines
developmental needs or rights of learners. During the programming phase, these needs can be translated into levels of habitability, or indications of environmental quality as perceived by
building users. If a building receives a high rating for habitability, it is found to be a satisfying place, highly livable across
body, mind, and spirit. The Roman Vitruvius first said it most
simply in the first century: to succeed, buildings must meet a
triple standard of firmness, commodity, and delight (as quoted
in Rybczynski, 2001, p. 4).

To explain this process of translation, I begin with an instrument architect Wolfgang Preiser and I developed years ago to
link educational and architectural needs during programming
(also see graphic in Tools for Thought). The "habitability framework" is loosely based on levels of human functioning outlined

by psychologist/philosopher Abraham Maslow. Maslow listed a hierarchy of human motivation beginning with physiological needs such as hunger or thirst, and reaching the highest-level need for self-actualization, or full realization of one's potential (Maslow, 1943, 1954). The Taylor and Preiser method groups Maslow's needs by body, mind, and spirit. Occupants' needs for the built environment (architecture) are then translated as habitability levels. The levels are expressed in terms of architectural habitability on three levels:

- ▸ Body or health and safety

- ▸ Mind or functional performance

- ▸ Spirit or psychological comfort and aesthetic satisfaction (Preiser & Taylor, 1983)

Physical learning needs are met at the health and safety level through adherence to codes and hygiene standards, avoidance of hazards and hazardous materials, and by meeting health, security, safety concerns throughout the facility. Architectural programs consider appropriate construction practices, public policy, access (Americans with Disabilities Act, or ADA), fiscal anticorruption controls, ecologically sound systems and practices, crime prevention, and land use policy. Overall design should speak to the advantages of wellness over intervention (an ounce of prevention is worth a pound of cure).

The mind is supported in the physical environment by adequate space, spatial relationships, adjacency, and communication systems. Technology, spaces that support changing educational delivery systems, multiple use, flexibility, adjustable lighting, storage, and deployability and ergonomics of furniture also support performance. An environment rich in cues or prompts for learning (known as manifestations; see chapter 7) supports learning, the mind, and cognition.

Psychological comfort and aesthetic satisfaction are enhanced through ambient qualities such as color or natural lighting, sensory stimulation, privacy/places for reflection, accessibility, control, adaptability, meaning, cultural connections, and links to nature and beauty (ecology and stewardship).

Qualitative standards for architecture that truly support school function, learning, and student happiness are *not* necessarily built into codes and educational specifications. Architectural adequacy standards establish the acceptable levels for the physical condition, capacity, educational suitability, and technological infrastructure of school buildings. Standards are vital for their

Harold G. Fearn Elementary School, Aurora, Illinois.
Sunlight patterns. Hallway with built-in cubbies, seating, and display. Perkins + Will Architects. Steven Turckes and Gaylaird Christopher, principal architects. Photograph courtesy of Gaylaird Christopher.

Capuano Early Childhood Center, Somerville, Massachusetts. The first-floor atrium corridor linking the classroom wing with public spaces brings daylight into the adjacent cafeteria via exterior and interior window walls. North-facing windows and energy-efficient glazing allow constant diffuse light without blinds to regulate light levels. Second-floor skylights illuminate both levels, and exterior window walls provide transparency between the center's main public space and the adjacent playfields outdoors. HMFH Architects, Inc. Photograph by Wayne Soverns Jr., and courtesy of SchoolDesigner president Joel K. Sims, AIA.

"watchdog" function and for the basic safety and access they provide for the users of public buildings. Unfortunately, in the interpretation of standards, square footage and efficiency have been set up against imagination and creativity, as if the two viewpoints were completely incompatible. More needs to be done to connect school facilities design to educational best practices and user satisfaction, and we need to expect more of all participants in the planning process.

Indeed, changing the educational specification process for school facilities design is one way to initiate progressive educational reform. According to Lang (2004), restrictive design standards often stymie creative innovation or meaningful change in school architecture. In Seattle, educators, district administrators, and local architects participated in a yearlong development process to create a set of flexible standards that could be applied autonomously to each individual school project in order to better support school reform through design. The participants drafted seven guiding design principles for high-achieving schools of the future:

1. Learner-centered

2. Personalizing environment

3. Program adaptability

4. Community connection

5. Aesthetics

6. Safety

7. Collaboration

The idea is to move beyond surface issues and mere redecoration to true transformation of school spaces (Lang, 2004).

The habitability levels represent a shift from hierarchical thinking to a holistic or parallel approach that sees all levels of habitability as being indispensable to the successful design of an educational facility. Perhaps the habitability levels can be used to improve the extant standards documents. Habitability levels are intended to help planners think in multiple ways about learning and design, moving well beyond the merely adequate and ruthlessly efficient to the truly uplifting.

Habitability and Basic Architectural Needs

During the programming process, most school architects work with their clients to define a generic list of basic needs for architectural spaces and elements. These architectural needs—for floors, walls, ambient features, and more—are common to most learning settings. The Basic Needs chart is an accessible design tool that describes the attributes of a prototype learning setting while minimizing redundant information. Stakeholders respond to the chart with revisions for their specific setting needs. Any variations to the basic needs are noted later in the program in detailed description of specific activity settings.

In my work with architect George Vlastos, we developed a Basic Needs chart for all three levels of habitability, so that the chart becomes the point of departure for descriptions of health and safety, functionality, and psychological and aesthetic needs for architectural spaces. Linking habitability levels to basic needs ensures that planners are considering the whole person across body, mind, and spirit when thinking about school facility design. As an example, I have provided a Basic Needs chart from a program written with CCC/HOK Architects for Nome Elementary School in Alaska in the early 1980s (please see the end of this chapter). At Nome, our Basic Needs chart was a concise one-page document that was made part of the programming book cover. It became a foldout back page for easy reference as architects accessed information on different activity settings in the book (see illustration).

To apply the Basic Needs chart in current practice, planners can modify the components to fit the particular demands of the project, include new research, update technical and security codes, and add requirements for green architecture.

The fold-out back cover of the programming document provides easy access for a Basic Needs chart. Illustration by Atsuko Sakai.

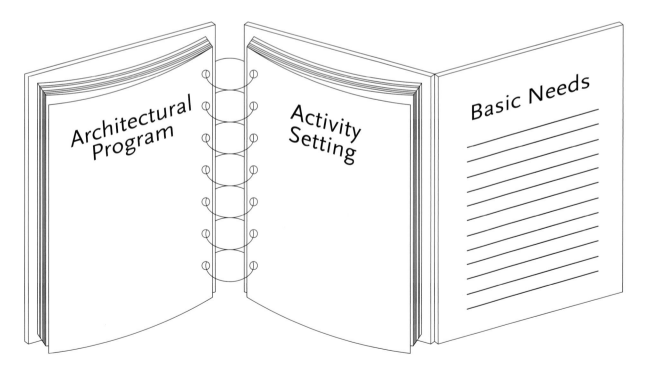

Circulation/Hallways Chart

Health and Safety (Body)	Functional (Mind)	Psychological and Aesthetic (Spirit)
Hallways	**Hallways**	**Hallways**
▶ Easily maintained	▶ "Meander circulation while ensuring supervision" (Lackney on security)	▶ Legibility
▶ Safety (list specific fire codes and adequacy standards or educational specifications for your area)	▶ Open up sight lines	▶ Wayfinding using color, graphics
	▶ Designed as learning spaces	▶ Sociality
	▶ Museums	▶ Student self-expression
	▶ Information centers	▶ Natural lighting
▶ Passageways suggested maximum area 17 percent of gross square footage	▶ No lockers	▶ Fenestration into classrooms (openness)
	▶ Break out spaces	▶ Skylights
▶ Transparency of interior walls for supervision while maintaining acoustical quality	▶ Galleries	▶ Curvilinear
	▶ Niches	▶ Soffits
	▶ Display	▶ Alcoves
▶ Natural lighting for health	▶ Avoid old model of double-loaded corridor	▶ Soft seating
	▶ Wide	▶ Plants
	▶ Well-designed signage/Braille/multilingual	▶ Mall-like
	▶ Many exits but one main entrance with sign-in for security	▶ Interior views
	▶ See "walls"	▶ Atrium, social gathering
		▶ "Main Street" concept used as link between school "neighborhoods"
		▶ Floor graphics

Habitability of hallways across body, mind, and spirit; analogous to Maslow's levels of human functioning.

BEYOND BASIC NEEDS

Once the basic needs are defined, variations or extensions to the basic needs are identified. In the Nome project, we created a separate page for each setting variation as part of the school's program document. It is not possible to list here all the architectural innovations that can and do occur to support learning in different settings, but an illustration serves to show how the program meets and then moves beyond basic needs to suggest new possibilities for building performance.

I will use as an example the basic need for hallways and a design solution that I would like to see eliminated for good: the double loaded corridor lined with identical, rigid, boxlike classrooms, an outdated industrial model still seen even in our newest schools. In broad terms, buildings are composed of circulation areas and places or destinations. Once basic safety codes are met, circulation areas such as corridors can be made into places or destinations by giving them additional functions. Please see the Circulation/Hallways chart, and note that the text of this chapter is accompanied by a series of illustrations that depict creative circulation solutions for schools serving different age levels.

The Circulation/Hallways chart expands the definition of a hallway to include all levels of satisfaction and to surpass basic needs, which paves the way for more creative and comprehensive design criteria. If we design all spaces within the school and on the school grounds to be learning spaces, then no space is wasted, minimized, or unused. All space is instructional space, which is essentially the most efficient use of square footage possible for schools.

What is Habitability for Schools According to the Latest Research?

Children spend many hours per day for most of their young lives in schools. The livability of schools does matter. A quick survey of the research indicates that in many ways children are especially vulnerable to environmental hazards such as poor air quality, lack of natural light, or noise. This is primarily because children's bodies are still developing and outside agents can disrupt that growth and development, putting health and performance at risk. Students' minds are at risk when environments do not functionally support innovations in learning and teaching theory; when distractions, crowding, and clutter interfere with understanding; or when poor conditions result in increased student and teacher absenteeism or changeover. Their spirits suffer when learning environments are dirty or in disarray, in need of repair, too large and impersonal, devoid of local culture or sociable elements and locked away from community, or lacking spaces for individual reflection and privacy. Time spent in poorly designed and unhealthy portables also sends a negative message. Good design responds to these threats to the habitability of learning environments.

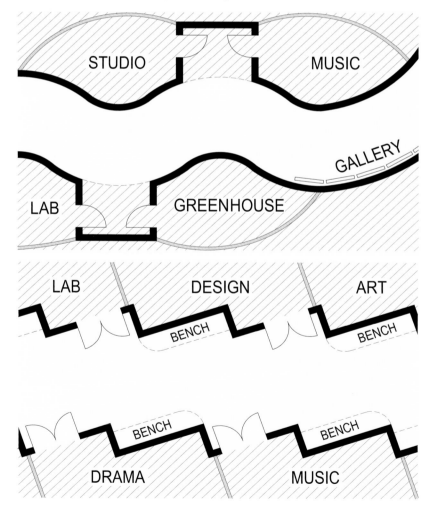

Why not make large circulation corridors into useful spaces with seating and exhibition areas? Illustrations by Atsuko Sakai. Designs by Anne Taylor.

Coe Elementary School, Seattle. Open space cluster. A symmetrical overlook is surrounded by learning spaces and multiple levels, providing interior views. Photograph courtesy of Mahlum Architects.

THE LINK BETWEEN HABITABILITY AND ECOLOGICALLY RESPONSIVE (SUSTAINABLE) DESIGN

What is good for the individual's well-being at all three levels of habitability is also sound ecological practice. For example, green school design aims to open buildings to daylight and views, with the general goal of saving on lighting energy costs and reducing energy loads for HVAC systems. Not only is this aesthetically pleasing, but Kats (2006) cites a study that shows workers with views performed 10 to 25 percent better on tests than those without views. A growing body of research shows a measurable relationship between physical characteristics of school buildings and student performance (Earthman, 2002). We need to make explicit this direct connection between sustainable design for schools and individual well-being and academic success. Ecologically responsive design meets energy conservation and cost saving goals while leading to better conditions for school facilities' users (Olson & Kellum, 2003). Healthier buildings mean healthier occupants and a healthier Earth.

Proper building maintenance is also a sustainability issue. When poor conditions are extreme they negatively impact learning (Higgins, et al., 2005). (Higgins et al. report that when minimum standards are met, the impact on performance is less clear.) In my visits to schools I have seen plenty of evidence that minimum standards are not being met and as a consequence quality of learning is suffering. I have encountered leaking roofs, faulty equipment, and airless portables with blinds closed to natural light. An investigative reporter in Albuquerque, New Mexico, recently revealed that many Albuquerque public schools have not undergone fire safety inspections "for years, if ever," and that many portable buildings lack fire extinguishers (KRQE News 13, 2008). The report resulted in increased fire inspections, but neglecting such problems endangers lives and sends a negative message to children and educators.

At a Greenbuild Conference in Denver (2006), U.S. Green Building Council CEO and president Rick Fedrizzi stated the problem:

> In America more than fifty-five million students and more than five million faculty, staff and administrators go to school every day. That's over twenty percent of America's population that spends about six hours a day in a school building. Twenty percent. Now you know how it works. Schools are built with tax dollars. In fact in 2007, over $35 billion of those tax dollars will be spent on K–12 construction. Typically they are built to code, and nothing more. They have poor ventilation, inadequate lighting, horrific acoustics, and antiquated heating systems. We send our kids off to prisons every morning and expect them to come home with A's and B's.

Using an Organizing System

Research also shows that minorities and students of lower socio-economic status suffer disproportionate burdens regarding poor environmental quality of school facilities such as indoor air quality (IAQ). Unsatisfactory conditions also contribute to teacher attrition (Schneider, 2002). In one study, 40 percent of teachers who rated their school facilities with a grade of C or lower considered leaving the school, and 30 percent considered leaving the profession entirely (Global Green USA, 2005).

The research also reveals other key points:

▸ Achieving ecologically responsive designs requires thinking about the whole building and its entire life cycle from initial planning to operation (Olson & Kellum, 2003; National Renewable Energy Laboratory, 2002).

▸ In a small study in New York City, schools reporting one or more unsatisfactory building components also reported higher suspension rates (up to 14 percent), lower test scores (minus 5 percent), and lower attendance in middle and high schools (2 to 3 percent) than those who did not report unsatisfactory building components (Boese, 2005).

▸ Savings from efficient energy use can be redirected toward other education needs, according to a brochure from the National Renewable Energy Laboratory (2002).

▸ Issues of inclusion and control during planning and operation of schools facilities remains important to teachers, who expect some ability to adjust temperature, light, ventilation, and acoustics in their classrooms (Heschong Mahone Group, 2002).

▸ Because teachers often find themselves cleaning their own classrooms and even doing some maintenance, I suggest they receive professional development in the management of their learning environments through use of green cleaning products. Research on performance benefits of green design would also enable teachers to make wise decisions in configuring environments, including fresh air and views, to best suit children.

A review of the National Clearinghouse for Education Facilities resource list reveals hundreds of articles addressing school facilities' conditions and factors affecting student performance and learning. LEED for Schools (2007) suggests remedies to poor

Kuoppanummi School, Finland. Wide corridors allow multiple uses of hallway space for individual work, conference, or small group meetings, with fenestration to the classroom for supervision. The attractive, modern setting is provisioned with stools on wheels, built-in seating, technology, storage, and plants. Perko Architects. Interior design and pedagogical furniture by Architects Meskanen & Pursiainen. Photo by Jussi Tiainen.

facility conditions through ecologically responsive, sustainable design criteria. These and other sources suggest concerns and solutions for high-performance schools. Four important environmental issues prevalent in the research include acoustics, IAQ, thermal comfort, and daylighting.

Acoustical Quality and Noise Control

Students do not learn when they cannot hear well (Global Green USA, 2005) and noise causes stress (Schneider, 2002). There is a link between noise and poor academic progress (Schneider, 2002; Dunne, 2006). Schools can have external background noise, inside noise from students themselves, noise from HVAC systems, and reverberations (reflections of sound that prolong it and can cause distortions). These affect learning for all students, those with hearing challenges and those without (Dunne, 2006). Environmental noise levels during regular school activities are approximately four to thirty-eight decibels above the levels determined to be optimal for speech recognition by normal-hearing children. In these conditions, first graders would recognize only 66 percent of the words spoken by the teacher (Picard & Bradley, 1997). Picard and Bradley also cite teacher voice fatigue and frustration caused by noisy conditions. Smith (2002) reports that as reverberation increases, word discrimination decreases, affecting the student's ability to hear and correctly interpret what others are saying. Noise is cacophony, the acoustical equivalent of clutter.

Ecologically sound design principles directly and indirectly address acoustics through better siting of learning facilities away from sources of noise, high-quality HVAC designs, and attention to life-cycle maintenance (U.S. Green Building Council, 2007; Olson & Kellum, 2003). The American National Standards Institute (ANSI) requires classrooms and other core learning spaces to meet standards for reverberation and acoustical performance including thick walls and roofs for absorbing external sounds, insulation, surface treatments, and/or configuration of spaces to separate noisy areas from quiet ones. Acoustical tiling is now offered in increasingly flexible sizes and shapes.

Indoor Air Quality

Care must be taken to balance the benefits of shelter provided by buildings with the quality of air contained within enclosed spaces. IAQ remains a serious concern for schools. A frequently cited statistic from the General Accounting Office (GAO, 1995) warns that fifteen thousand American schools have unfit air (Kats, 2006; Schneider, 2002).

Top: James Monroe Middle School, Albuquerque, New Mexico. The design for this middle school was inspired by Chaco Canyon with windows open to views of the mountains. Jane Mahoney of the *Albuquerque Journal* described the hallways as "light-soaked curving corridors." Van H. Gilbert Architect PC. Photograph by Robert Reck.

Bottom: Galleries and museums with cultural realia adjacent to the hallway in an open area with trees and plants, in a Fairbanks, Alaska, library. Photograph courtesy of CCC/HOK Architect.

Using an Organizing System

Primary sources of poor IAQ include contaminants and faulty or poorly operating HVAC systems (Olson & Kellum, 2003). Schneider characterizes poor IAQ as a lack of fresh air (poor ventilation), and indoor pollution of chemical or bacterial origin, mold buildup, and other issues often caused by inadequate maintenance. These environmental conditions can negatively affect the health and well-being of school users. According to Schneider, "sick building syndrome" symptoms include upper respiratory infections; irritated eyes, nose, and throat; nausea; dizziness; headache; and fatigue. When CO_2 levels rise, building occupants experience headaches, drowsiness, and the inability to concentrate. Fifteen to twenty cubic feet of air per minute per person (Schneider, 2002) is recommended for proper ventilation, and because children are often packed into learning spaces, higher ventilation levels may be required for schools than for office buildings. In addition, Cavanaugh (2003) reports that indoor pollution is even worse in portable classrooms than in traditional ones.

The health costs of poor IAQ are enormous. The American Lung Association's Children and Asthma Fact Sheet (2007) lists asthma, which is exacerbated by poor IAQ, as the leading cause of absenteeism, resulting in 12.8 million lost school days each year. The student performance costs of poor IAQ are often hidden within statistics on absenteeism and sick days for teachers (Kats, 2006). According to Boese (2005), "Students who attend schools with environmental hazards that impact IAQ are more likely to miss class, and therefore lose learning opportunities" (p. 3).

The Occupational Safety and Health Administration (OSHA) sets regulations to protect building occupants, but these have not been adapted specifically for children or schools, according to Boese (2005). LEED (2007) awards points in its ratings system to schools for outdoor air delivery monitoring with alarms if needed, automatic measurement and controls, additional ventilation, and for attention paid to IAQ during renovation or construction. Operable windows also are helpful. To lower contaminant levels, green supplies and products reduce toxic compounds and their emissions into the learning environment. Low-emitting building materials and design that minimizes entry of outdoor pollutants (site, orientation, and transportation issues), all play a part in improving air quality, which is also tied to thermal conditions and humidity.

Thermal Comfort

Recommended humidity levels for indoor environments fall between 40 and 70 percent, and the range for temperature is 68 to 74 degrees Fahrenheit for maximum student/worker performance (Schneider, 2002). *Mold Remediation in Schools and Commercial Buildings*, an EPA guide, states that the key to mold control is moisture control. Mold contributes to poor IAQ and health problems, as discussed above. A Global Green USA fact sheet cites a study in which students in an environment without air-conditioners performed at three to twelve percentage points in various measures below those with air-conditioning (2005). In my own state many schools are hot in the fall and spring, up to 90 degrees Fahrenheit, which makes classrooms unbearable.

East San José Elementary School, Albuquerque, New Mexico. The rhythmic and playful patterns in uplighting and circular floor demarcation for group use are part of a school reorganization and addition project. The corridor was designed as a learning space to be used by class groups with an exhibit gallery, audio/visual theater, nature center, and assembly area. Photograph courtesy of Garrett Smith Ltd.

Top: Erie High School, Erie, Colorado.
Interior commons. H + L Architecture.
Photograph courtesy of Chad Novak
and SchoolDesigner president
Joel K. Sims, AIA.
**Bottom: Roosevelt Middle School,
Tijeras, New Mexico.** Floor graphic
depicting cardinal directions. Photograph
courtesy of Garrett Smith Ltd.

On the positive side, better HVAC systems are available and rating systems such as Energy Star ensure that the systems are appropriately sized to the facility and have adjustable controls (Green Global USA, 2005). As with other IAQ considerations, high-efficiency windows, double-paned windows, careful building envelope (exterior building shell) design, siting for solar access and ventilation, and high R-values in insulation all affect building performance while saving energy costs (Olson & Kellum, 2003; National Renewable Energy Laboratory, 2002).

A better-performing building increases comfort levels for building occupants. Solar design and daylighting also impact temperature and should be considered as part of the whole building concept. For example, using more daylight reduces heat from light fixtures and improves ventilation through operable windows and proper shading and diffusion of natural light. As stated earlier, teachers prefer some control over environmental conditions. Also important are HVAC standards for operation, maintenance, monitoring, and assessment, which should occur in an integrated fashion. Appropriate air temperature, radiant temperature, air speed, and relative humidity enter into the quality of the thermal design (LEED, 2007).

The concept of "bioclimatic architecture," which takes into account climate and environmental conditions to help achieve thermal comfort indoors, is gaining interest. The focus of bioclimatic architecture is on design and architectural elements that avoid mechanical systems, which are regarded as support.

Daylighting

Many of our schools were designed in the 1970s with the mistaken notion that buildings without windows saved energy, which created dark buildings with extreme opacity. This must be remedied immediately. Daylighting improves test scores, reduces off-task behaviors, and plays a significant role in student achievement (Kats, 2006). Using daylighting to improve lighting conditions while conserving energy is also one of the primary aims of sustainable design. Daylighting can cut buildings' lifetime energy expenses by 30 to 70 percent through the use of diffuse light from baffles, roof monitors, skylights, and clerestories (Olson & Kellum, 2003). A commonly cited daylighting study found that students in classrooms with the most daylighting progressed 20 percent faster in one year in math tests and 26 percent faster in one year in reading tests than their counterparts with the least amount of natural light (Heschong Mahone Group, 2002).

There is evidence that daylighting provides the best lighting conditions (Schneider, 2002). According to the Green School Initiative (Global Green USA, 2005), daylight provides biological stimulation that regulates body systems and mood, saves costs, and offers the benefits of natural ventilation. Siting, location of windows, transparency throughout a school, and diffusion of light remain issues important to light quality. Kats (2006) describes a study in which workers performed 15 percent better in offices with no glare than in those with glare. Low-e glazing (a window treatment that reduces the transmission of light and heat) minimizes temperature change and offers the side benefits of good daylighting, including downsized HVAC systems that save energy and reduce noise while enhancing the health, comfort, and performance of students and teachers (National Renewable Energy Laboratory, 2002). Light shelves and window treatments used for shading or allowing sunlight to enter combine with solar orientation and other siting decisions to achieve appropriate sunlight levels throughout the year.

LEED (2007) also stresses the connection between indoor and outdoor environments and views. Designers can maximize interior lighting through multiple means: siting of the building, orientation of structures, increasing building perimeter, employing shading devices, installing windows in 90 percent of all regularly occupied areas, lowering partition heights, and using interior glazing and automatic photocell-based controls.

I must reiterate the importance of interconnectedness and integrated thinking to sustainable design. Buildings are complex and no environmental factor exists in isolation. An "eco-poetic" aesthetic, or the ambient quality of mixed elements—color, ergonomics, flexibility, and deployable furniture—contributes to the effect of the whole. Acoustical quality, IAQ, thermal comfort, and daylighting are by no means the only attributes for learning environments suggested by current research. Other high-performing elements also offer higher levels of habitability:

- Artificial lighting (full-spectrum and task lighting)

- Circulation (socialization and wayfinding)

- Community access (multiuse and shared use)

- Constructivism (classrooms as design studios, labs)

- Culture (local representation)

- Display (student-based, museum-quality galleries)

- Environmentally responsive green design (sustainability and constant maintenance)

- Fitness and balanced nutrition

- Furniture (modern, ergonomic, flexible, deployable)

- Inclusion (universal design, multiethnic)

- Indoor/outdoor relationships (views, access, transparency, transitional zones)

- Learning landscapes (academic use of outdoor spaces; see chapter 10)

- Limited use of portables (or redesigned portables)

- Privacy (alcoves, retreat spaces, "cave" space)

- Personalized learning (home base with personal workstation, personal storage versus lockers)

- Signage/graphics (readable, attractive, bilingual, Braille)

Auburn Career Center, Auburn, Ohio.
A vocational center with a continuing education facility, skylight vault, and seating within the circulation space. Photograph by Eric Hanson and courtesy of Richard Fleischman + Partners Architects, Inc.

Benjamin Franklin Elementary School, Kirkland, Washington. Interior fenestration. Decreasing the isolation of the individual classroom and introducing a light, open feel to corridors. Photograph courtesy of Mahlum Architects.

- Security (environmental design for crime prevention rather than over reliance on technology)

- Small learning communities, small school size, and small class size (fifteen to seventeen students)

- Storage (floor to ceiling, thirty feet long, deployable, orderly, project-based, accessible, and more of it)

- Technology (ubiquitous digital access)

- Varied learning group spaces and adjacencies (individual, small group, presentation promoting movement)

- Visual comfort (transparency, vistas indoors and out)

- Welcoming entry (special thanks to Prakash Nair and Randall Fielding)

Moving from Program to Design

George Vlastos and I use the habitability framework to plan learning environments' architectural elements so that design elements become active learning tools and have educational benefits for the user. The next chapter examines how design elements we call "manifestations for learning" are selected and built into the learning environment. We ask all stakeholders and the architect to question every design choice by asking: What is the educational implication or learning potential of this design decision?

The Habitability Framework:
Transfer of Maslow's Levels of Human Functioning to Habitability Levels of Architecture

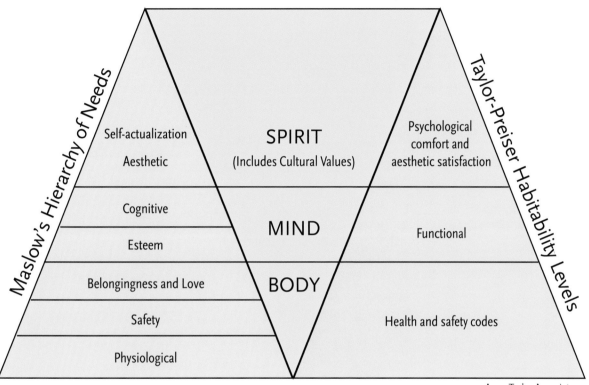

Maslow's Hierarchy of Needs

Taylor-Preiser Habitability Levels

Self-actualization

Aesthetic

SPIRIT
(Includes Cultural Values)

Psychological comfort and aesthetic satisfaction

Cognitive

MIND

Esteem

Functional

Belongingness and Love

BODY

Safety

Health and safety codes

Physiological

2007 Anne Taylor Associates

The Taylor-Preiser habitability levels parallel Maslow's hierarchy of needs, revealing the inverted triangle that emphasizes highest levels of spiritual satisfaction with architecture of schools.

Sample Basic Needs Chart from Nome, Alaska

H Health and Safety	**F** Functional	**P** Psychological and Aesthetic
1 Occupant Load: See activity setting	**1 Occupant Load:** 24 students; 1 teacher. See furniture and equipment provisions	**1 Occupant Load:** Teacher and student interaction and achievement
2 Area Requirement: Not crowded	**2 Area Requirement:** 30 sq. ft./student x 24 students = 720 sq. ft.	**2 Area Requirement:** Large/multipurpose/closed/private
3 Floors: Easily maintained, durable	**3 Floors:** Warm: carpet should be durable and easily patched; some hard, washable areas	**3 Floors:** Clean, muted, and soft
4 Ceiling: Easily maintained	**4 Ceiling:** Flat acoustical grid system/accessible, 80 percent reflectance	**4 Ceiling:** Bright/finished; flat white-non glare
5 Walls: Easily maintained	**5 Walls:** Vertical: chalkboard with flexible height; all walls tackable; sq. corners; 70 percent reflectance	**5 Walls:** Bright/finished; flat white, nonglare
6 Height: See activity setting	**6 Height:** 9'0"	**6 Height:** Flat, level
7 Lighting: Seventy-foot candles	**7 Lighting:** Parabolic fluorescent with zoned switching controls	**7 Lighting:** Uniform/quiet/nonglare
8 Special Electric: N.A.	**8 Special Electric:** Plug mold below chalk rail	**8 Special Electric:** N.A.
9 Natural Light: Health benefits	**9 Natural Light:** NonOperable; 20 sq. ft. minimum with blinds	**9 Natural Light:** Relationship to outside; improved performances
10 Solar Oriented: See activity setting	**10 Solar Oriented:** Exterior window with south or east exposure	**10 Solar Oriented:** Direct sunlight; warmth; biotic
11 Ambiance: Clean and uncluttered	**11 Ambiance:** Multipurpose/closed	**11 Ambiance:** Homelike: simple/modern/ unusual/contained/finished/ friendly/imaginative
12 Color: Varies	**12 Color:** Off white; see research on color	**12 Color:** Accent colors: light/nice/bright; minimal application
13 Graphics: Exits clearly marked	**13 Graphics:** Signage as locational logic	**13 Graphics:** Homelike: supports developmental needs; cultural/geographic; distinctive/modern/unusual/ imaginative
14 Storage: Some locking	**14 Storage:** See furniture and equipment provisions	**14 Storage:** Simple; accessible

H Health and Safety	**F Functional**	**P Psychological and Aesthetic**
15 Time Required: N.A.	**15 Time Required:** Standard school day	**15 Time Required:** N.A.
16 Security: Open up sight lines	**16 Security:** Secure entry keyed individually with masters and submasters, teacher's unit	**16 Security:** Protected; atmosphere of trust
17 Ventilation: Nondraft	**17 Ventilation:** Time clock shut off; 2 air changes per hour	**17 Ventilation:** Not stuffy, alert
18 Heating: Constant uniform	**18 Heating:** 68°–72° during standard school day with time clock set back	**18 Heating:** Comfortable, alert
19 Sound: Acoustical codes	**19 Sound:** Noise criteria: NC 30–40 Sound transmission: STC 45–50	**19 Sound:** Isolated and quiet
20 Hazards: N.A.	**20 Hazards:** N.A.	**20 Hazards:** N.A.
21 Flexibility: N.A.	**21 Flexibility:** Nonbearing walls or demountable partitions with flexible HVAC and lighting	**21 Flexibility:** Autonomy of learners; deployable choice
22 Visual Access: Varies	**22 Visual Access:** One door with light; one window	**22 Visual Access:** Outward
23 Adjacency: See activity setting	**23 Adjacency:** Accessible to everywhere	**23 Adjacency:** Simple/free
24 Communication Technology: Varies	**24 Communication Technology:** Clock/fire alarm/smoke detector/computer jack/TV jack/voice (two-way with privacy)	**24 Communication Technology:** Student-centered
25 Socialization: See activity setting	**25 Socialization:** Teamwork opportunities	**25 Socialization:** Internal/friendly/private
26 Furniture and Equipment: Ergonomically correct for all students promoting health and posture	**26 Furniture and Equipment:** Functionally appropriate for subjects being taught and learning styles; studio workspace with tables/storage	**26 Furniture and Equipment:** Contemporary design, some older furniture of good design could be refinished
27 Handicapped Accessibility: Sound attenuation where needed; Braille signs; accessibility to all areas; meet ADA requirements	**27 Handicapped Accessibility:** Total indoor environment negotiable by physically and mentally challenged students, especially for inclusion in regular classrooms	**27 Handicapped Accessibility:** All assistive technology and ramps of high aesthetic quality and design; universal design
28 Portables: Not a solution for reduction of class size or overcrowding		**28 Portables:** District should insist on better and contemporary design if portables are necessary

The Three-dimensional Textbook

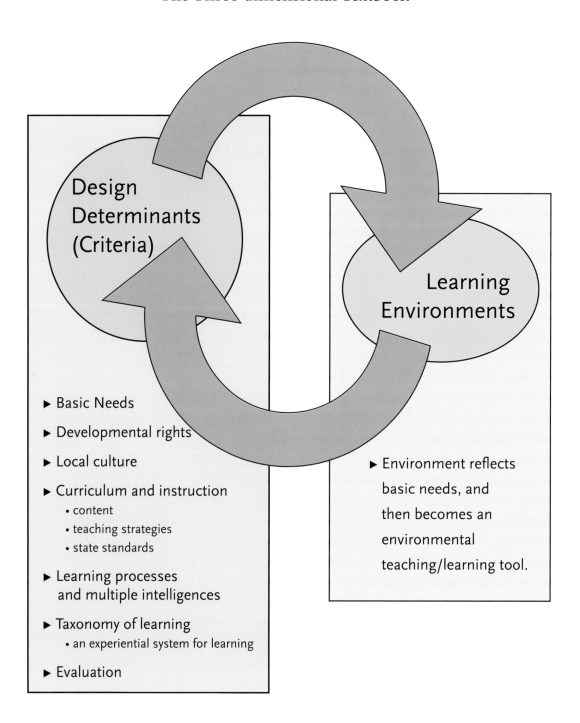

Design
Determinants
(Criteria)

Learning
Environments

► Basic Needs

► Developmental rights

► Local culture

► Curriculum and instruction
  • content
  • teaching strategies
  • state standards

► Learning processes
  and multiple intelligences

► Taxonomy of learning
  • an experiential system for learning

► Evaluation

► Environment reflects
  basic needs, and
  then becomes an
  environmental
  teaching/learning tool.

*Following the chapter on programming, two designer perspectives
address basic programming concerns for the school facility, indoors
and out. First, Wolfgang Preiser shows how informed decision making
and assessment lead to continuous improvement for school designs.
Seven principles of universal design follow Preiser's contribution.*

*A second designer perspective article from Baker Morrow and
Elizabeth Calhoon gives the ground rules for access and safety for school
playgrounds. Although my vision for "learning landscapes" moves beyond
the typical playground (see chapter 10), it is essential that such spaces
remain positive forces in the lives of children through safe design.*

The Triad of Programming, Post-occupancy Evaluation, and Universal Design

*Toward Continuous Quality Improvement
(Including the Seven Principles of Universal Design)*

Wolfgang F. E. Preiser

Professor of architecture (retired), University of Cincinnati

The relatively young subfields of programming, POE, and universal design have made, and will continue to make, significant contributions to architecture in the quest for improving the quality of the built environment. This applies to school design as well, which has seen several significant transformations in the past thirty years, including the trend toward flexible plan schools, sustainable schools, integrative schools from grades K–12, magnet schools, compact urban schools, and others.

As subdisciplines of architecture, programming began in the 1950s, while POE started in the mid-1960s, and universal design in the mid-1980s. All these subfields are concerned with the quality of the built environment as the end users experience it and, thus, these subfields are process driven.

The subfield of programming started in school buildings with a method called "problem seeking," which the firm of Caudill, Rowlett, and Scott (CRS)

Building Performance Evaluation (BPE) Process Model

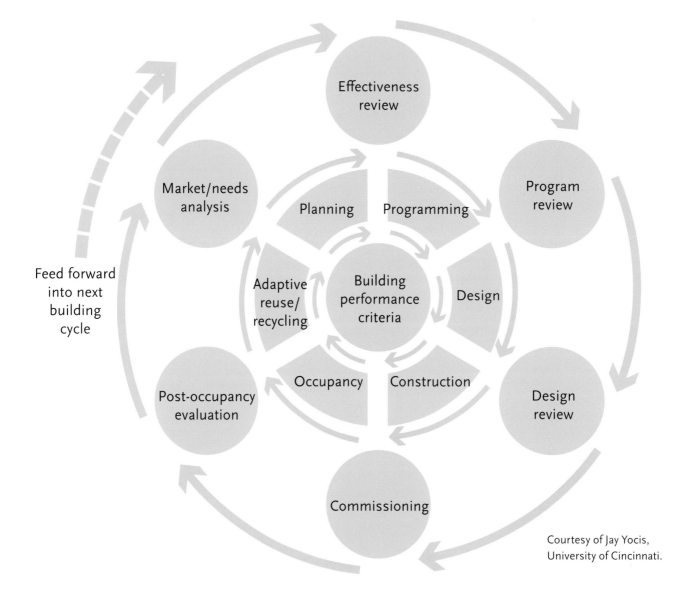

Courtesy of Jay Yocis,
University of Cincinnati.

developed in Texas (Peña, Parshall, & Kelly, 1987). It is a much-used top-down programming approach that seeks to extract key programming concepts from the stakeholders, i.e., teachers, students, administrators, parents, and the community at large, through so-called squatter sessions. In these sessions, the stakeholders identify and prioritize important considerations in the programming and design of a school. A facilitator helps organize the data, which are noted on five-by-seven-inch cards and placed on the walls of the squatter session venue. After two days of such an exercise, key concepts essential to effective programming are typically distilled and documented.

Value-based programming, as described by Hershberger (1999), and research-based programming both attempt to identify the value positions and their relative importance as identified by major stakeholders in a given school project. One such example is the Schoolhouse of Quality approach (Hammond & Schwandner, 1997), which is similar to the problem-seeking approach in that important values are first identified, and then ranked in importance. The difference in the method is that when all is said and done and the building is occupied, the programming team returns and conducts an evaluation of whether the values have in fact been delivered to the stakeholders. In other words, this system goes full circle with a methodology derived from the business world.

As a feedback mechanism, POE has evolved into an integrative framework for building performance evaluation (Preiser, 2003), focusing not only on the built outcome at the time of occupancy and post-occupancy, but also on the entire building delivery and life cycle.

This is particularly relevant to growing school districts, where the lessons learned from one generation of school buildings can be applied to the next, with successes repeated and mistakes avoided. Implicit in such a feedback system is a systematic categorization and collection of data about the performance of school buildings and, thus, the "data capture" assures that expertise does not only reside in the brains of programmers and designers, but also in in-house databases. Systematic POEs can help document the condition of school buildings in a facility audit, make strategic decisions about renovations and replacements or additions of new schools, and, when properly documented, justify funding requests to the state legislature by being able to prioritize school districts' needs and expenditures (Petronis, 1993).

Enter universal design, the new design paradigm for the twenty-first century, which seeks to make products, buildings, transportation systems, and information technology accessible to all people, regardless of disabilities, ethnicity, or culture. It follows the democratic principle of equality for all, something that school design should exemplify by not discriminating against anyone, but rather by being inclusive and diverse. In the *Universal Design Handbook* (2001), Preiser and Ostroff described examples of applying the seven universal design principles.

What specific features would a universally designed school have? For example, such schools might have facilities that the community can utilize after hours: workshops, libraries, access to information technology and databases, and performance facilities. In a suburban community of Cincinnati

Institutional Audit

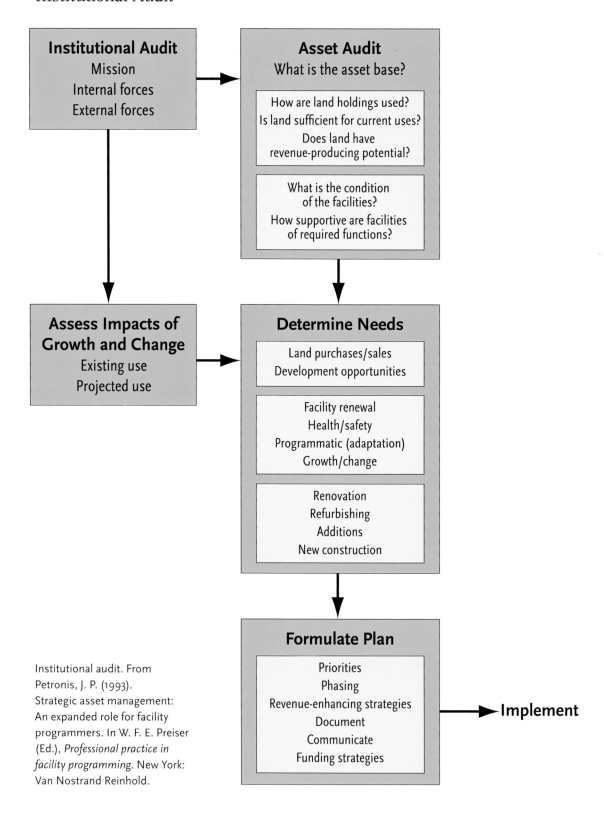

Institutional Audit
Mission
Internal forces
External forces

Asset Audit
What is the asset base?

How are land holdings used?
Is land sufficient for current uses?
Does land have
revenue-producing potential?

What is the condition
of the facilities?
How supportive are facilities
of required functions?

**Assess Impacts of
Growth and Change**
Existing use
Projected use

Determine Needs

Land purchases/sales
Development opportunities

Facility renewal
Health/safety
Programmatic (adaptation)
Growth/change

Renovation
Refurbishing
Additions
New construction

Formulate Plan

Priorities
Phasing
Revenue-enhancing strategies
Document
Communicate
Funding strategies

Implement

Institutional audit. From
Petronis, J. P. (1993).
Strategic asset management:
An expanded role for facility
programmers. In W. F. E. Preiser
(Ed.), *Professional practice in
facility programming*. New York:
Van Nostrand Reinhold.

Harding High School, Ohio. Commons. Courtesy of Steed Hammond Paul, Inc., Cincinnati, Ohio.

there was no town center, so the programmers and designers created the "commons" concept at Harding High School in Ohio, thus allowing the community to hold events there.

As a movement, universal design or "design for all," as it is called in the United Kingdom, has expanded since its origins in the 1980s into a global movement that is supported by a number of federally funded research centers in the United States. The movement remains strong in the United Kingdom and Japan, where the demographic trend toward ever-older seniors is already quite dramatic.

Taken together, the triad of programming, POE, and universal design holds great promise for improved quality of school environments of the future.

The Principles of Universal Design

Version 2.0, April 1, 1997
The Center for Universal Design
North Carolina State University

Compiled by advocates of universal design, listed in
alphabetical order: Bettye Rose Connell, Mike Jones, Ron
Mace, Jim Mueller, Abir Mullick, Elaine Ostroff, Jon Sanford,
Ed Steinfeld, Molly Story, and Gregg Vanderheiden

UNIVERSAL DESIGN

The goal of universal design is to create products and environments to be usable by all people to the greatest extent possible without adaptation or specialized design.

Principle One: Equitable Use

The design is useful and marketable to people with diverse abilities.
Guidelines:
    1a. Provide the same means of use for all users: identical whenever possible and equivalent when not.
    1b. Avoid segregating or stigmatizing any user.
    1c. Make provisions for privacy, security, and safety equally available to all users.
    1d. Make the design appealing to all users.

Principle Two: Flexibility in Use

The design accommodates a wide range of individual preferences and abilities.
Guidelines:
    2a. Provide choice in methods of use.
    2b. Accommodate right- and left-handed access and use.
    2c. Facilitate the user's accuracy and precision.
    2d. Provide adaptability to the user's pace.

Principle Three: Simple and Intuitive Use

Use of the design is easy to understand, regardless of the user's experience, knowledge, language skills, or current concentration level.

Guidelines:

3a. Eliminate unnecessary complexity.

3b. Be consistent with user expectations and intuition.

3c. Accommodate a wide range of literacy and language skills.

3d. Arrange information consistent with its importance.

3e. Provide effective prompting and feedback during and after task completion.

Principle Four: Perceptible Information

The design communicates necessary information effectively to the user, regardless of ambient conditions or the user's sensory abilities.

Guidelines:

4a. Use different modes (pictorial, tactile) for redundant presentation of essential information.

4b. Maximize "legibility" of essential information.

4c. Differentiate elements in ways that can be described (i.e., make it easy to give instructions or directions).

4d. Provide compatibility with a variety of techniques or devices used by people with sensory limitations.

Principle Five: Tolerance for Error

The design minimizes hazards and the adverse consequences of accidental or unintended actions.

Guidelines:

5a. Arrange elements to minimize hazards and errors; the most frequently used elements should be the most accessible; hazardous elements should be eliminated, isolated, or shielded.

5b. Provide warnings of hazards and errors.

5c. Provide fail-safe features.

5d. Discourage unconscious action in tasks that require vigilance.

Principle Six: Low Physical Effort

The design can be used efficiently and comfortably and with a minimum of fatigue.

Guidelines:

6a. Allow the user to maintain a neutral body position.

6b. Use reasonable operating forces.

6c. Minimize repetitive actions.

6d. Minimize sustained physical effort.

Principle Seven: Size and Space for Approach and Use
Appropriate size and space is provided for approach, reach, manipulation, and use, regardless of user's body size, posture, or mobility.

Guidelines:

7a. Provide a clear line of sight to important elements for any seated or standing user.

7b. Make reach to all components comfortable for any seated or standing user.

7c. Accommodate variations in hand and grip size.

7d. Provide adequate space for the use of assistive devices or personal assistance.

Credits: *© 1997 North Carolina State University. Major funding provided by the National Institute on Disability and Rehabilitation Research. For more, see Story, M. F. (2001). Principles of universal design. In Preiser, W. F. E., & Ostroff, E. (Eds.), Universal design handbook (chapter 10). New York: McGraw-Hill.*

Kids Outdoors in the New Century

Notes on Playground Design

Baker Morrow,
   Fellow, American Society of Landscape Architects, and
Elizabeth Calhoon,
   American Society of Landscape Architects

Morrow Reardon Wilkinson Miller, Ltd.,
Landscape Architects, Albuquerque

Many of us can remember the playground of the past consisting of one climbing structure, one set of swings, one tetherball pole, which never had a ball, and a backstop all located on solid, compacted dirt. A colleague who attended one such school says she will never forget the day when one of her classmates decided to "bail out" of the swing, resulting in a compound fracture of his leg. Tough landing, hard surface, and an important lesson learned.

Since the 1970s and 1980s, the U.S. Consumer Product Safety Commission and the American Society for Testing Materials (ASTM) have done multiple studies of playgrounds and play equipment, resulting in a useful set of playground safety design standards for play equipment and play area design. There are some in the teaching and design professions who might argue that these standards have resulted in play environments and equipment that are "sterile." When faced with the responsibility of designing safe places and structures for children to use for play, however, we must find ways to work within these standards to make our play areas and equipment as exciting, fun, and adventuresome as possible.

Among the important safety considerations when designing a playground are the slope of the site, site drainage, site exposure, utilities (underground and overhead), access, and fencing. Existing vegetation may also be important.

Top: Keystone Early Learning Center, Montgomery, Alabama. Safe slides and hillsides. Slides are built into a berm with a tunnel beneath for a tricycle trail. Steven Bingler, Concordia LLC. John Chambless, Brown Chambless Architects.
Bottom: Shade and site exposure. Photo courtesy of Baker Morrow and Elizabeth Calhoon.

SLOPE

The slope of the site matters because of handicapped (ADA) access and also because, in most cases, the area in which the play equipment is to be located has to be perfectly level. This is because the safety surfacing (sand, wood fiber, etc.) used in most play areas is "fluid." Therefore, in order to maintain a minimum depth of this protective fall-surface material beneath the play equipment, the area should be level and contained by a border or wall, preferably made of concrete and set well away from the play structures. If budget allows, a poured-in-place safety surfacing can be used. The play equipment area can have up to a 2 percent slope.

SITE DRAINAGE

Play areas and adjacent surfaces should not be used to pond storm water. Drainage should be directed away from these areas. If drainage is allowed to enter the play areas, the protective fall-surface materials will compact, causing constant safety and maintenance issues. It is important that the adjacent surfaces drain easily to allow for use by the children immediately after a rain or snow.

SITE EXPOSURE

Children should be able to play freely in the shade, especially in hot climates. Some sun is beneficial, of course, but leafy trees and shade structures are key design elements in and around playgrounds and play areas. The landscape architect or other designer needs to be careful in tree selection: trees with thorns or trees that produce large amounts of pollen are poor choices for children's areas. They may violate local plant selection ordinances, as well. Select trees such as sycamores, ashes, or oaks that are hardy and can be pruned cleanly into high, shade-producing canopies. If the play area is large enough, a small path among the surrounding trees can be punctuated with tree-identifying labels or plaques, thus allowing the children to learn about the plants as they play.

Winter and spring winds can be problematic around play areas. Rolling berms placed perpendicular to the direction of local prevailing winds can be very effective in protecting the children, and may themselves serve as play features. Grassy berms in the right places can be particularly appealing. Lines of trees or hedges (especially if they include evergreen species) may also protect play areas from the chilly winds of fall and winter. The landscape architect should always be sure that safety is not compromised by hedge placement; good play areas need to remain highly visible from many directions.

UTILITIES

Utilities, including gas, water, sanitary and storm sewers, power and telephone lines, and others, are usually best kept at some distance from a playground. Children's play is spontaneous, quick, and very much of the moment, and no child should be expected to keep an eye out for manhole covers, low-slung power lines, or sewer cleanouts. Even access to *buried* utilities in a kids' play area may be problematic, as the play structures may need to be displaced during servicing, and burst or leaking lines can create hazards to recreation.

Wherever possible, utilities should be located at some distance outside the boundaries of the play area. Where an intrusion of utility lines (such as those needed for irrigation service) is simply necessary to accomplish the playground design (watering play area shade trees, for instance), the lines should be laterals or secondaries—not primaries.

ACCESS

Quick and safe access to play areas from nearby school doors is desirable from a number of viewpoints.

1. It allows students and their teachers to make the most of what may be limited playtime. In smaller schools, good, close access to play may allow a teacher to keep an eye on the children from the classroom itself.

2. The play area, if well sited and shaded, can be seen by the children as a simple and natural extension of the school itself. Play is natural, and its benefits can extend to formal schooling as well. Indoor and outdoor learning should go together, and both can be supported through access and openness.

3. Ease of access better integrates children with disabilities into both the play areas, with their lively activities, *and* overall student life at the school. Many—if not most—young students may at some time suffer from an injury or condition that limits their movement. Examples include a broken arm, a sprained ankle, an allergic condition, or perhaps something more serious and lasting. Ease of access to play and play equipment, and the integration of children who have an unusual need or two into normal recreation, will benefit everyone.

Top: Longfellow Elementary School, Albuquerque, New Mexico. Fencing alternative to chain link. Photograph courtesy of Anne Taylor.

Bottom: Arroyo del Oso Elementary School, Albuquerque, New Mexico. Local concepts extend to the playground design with a bridge, an arroyo (dry river bed or wash), and sculptural forms representing trees. Photograph courtesy of Garrett Smith Ltd.

FENCING

The relatively modern phenomenon of the general fencing of play areas may serve two distinct purposes.

The first involves limiting access to school play areas by the general public. In this case, necessary fencing may enclose an entire schoolyard. Only teachers, coaches, students, and staff may be allowed into a play area, and then only for carefully designated intervals. The purpose of this cautionary control is, of course, to keep the children safe from social predators, and in many instances it may be quite justified.

The second sort of fencing may involve special play areas for different age groups of children, or perhaps unusual play features such as skate parks whose use might need to be restricted.

The best sorts of fencing for these purposes should be "see-through" (not opaque). Ornamental metal or chain link in its many varieties will often be used, but should not be taller than a maximum of six feet, have rough or cutting edges, and never make a play area—or, for that matter, a whole school—feel prisonlike or besieged. A good fence should serve the children well as they play. It should *not* simply be placed around a playground as a convenience to the nervous adults who may be responsible for a boisterous set of youngsters.

CONCLUDING NOTES

The thoughtful siting of a play area involves effective slope treatment, good access, adequate drainage, careful utility placement, and a number of related factors in a feat of inspired integration. Good play equipment is also essential for a successful playground. Durable steel, treated wood, hard plastic, and long-lasting rubber have all been popular, both together and individually, in recent decades.

Which is the best?

The current choice in play equipment seems to be bright, colorful, powder-coated and vinyl-coated steel with molded plastic elements. It is flexible but strong, it lasts, and it is comfortable for the kids to use. There are no splinters, and it is neither too hot nor too cold to the touch. It adapts to the seasons. It also lends itself well to the design of play pieces in small and large sets.

Could coated steel and plastic be the ultimate answer? Probably not, though it is quite a good one for today. Practical experience tells us that the need for play in our kids and its healthy expression are the true constants. The materials and equipment that we employ in our playgrounds will likely always change.

Top: Durable, bright playground equipment is currently popular. See chapter 10 for new playground possibilities and learning landscapes. Photo courtesy of Baker Morrow and Elizabeth Calhoon.

Bottom: *Denise Louie Dragon*, Seattle. A fantasy sculpture for play with elements created by children. Dragon designed and built by Steve Badanes with Joan Heaton and Dave Robertson. Mosaic toes by Linda Beaumont and the children of Denise Louie Head Start Center. Photograph by Jared Polesky.

Phyllis Nye Bilingual Early Childhood Center,
Santa Fe. Van H. Gilbert Architect PC, design
architect. Karen Marsh, project architect.
Photographs by Robert Reck.

Architectural Programming for the Learner

INTRODUCTION

This section of articles and case studies is dedicated to the individual learner and to lifelong learning, organized from early childhood to the university level and beyond. To summarize, the architectural programming and design process that truly respects learners is informed by the physical, developmental, and curricular needs of children throughout their education and into adult life. An understanding of the learner and learning styles grows into an appreciation for diversity. Most importantly, educators and architects must share in the quest to meet the individual rights of every single person, and to value every person born.

At the concrete level, school designers must deal with issues of scale and ergonomics for the student and adult populations using the facility. In terms of furniture, interior designers must be trained to consider the special ergonomic requirements of children in the learning setting. *The Measure of Man and Woman: Human Factors in Design*, a volume from Alvin R. Tilley and Henry Dreyfuss Associates (1993), is a great source for information about anthropometrics and design. It contains more than 180 diagrams of human measurement data from childhood to old age, including factors for people who are differently abled. Human factors data include temperature, noise, lighting, and other environmental conditions. Issues specific to children include adjustable, adaptable furniture that encourages movement during their highly sensitive growing years. VS Möbel designs ergodynamic furniture to reduce the negative consequences of a sedentary lifestyle, which can include damaged posture, back pain, and even concentration problems. Continually adjustable furniture offers children an alternative to the rigid and upright postures they must endure while using most school furniture (VS America, Inc., 2007).

Child's Age in Years	Average Vertical Grip Reach	Ave. Lateral (Side Reach) Grip
2.0–3.5	42.2"	20.8"
3.5–4.5	45.9"	22.1"
4.5–5.5	49.8"	23.5"

Measuring the human form at different stages of development and using the information in school facility design increases the child's ability to interact effectively with the environment.
Original illustration by George Vlastos.
Adapted by Myrna Marquez.

Continually adjustable furniture is available, and yet 80 percent of children spend their time sitting in rigid postures in school settings with inappropriate furniture.

Preiser's article in this book and his manual on universal design offer many guidelines that are essential to design for all types of learners, the point being that all students benefit from designs that also accommodate the differently abled. Colorado's Winter & Company has developed a "special needs design studio" to go beyond the many laws that ensure access for all, and to address planning, assessment, and design issues for blind and deaf students, including homelike environments, issues of communication access, space usage and lighting, and assistive technology (Winter & Company, 2007). Today's classroom is becoming increasingly inclusive, with new programs that bring students with disabilities into the regular education classroom. Correspondingly, there is a need for spatial accommodations to support inclusion. L-shaped classrooms and deployable partitions, for example, address this requirement by providing openness and connection while allowing room for pullout activities or quiet time. Technology can also support visual learning styles of many children with learning disabilities.

MULTIPLE INTELLIGENCES THEORY

Tailoring the environment to the individual learner also requires awareness of varying learning styles, as introduced in chapter 5. Howard Gardner, a professor and psychologist at Harvard University, developed a theory of multiple intelligences that has challenged former assumptions about human competencies. After researching, reviewing, and compiling data from diverse sources including studies of prodigies, brain-damaged patients, and normal children and adults from various cultures, Gardner identified several "frames of mind" or intelligences. Gardner defines an intelligence as a set of problem-solving skills that allow an individual to resolve genuine problems, fashion effective products, and acquire new learning. An intelligence also must be valued by a culture as useful and important.

Gardner identified eight intelligences or competencies:

Verbal/linguistic: Thinks in words, is sensitive to language

Logical/mathematical: Approaches problems logically, discerns numerical patterns

Visual/spatial: Perceives the visual world accurately, thinks three-dimensionally

Bodily/kinesthetic: Uses one's body to sense the environment, communicate, and solve problems; has manipulative skills

Musical/rhythmic: Is sensitive to nonverbal sounds in the environment; has ability to produce and appreciate music

Interpersonal: Is sensitive to the feelings and moods of others

Intrapersonal: Is sensitive to one's own feelings; knows self

Naturalistic: Is sensitive to the natural world and natural cycles (Gardner, 1983, 1999)

IMPLICATIONS OF MULTIPLE INTELLIGENCES THEORY FOR ARCHITECTURE OF SCHOOLS

Here are a few ways environment can support these identified intelligences:

Verbal/linguistic: Signage in multiple languages, a theater in every school, multimedia communication centers

Logical/mathematical: Patterns built into the floor or walls, structural features revealed, places for technology, geometric form

Visual/spatial: Architecture teaches through a variety of spaces, sculpture, and wall graphics; galleries in schools; hallway museums; windows and interior views

Bodily/kinesthetic: Fitness trails, gymnasium, dance studios, tools to manipulate

Musical/rhythmic: Acoustics, music practice rooms, performance venues

Interpersonal: Deployable and movable furniture, places for teamwork, large horizontal work surfaces versus individual desks, gathering spaces indoors and out, conference rooms

Intrapersonal: Outdoor seating, study alcoves, private areas, quiet rooms

Naturalistic: Habitats, recycling venues, nature trails, green architecture

There is more than one way to learn. The design process naturally touches on many of the intelligences identified by Howard Gardner: verbal/linguistic skills to research and present projects; logical/mathematical to measure and plan; visual/spatial to create drawings and three-dimensional models; bodily/kinesthetic to build structures and manipulate tools; interpersonal intelligence to work in teams; intrapersonal to communicate personal intuitive beliefs through design; and naturalistic to embed designs in landscape settings or use sustainable design principles. Photograph courtesy of Anne Taylor.

REACHING MULTIPLE INTELLIGENCES AT THE BOSQUE SCHOOL, ALBUQUERQUE, NEW MEXICO

Sensitivity to differences in learning styles can and does inform successful school design at the Bosque School. This college prep school serving grades six through twelve is a convergence of environmental studies, natural beauty of the site, and sustainable design by Mazria Inc. Odems Dzurec Architecture/Planning. Architects included water harvesting features, wetlands, indoor and outdoor classrooms that orient to the bosque (river-edge forest), materials and colors that blend into the shadows of the natural setting, daylit spaces, and passive solar heating and cooling. To aid in interactive learning, the school is composed of small buildings organized to form a plaza, courtyards, and paths for informal meetings between students and teachers.

Bosque School, Albuquerque, New Mexico.

Top: Aerial view. The school is situated along the bosque, a narrow wooded area that follows the course of the Rio Grande through Albuquerque. Among other environmental concerns, students help monitor and maintain the site and study groundwater levels and quality as part of the Bosque Ecosystem Monitoring Program. Photograph © Ed Taylor.

Center: Architect Robert Peters worked with Bosque students to create an educational installation for three overlooks on the city's Montaño Bridge. Students researched plant and wildlife in the area, worked with a wildlife illustrator, and translated text to Spanish with the help of a professor as they planned and designed panels depicting life along the bosque (Schoellkopf, 2004). Here Bosque parent Barbara Gorham stands at one of the overlooks. Photograph by Marisa Gay.

Bottom: Bosque clean up and tree planting projects. Naturalistic intelligence and interpersonal skills of community service and volunteerism are part of graduation requirements for each grade level at Bosque School in Albuquerque, New Mexico. Photograph by Marisa Gay.

THE ALOHA EXPERIMENT: ADDRESSING SPIRIT

The Polynesian Cultural Center near Honolulu demonstrates an excellent service learning model for higher education with culture as its architectural theme as well. The center's mission, with the help of students from Brigham Young University's Hawaii campus, is to preserve the cultural heritage of Polynesia. Many of the university students are working their way through school as guides, musicians, dancers, demonstrators, and service personnel at the center. Maintaining a well-attended cultural center (with some 30 million visitors since 1963) involves students in a real and viable project and produces young scholars who are not only beautiful and healthy representatives of their heritage, but also purposeful in their pursuit of a career, knowledgeable, and spiritually committed to their own history (Polynesian Cultural Center, 2006).

Top: Brigham Young University–Hawaii students preserve their heritage through service learning at the Polynesian Cultural Center. Image courtesy of the Polynesian Cultural Center, Hawaii.

Bosque School, Albuquerque, New Mexico.
Center: Students capture and band a porcupine as part of a local wildlife identification project at Bosque School in Albuquerque, New Mexico. Photograph by Adam Gebauer.
Bottom: Irrigation reflections near Bosque School, Albuquerque, New Mexico. The beauty of the site inspires visual/spatial and contemplative intrapersonal intelligences. Photograph © Miriam Hall, 2004.

Mid-Pacific Institute, Honolulu, Hawaii. The digital generation expects more of our schools, having moved beyond the passive absorption of facts to a new interactive paradigm. Photograph courtesy of the Mid-Pacific Institute and Scott Allen, photographer.

LISTENING TO YOUNG PEOPLE

Young people have imaginative contributions to make regarding what they want in learning environments. A narrative that Mahlum Architects submitted to CEFPI reports that planning and visioning workshops for Cedar Valley Community School in Washington State asked children to draw the perfect learning environment. They came up with apple orchards, Puget Sound, and submarines. These children and others everywhere seek connections to the culture and world they know. Lois Brown Easton, writing for *Education Week* (2002), described listening to high school students whose main wish was to be engaged in their learning. Students revealed that engagement comes through authentic and open-ended questioning, hands-on learning, personalized learning, assuming active roles in the learning process, and being held to a certain standard or level of challenge. Contrary to the stereotypical image of the high school student asleep at his desk, these young people truly want to learn.

Technology will increasingly aid the personalization of instruction (see more in chapter 9). Randy Hinrichs, group research manager at Microsoft, predicts that technology will allow learners to build personalized digital libraries that stay with the learner for life. As described in *Threshold* magazine, learners accumulate data and resources through a kind of lifelong "clipping service." A look back becomes an "updated re-immersion in the subject matter, a kind of academic band between learning experiences" (Callison, 2004).

Contributors to this forum show their respect for children and young adults by considering their individual needs and listening to their ideas.

PROFESSIONAL DEVELOPMENT

Of equal importance to successful design of schools is the issue of lifelong learning, including professional development for teachers and other educational facilitators. In 1997, GLEF published *Learn & Live*, a book and film documentary to be used by colleges of education, teachers, business leaders in partnerships with schools, in-service training programs, and school boards to envision the future of education. *Learn & Live* reaffirms the value of education and redefines the role of educators with the aim of reducing the isolation of schools and learners through new technology and better design. Higher education must also offer better learning environments and newer models for teaching educators than those that now exist. Even today at some college-level teacher training institutions, classroom instructional aids remain at the level of an overhead projector!

Educators can learn in prototype settings that embody the future for school design rather than sitting through the usual lectures in outmoded classrooms. This provides continuity for the entire learning process.

Educators trained in outdated environments will not have the necessary information, instructional methodology, and digital skills to teach the next generation of technology users, and are unlikely to be hired in the future. To counter this lack, Creative Learning Systems (CLS), designer of technology

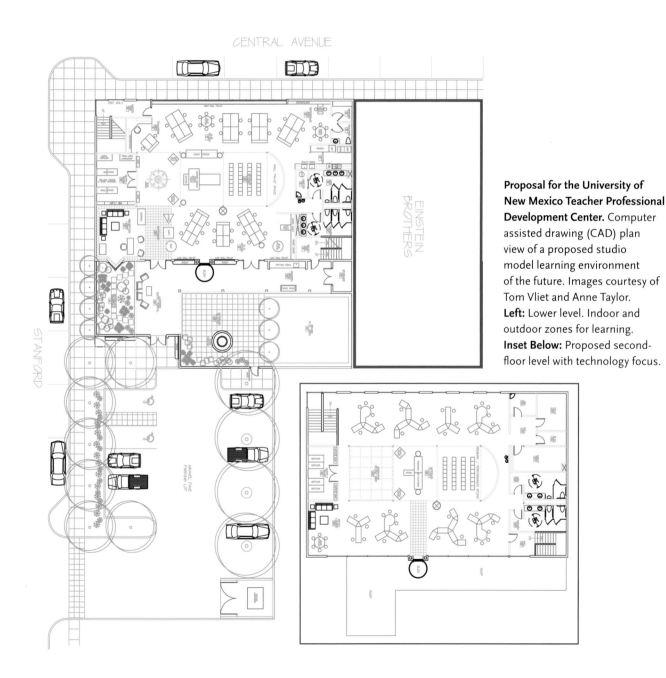

Proposal for the University of New Mexico Teacher Professional Development Center. Computer assisted drawing (CAD) plan view of a proposed studio model learning environment of the future. Images courtesy of Tom Vliet and Anne Taylor. **Left:** Lower level. Indoor and outdoor zones for learning. **Inset Below:** Proposed second-floor level with technology focus.

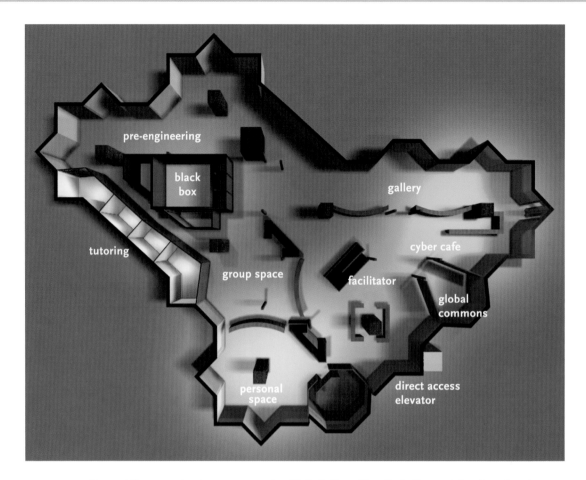

Concept for an academic resource center, Wells College, New York. Concept drawing of a cyber research and library learning center of the future for higher education. UNM architecture students Julio Dominguez, Timothy Stephens, Jeremy Trumble, and Andrew Werth.

environments for schools, offers a teacher professional development program using CLS environments (see more about CLS in chapter 9). The training takes place on-site within the specially designed CLS technology environment. Course content includes project-based learning, collaborative learning, facilitation methods and processes, student self-assessment techniques, evaluation portfolios, and the technical aspects of the CLS environment capabilities and their management. Follow-up after training is also important. Learners gather after one year of using the new learning environments installed in their schools to attend and earn university credits at a conference for sharing CLS experiences and new ideas (Dando, personal communication, February 14, 2006).

To encourage teamwork and shared learning for educators, school designers can rethink adjacencies, redesign, and reconfigure teacher workrooms, lounges, and offices to become collaborative centers that encourage communication in a profession that often isolates teachers.

Technology is changing the library or media center, too. The role of librarians is linked to the role of the public library as a central democratic repository

George Pearl Hall, School of Architecture and Planning, University of New Mexico. Left: Note the light shelves on the south side of the building and the outdoor amphitheater. Architect Antoine Predock designed a learning environment that teaches through many exposed architectural elements. The design reveals infrastructure and exposed systems and how plan and section are connected through the relationship of daylight, spatial flow, and structure. A planned sustainable demonstration green roof features native grasses that are drought and heat resistant. A cistern collects water from the roof. **Right:** Night view. Built of glass and stucco, this modern interpretation of the traditional Pueblo Revival style, a four-story building, has a spacious center atrium and 108,000 square feet of round-the-clock studios, smaller instructional spaces, and a twenty-six-thousand-square-foot fine arts library. Note a cantilevered outdoor projection screen for movies. Antoine Predock Architect PC. Jon Anderson, project architect. Photographs by Kirk Gittings.

for learning in the digital age. In a way, the role remains the same: to support lifelong learning, preserve cultural heritage, and ensure equitable access for all learners. The method of fulfilling that role has changed and must be supported by design. Today's library media specialists must be taught to act as "mentors and models of critical and creative thinking" (Callison, 2004). The emerging "library learning laboratory" is a facility "composed of many small pods for small group work, each with access to online information terminals, video-editing stations and telecommunications for interviews with content experts" (p. 16). The librarians who manage these spaces must become experts in new forms of interactive information technology, and would best do so by receiving their professional development within the new library learning laboratory model.

The case studies and articles in stewardship forum 2 illustrate how educators and designers pay careful attention to developmental needs of learners of different ages, direct their planning toward the special needs of learners and the diversity of learners, and involve children and community in the programming and design process.

School planners often need to expedite school building projects. How do we do this without sacrificing input from multiple stakeholders, including children who will use the facility? John Petronis uses a workshop system to focus decision making during planning. Petronis writes that the variety of client interests in programming of educational facilities offers both a challenge and an opportunity. The challenge is to manage the flow of information in a valid and timely way. The opportunity comes when planners capitalize upon the unique expertise of participants, usually through the formation of planning committees representing a variety of perspectives.

Facility Programming
Focused Decision Making

John Petronis

*American Institute of Architects,
American Institute of Certified Planners*

*Founder and president of Architectural Research
Consultants, Inc. in Albuquerque, New Mexico*

A program defines the goals, facts, concepts, and needs of the project, and it forms the basis for developing and evaluating design solutions. It also includes specific information about the type, number, size, and characteristics of each space needed and realistically reflects the target project budget. While the facility program should thoroughly describe the owner/user requirements, it should not be so constrained that it restricts opportunities for enrichment by insights of the design architect.

PROGRAMMING WORKSHOPS

A programming workshop is one method that successfully makes use of the expertise and knowledge of participants. In a series of workshops, programming information is presented in a logical and focused manner that moves sequentially from broad to specific issues. After an initial kickoff meeting, it usually takes three workshops to develop a program, as outlined below.

> ▶ At an initial **kickoff meeting**, the facility programmer introduces the planning participants, identifies expectations, and describes the facility programming process and how it fits into the overall building development process. Methods for collecting information and schedules are discussed.

During this urban planning exercise, children learned the language of architecture, cooperation, and teamwork by working with paper strips to create three-dimensional architectural models. Preparing stakeholders for the programming process through workshops encourages effective community input from all age levels.
Photograph by Brian Lucero.

▶ The focus of the **first workshop** is to present to participants information about the facility's requirements collected in questionnaires, interviews, and other sources, including research of similar facilities. Preliminary project goals and facts of the project are presented for discussion and validation. Facts or issues that need further study are identified.

▶ The **second workshop** recaps goals and key facts, including any changes and additional research identified during the first workshop. Overall programmatic concepts about how to achieve the goals are presented for discussion. For example, programmatic concepts might include the ways in which the project should provide for flexibility to meet new educational requirements over time. Diagrams can also be used to describe various functional requirements. In this workshop, specific space needs are presented that detail the number, type, size, and broad characteristics of spaces in the program. Participants review the information and identify priorities in order to balance the total amount of space with the amount of budget available.

▶ The **third workshop** presents the preliminary program and resolves any remaining details. The facility program can be finalized on the basis of the input from this workshop.

This workshop-based programming approach provides specific opportunities to

▶ Activate the specific expertise of participants, add depth to the understanding of project issues, and enhance the quality of final decisions

▶ Encourage consideration of all points of view and debate and discuss any important issues that will impact the future of the project (this process also helps to distinguish between wants and actual needs)

▶ Enhance decision making; since representatives of both client/owner and client/user groups are involved throughout the process, decisions reflect all interests and are respected as the project moves forward, and

▶ Educate all parties about architecture and the building development process; facility programming provides an excellent venue to discuss good and bad architectural experiences and the roles and responsibilities of all parties in the building development process.

The Keystone project combined the efforts of Steven Bingler, Concordia LLC; John Chambless, Brown Chambless Architects; and Anne Taylor Associates.

A Learning Model in Practice
Keystone Early Learning Center, Montgomery, Alabama

Dee Trout
Early childhood educator

THE ORCHARD

Why would children want to save the Earth if they're never allowed to play in the dirt, make mud pies, plant seeds in a garden, and watch the seeds grow? Why are so many playgrounds devoid of plants? Children need to plant seeds with their own hands and see those seeds come to life with their help and the help of water from the rain and warmth from the sun. We had a nice little orchard at Keystone that had blueberry bushes and pear, apple, and fig trees. The children could go into the orchard during each season and look at the different leaf shapes and gather the leaves to make collages, paintings, rubbings, or even leaf people. When the fruit came on the trees the children got to see it grow from small to fully developed and to see which trees grew which fruit. They picked their own fruit from those trees and ate it, cooked with it, and tried printmaking with it.

Keystone Early Learning Center, Montgomery, Alabama. Above: Entry. **Right:** Entry gallery for student art. Features standard-sized frames for easy change of artwork. The entry also contained museum-quality display cases for three-dimensional works. Steven Bingler, Concordia LLC. John Chambless, Brown Chambless Architects. Photographs courtesy of Anne Taylor Associates.

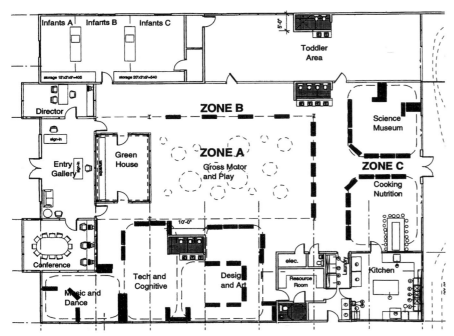

Keystone Early Learning Center, Montgomery, Alabama.
Floor plan. The interior space of the center was divided into an entry suite, an infant zone, toddler area, and preschool. Around the perimeter of the preschool's large central open space, Zone A, were learning zones for art, music, cognitive development, and cooking. Appropriate mobile storage was housed in each of the learning zones. The preschool was a large open forum that connected to the outdoor garden, small orchard, and learning landscape consisting of two playgrounds, one for toddlers and the other for older children. Plan view adapted from the original by Jerod Bosey. Original plan view courtesy of Concordia LLC and Brown Chambless Architects. Programming by Anne Taylor.

THE AQUARIUMS

Parents and children entered Keystone through the art exhibit gallery and were greeted by two 450-gallon fish tanks, one for saltwater and one for freshwater life. The children enjoyed watching both tanks and making comparisons. Children learned about coral, what the saltwater fish, crabs, and starfish ate, how they reacted to each other, and how the water was treated so it stayed clean and clear. They learned how salt was added to the water to maintain the appropriate level and about the filtering systems of both aquariums.

THE GREENHOUSE

Children helped me clean the indoor greenhouse and feed the animals living there. In the greenhouse we had spring frogs, red-eyed tree frogs, and South American barking frogs. The animals were a wonderful experience for the children, especially the barking frogs. Parents, grandparents, and visitors were always asking me if I had puppies in the greenhouse. In the spring there would be shallow places in our playground garden that would fill up with water. The children would dip tadpoles out of these pools and put them in a tadpole pond in the greenhouse. Children fed the tadpoles, maintained the water level, and watched the tadpoles metamorphose into frogs. Parents and children would bring toads, lizards, bugs, and turtles they had found and put them in the greenhouse. They especially enjoyed naming the animals they found.

Greenhouse entry. Bringing the outdoors indoors. Photograph courtesy of Anne Taylor.

Keystone Early Learning Center, Montgomery, Alabama.
Left: Windows were designed for infants, scaled low and accessible from the floor. **Right:** An infant feeds a rabbit in the greenhouse. Photographs by Dee Trout.

Birds also lived in our greenhouse, and the children enjoyed watching them gather twigs and hay to build nests, eat, and take baths. The children were very excited when the birds laid eggs. We talked about the eggs and how many days it would take for them to hatch. We made a calendar and counted the days off as they went by. How happy and proud the children were to see their little birds when they were big enough to fly from the nest.

THE WINDOWS

Keystone was full of windows that let in plenty of natural light. I've seen a child standing at a window in awe at all the rain coming down, completely in tune with nature. There were low, floor-level windows in the infant rooms for children who were not standing or walking yet. A large window in the infant room would let the sunshine in on the floor at a certain time of day. The butterflies would usually be in the flowerbeds outside the window. As they fluttered from flower to flower, their shadows would fall on the floor in the room. The infants would crawl and chase and try to catch the butterfly shadows.

I believe that daycare centers are built for the children, not for adults. The philosophy of the Keystone Early Learning Center celebrated the image of the child as strong and competent. The openness of the center gave the children enough space and freedom to have their own visions for learning and to build and create with those visions.

Sadly, after serving for three years as an inspiring model for educational excellence, the facility was razed and in its place was constructed a baseball diamond and park.

Karen Marsh writes that when a school has been operating for years in substandard conditions, the teachers, children, and even the parents become accustomed to just getting by. This was the case at an early childhood center in Santa Fe, New Mexico, until the programming process for a new learning environment addressed the children's special needs, paving the way for an apt architectural response.

Designing for Special Needs at the Nye Bilingual Early Childhood Center, Santa Fe, New Mexico

Karen Marsh

Registered architect in the District of Columbia and New Mexico

The Nye Bilingual Early Childhood Center (BECC) served three- to six-year-old children with a variety of learning styles, developmental ability levels, and ethnic and cultural backgrounds. When the programming phase for a new school building began, it was clear in the beginning that the teachers were used to making do and might have a hard time thinking beyond their concrete block walls and portables. With the techniques for programming brought forward by Anne Taylor, however, the programming team (consisting of a number of teachers, a speech therapist, occupational therapist, physical therapist, and an architect) soon created a new program for the school.

The architectural response to the program involved the following:

1. Identity: Creating a distinct identity for the BECC, separating it from the large elementary school of which it was also a part. This was accomplished by placing the BECC at one end of the school with its own entrance, parking area, and vehicular access.

2. The plaza: The design of the plaza involved colliding a wavy *S* curve with a nonwavy *S* curve. This layout enabled the designer to align distinct learning environments along the curves.

3. The entry: Each child is signed in and out at the BECC. A large portion of the receptionist's desk incorporated a very long, low counter where the child would be involved in the process. Below the counter, additional shelving was provided for additional paper or supply storage.

4. Hallway: Most of the faculty and volunteer workrooms and offices were located near the entry so that a relatively long corridor had to be created to access the plaza. The length of the corridor provided the opportunity for more interaction with the child. A key element to the success of this long space was the incorporation of natural light.

Nye Bilingual Early Childhood Center, Santa Fe. Top: Long, curvilinear plaza. Learning activities, seating, storage, skylights, and child- and adult-scale doors to classrooms. **Bottom:** Plaza view. A variety of activity zones, including technology desks built into the curvilinear spaces at left. Van H. Gilbert Architect PC, design architect. Karen Marsh, project architect. Photographs by Robert Reck.

5. Mini-museum: The wall directly at the end of the corridor was built out with a mini-museum that had wall display capabilities and low shelves where items could be seen, touched, and manipulated as part of the theme.

6. Mail kiosk: Within the same space and adjacent to the mini-museum was the mail kiosk, a structure with a round, child-high counter for drawing pictures or writing notes that could then be placed in the mailbox at the center of the kiosk. The mailbox wall, also adjacent to the mini-museum, had a mailbox for each child, volunteer, and teacher in the school.

7. Activity zones: The plaza design, due to its large size, provided a place for individual as well as group activities. Some activity zones included

Reading pit: One corner of the room was built with a two- or three-step pit in a quarter-round shape. The steps were carpeted and sized for a dozen or so children to sit facing the corner, which was built out with shelving for books—a sort of mini-library. Curvilinear soffits in the ceiling offered indirect lighting.

Art zone: In the center of the plaza a piece of casework housed art supplies. The art supply casework had two sinks, one at handicap-accessible height (for children) and one at a regular child height. Tack boards were provided on the back of the casework. In close proximity to the supplies was four or five child-sized round tables and chairs.

Gross motor play: This learning zone was a large area with padded blocks and mats for tumbling and playing. Along one side of the space full-length mirrors were installed so that children could gain self-awareness and confidence as they saw themselves practicing various movements.

Role-playing: A small stage with a few steps up built into the flooring material was located in this zone. Nearby hooks for dress-up clothing and adjacent mirrors were installed.

Technology area: Computer desks had rounded fronts so that they fit into the geometry of the plaza and were located so that the screens would not reflect nearby windows.

8. Therapy room: Most of the children at the BECC had special needs that required special attention, so physical, speech, and occupational therapists were part of the permanent staff. Each of their rooms was especially designed for their respective therapies. For example, in the physical therapy room the roof structure was exposed and sized to support a long beam. The beam was fitted with hooks to suspend some of the equipment used in therapy. All of the therapy rooms were equipped with mirrors.

9. The learning environments: Being designed along a curve, the learning environments were pie-shaped. The large curved end opened to the outdoor playground. This wall was primarily a large window with a low bench at the bottom of the window. The side walls were equipped with deep, full-height casework, including places for the children's personal items as well as most of the supplies to be used in the room. Low doors scaled to children and adult doors opened to the plaza area. Each learning environment was equipped with sinks and toilet rooms. The bathrooms had low toilets for easy use by children, as well as diaper-changing facilities. All of the equipment in the toilet room was placed so as to be easily accessible to the child, instilling independence and self-sufficiency.

Because the BECC was part of the Santa Fe Public Schools system, it was built with public funds. Construction of the center happened to be a small part of the construction of a large elementary school. This meant that the bidding process was extremely competitive, as very large projects are desirable among contractors. As a result, the BECC was fortunate that all of the very important casework and items that were planned from the beginning remained in the project.

Why do some designs endure? The Crow Island Elementary School in Winnetka, Illinois, built in 1940 as an expression of progressive education, still serves as inspiration to a new generation of school designers.

School Design that Lasts
Harold G. Fearn Elementary School

Gaylaird Christopher
Principal architect of Architecture for Education, Inc.

After visiting several new state-of-the-art facilities, Fearn's community planning committee found itself captivated by the seventy-year-old Crow Island Elementary School in Winnetka, Illinois. They were struck by the school's large, flexible L-shaped classrooms with their direct relationships to the outside and generous common facilities.

Fearn Elementary School's layout is organized around a wide public street or corridor that connects one end of the school to the other. The classroom clusters are on one side of the street and the public or support spaces of the school are on the other. By separating classrooms from the larger, noisier activities, the classroom clusters take on their own identity, giving students a peaceful setting that is seldom experienced in larger school facilities.

The school, which opened in August of 2002, creates a series of small learning communities that consist of four classrooms surrounding a shared resource area. The planning committee's visit to Crow Island had resulted in the teachers' desire to have larger learning environments. In response to this need, the library was decentralized, which had the benefit of adding more than one hundred square feet to every classroom.

Harold G. Fearn Elementary School, Aurora, Illinois.
This Page: Corridor with student storage and seating at left and classrooms with fenestration giving an open feel to the hallway or "street." Photograph courtesy of Gaylaird Christopher, Architecture for Education, Inc. **Facing Page:** Classroom with view to outdoors. Photograph courtesy of Greg Murphey.
Perkins + Will Architects. Steven Turckes and Gaylaird Christopher, principal architects. Dr. Sherry Eagle, former superintendent of schools.

Another planning idea from Crow Island called for each classroom to have its own private restroom. Having bathrooms directly accessible to the classroom creates a more homelike setting and the proximity results in more instructional time. Custodians say that maintenance is much easier since students and teachers both supervise and maintain their restrooms.

The school houses a unique resource in the Aurora University teacher training center. A prospective teacher entering his or her freshman year at the university can spend time at Fearn supporting classroom activities through student and apprentice teaching. A scholar-in-residence who is employed by the university becomes an added resource and leader for the elementary school. This professor of education teaches instructional methods and philosophy classes in the large multipurpose room provided and paid for by Aurora University. Fearn is part of the second phase of a campus that includes Gary Jewel Middle School. The two schools share the thirty-acre campus with the North Aurora Parks Department.

With the help of Sherry Eagle, a visionary superintendent, architects and planners were able to bring the community together to create innovative, high-quality learning environments while absorbing the spirit of schools that last.

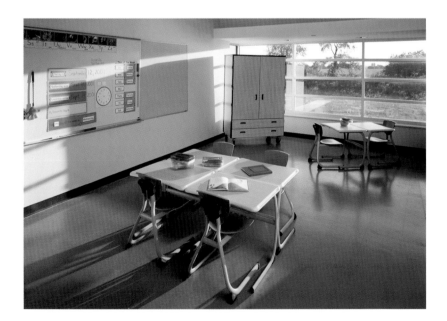

This school was programmed but not built; however, the design concept is still informative. The school facility was designed as a three-dimensional textbook for three grade levels. Each grade "house" had the same floor plan but differing orientations on the site, resulting in a symbolic representation of themes specific to adolescence, including personal identity and growth through the age levels.

The Middle School at High Desert
Excerpts from a Design Narrative

Amy Yurko
American Institute of Architects

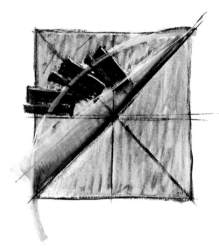

High Desert Middle School, Albuquerque, New Mexico.
Concept sketch. The arc of the datum wall links three grade houses. Illustration by Amy Yurko.

The Middle School at High Desert was to be a new independent, nonprofit school located on a dramatic site at the foothills of the Sandia Mountains in Albuquerque, New Mexico. On ten acres of sand and rocky desert terrain, the building design accentuated the natural slope of the site, an approximately forty-foot drop in elevation from its northeast to southwest limits.

MODEL FACILITY

Intended to be a model for public and private educational facilities in New Mexico and across the country, the new school was designed to comply with Albuquerque Public Schools guidelines and cost models. However, its educational approach was markedly different. Without the use of traditional textbooks, the building itself—supported by the use of advanced instructional technology—would serve as a three-dimensional learning tool. Supporting sixth-, seventh-, and eighth-grade-level developmental objectives as well as traditional curriculum subjects such as geometry, physics, history, English, and science, the building would display its various systems to create opportunities for interactive and cross-disciplinary learning.

COMPONENTS

Program spaces such as administration, food service, music, performing arts, and a gymnasium were grouped together in a continuous masonry wedge of volume. Each grade was to be housed independently. A primary open public space served as the link between support spaces and the three learning communities, and it contained a multipurpose great hall and stepped performance/dining area. A bi-level kiva incorporated into this area provided insight into the cultural context of the project. A datum wall feature emerged from the apex of the site and gently curved through the natural grade, intersecting building and landscape components. The site area on the convex side of this arc remained primarily natural, while the area inside the arc was to be modified in various ways to support multiple learning objectives. The datum feature maintained a constant absolute height such that at one end it would be level with the ground, and at the opposite end the site would drop away to reveal a masonry wall approximately forty feet high.

GRADE HOUSES

Each of the grade-level learning communities were identical in plan but singular in their specific three-dimensional geometric relationships to the sun, views, topography, main interior public spaces, support portions of the building, and to the curved datum wall feature.

▶ The sixth-grade house was partially embedded into the higher end of the site and was embraced by the exterior datum wall in its focus of **self-awareness/independence**.

▶ The seventh-grade house's floor level matched the natural site level at its location. This grade's identity of **community and cultural awareness/ interdependence** was maintained in its adjacency to the main entry and great hall as well as its central location within the facility. The datum wall equally divided the seventh-grade house.

▶ The eighth-grade house hovered above the natural grade at this site's low point and was almost entirely outside of the radius of the datum wall in its manifestation of the identity of **global awareness/transitions**. The identity of this grade was accented by its alignment with true north—the only building component with this true orientation on the site.

MEDIA CENTER

An unusual interpretation of "library" took place in this project as the entire building was designed as a media center where each student would carry a personal laptop computer with access to local, regional, and global networks. However, a traditional reading room was included to serve as a place for students to curl up with a book. This space was furnished with comfortable couches and chairs. Provisions for a rotating book collection were to be coordinated with the Albuquerque Academy and the University of New Mexico.

ENGINEERING

Engineering systems would be designed and located to provide educational opportunities. Included were evaporative cooling, radiant floor heating, hard-wired and infrared computer network connections, gray-water reclamation and an ecology pond, and vision panels into service rooms. Structural design included exposed modified bowstring trusses in the grade houses, which visually and geometrically explained their components of tension and compression.

CREDITS

Perkins + Will architects were responsible for the educational facility design. Architectural development was a collaboration between local architect Garrett Smith Ltd. (GSL) of Albuquerque and Perkins + Will. Educational programming was a joint effort, with Anne Taylor Associates as programming consultants, and included a user's manual explaining the potential educational uses of the building itself. Perkins + Will provided project engineering services. Principals in charge were Ray Bordwell of Perkins + Will, and Garrett Smith of GSL. The project design architect and project manager was Amy Yurko, also of Perkins + Will at that time.

Spaces Teachers Need to Be Effective

Eeva Reeder

Instructional coach and former high school math teacher

One of the best summaries I've heard of the past three decades of research on how people learn is from an interview with cognitive scientist Howard Gardner:

> There is now a massive amount of evidence from all realms of science that unless individuals take a very active role in what it is they're studying, unless they learn to ask questions, to do things hands-on, to essentially recreate things in their own mind and transform them as is needed, *the ideas just disappear* (George Lucas Educational Foundation, 1997).

Best instructional practice is not the open question now that it was even a dozen years ago. Teachers who want learning to stick must design learning activities for their students that engage the mind, and whenever possible, the heart of the learner; that are inquiry-driven and problem-based; that require students to build, troubleshoot, persuade, and redesign on the basis of new knowledge; and that provide the time and structure for deep reflection.

LEARNING SPACES THAT WORK

Just as different learning goals require different learning strategies, different instructional strategies require different learning spaces. The Wright brothers needed a place to research and design their aircraft. They needed a different space in which to build and refine the prototypes, and obviously an altogether different one in which to test them. Learning spaces suited to technology-based learning and the active learning that cognitive researchers recommend are quite different from what most of us are used to.

We need new structures flexible enough to accommodate our necessarily evolving definition of the purpose of schooling; otherwise, we will put teachers in the difficult position of trying to use teaching strategies in spaces not designed for them (trying to build aircraft in rooms designed for lectures).

The other great challenge for school planners and architects is to convince stakeholders and decision makers that certain cost-saving measures in building design do not result in long-term gain. Because we know better now, funding the construction of structures that cannot support best practices is unconscionable. Would we build new hospitals or sports stadiums this way? Especially given the half-century life expectancy of most school buildings, it is not smart to erect ones that will keep teachers using outmoded and ineffective instructional strategies.

A poorly designed building has a ripple effect of diminishing returns on other investments as well. Costly professional development programs for teachers, millions spent on smaller-learning-community initiatives, and expensive classroom technology purchases may all result in unremarkable gains in student achievement if otherwise willing and knowledgeable teachers are largely prevented by physical constraints from making the most of them. We risk losing some of our hardest working and most talented teachers when we put them in situations in which they cannot act on their knowledge of how to affect learning. We cannot reasonably expect a person to go to work and swim upstream every day and sustain that effort for very many years. The limited and inflexible spaces in which teachers must accomplish their extremely demanding task make especially little sense given the high percentage of teachers who leave the profession within the first few years and the decreasing number of people choosing to enter it in the first place.

A CAUTION

A poorly designed building can prevent meaningful reform of instruction, but a well-designed one cannot cause it to happen.

Designing and building the proper learning space is one of the first orders of business in education reform, but it must be simultaneously accompanied by rigorous, practical, and ongoing staff development that equips teachers to keep pace with findings from educational research and changing technology.

In my observations as a school instructional coach, the primary drag on instructional reform is teachers' lack of skill or knowledge in how to do things differently, not so much an unwillingness to try new things. For example, most teachers need help knowing what to leave out of the curriculum in order to make room for investigations and projects while still preparing students for standardized tests. They need to know how to design worthwhile, academically rigorous learning tasks; how to apply practical techniques and scaffolds for helping students become more skillful thinkers; and how to determine whether students' products and performances give adequate evidence of learning and competence. They need proven ways to use technology to enhance learning. Maybe hardest of all, teachers need help relinquishing the belief that they can control student learning outcomes as their students begin to investigate complex topics, wrestle with nuance, and start formulating their own answers to hard questions and problems.

In the end, teachers cannot force students to learn. They can only create learning environments in which the desired learning is *most likely* to occur. We have models for what works in both instructional design and building design. A good building design in these rapidly changing times is more like a score for a jazz band than a marching band—it invites improvisation and allows interpretation, not assuming it will be played the same way year after year.

Top: Teachers and students are well aware that many schools cannot keep up with rapidly changing technology, as seen in this timeline of computers in one classroom. Photograph by Murray Enggass, teacher.
Bottom: As part of an architect-in-the-schools program from the National Endowment for the Arts, architecture students reconfigured a basement classroom into this multileveled, plant-landscaped drafting room in a New Jersey high school. Photograph courtesy of Aase Ericksen.

Stephen Wheeler's instructional methods not only help architecture students develop informed responses to the world and issues of sustainability, but they can also be adapted and used as exercises during the programming process to reawaken the long-forgotten sensibilities of childhood and develop the capacities of the knowing eye.

A Pedagogical Framework for Active Learning
Education and Sustainability

Stephen Wheeler

Former assistant professor, Community and Regional Planning Program, School of Architecture and Planning, University of New Mexico, now at University of California–Davis

Field survey in the Galisteo Basin, New Mexico. Even higher education students need to get out of the classroom and learn in the environment. Photo courtesy of Bill Fleming and Stephen Wheeler.

My general philosophy of teaching architectural students emphasizes the process of "learning by doing," through which students work actively with material and develop and apply their own ideas. This approach is especially applicable to the study of sustainability issues in that it requires students to interact with and respond to the real world. Such methods give students a sense of how environments around them could be different, and how they themselves could contribute to such change.

I try to promote this activity by keeping traditional lectures to a minimum and including group discussions, role-plays, graphic exercises, student presentations, and field trips as an integral part of course material. Even within lectures students engage in extensive Socratic dialogue, often filling in arguments behind a particular point of view or responding to one another's arguments. Follow-up questions require students to enunciate their own design values and assumptions. Students also complete a number of short written and graphic assignments to work on writing, critical thinking, and presentation—all valuable tools for advocating sustainable practice in the future.

I usually ask students to state their design goals and strategies explicitly, and to make explicit connections between values and design strategies. To get students to question their own beliefs, I often start a semester by having them create a cognitive map of a childhood environment and also by having them map their ideal community. We then put these two graphics up on the walls side by side and examine relationships between them. If the class is large, I have students explain their maps to several peers in a small group.

In role-plays we use fictionalized biographies of community members or local politicians, and I ask students to play characters against type. Environmentally oriented students get to be developers, and the more conservative students get to be environmentalists or social justice advocates. We have often done role-plays around a development approval decision (a mock city council hearing) or a community design charrette (workshop).

Walking tours are a standard part of my classes. Students need to learn the skill that Allan Jacobs called "looking at cities." I stop the group every block and ask them to tell me what is going on in that place, what happened in the

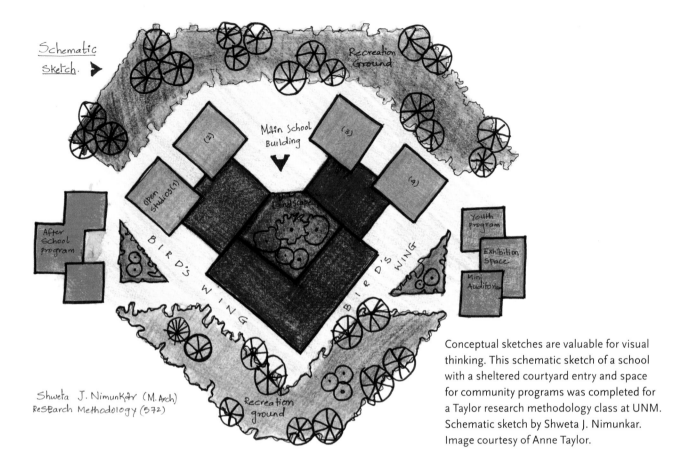

Schematic
Sketch. ▶

Recreation
Ground

Main School
Building
▼

(2)

(3)

(4)

Open
Studios (1)

Landscape

After
School
program

BIRD'S WING

BIRD'S WING

Youth
Program

Exhibition
Space

Mini
Auditorium

Shweta J. Nimunkar (M.Arch)
Research Methodology (572)

Recreation
ground

Conceptual sketches are valuable for visual
thinking. This schematic sketch of a school
with a sheltered courtyard entry and space
for community programs was completed for
a Taylor research methodology class at UNM.
Schematic sketch by Shweta J. Nimunkar.
Image courtesy of Anne Taylor.

past, and what opportunities might exist for future redesign. We imagine how it might feel for different types of people—the young, the elderly, the disabled, men, women, and members of minority groups—to experience particular spaces.

Many other sorts of field exercises are possible. In one class, groups of students walked the length of the city's waterways, taking systematic notes on the condition of these streams and possible opportunities to restore them. The resulting report was given to the city's planning staff. Ecological education programs in many other locations worldwide have emphasized wilderness trips, hands-on environmental cleanup, mapping exercises, and schoolyard gardening projects. Experiments such as the "edible schoolyard" project initiated by Alice Waters in Berkeley are increasingly well known.

GREEN SCHOOL FACILITIES

In 2003, the University of California regents voted to require all new buildings to be LEED-certified; local school boards

in some communities have also taken similar steps. Perhaps someday soon educators at all levels will teach in facilities that in fact exemplify the sustainability principles that we would like our students to learn. My own experience, however, has generally been of educational facilities that provide examples of what *not* to do in terms of sustainability. As a class we often prepare critiques of the classroom, noting for example dependency on artificial lighting during the day, inefficient heating and cooling systems without user controls, the lack of windows, and the presence of carpeting or building materials that are likely to degrade indoor air quality. Such a critique can be a valuable learning experience. But it would be so wonderful instead to have buildings that illustrate a new consciousness of environmental and social factors.

Overall I see my role not as helping students learn a particular subject matter, but as helping them learn to think, know themselves, see the world, and develop strategies for action. If my students can develop these skills I think they'll be much better designers in the long run.

The Technology Learning Center proposed in the excerpted piece below addresses a basic need for teacher professional development that models current best practices in educational theory. If teachers are trained using obsolete methods, those methods will continue to be passed on to the next generation of learners in our schools. Teaching multiple ages using the same centralized facility ensures continuity in learning that has been lacking in the educational system as a whole.

The Technology Learning Center

Robert Lurker, Joyce Downing, and Diane Wilson

Central Missouri State University

A PROJECT BRIEFING

The twentieth century was characterized by increasingly rapid innovation and technological advancement. As a result, public schools and teacher training institutions of higher education have been challenged by both the private and public sectors to change the basic principles underlying the K–16 learning process. Curriculum and instruction at the secondary and postsecondary levels must be altered to nurture and develop a different set of learner skills that include individual goal setting, problem solving, communication and collaboration, innovation, self-evaluation, and an understanding of the technology that envelops our lives. Central Missouri State University (CMSU) proposes to create a hands-on, multifunction technology laboratory—the Technology Learning Center (TLC)—that would bring together university faculty, students, public school teachers and students, and community stakeholders in business and industry.

FIVE MAJOR OBJECTIVES

The TLC is designed to achieve five major objectives supporting P–16 and lifelong education:

- To provide **preservice training** for all CMSU teacher education candidates. Future educators will gain hands-on experience with a broad range of technological processes and methodologies, equipment, and computer-based hardware and software. In addition, future teachers will have opportunities for direct interaction with public school students using the center, thus increasing their field experience hours.

- To provide extensive hands-on **in-service training** for K–12 public and charter school teachers and CMSU faculty. K–16 educators from a variety of academic disciplines will receive extensive training in the center, with a focus on evaluating and applying cutting-edge technology in their own classrooms.

- To provide **incentives for technology integration and research in P–12 classrooms and the community**. This involves enhancing existing classes in the public schools and at the university level as well as developing new curriculum based on state and national standards and piloting new materials and methods using action research methodology.

- To provide **public school access** to advanced technology for students in grades six through twelve in the Warrensburg/Kansas City area. A cadre of faculty from colleges at CMSU and participating public schools will be trained as facilitators annually.

- To **provide community/stakeholder group access** to technology and training opportunities for public and private sector businesses and agencies, including law enforcement and nearby Whiteman Air Force Base personnel.

These objectives are designed to improve the knowledge and ability of future teachers to better use technology in their teaching practices, to provide students with additional learning opportunities, to provide continuity of technology learning from kindergarten through twelfth grade, and to improve the quality of teacher preparation programs.

Technology Learning Center—Building Occupancy

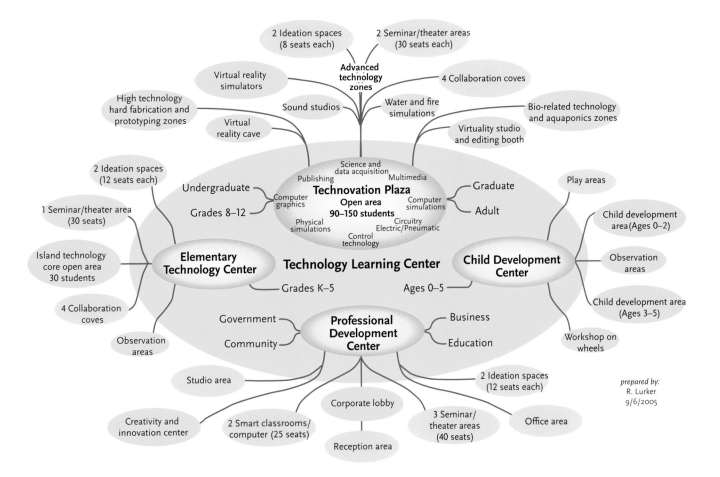

Proposed Technology Learning Center (TLC), Central Missouri State University (CMSU).
The eighty-two-thousand-square-foot multistory green design is envisioned to bring
together four major use areas (as shown in the green disks): the Technovation Plaza,
the Professional Development Center, the Elementary Technology Center, and the
Child Development Center. The proposed TLC will serve thousands of CMSU students,
classroom teachers, preschool to college-age students, and community members each
year. The Technovation Plaza area developed by Creative Learning Systems in 2004
functions as the main laboratory, surrounded by advanced technology and collaboration
areas. Image prepared by Robert Lurker.

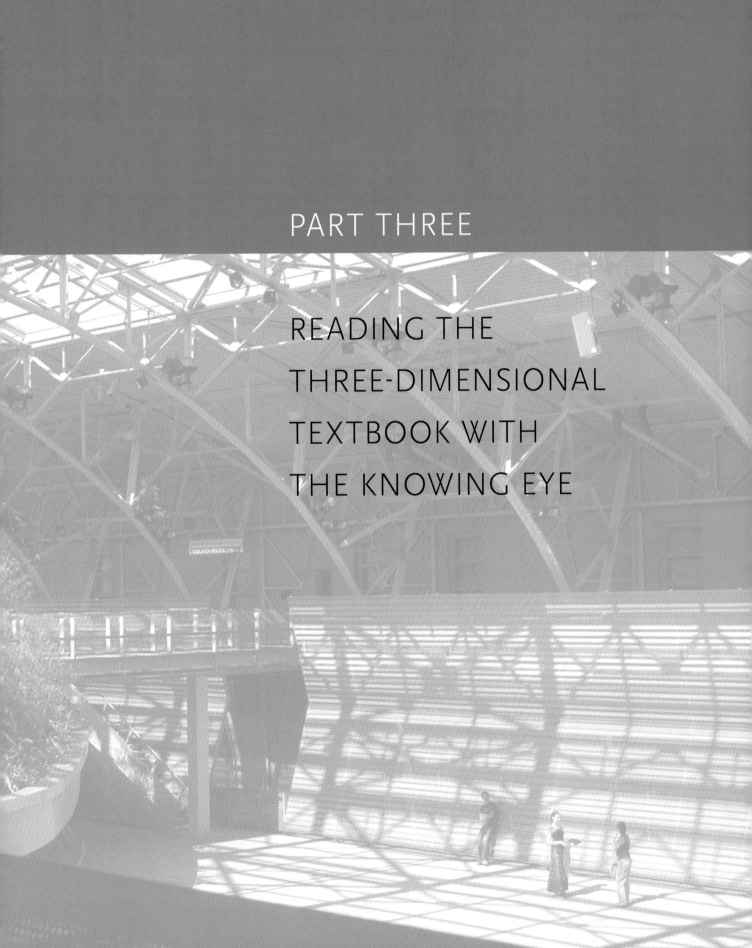

PART THREE

READING THE
THREE-DIMENSIONAL
TEXTBOOK WITH
THE KNOWING EYE

Science Center School, Los Angeles,
California. Morphosis Architects.
Thom Mayne, principal architect.
Photo by Pavel Getov.

CHAPTER SEVEN

Manifestations for Learning

Introduction:
Learning from the Physical Environment

Educational concepts can be woven into the structure of a school, making it an active rather than a passive space for learning. The "informed" learning environment is a three-dimensional textbook or teaching tool intentionally filled with rich cues or prompts for learning. A cue is defined in Merriam-Webster's Collegiate Dictionary as a "feature indicating the nature of something perceived." A prompt is something that moves us to action. A cue or prompt in the physical world is a material or concrete object that incites students to learn not only about subject matter areas, but also leads them to an understanding of the underlying ideas, patterns, and principles of the universe. Steven Bingler, Bonnie Sherk, and I coined the term *manifestations* to refer to the physical objects that make up the three-dimensional textbook from which we learn. Students interact with and use these manifestations in the environment as experiential guides or learning tools. Understanding the physical environment as a physical manifestation of ideas or concepts is an example of the wisdom gained from the knowing eye.

Found Objects and their Educational Implications

Some manifestations are simply found and exploited by those who are trained to know what to look for in the environment. A geologist uses soils and landforms to illustrate the Earth science concept of the rock cycle. Social studies students map the existing buildings in a neighborhood or use global imaging systems to learn the concepts of history, land use, urban planning, and geography. A Navajo weaver brings a rug to the classroom to inspire a discussion of mythology and symbolism in Native cultures, before children weave their own symbolic rugs.

Plateau Senior High School, Seattle, Washington.
Learning from school grounds and "found" beauty.
If there is a stand of trees on the site, leave it! Richard
Fleischman + Partners Architects, Inc. Photograph by
Eric Hanson.

Although much of the above information can be summarized in books, concrete, real-life learning offers a more meaningful, immediate, and intuitive experience for students. Real-life experiences allow for student self-identification with the subject matter, thus optimizing the learning process.

Architects can support the realm of found objects and their potential for learning by incorporating them into their macro and micro designs and allowing the natural, built, and cultural environment of a school to shine through. If the site is near a stream, the stream is not diverted or sent into a culvert; instead, it becomes part of a learning landscape. The geometry of structure is not hidden, but is revealed and made obvious through exposed trusses or beams or accented through use of color, repetition, and signage. Siting and choice of materials can ensure that schools appear to be a part of the community and its landscape, not isolated from the local culture or patterned after the "big box" mentality. Materials for building can also be green and biobased, reinforcing our connections to nature and the local life zone, thus promoting ecoliteracy.

Manifestations Designed into the Learning Environment

Architecture is the science and the art of building, "or to be more poetic, the moment that a building is imbued with a knowing magic that transforms it from mere shelter into that of a self-conscious work of art" (Glancey, 2000, p. 9). Schools are much more than places to stow children during the day. Architecture is pedagogy. Architecture for education becomes art only when the architecture itself teaches; when design elements highlight concepts across disciplines, forming an environmental curriculum; when the facility meets the highest aspirations of the architectural profession; and when a school is endowed with beauty and imagination.

Science Center School

Los Angeles, California

Science Center School is a hybrid institution, combining a K–5 elementary school and teacher training program with the resources of a major museum.

 The adaptively reused armory, dating from 1919, has been converted into a flexible, open, two-story atrium dominated by a large interior bamboo garden. The bamboo garden is pierced midway by skywalks, and it forms the heart of the Science Education Resource Center.

Science Center School, Los Angeles, California. Morphosis Architects. Thom Mayne, principal architect. Photo by Pavel Getov.

Top: La Mesa Elementary School, Albuquerque, New Mexico. Photograph courtesy of Garrett Smith Ltd.
Bottom: George Vlastos designed this gear ratio and pulley for lowering a table from the ceiling to be operable by children. Image courtesy of Anne Taylor.

Successful Models

It is impossible to list every manifestation that an architect might design into a school. The main point is that the physical environment is a potent, influential "silent curriculum" that deeply affects learning and behavior. A few examples illustrate the potential for designers:

- ▸ Provide playground fencing that embodies math/geometry concepts and aesthetically surpasses the usual chain link. Architect Garrett Smith designed fencing at La Mesa Elementary School as a learning tool. Students can study the fencing to explore the concept of "line" (curved, straight, parallel, diagonal, vertical, horizontal, grid). Other math ideas embedded in the fencing include repetition, rhythm, pattern, measurement, and counting/numbers. Even musical scale concepts can be embedded in fence designs.

- ▸ Provide space and irrigation/water for garden environments to teach science concepts, including heath and nutrition. In the King Middle School in Berkeley, a large asphalt surface was transformed into an Edible Schoolyard Project with the help of Alice Waters, a restaurant owner. Sixth and seventh graders care for the half-acre garden. The school's science curriculum for these two grades focuses on the garden and a kitchen where students learn about foods and nutrition, including foods from other cultures. Learn more online at the project's Web site, http://www.edibleschoolyard.org.

- ▸ Incorporate simple machines into the learning environment. The gear ratio and pulley system shown here, which is operable by children, was used to raise and lower a space frame table to create open space in the classroom or to add working surfaces as needed.

- ▸ Provide language arts and visual arts concepts through well-designed signage. The signage at Solana, an industrial commercial park located outside Dallas, links clear, aesthetically pleasing fonts with eye-catching visual sculptural elements. Other concepts in signage include bilingual learning and use of Braille.

▸ Provide fitness rooms in schools. Schools are changing the focus of physical education classes from sports and athleticism to fitness, according to the health section of the *Albuquerque Journal* (Sweet, 2003). The movement is in response to current crisis levels in student obesity, and it stresses lifelong exercise for everyone, not just the physically gifted. Places for individual workouts, aerobics rooms, fitness centers or trails and equipment, weight rooms, climbing walls, and medical monitoring equipment (heart monitors, software to analyze fitness, pedometers, etc.) all support the shift from traditional gymnasium to fitness center.

▸ Provide biology concepts through landscape architecture. Robin Moore's *Plants for Play* (1993) is a valuable plant selection guide that helps architects and educators understand the multisensory learning possibilities for outdoor environments. Categories covered explore sensory variety, play value, nature's bounty, seasonal interest, shade quality, screens (visual barriers, windscreen), wildlife enhancement, erosion control, and drought tolerance. Every plant selected for school grounds can become a teaching tool.

▸ Support literacy through spatial organization, provisioning, and arrangement of materials in reading and writing environments. The functional use of print as a teaching tool can be supported architecturally by display areas, message centers, mailboxes, signage, digital displays, places to record data, media centers, and a variety of stimulating objects in the environment. Provide spaces that allow sharing, browsing, and contemplation of literary materials (Loughlin & Martin, 1987).

Top and Center: Quality signage with sculptural elements at Solana, an industrial commercial park near Dallas, Texas. Solana owner and developer: Maguire Partners. Legorreta + Legorreta Architects. Solana sign by Debra Nichols Design.
Bottom: Positive form and negative space, reversed for visual interest. Solana owner and developer: Maguire Partners. Legorreta + Legorreta Architects. Solana signs by Debra Nichols Design.

▶ Turn the school environment into a celebration of culture and architecture. Patterson Architects designed a prototype of a Texas elementary school media center to include architectural elements such as a bridge, tower, loft, spiral staircase, and a homelike structure housing a reading area. Other designs explore multicultural hallways and entry treatments for elementary schools.

Left top: Prototype design for Alton O. Bowen Elementary School, Bryan Independent School District, Texas. School media center with cultural wall elevations and architectural elements including a library loft, bridge, tower structure, reading house, circular layout, hanging displays, curvilinear stairs, movable stools for seating, and plants. These constitute "places within spaces," as in theatrical set design. Patterson Architects. Photograph by Charles D. Smith.
Left bottom: The fairytale castle corner serves two purposes, acting as a gateway to the kindergarten pod and as an imaginative alternative learning center in the hallway. Patterson Architects. Photograph by Charles D. Smith.

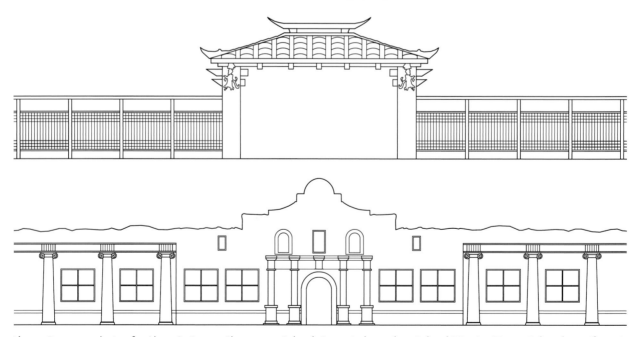

Above: Prototype design for Alton O. Bowen Elementary School, Bryan Independent School District, Texas. Cultural manifestations. Facades with different cultural and historical motifs convert wall space into learning zones in this prototype design. Wall elevations by Atsuko Sakai, adapted from blueprint drawings from Patterson Architects.

▶ Use paint as an inexpensive and versatile architectural membrane to teach all subject matter areas through graphics, maps, and murals. Perkins + Will, architects of Perspectives Charter School in Chicago, used colossally scaled, multilingual graphics in the school's open multiuse space to express the core values and philosophy of the school. Simply painting walls can also brighten a school. Publicolor, a nonprofit group, is devoted to getting rid of those bland institutional colors and replacing them with vibrantly colored walls that students help paint. The program has enlisted more than five thousand students, who learn not only painting skills, but also to appreciate the schools they upgrade and to stay in school (National Clearinghouse for Educational Facilities News, 2006).

Above: Optical Illusions, geometry, and scale. John Steele, designer.

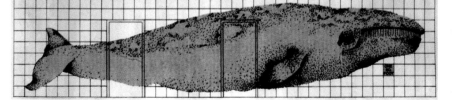

Eagle River, Alaska

Vlastos and Taylor were artists-in-residence and facilitators for the project executed by students in Eagle River, Alaska. **Clockwise from top left:** Fifth graders prepare cutouts for physical education exercise stations. Exercise stations with overlapping images and color graphics. A whale drawn to scale on a brick grid illustrates math concepts in Eagle River, Alaska. Mural by George Vlastos, architect. Photographs courtesy of George Vlastos, architect, and Anne Taylor.

The Pond: The wetland as an interdisciplinary manifestation for learning

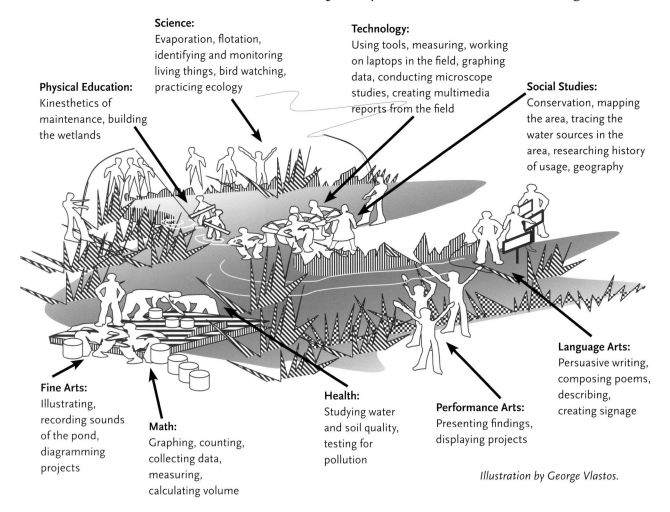

Science:
Evaporation, flotation, identifying and monitoring living things, bird watching, practicing ecology

Technology:
Using tools, measuring, working on laptops in the field, graphing data, conducting microscope studies, creating multimedia reports from the field

Physical Education:
Kinesthetics of maintenance, building the wetlands

Social Studies:
Conservation, mapping the area, tracing the water sources in the area, researching history of usage, geography

Fine Arts:
Illustrating, recording sounds of the pond, diagramming projects

Math:
Graphing, counting, collecting data, measuring, calculating volume

Health:
Studying water and soil quality, testing for pollution

Performance Arts:
Presenting findings, displaying projects

Language Arts:
Persuasive writing, composing poems, describing, creating signage

Illustration by George Vlastos.

The Environment Is Interdisciplinary

No single discipline fully explains our world. Through interaction with objects, children encounter integrated concepts from math, science, social studies, language arts, physical education, and the arts. As children discover the richness of the environment, they learn to view their surroundings in multiple ways, increasing their problem-solving abilities with ideas and strategies taken from all subject matter areas. Davis and coauthors (1997) write that interdisciplinary learning automatically aids higher-order thinking skills by requiring learners to compare, synthesize, and innovate.

My work in California with Bonnie Sherk (1994), landscape architect and founder of A Living Library, illustrates how an interdisciplinary approach can arise naturally from a single provocative environmental manifestation, or centerpiece for learning. The environmental pond was conceived as a teaching tool for Lincoln High School West in California (see illustration above). The ideas behind this manifestation related to the humanities, science, social studies, math, and the arts. The pond also would be understood in its broader relation to the larger water environments of the school district, the town of Stockton, the delta region, California's waterways, and the sea.

The environmental pond as an integrated curriculum manifestation was intended to involve the students in multiple learning experiences and reinforce their different learning styles through a strategy similar to the ATA Taxonomy outlined in chapter 5. The learning opportunities of the "whole design experience" included all phases and aspects of the pond from its inception: the schematic landscape design, design development, and construction of the pond, as well as ongoing growth, use, maintenance, observation, measurement, and testing of the pond. Interdisciplinary study was designed to result in higher-order valuing and stewardship themes that would develop an ecohistoric sense of place in students (Taylor & Sherk, 1994).

Translating Architectural Elements into Learning Opportunities

An entire school facility inside and out can teach if its functions and spaces are visible and accessible to children. Support areas such as administration, the cafeteria, the nurse's office, custodial closets, grounds maintenance storage, and more can be designed so that children observe and learn about careers and participate in maintaining and caring for the school.

The charts in the Tools for Thought section at the end of this chapter show how common architectural elements can be designed for their maximum potential as learning manifestations. The charts emphasize design over technical architectural information and show how learning opportunities can emerge from carefully designed places and objects. The chart format is a planning tool that

- ▶ Identifies the architectural element or system (manifestation)

- ▶ Describes ways to enhance the design potential of the element

- ▶ Lists educational implications or concepts embedded in the architecture, and

- ▶ Suggests learning experiences arising from student interaction with the manifestation, based on the ATA Taxonomy described in chapter 5.

The first chart provided here highlights **school-wide systems** (floors, heating, ventilation, and so on) as three-dimensional textbooks for learning. A second chart moves to **outdoor learning zones**, which are conceived as part of the total academic picture for school design. (For more about transforming our neglected school grounds into learning landscapes, see chapter 10.)

Rather than relying on traditional textbooks and rote learning, a new, integrated curriculum must be written based on themes from environmental manifestations by taking an object or entity, examining its form and function, and then translating perception of the object into ideas, knowledge, understanding, creative problem solving, and self-expression.

Manifestations: Learning from School-wide Systems

Architectural Element: Acoustics/Sound Attenuation

Enhanced Design Potential	Educational Implications (Concepts)	Active Learning Experience (ATA Taxonomy)
▶ Design with different materials that deflect sound in different ways (glass, concrete, fabric). ▶ Design shape of spaces to affect sound (angle walls slightly, change ceiling plane, use convex curved finish panels on ceiling). ▶ Consider size of spaces and small group usage. ▶ Stagger wall planes. ▶ Devise separation, diffusion, and noise cancellation systems. ▶ Demonstrate effects of different sound insulation techniques (gypsum board wall constructions). ▶ Install whisper tube. ▶ Use hearing-disabled standards throughout.	▶ Decibel ▶ Measurement ▶ Physics of sound (wave, echo, reverberation, reflection) ▶ Types and intensity of sounds ▶ Hearing/ear ▶ Music concepts ▶ Sound technology ▶ Sound attenuation	**Observation and multisensory discovery:** Take a blindfold tour to emphasize hearing. Listen to sounds indoors and out. Play with synthesizers. **Data collection:** Measure sound, experiment with materials and sound using enhanced design environments, record sound. **Concept formation:** Create and label a diagram of how the human ear works. **Problem solving:** Create a sound garden outdoors. **Valuing:** Listen to your favorite music, sing or play an instrument. **Stewardship:** Investigate noise pollution around your school and offer solutions.

NOTES

_____

_____

_____

_____

_____

_____

_____

Architectural Element: Artificial Lighting

Enhanced Design Potential	Educational Implications (Concepts)	Active Learning Experience (ATA Taxonomy)
▸ Full-spectrum lighting ▸ Uplighting ▸ No fluorescent lighting ▸ Bundle cables, color code by function, and expose with signage ▸ Task lighting ▸ Multiple lighting systems flexible for use by students ▸ Light tables ▸ Shadow wall ▸ Timed light controls ▸ Color of lights and changing color	▸ Health (proper lighting, vision) ▸ Physics of light ▸ Electricity ▸ Electrician ▸ Safety ▸ Science ▸ Color/spectrum ▸ Opaque ▸ Transparent ▸ Design ▸ Lighting applications (aesthetic use of lighting in theater, dance, architecture, art, and creating art out of light) ▸ See also "natural lighting"	**Observation and multisensory discovery:** Play with light tools, light tables, color. Explore differences: high pressure sodium, fluorescent, full spectrum. **Data collection:** Describe all light sources you can find at school. **Concept formation:** Make a chart of lighting sources and designs through the centuries. **Problem solving:** Create an electrical circuit. **Valuing**: Design lighting for a student performance. **Stewardship**: See how much energy you can save through smart artificial light usage and natural lighting. How do white ceilings affect interior lighting?

NOTES

_____

_____

_____

_____

_____

_____

_____

Manifestations: Learning from School-wide Systems *(continued)*

Architectural Element: Ceilings

Enhanced Design Potential	Educational Implications (Concepts)	Active Learning Experience (ATA Taxonomy)
▶ Grid system or space frame for hanging objects ▶ Acoustics, sound attenuation (curved elements) ▶ Acoustical tiles ▶ Exposed truss and/or ventilation system ▶ Up lighting ▶ Skylights or glass ceilings ▶ Drop-down furniture ▶ Reflectivity and light ▶ As cultural learning tools (historical precedents) ▶ Clouds (suspended ceiling)	▶ Positional concepts ▶ Shapes and forms (geometry) ▶ Architecture ▶ Structural systems ▶ Air circulation ▶ Sound ▶ Display ▶ Measurement (height, area)	**Observation and multisensory discovery:** Observe ceilings in different parts of the school. **Data collection:** Visually record (sketch) exposed truss system. **Concept formation:** What is the difference between a ceiling and a roof? For older children: Compare ceilings of churches, homes, and indigenous dwellings. **Problem solving:** Calculate the ceiling area of your room or for the entire school. Count ceiling tiles, length and width, to calculate room size. **Valuing:** Use bodies to imitate and feel forces on structural systems such as trusses and domes. **Stewardship:** Visit a planetarium and see how it is constructed and how it works. Think about the night sky. What is light pollution?

NOTES

Architectural Element: Circulation/Wayfinding

Enhanced Design Potential	Educational Implications (Concepts)	Active Learning Experience (ATA Taxonomy)
▸ Avoid long narrow double-loaded corridors ▸ Install galleries and display systems ▸ Make hallways wide, as possible pull-out space ▸ Color code and use consistent signage for visual/verbal literacy; graphics ▸ Security: limit entryways, maximize exits; open up sight lines ▸ Furnish small areas for socialization and learning: niches, study areas, technology zones ▸ Concepts of the street, mall, atrium, etc. ▸ No lockers in hallways ▸ Skylights/natural lighting ▸ Interior fenestration and views ▸ Cultural influences ▸ In temperate climates, hallways and gathering spaces can be outside. ▸ Single loaded for natural light	▸ Art ▸ Display/gallery ▸ Expression ▸ Socialization ▸ Culture ▸ History ▸ Technology ▸ Urban systems ▸ Spatial configuration ▸ Pedestrian ▸ Safety ▸ Fire drill (diagram, map, route) ▸ Exit	**Observation and multisensory discovery:** Map the school. **Data collection:** Find out about local codes and fire safety. Measure the distance you walk each day. **Concept formation:** Compare school circulation system to other buildings and to cities. What patterns do you find? **Problem solving:** Design a treasure hunt using accurate distances for your school hallways. **Valuing:** Create art for display, or organize and curate a visiting cultural show for public space at school. **Stewardship:** Discuss why plants are important. Next, organize a fund-raiser to place potted plants in school hallways, and design a system for plant care.

NOTES

_____

_____

_____

_____

_____

_____

TOOLS FOR THOUGHT

Manifestations: Learning from School-wide Systems *(continued)*

Architectural Element: Communication Technology

Enhanced Design Potential	Educational Implications (Concepts)	Active Learning Experience (ATA Taxonomy)
▶ Models of technology systems, or transparent windows to technology ▶ School wired for networking, Internet, or wireless environments ▶ Increased flexibility to support changing technology (furniture, spaces) ▶ Cyber café ▶ Ubiquitous technology ▶ Laptop docking systems ▶ Intercom ▶ AV/TV integrated into storage system or on a cart for flexibility ▶ Ergonomic considerations: TV bolted near ceiling is not advisable for children ▶ Lighting considerations with technology (diffused) ▶ Library becomes multimedia production lab ▶ Electronic informational signage	▶ Literacy ▶ Language ▶ Drama ▶ Writing ▶ Schedule ▶ Calendar ▶ Manners and safety (telephone, Internet use) ▶ Technology, computers ▶ Fine motor coordination ▶ Videography ▶ Critical thinking ▶ Multimedia presentations	**Observation and multisensory discovery:** Use technology equipment. **Data collection:** Use technology to graph, chart, and create databases for your projects. **Concept formation:** Research new technologies and present the information to the school board. **Problem solving:** Create a class Web site for parents to access and keep it updated; use multiple forms of media to design projects. **Valuing:** Students use the school announcement system to learn value of news/giving messages, and to appreciate the importance of evaluating the information they receive. **Stewardship:** Care for, maintain, and clean equipment. Study manners, technology, and safety online.

NOTES

_____

_____

_____

_____

_____

Architectural Element: Entry, Exits, Access

Enhanced Design Potential	Educational Implications (Concepts)	Active Learning Experience (ATA Taxonomy)
▶ Handicap access/universal design ▶ Child scale door/access ▶ Doors with levers ▶ Windows in doors ▶ Signage ▶ Design of entry reflects local culture, welcoming ▶ Consider adjacencies that reflect project-based, student-centered learning, i.e., decentralized resources, break-out rooms, transitions to outdoors. ▶ Nurse, social, health, and recreation services have community access. ▶ Administration has view of entry for security. ▶ Portal walkway and courtyard entry can reflect local culture through design and display. ▶ Entry can contain living things: aquarium, terrarium, container plants, insect zoo. ▶ Magnetic door closures (for fire drills)	▶ Respect ▶ Valuing ▶ Inclusion ▶ Laws, codes (civics) ▶ Health ▶ Gross and fine motor skills (opening and closing doors; prehensile grasp of levers, knobs) ▶ Mechanics (hinge, lever, fulcrum) ▶ Positional concepts ▶ Angles (turning wheelchair) ▶ Reading ▶ Following directions ▶ Mapping ▶ Culture and architecture ▶ Structural systems (arch, post and beam, cantilever)	**Observation and multisensory discovery:** Observe and diagram how a door works. What are different doors made of? How wide are different doorways? Why? How do locks, knobs, hinges, and levers work? **Data collection:** Take a neighborhood walking tour and sketch examples of entries. **Concept formation:** Identify and trace international symbols for transport, access, public spaces, etc. **Problem solving:** Design a new entry for your school and make a model to scale. **Valuing:** Use a wheelchair to get around your school. Write about the experience. **Stewardship:** Maintain and care for living things that are part of the design. Create a garden walkway that leads to the entry.

NOTES

TOOLS FOR THOUGHT

Manifestations: Learning from School-wide Systems *(continued)*

Architectural Element: Floors

Enhanced Design Potential	Educational Implications (Concepts)	Active Learning Experience (ATA Taxonomy)
▶ Soft carpet in identified spaces ▶ Washable floors in project areas or near water sources ▶ Floor graphics ▶ SmartSlab (load-bearing, interactive image screens that can be used on floors, walls, and sidewalks for global simulcasts and remote data transfer) ▶ Prewired floor systems ▶ Consider life cycle energy of products used. ▶ Maintain with safe products (indoor pollution). ▶ New products in floor systems, including antistatic and antimicrobial properties; renewable natural ingredients such as flax, pine rosin, wood flour and jute; and bamboo flooring	▶ Products ▶ Materials ▶ Structure ▶ Pollution/conservation ▶ Resources ▶ Textures ▶ Traction/friction ▶ Games/sports/courts ▶ Graphics (can represent multiple concepts in any subject matter area) ▶ Measurement, area ▶ Health ▶ Safety	**Observation and multisensory discovery:** Take off your shoes and explore different textures of surfaces and describe. **Data collection:** Measure floor area using informal and formal measurement tools (taking steps as compared to using a meter stick). **Concept formation:** Look up the word *floor*. Think of rhymes for *floor*. **Problem solving:** Design a floor graphic that teaches a math concept. **Valuing:** Bounce a ball in the gym and on carpeting. Compare. What surfaces are best for different sports? Why? **Stewardship:** Investigate materials used in creating floors. Sort by type: renewable, nonrenewable, recyclable, natural resource, man-made, etc. Clean the floor. Sample cleaning materials.

NOTES

_____

_____

_____

_____

Manifestations: Learning from School-wide Systems *(continued)*

Architectural Element: Furniture

Enhanced Design Potential	Educational Implications (Concepts)	Active Learning Experience (ATA Taxonomy)
▶ Tables as desks ▶ Flexible, deployable, movable (wheels) ▶ Collapsible ▶ Stackable ▶ Tables with vertical fold possibility, on wheels ▶ Shelves on wheels ▶ Ergonomic chairs ▶ Large horizontal working surfaces versus desks ▶ Arrangement of furniture reflects best educational practices (not oriented toward teacher at front, but geared to teamwork, project-based learning, cooperation, new technology). ▶ Partitions deployable by students ▶ Gallery-type framing system for student and public art ▶ See also "storage"	▶ Measurement ▶ Studio ▶ Adjustable ▶ Flexible ▶ Movable ▶ Presentations ▶ Projects in all subject matter areas ▶ Teamwork ▶ Social skills ▶ Cooperation, sharing ▶ Responsibility for own learning ▶ Respect ▶ Cultural valuing ▶ Art, art history ▶ Gallery ▶ Display ▶ Technology ▶ Body systems ▶ Health (ergonomics) ▶ Mechanics (wheel, hinge, etc.)	**Observation and multisensory discovery:** Compare chairs throughout your school. Which is most comfortable for you? Why? **Data collection:** Measure height and reach of each student and graph results. Name as many kinds of furniture as you can. **Concept formation:** Write a description of a piece of furniture in your room as if for a catalogue. Label features and parts. **Problem solving:** Reorganize your classroom to support work on a team project. **Valuing:** Maintain a student gallery. Participate in furniture choice and state preferences. **Stewardship:** Create and maintain an outdoor seating area or refinish outdoor tables. Study different indoor furnishings to find low-emitting products.

NOTES

Manifestations: Learning from School-wide Systems *(continued)*

Architectural Element: Green Architecture

Enhanced Design Potential	Educational Implications (Concepts)	Active Learning Experience (ATA Taxonomy)
▶ Research references ▶ LEED certification ▶ Green Alliance 924 Park Ave. SW Albuquerque, NM 87102 ▶ *Cradle to Cradle* by William McDonough ▶ *Green Architecture* by James Wines. Wines's eco-friendly checklist includes modest scale, use of recycled and renewable materials, low-embodied-energy materials, harvested lumber, water catchment systems, low maintenance, recycling of buildings, reduction of ozone-depleting chemicals, preservation of the natural environment, energy efficiency, solar orientation, integration of architecture and landscape. ▶ New "green" technology such as intelligent facades; advances in photovoltaics ▶ Remodeled/reused space ▶ Insulation ▶ Natural light usage	▶ Ecology ▶ Holism ▶ Environment ▶ Cycles ▶ Networks ▶ Coevolution ▶ Scale and limits ▶ Dynamic balance ▶ Consumption ▶ Natural resources ▶ Earth science ▶ Renewable resource ▶ Conservation ▶ Energy, alternative energy ▶ Sustainability ▶ Stewardship ▶ Change ▶ Architecture ▶ Earth-centric philosophy ▶ Connectedness ▶ Culture ▶ See "Outdoor Learning Zones" chart	**Observation and multisensory discovery:** Use magnifiers to study plants and insects. **Data collection:** Record and identify plants and animals found on the school grounds. Collect data about air and water quality. **Concept formation:** Use the Internet and green technology provided in the school design to study ecology and make signage. **Problem solving:** Design a habitat for your school grounds (from a terrarium to wetlands, insect garden to fish pond, etc.). Maintain and monitor the habitat. **Valuing:** Keep track of how much energy you save by using natural lighting. Why is it important to conserve? **Stewardship:** Compost lunchroom garbage for gardens. Set up a school recycling center and study materials usage.

NOTES

Manifestations: Learning from School-wide Systems *(continued)*

Architectural Element: HVAC—Heating, Ventilation, and Cooling

Enhanced Design Potential	Educational Implications (Concepts)	Active Learning Experience (ATA Taxonomy)
▶ Measure whole cost of ventilation systems over time and maintenance issues. ▶ Leave part of system open to visibility to act as a museum. Label parts. ▶ Paint exposed portion of duct system, color-coded to show intake and return. ▶ Map the duct system. ▶ See also recommendations of "green" design, including use of solar orientation, solar energy, ground cooling systems, etc. ▶ Provide museum-quality displays of wall structure, insulation and materials. ▶ Use nonpolluting materials for high air quality. ▶ HVAC monitoring systems accessible to students	▶ HVAC (heating, ventilation, cooling) ▶ Measurement ▶ Temperature ▶ Thermostat ▶ Circulation (including human body systems as related to building systems) ▶ Properties of matter (hot and cold) ▶ Climate/microclimate ▶ Heat flow, conduction ▶ Pollution ▶ Mapping ▶ Conservation ▶ Solar energy ▶ Health (air quality) ▶ Stewardship ▶ Mechanics ▶ Electricity ▶ Sound (measurement and acoustics) ▶ Diagrams ▶ Convection (air) ▶ Radiation (radiator) ▶ Conduction (electric stove)	**Observation and multisensory discovery:** What does the building feel like to you? Take a walking tour to map hot, cold, stuffy, well-ventilated, noisy, and quiet. **Data collection:** Measure temperature and air quality. **Concept formation:** Research indoor pollution. **Problem solving:** Diagram or make models of the human circulatory system and compare them to building systems. **Valuing:** Use the arts to express your favorite season, temperature, and/or climate. **Stewardship:** Monitor, present results, and apply ecologically responsive HVAC measures at school.

NOTES

Manifestations: Learning from School-wide Systems *(continued)*

Architectural Element: Natural Lighting

Enhanced Design Potential	Educational Implications (Concepts)	Active Learning Experience (ATA Taxonomy)
▶ Fenestration for energy conservation ▶ Operable windows ▶ Southern window treatment ▶ Orientation and siting of building ▶ Solar/passive solar ▶ Greenhouse ▶ Durable blinds ▶ Perforated shades ▶ North light is beneficial for art studios. ▶ Skylights ▶ Clerestory ▶ Light shelves up high ▶ Controls for natural light such as shades, louvers, remote control blinds, etc. ▶ When you maximize daylight, you minimize the need for applied decoration. ▶ Use of courtyards ▶ Placement of furniture for maximum benefit	▶ Shadows, light, dark ▶ Solar system ▶ Reflection ▶ Refraction ▶ Absorption ▶ Cardinal directions ▶ Day, night ▶ Seasons ▶ Physics (light) ▶ Vision, eyes ▶ Temperature ▶ Weather ▶ Art (sun prints, window views, tracing, elements of art) ▶ Botany ▶ Green architecture ▶ Mechanics (window, solar design) ▶ R-value (range of temperatures) ▶ Cultural implications (Native American site orientation, role of sun in religions, writing about the sun) ▶ Spatial concepts (inside, outside, up, down, open, closed, etc.)	**Observation and multisensory discovery:** Use vision tools (lenses, prisms, magnifiers, mirrors) to play with natural light. **Data collection:** Keep a daily record of the weather; track the path of the sun throughout the school year; observe and draw the movement of shadows on school grounds; track sunlight coming in windows. **Concept formation:** Diagram how the eye works. **Problem solving:** Plan and host a solar picnic. Design solar ovens and use them to cook hotdogs. **Valuing:** Find examples of natural light and windows in art. Discuss them and then create your own window art. **Stewardship:** Design a pamphlet for parents that shows how your school uses natural lighting to save energy. Take photos.

NOTES

Architectural Element: Plumbing

Enhanced Design Potential	Educational Implications (Concepts)	Active Learning Experience (ATA Taxonomy)
► Use transparent pipes under sink area (system open to visibility). ► Ergonomics: use sinks with adjustable height feature; child scale toilets ► Lever faucets ► Smart plumbing with signage about how it works ► Provide a diagram of the entire water system from the water fountain to the sewage treatment plant. ► Investigate water recycling systems, including natural systems such as wetlands ► Hygiene and grooming signage in restrooms	► Water systems and sources ► Waste management, sewer systems, water treatment plants ► Human body waste system (digestion) ► Gravity ► Measurement (volume) ► Flow, cohesion (properties of water) ► Hygiene ► Mechanics (levers) ► Temperature ► Health (water quality) ► Chemistry (water testing) ► Conservation ► Community water issues (persuasive writing, speaking) ► How smart plumbing works	**Observation and multisensory discovery:** Drink bottled water and water from the tap and compare. How do they taste? **Data collection:** Make a graph of your monthly water bills at home and at school. **Concept formation:** Research plumbing around the world and throughout history. **Problem solving:** Conduct experiments to discover properties of water. **Valuing:** Discuss conservation. Think of ways your school can save water, and implement them. **Stewardship:** Study how nature recycles and cleanses water (wetlands, water cycle, etc.). Apply what you've learned to the school grounds.

NOTES

_____

_____

_____

_____

_____

TOOLS FOR THOUGHT

Manifestations: Learning from School-wide Systems *(continued)*

Architectural Element: Power

Enhanced Design Potential	Educational Implications (Concepts)	Active Learning Experience (ATA Taxonomy)
▶ Clear plate over light switch to show circuitry or other exposed systems (electricity museum) ▶ Solar panel/photovoltaic ▶ Meet technology needs with plenty of electrical outlets ▶ Windmill on playground ▶ Wireless technology ▶ See "green" architecture, "HVAC," and "natural lighting" ▶ Monitoring systems ▶ Use the power of natural light to increase efficiency: add photovoltaic capacity to existing building components such as awnings, canopies, rooftop arrays. ▶ Greenhouse	▶ Electricity ▶ Power sources and systems ▶ Photovoltaics ▶ Wireless technology ▶ Generation ▶ Magnetism ▶ Mechanics of switch ▶ Model-making (for example, solar powered vehicles) ▶ Safety ▶ Technology, computers ▶ History of electricity ▶ Alternative energy, conservation ▶ Weather, climate	**Observation and multisensory discovery:** What is static electricity? What is lightning? **Data collection:** Collect, compare, and graph electricity use data from all schools in your district. **Concept formation:** Trace the path of the power your school uses, from source to outlet. Look up *power* in the dictionary and see its different meanings. **Problem solving:** Use a science kit or Internet research to learn how to wire an electrical circuit. **Valuing:** Discuss what happens when the power goes out. In how many ways does electricity make life easier? **Stewardship:** Visit and research a wind farm, power plant, dam, solar powered building, etc.

NOTES

_____

_____

_____

_____

_____

_____

Architectural Element: Security

Enhanced Design Potential	Educational Implications (Concepts)	Active Learning Experience (ATA Taxonomy)
► "All hazards" approach to safety ► Include signage for how systems connect to community resources (fire station, security office, etc.). ► Color-coded exit system ► Consult local law enforcement and other experts during programming. ► Controlled access to school grounds, different areas of the school at different times of day, lockdown capability ► Outdoor lighting ► Aesthetically pleasing boundary treatments: fencing, plantings ► Surveillance: open views through fenestration, offices near entries, open sight lines, etc. ► Police substation on site ► Technology: cameras, sensors, thumbprint access, card swipe systems, hazard radios, lighting ► Use computer-aided design (CAD) building drawings to aid in emergencies.	► Public safety and careers ► Fire drill ► Following directions ► Maps ► Exit/entrance ► Literacy, reading ► Diagram ► Sound ► Measurement (time) ► Homeland Security ► Emergency ► Preparation ► Camera ► Urban design ► Shelter ► Control room	**Observation and multisensory discovery:** Older students can observe behaviors in different areas of the school. **Data collection:** Compile above observations into a report on the safest/least safe areas of your school. **Concept formation:** Write a paragraph about what environmental characteristics make you feel secure or insecure. **Problem solving:** Design a team project that will make your school safer (fund-raiser for extra lighting; signage; cleaning up an outdoor space, etc.). **Valuing:** Debate: Does increased surveillance lead to safer environments, and at what cost? **Stewardship:** Develop a code of conduct that details how you will treat others in such a way as they feel safe and secure.

NOTES

_____

_____

_____

_____

_____

Manifestations: Learning from School-wide Systems *(continued)*

Architectural Element: Storage

Enhanced Design Potential	Educational Implications (Concepts)	Active Learning Experience (ATA Taxonomy)
► Floor-to-ceiling wall units with modular parts ► Teacher storage above, child scale access below ► Drop down tables ► Retractable shelves ► Large portfolio and project storage capacity ► On wheels with brakes ► Tackable or writing surfaces ► Units or storage with doors ► Sliding door/panels ► Personal storage spaces (cubbies, in-room cabinets, not hall lockers) ► Storage located in transitional spaces: class entry zone	► Stewardship ► Organization ► Order, sorting ► Responsibility ► Preservation ► Respect ► Valuing ► Writing ► Display design ► Long-term, project-based learning	**Observation and multisensory discovery:** Students organize and sort objects. **Data collection:** Take an inventory of class manipulatives and equipment. **Concept formation:** Learn how to properly "store," organize, and retrieve information on a computer, i.e., create and name folders. **Problem solving:** Use the storage/display options in your classroom to create an art museum or science fair and invite parents and peers. **Valuing:** Take before and after pictures of a cluttered space that you clean up. **Stewardship:** Students are responsible for maintaining classroom organization and reducing clutter.

NOTES

_____

_____

_____

_____

_____

Architectural Element: Walls and Display

Enhanced Design Potential	Educational Implications (Concepts)	Active Learning Experience (ATA Taxonomy)
▶ Wall mounted technology/ equipment (SMART Boards, electronic ticker, video screens) ▶ Magnetic marker board ▶ Gridded whiteboard ▶ Roll down marker surfaces ▶ Tackable space versus bulletin boards ▶ Floor to ceiling pinable display space ▶ Access to display for all developmental ages ▶ Explore pivotal walls and doors; sliding boards ▶ Vary textures and colors ▶ Window cut in wall to show R-values (range of temperatures) of different structural materials (wood, steel, wall finishes/color, insulation, gypsum board, glass) ▶ Use environmentally sensitive building products to avoid sick building syndrome (paints) ▶ See "natural light" (fenestration) ▶ Corridor display systems	▶ Writing ▶ Reading ▶ Math ▶ Graph, grid ▶ Spatial concepts (high, low, up, down) ▶ Photography, film ▶ Display/art and design/graphics ▶ Electronic display ▶ Building materials and their properties ▶ Transparent/opaque ▶ Conservation ▶ Production ▶ Shelter (multicultural, homes) ▶ Measurement (dimensions, area) ▶ Texture ▶ Multimedia presentations ▶ Message/mail boards ▶ Communication ▶ Elements of art (color mixing, shade) ▶ Magnets ▶ Health, safety	**Observation and multisensory discovery:** Take rubbings of different surfaces. Write on different surfaces, or use the smart technology. **Data collection:** Use walls and windows to measure height, width, and area. **Concept formation:** Investigate homes in different cultures, what materials go into their construction, and display your findings. **Problem solving:** Hold a contest to design a wall graphic. Use scale and grid system to enlarge the winning entry and transfer it to the wall for painting. **Valuing:** Why do we build walls? What do walls do? **Stewardship:** Visit an art museum and study how the works are displayed. Talk to the museum curator and director about preservation, and restoration of artwork.

NOTES

_____

_____

_____

_____

Manifestations: Outdoor Learning Zones

Architectural Element: Entrance

Enhanced Design Potential	Educational Implications (Concepts)	Active Learning Experience (ATA Taxonomy)
► Careful siting and orientation toward solar and cultural landmarks ► Portal/shade/protection ► Clear, welcoming signage ► Bilingual, Braille signage ► Open transition to administrative spaces (visible from exterior) ► Courtyards, plazas ► Large work of art relating to school themes, cultures, or school logo/identity ► Sundial ► Built-in seating ► Plants, planters ► Separate entrance areas for students and after hours programs/community outreach ► Child scale approach, entry ► Outdoor display space ► Access for all ► Link with pathways, life zone design, traffic	► Cardinal directions ► Solar orientation ► Landmark ► Architecture ► Scale, proportion, symmetry, size ► Spatial concepts (inside, outside, near, far, left, right) ► Languages, reading ► Vocabulary: entrance, entry, enter ► Graphics ► Art (sculpture, relief sculpture, painting) ► Diversity ► Public events ► Time ► Sun, shadow, seasonal change, solar path ► Garden ► Plants/parts of plants ► Flags	**Observation and multisensory discovery:** Study animal entrances. **Data collection:** Make a list of what you see, in order, as you approach the front of your school. What does it say to you? **Concept formation:** Study kinds of handicapped access. What designs help everyone feel welcome? **Problem solving:** Design a school spirit T-shirt that uses the entrance to your school as part of the design. **Valuing:** Write a poem comparing how it feels to be inside and outside in different seasons, types of weather, etc. **Stewardship:** Classrooms take turns maintaining, sweeping, and weeding the entrance area. Plant bulbs to bloom each spring.

NOTES

_____

_____

_____

_____

Architectural Element: Equipment

Enhanced Design Potential	Educational Implications (Concepts)	Active Learning Experience (ATA Taxonomy)
▶ Optimize organic placement of equipment (slides built into hillsides, built-in seating, platform built around a tree, etc.) ▶ Architectonic structures designed for imaginative play, rather than commercial/prefab plastic; bridges, platforms, geodesic domes, tunnels, containers ▶ Level changes: ramps, steps that double as seating, pit seating ▶ Movable elements ▶ Loose parts ▶ Places for manipulative play or work (sand, water, gardening, technology) ▶ Shade structures ▶ Equipment for outdoor classrooms (lab, animal pen, solar collector, data collection devices, etc.) ▶ Adequate outdoor storage zones ▶ Fitness parcourse, signage, and access for community	▶ Health and fitness ▶ Exercise ▶ Safety ▶ Gross motor development ▶ Fine motor development ▶ Imagination ▶ Architectural elements (bridge, tunnel, dome) ▶ Positional concepts (high, low, up, down, inside, outside) ▶ Concepts related to outdoor study of all kinds (biology, physics, weather, measurement) ▶ Stewardship ▶ Inventory of play equipment	**Observation and multisensory discovery:** Use all types of equipment outdoors. Exercise to build upper and lower torso strength. **Data collection:** Keep an inventory of equipment. Photograph. Investigate safety issues. **Concept formation:** Set up an obstacle course using your playground equipment and movable elements. **Problem solving:** Design and build a model of a bridge structure to cross a ditch, stream or other obstacle on your school grounds. Build a real bridge. **Valuing:** Research the value of exercise. Create signage for a fitness trail and start a fitness club. **Stewardship:** Work with adults to maintain and repair damaged equipment.

NOTES

_____

_____

_____

_____

_____

Manifestations: Outdoor Learning Zones *(continued)*

Architectural Element: Fencing and Boundaries

Enhanced Design Potential	Educational Implications (Concepts)	Active Learning Experience (ATA Taxonomy)
▶ Provide a protecting perimeter without chain link ▶ Use natural boundaries: trees, bushes, hedges ▶ Fence murals painted by children or local artists could change every six months. ▶ Boundaries separate age groups on playgrounds. ▶ Patterns incorporated into fencing ▶ Musical eight-tone scale fence ▶ Variety of edging materials, textures for visual interest ▶ Movable boundaries so that students can configure their own spaces ▶ Some areas can be closed off while others remain open to the public. ▶ Use different types of fencing related to local building styles or to historical styles. ▶ Design attractive gates. ▶ Investigate new choices for security mesh in cities. ▶ Visibility/supervision ▶ Activity stations/zones	▶ Positional concepts (edge, inside, outside, around) ▶ Repetition, counting ▶ Lines, angles, shapes, forms, patterns (geometry) ▶ Compass ▶ Architecture and history ▶ Structural systems ▶ Materials ▶ Math: height, width, perimeter, area, measurement ▶ Sound/music ▶ Display/art ▶ Graphics, color ▶ Botany ▶ Games, sports concepts (out of bounds) ▶ Privacy ▶ Supervision	**Observation and multisensory discovery:** Draw fences in your neighborhood. **Data collection:** Measure fencing around your school. Research materials used in fencing, or types of fences. **Concept formation:** Trace maps and define concepts of fence, boundary, border. **Problem solving:** Figure out how much money it would take to replace chain link fencing with another type of boundary. Design a new boundary. Compare prices and write a proposal for change to the school board. **Valuing:** Discuss: Do fences make good neighbors? **Stewardship:** Design a memorial area or place for contemplation using natural elements to define the boundaries of the space.

NOTES

Architectural Element: Gardens

Enhanced Design Potential	Educational Implications (Concepts)	Active Learning Experience (ATA Taxonomy)
▶ Raised bed gardens of all kinds ▶ Container gardens ▶ Vary types of gardens for learning: vegetable, herb, insect, ethnic/cultural, rock, flower, butterfly, historical. ▶ Consider access for the community when school is in session and during summer. ▶ Water/irrigation systems ▶ Water recycling systems, cisterns for rain collection, canales ▶ Farms: trees, orchards, crops ▶ Provide composting bins. ▶ Tool sheds ▶ Greenhouse with seed bank ▶ Landscaping, bulbs, etc., around all schools ▶ See designer perspective forum articles about agriculture in the classroom and the school farm.	▶ Biology (parts of plants, animals, insects) ▶ Life cycle ▶ Growth ▶ Health, nutrition ▶ Food groups ▶ Earth science ▶ Fine and gross motor skills ▶ Ecology ▶ Habitat ▶ Agriculture ▶ Irrigation ▶ Food distribution systems ▶ Commerce ▶ Symmetry ▶ Counting ▶ Vocabulary, labeling ▶ Intergenerational social interaction ▶ History ▶ Stewardship ▶ Cooperation ▶ Community ▶ Cultures ▶ Volunteer ▶ Solar cycles, seasons	**Observation and multisensory discovery:** Work in gardens, smell flowers, taste foods, examine textures, and compare. **Data collection:** Dissect plants and label parts. **Concept formation:** Plant a seed, measure and record its growth and diagram the life cycle. **Problem solving:** Conduct scientific experiments with plants. What do they need to survive? Plant insect gardens and collect specimens. Create a geometrical garden layout. **Valuing:** Partner with a local charity and grow food to help feed others. Ask community members for gardening tips and help. **Stewardship:** Investigate ways to recycle and collect rainwater and use it to water gardens.

NOTES

_____

_____

_____

TOOLS FOR THOUGHT

Manifestations: Outdoor Learning Zones *(continued)*

Architectural Element: Gathering Space

Enhanced Design Potential	Educational Implications (Concepts)	Active Learning Experience (ATA Taxonomy)
▶ Amphitheater (large group forum as stepped climbing structure, or round depression, or built into a hillside) ▶ Outdoor stage ▶ Accommodate small, medium, and large groups ▶ Shade structures (see "shade") ▶ Solar orientation ▶ Plazas, courtyards ▶ Small group areas with seating (benches, bench/trellis, bancos, low walls) ▶ Transitional spaces such as patios, decks, porches, overhangs, covered walkways ▶ Focal points: fountains, sculpture, landmark, ancient oak, etc. ▶ School as park ▶ Role-play areas	▶ Literacy ▶ Language ▶ Drama ▶ Story, play ▶ Music ▶ Dance ▶ Performance ▶ Speech ▶ Fine and gross motor skills ▶ Size, shape ▶ Shade, solar orientation, shadow ▶ Cultural events ▶ Public art ▶ Socialization	**Observation and multisensory discovery:** Use outdoor space for assemblies, meetings, and classes, as well as recess. **Data collection:** See how often outdoor spaces at your school are used. How many people can fit in the amphitheater? Are there some areas that are never used? Why? **Concept formation:** Name types of public gathering spaces in your city or town. Make a chart of indoor and outdoor locations and how they are used. **Problem solving:** Stage a play, a dance, or hold a concert outdoors. **Valuing:** Plan a year-end event outdoors that celebrates all the volunteers at your school. **Stewardship:** Plan a school grounds cleanup day and invite the community.

NOTES

_____

_____

_____

_____

_____

_____

Architectural Element: Life Zone Design

Enhanced Design Potential	Educational Implications (Concepts)	Active Learning Experience (ATA Taxonomy)
▸ Design to fit the natural landscape and climate rather than to conquer it. Xeriscape in dry climates, for example. ▸ Use native plants. ▸ Use indigenous materials and building techniques. ▸ Preserve, restore, or create habitats for native creatures. ▸ Build for energy play (solar collector, sundial, windmill, weather stations). ▸ Ethno-gardening ▸ Include signage about the life zone as a learning tool. ▸ Include connections to local agriculture or landforms to emphasize individualized sense of place (orange grove in Florida, cactus garden in Arizona, wind shelters in Alaska, siting toward sacred mountains in New Mexico). ▸ Leave some natural open space. ▸ Lose some asphalt!	▸ Earth science ▸ Life zone ▸ Ecology ▸ Nature ▸ Climate ▸ Weather ▸ Conservation ▸ Habitat ▸ Native ▸ History, culture ▸ Preservation ▸ Energy ▸ Garden ▸ Topology (soils, rocks, erosion, contours) ▸ Sense of place ▸ Agriculture ▸ Geology ▸ Geography	**Observation and multisensory discovery:** Hike in the local area with a visiting U.S. forest ranger. Which life zone are you in? **Data collection:** Identify, photograph, and compile a list of native plants and animals that survive on your school grounds. **Concept formation:** Make posters describing each of the major life zones on earth. Create a map. **Problem solving:** Trace a resource from your local area. Follow its journey to become a finished product. **Valuing:** Invite senior citizens to the school to demonstrate their use of local materials in building, gardening, weaving, etc. **Stewardship:** Research endangered species in your area. Clean up a local stream or woods. Create a seed bank based on local plants.

NOTES

TOOLS FOR THOUGHT

Manifestations: Outdoor Learning Zones *(continued)*

Architectural Element: Pathways

Enhanced Design Potential	Educational Implications (Concepts)	Active Learning Experience (ATA Taxonomy)
▶ Use a variety of ground surfaces and textures. ▶ Vary path widths. ▶ Vary curved, straight, angles, intersections ▶ Handicap access (no sharp drop-offs at edges, width, surfacing, inclines) ▶ Fitness courses with information about body systems ▶ Running/jogging tracks ▶ Nature trails with signage ▶ Bike trail/tricycle track ▶ Obstacle course ▶ Child scale traffic signage ▶ Vary ground levels and inclines ▶ Link to destinations such as those outlined in gathering spaces ▶ Buildings themselves can suggest pathways or can frame vistas. ▶ Continue pathways from the exterior indoors.	▶ Surface ▶ Texture ▶ Types of lines, angles, etc. ▶ Distance ▶ Fitness, health ▶ Body systems ▶ Exercise ▶ Nature ▶ Safety ▶ Spatial concepts	**Observation and multisensory discovery:** Use paths, trails, and fitness courses. **Data collection:** Use a pedometer to calculate the distance of different pathways, or to record how far you walk. **Concept formation:** Research and write the information needed for signs about body systems. Work with an architect and artist to put the signs in place. Learn about trail-blazers Lewis and Clark and others. **Problem solving:** Use the Internet to determine what safety items hikers need. Put together a kit for hikers. **Valuing:** Plan an exercise program. Start a walking club. Why is exercise important? **Stewardship:** Maintain and use a nature trail at school, or volunteer as a group to help maintain a local trail.

NOTES

_____

_____

_____

_____

_____

Architectural Element: Shade

Enhanced Design Potential	Educational Implications (Concepts)	Active Learning Experience (ATA Taxonomy)
▸ Use a combination of natural shade and man-made structures. ▸ Vary tree canopy. ▸ Vary tree types. ▸ Ideas for built structures include ramadas, pergolas, open lattice, patio covers, tensile structures, portals, tree houses, a trellis with a bench, covered walkways, walls built for shade at different times of day (solar orientation) ▸ Built structures reflect local architecture or cultures. ▸ Container structures (could be movable) ▸ Deployable structures ▸ Shade as part of personalized spaces for reflection ▸ Shaded parking lots ▸ Houselike structures ▸ Thermometers outdoors	▸ Shade, shadow ▸ Sunlight ▸ Temperature ▸ Thermometer ▸ Measurement ▸ Solar orientation ▸ Shelter ▸ Materials ▸ Architecture and design ▸ Natural ventilation ▸ Homes ▸ Tree (life cycle, importance to environmental air quality, leaf collections, parts of trees, etc.)	**Observation and multisensory discovery:** Experience areas in terms of sunlight and shade. Visit areas at different times of day. **Data collection:** Use thermometers, Celsius and Fahrenheit. **Concept formation:** Trace movement of tree shadows over time, either during the day or each day during the school year. Keep visual records of the changes (sketch, photo). Explain what is happening. **Problem solving:** Design and build a shade structure. **Valuing:** Draw different kinds of shelters (homes) from around the world. Discuss how shelters protect us from the elements. **Stewardship:** Discuss global warming. Brainstorm actions you can take to improve the situation.

NOTES

_____

_____

_____

_____

_____

Manifestations: Outdoor Learning Zones *(continued)*

Architectural Element: Traffic and Parking

Enhanced Design Potential	Educational Implications (Concepts)	Active Learning Experience (ATA Taxonomy)
▶ Plan for separated circulation of vehicles and pedestrian flow. ▶ Separate bus from parent traffic. ▶ Plant parking areas with trees and grass islands to reduce heat and filter runoff. ▶ Sheltered bus waiting areas for extreme climates ▶ Use alternatives to black asphalt (white concrete). ▶ Careful siting for idling buses to reduce indoor pollution/proximity to HVAC systems ▶ Siting and access to public transport ▶ Multiple purposes for parking structures: green roof, photovoltaic panels ▶ Links to city bike trail systems	▶ Vehicle ▶ Pedestrian ▶ Traffic rules and signage ▶ Public transportation ▶ Air quality ▶ Pollution ▶ Temperature ▶ Microclimates ▶ Heat absorption ▶ Reflection ▶ Properties of light ▶ Urban warming ▶ Plants ▶ Geometry (lines, angles) ▶ Measurement (time, distance, temperature) ▶ Laws, rules, regulations ▶ Social studies (patterns of circulation and flow, transportation, usage, streets, maps) ▶ Safety	**Observation and multisensory discovery:** Observe traffic patterns at your school. Are there problem areas? **Data collection:** Measure temperatures in the parking lot. Compute turning angles from curbs for various vehicles. **Concept formation:** Use light tables to trace roadmaps of major cities. **Problem solving:** Test the concept of urban nighttime warming using different parking lot surfaces. Design experiments with different materials and their heat-absorbing or reflecting qualities. **Valuing:** Discuss traffic safety at age-appropriate levels. **Stewardship:** Each class designs and maintains one parking lot "island" of greenery.

NOTES

_____

_____

_____

_____

_____

Architectural Element: Water Usage

Enhanced Design Potential	Educational Implications (Concepts)	Active Learning Experience (ATA Taxonomy)
▸ Design water or wetlands habitat on-site ▸ See Morrow and Calhoon's designer perspective on drainage and playgrounds. ▸ Set up gray water recycling systems (roof, runoff, canale or downspout, cistern). ▸ Use signage and labeling for any water systems (work stations act as museums for learning). ▸ A cooling tower with adjacent ponds, usually located under a ramada or shade structure, can lower temperatures forty degrees. ▸ Plan for irrigation of school gardens and farms, and access to water. ▸ Hydroponics station	▸ Properties of liquids/water (adhesion, absorption, surface tension, freezing, boiling, evaporation) ▸ Water cycle ▸ Bodies of water (geology, Earth science, geography) ▸ Erosion, flooding ▸ Gravity ▸ Climate, weather, precipitation ▸ Temperature ▸ Aquatic life ▸ Measurement, volume ▸ Drainage and irrigation systems ▸ Garden ▸ Habitat ▸ Animals ▸ Plants ▸ Water conservation, pollution, quality, chemistry of water ▸ Microscope ▸ Language, labeling	**Observation and multisensory discovery:** Plan water play for young students. Take trips to water habitats at school and elsewhere. **Data collection:** Measure water quality at different locations. Share findings on an ecology web page. **Concept formation:** Design a large wall graphic of the water cycle with labeling/signage. **Problem solving:** Maintain and study a water system on school grounds: build a wetlands, investigate pond life, or set up a recycling system. **Valuing:** Use watercolors to paint outdoors. **Stewardship:** Plan a PowerPoint presentation on how your school recycles water or how your cooling tower works, etc. Show it at other schools and to school boards.

NOTES

_____

_____

_____

_____

Earlier in this book I suggested that the children's museum can be a model for the ideal learning environment, a merging of active, hands-on learning with professionally designed spaces and display. Two designer perspectives complement that view. First, architect Ron Jacobs provides sketches that reveal some of the architectural brainstorming (visual thinking) that went into programming for ¡explora!, an Albuquerque children's science and art museum. Second, ¡explora! museum associate director Paul Tatter outlines his thoughts on environments designed for thinking and learning.

A Visual Explosion of Manifestations (Sketches)

Ron Jacobs
Architect

Sketches courtesy of Mahlman Studio Architecture

This portfolio of sketches (see pp. 217—19) shows the informal visual thinking process that architects often use to stimulate ideas. Post-it notes reproduced here reveal the range of curricular opportunities that can be manifested in the design of a learning facility. The adoption of just one of these concepts could lend identity and personality to a school site.

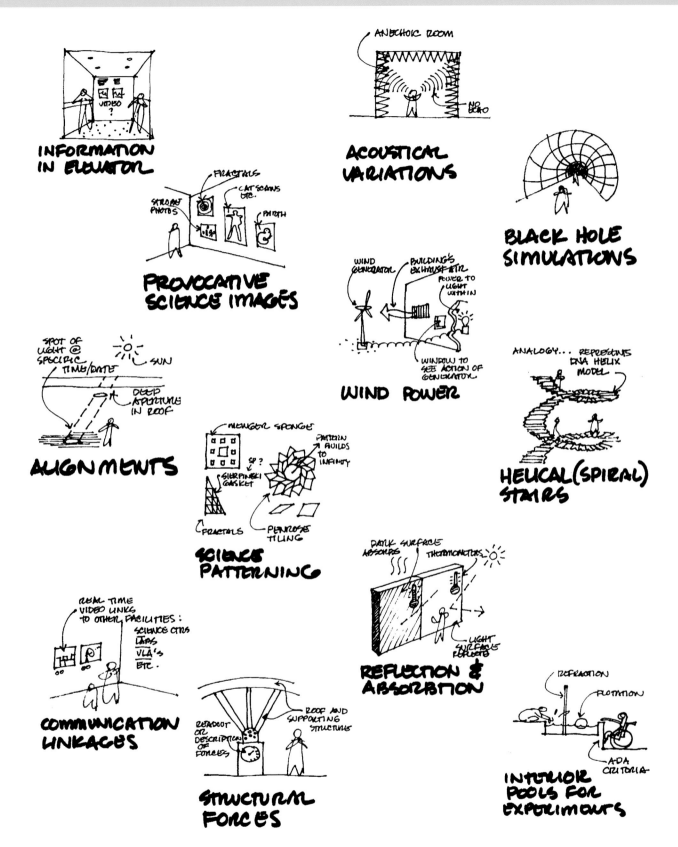

INFORMATION IN ELEVATOR

ACOUSTICAL VARIATIONS
ANECHOIC ROOM
NO ECHO

BLACK HOLE SIMULATIONS

PROVOCATIVE SCIENCE IMAGES
FRACTALS
CAT SCANS ETC.
STROBE PHOTOS
MOTH

WIND POWER
WIND GENERATOR
BUILDING'S EXHAUST ETC.
POWER TO LIGHT WITHIN
WINDOW TO SEE ACTION OF GENERATOR

ALIGNMENTS
SPOT OF LIGHT @ SPECIFIC TIME/DATE
SUN
DEEP APERTURE IN ROOF

HELICAL (SPIRAL) STAIRS
ANALOGY... REPRESENTS DNA HELIX MODEL

SCIENCE PATTERNING
MENGER SPONGE
SP?
SIERPINSKI GASKET
FRACTALS
PENROSE TILING
PATTERN BUILDS TO INFINITY

COMMUNICATION LINKAGES
REAL TIME VIDEO LINKS TO OTHER FACILITIES:
SCIENCE CTRS
LABS
VLA's
ETC.

STRUCTURAL FORCES
READOUT OR DESCRIPTION OF FORCES
ROOF AND SUPPORTING STRUCTURES

REFLECTION & ABSORPTION
DARK SURFACE ABSORBS
THERMOMETERS
LIGHT SURFACE REFLECTS

INTERIOR POOLS FOR EXPERIMENTS
REFRACTION
FLOTATION
ADA CRITERIA

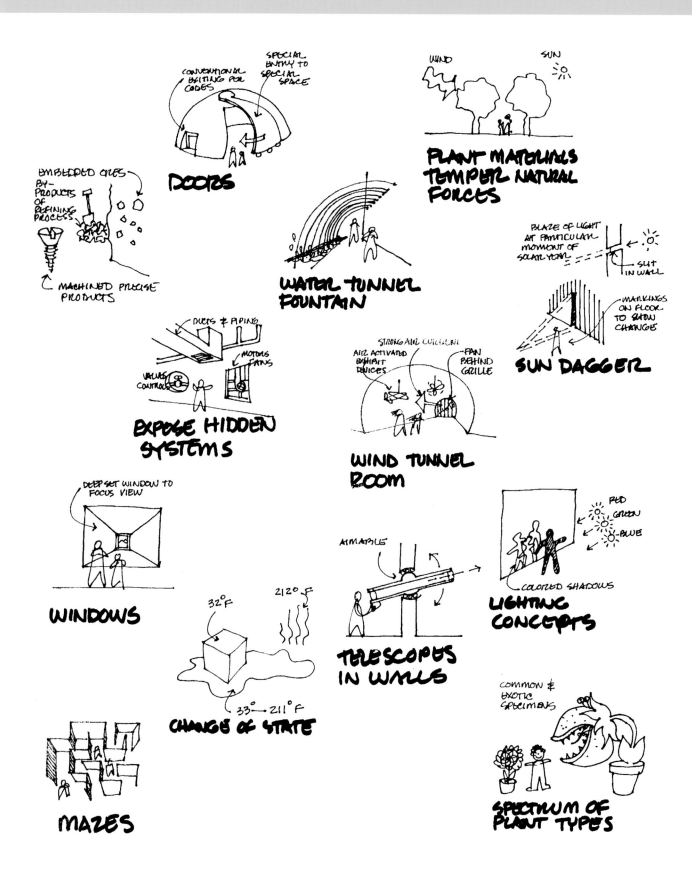

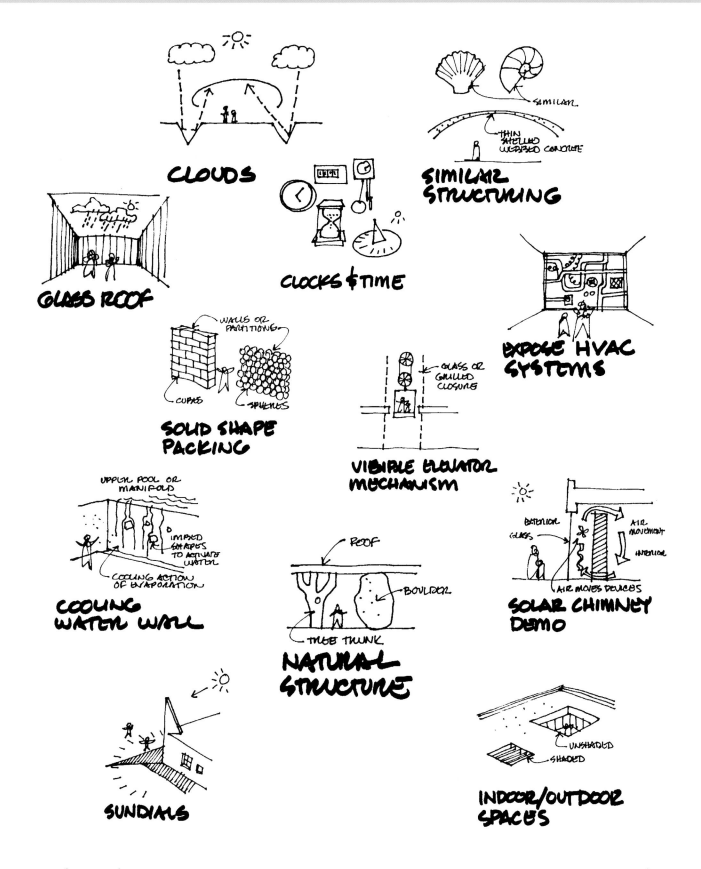

CLOUDS

SIMILAR STRUCTURING

SIMILAR

THIN SHELLED WEBBED CONCRETE

CLOCKS & TIME

GLASS ROOF

EXPOSE HVAC SYSTEMS

WALLS OR PARTITIONS

CUBES

SPHERES

SOLID SHAPE PACKING

GLASS OR GRILLED CLOSURE

VISIBLE ELEVATOR MECHANISM

UPPER POOL OR MANIFOLD

IMPLIED SHAPES TO ACTIVATE WATER

COOLING ACTION OF EVAPORATION

COOLING WATER WALL

ROOF

BOULDER

TREE TRUNK

NATURAL STRUCTURE

EXTERIOR GLASS

AIR MOVEMENT

INTERIOR

AIR MOVES DEVICES

SOLAR CHIMNEY DEMO

SUNDIALS

UNSHADED

SHADED

INDOOR/OUTDOOR SPACES

Paul Tatter envisions the following traits could play a role not only in the design of children's museums, but for schools everywhere.

The Meaning Is the Use

Characteristics of Environments for Thinking and Learning

Paul Tatter

Former Associate director, ¡explora! Children's Museum, Albuquerque, New Mexico

An environment consists of all the things, nonmaterial and material, nonliving and living (including people), all the forms of behavior, interaction, and transaction among these things, and all the embedded meaning and aesthetic and emotional qualities within a coherent space and time.

It is useful to ask how (1) the physical design of the space, (2) the qualities of the material available, and (3) the actions of the staff support each of the following characteristics of an environment for thinking and learning.

> ▶ The environment has a sense of history, rich with meaning. There is evidence of past activity, uses, established forms of behavior, and traditions.

> ▶ There is a feeling of work in progress, supporting the tentative quality of conclusions, with opportunities to change one's mind, make corrections, improvements, additions, and modifications.

> ▶ The space is designed to physically slow down activity. There are opportunities for lingering, sustaining concentration and focus, and a patience for wasting time and for making new connections.

- ▶ The environment draws upon curiosity by combining familiar and unfamiliar materials or procedures and encourages spontaneous small group collaborations, acknowledging learning as a social process.

- ▶ There is freedom of movement with a leisurely pace, a sense that thought and action are voluntary and that behavior is under personal control.

- ▶ There is the sense that the environment is sustained through the efforts of many individuals acting as contributors and collaborators.

- ▶ Conflict and disagreement are valued and utilized as sources for understanding and the development of new perspectives.

- ▶ The space supports multiple modes and forms of communication and provides reasons for communicating and for making ideas clear.

- ▶ There are opportunities for participation in decision making and evaluation.

- ▶ The environment legitimizes personal history as a source for inference, judgment, comfort, and expression. It accommodates personal differences in style, skill, interest, and role.

- ▶ All the components in the environment are designed to allow for a broad range of entry skills. Most instructions are facilitative rather than directive. The materials allow possibilities for elaboration at many levels.

¡Explora! Children's Museum, Albuquerque, New Mexico. Top left: Exterior landscaping with a geodesic dome that also serves as a picnic shade structure on the upper level. Image courtesy of Mahlman Studio Architecture and Paul Tatter. **Top right:** The exterior counterweight for a trapeze bike inside the museum. Photograph courtesy of Anne Taylor. **Bottom:** The concept of Fibonacci numbers was incorporated into the progression of shelflike protrusions on the museum exterior. Image courtesy of Anne Taylor.

¡Explora! Children's Museum, Albuquerque, New Mexico.
Top: The museum interior is spacious and full of light with two lofty stories linked by a cantilevered spiral staircase encircling a fountain. Note the sailcloth banners overhead. **Bottom:** Partitions and view from the stairs. Floor space is broken up by a variety of two-inch curvilinear and angled partitions into diverse and unpredictable personal spaces for learning. Photographs courtesy of Anne Taylor.

▶ There is evidence for valuing aesthetics and humor and joy in the surroundings, events, material, interactions, and work products.

▶ There are provisions for physical and emotional comfort.

▶ The environment supports the creation and use of models of objects, ideas, and processes, and models of interactions among objects, people, ideas, and systems, through experiment, construction, role-taking and play.

▶ Everything in the environment can be manipulated and changed. The scale is proportional to the people within it. There are loose parts. The inhabitants feel some control over the materials.

▶ There is a wide range of materials in close proximity, allowing use of the materials in different contexts for different applications and purposes. Materials have multiple uses.

▶ There is voluntary access to tools for use in observation, manipulation, and creation.

It is customary to think about most of the above-mentioned characteristics as procedural, and, consequently, to assume that they may be accounted for by appropriate practices within any physical environment. Rarely is the impact of physical environmental design considered to be crucial to the very possibility of sustaining an environment for thinking and learning. It is unlikely, however, that such an environment can be maintained without the support of a physical context conducive to its nurturing.

The Architectural Master Plan for ¡explora! Children's Museum

The ¡explora! master plan program document from Mahlman Studio Architecture examines the "architecture as exhibit" concept. Plaza paving displays mosaics of intricate geometric patterns, alternate exposed HVAC systems demonstrate science principles, and visual and acoustic illusions or puzzles provide interactive learning opportunities in the entrance/waiting area. Exhibit gardens and courtyards use landscape elements to create a variety of multisensory and perceptual experiences, including small animal habitats, sand and water play, creative clocks such as sundials or water clocks, and writing and drawing chalkboards positioned for informal discussions and diagrams. All spaces can teach, and can do so with humor. For example, the program calls for graphics of microscopic bacteria and viruses in the public washrooms, as well as display systems to explain the technology of washroom fixtures. A large freight elevator is decked out as a living room complete with a couch and rocking chair, ready for an informal conversation as one rises or descends.

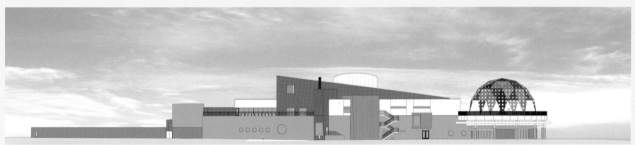

NORTH ELEVATION

WEST ELEVATION

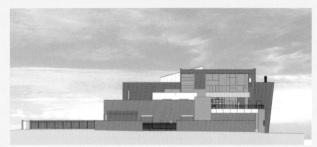

EAST ELEVATION

SOUTH ELEVATION

¡Explora! Children's Museum, Albuquerque, New Mexico. Elevation drawings.
Image courtesy of Mahlman Studio Architecture and Paul Tatter.

George Pearl Hall,
School of Architecture and Planning,
University of New Mexico.
Antoine Predock Architect, PC.
Photograph by Terry Schreck.

CHAPTER EIGHT

Connecting Manifestations to Learning through Curriculum and Post-occupancy Evaluation

Architects become educators when they design potent learning environments. They expand their role when they compile and write guidelines for occupants of buildings, just as manufacturers produce manuals and DVDs explaining how to use the products and appliances we buy. This can be done in many ways. David Macaulay's *The Way Things Work* (1988) is an excellent example of an illustrated user guide that reveals the function of common objects in our environment. Macaulay uses diagrams, illustrations, and narrative to demonstrate how machines work and to detail the scientific principles behind the devices we use every day. Similarly, an architect can provide design drawings accompanied by text about the location, usage, and interdisciplinary learning activities suggested by the manifestations built into the school. Over time, teachers and students can learn from and expand the guide with their own ideas. Thus, the user's manual becomes an evolving, dynamic, and ever-growing curriculum attesting to the value of the learning environment as a teaching tool. It explains how the school functions as a three-dimensional textbook for interdisciplinary learning.

Mazria Inc. Odems Dzurec Architecture/Planning of Santa Fe, New Mexico, designed the Edward Gonzales Elementary School as a prototype solar school for Albuquerque Public Schools. To educate the building's users about daylighting and passive solar design features, Mazria's firm wrote a brief user's manual that begins with facts about energy usage, includes a school floor plan diagram and list of design features, and provides an illustrated section on "how your classroom works." Full benefits of environmentally sound design cannot be realized without a clear understanding on the part of the building's users. (Please see appendix C for a copy of the user's manual.)

Organization of a User's Guide

A guide to the school's manifestations can be organized in any number of ways. The guide might be

- An alphabetical list of spaces and their learning implications

- An educational inventory of objects and spaces illustrated with photographs or drawings (could be digital)

- A visual dictionary of manifestations similar to a picture dictionary

- A self-published illustrated book about the school, written by students

- A map or master plan of the school campus with informative entries numbered and keyed to the location of manifestations on the map

- A pocket field guide to the school site

- A list of district standards tied to key locations on the school site

- A manual or digital program for scheduled maintenance of district HVAC systems and other infrastructure, similar to the recommendations provided by car dealers for ensuring proper car care

- A system of informative and interactive signage similar to that found in museums or along nature or fitness trails, integrated into the environment

- An audio recording used with headphones for guided architectural tours of campus manifestations

- A digital slide presentation or video, and/or a Web site with links to community resources.

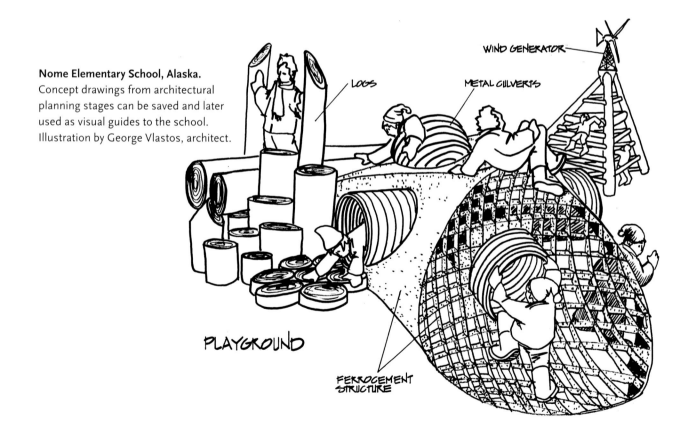

Nome Elementary School, Alaska. Concept drawings from architectural planning stages can be saved and later used as visual guides to the school. Illustration by George Vlastos, architect.

WIND GENERATOR

LOGS

METAL CULVERTS

PLAYGROUND

FERROCEMENT STRUCTURE

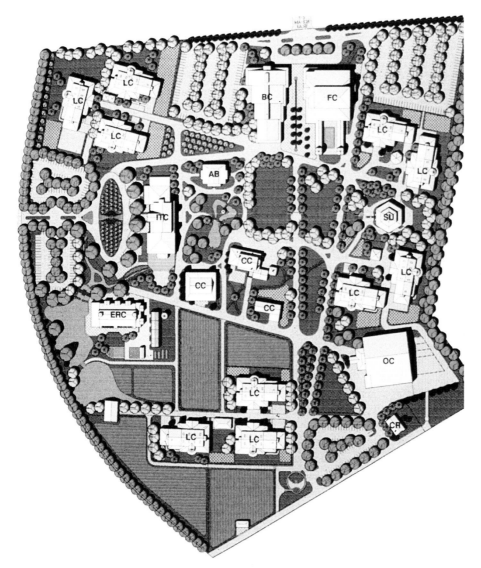

Lincoln High School West, Stockton, California. User's guide. The document opens with an aerial map of the campus. Letters are then placed at key locations. Each location is represented by a full page listing the manifestations at that location and how the manifestations can be used for environmental teaching and learning. An entire curriculum could be developed from the hundreds of manifestations ranging from aquaculture ponds to ductwork transitions, school bus routes, windmills, and more. Taylor, A., Sherk, B., Wolf/Lang/Christopher Architects, Inc., & Concordia LLC. (1994). *User's guide: West Campus Lincoln High School.* Unpublished programming document.

The guides may be arranged thematically or by subject matter discipline, or on a computer database retrievable through several keywords, places, interdisciplinary themes, or learning concepts. Another approach is to design a simple format or checklist for observing and evaluating manifestations. The data collected using the formats is assembled into a loose-leaf notebook or Web links that can be updated as students and teachers uncover new possibilities for learning.

The concept of a user guide can be extended to form an environmental curriculum for learning from the total school surroundings. This happens when architects and educators collaborate to develop specific activities or learning experiences based on the manifestations built into the school. The ATA Taxonomy and similar educational models introduced in chapter 5 can provide strategies for teaching and learning from the environment.

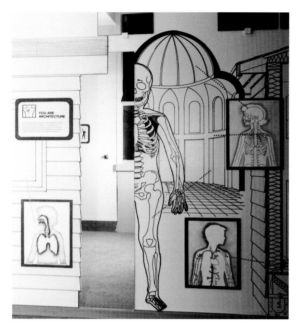

Signage for an architecture exhibition explores the theme, "You are architecture." The exhibit compares body systems with building systems and includes a mirror as part of the display for children to make personal connections (see the left half of the skeleton). Such signage could be incorporated into school displays consistently throughout a building, forming an integrated user's guide. Courtesy of Anne Taylor.

Curriculum Planning Formats

As part of my consulting work, I have designed "planning wheels," workshop guidebooks, matrices, and charts that show how the environment teaches concepts across subject matter disciplines (please see the Tools for Thought section at the end of the chapter for examples). My colleagues and I have designed learning experiences in poster form to accompany design workshops or to be posted in classroom design centers. Simple formats such as these provide consistency, allowing all participants to contribute to curriculum development and write their own learning activities while using a common language. Formats make sure all bases are covered and can be adapted to fit individual schools.

The wheels and other formats are versatile systems for curriculum development that can be used by both architects and educators before, during, and after the building project has been completed. During architectural programming, the planning team uses the format to delineate potential uses for an activity setting in order to set design criteria. The wheel or chart later becomes a tool for teachers analyzing the setting for teaching ideas, strategies, and underlying concepts. The formats also serve as evaluation tools. Educators and architects can use the formats after the school facility is built to determine whether the learning that occurs matches the intent of the design.

Manifestations and Implications for Professional Development

In Alabama, I worked as an educational consultant with Steven Bingler of Concordia LLC, architect John Chambless, and others to develop and conduct workshops to familiarize teachers with a new preschool facility that had been expressly designed as a teaching and learning tool. The *Basic Guide* (Concordia LLC, 1999) that accompanied these workshops evolved from the architectural program to act as a user's guide for educators. The topics covered were aimed at learning to truly see the school environment—developing the knowing eye:

- ▸ Examining a single object for meaning (see Tools for Thought)

- ▸ Examining multiple objects in multiple ways

- ▸ Techniques for self-expression, including problem solving with recycled materials in art

- ▸ Composing a bill of rights for early learners

- Photography, use of a video camera, and point of view

- Creating plan views, landscape designs, and maps for analyzing the environment and its use

- Understanding documentation and display

The aim of an environmentally based professional development program is to facilitate teachers' spontaneity and creativity through their familiarity with the environment as a learning tool, and to show how every object in the carefully crafted learning space has a logic or idea behind it and can be used to teach concepts. My hope is to break the usual verbal and logical stranglehold on curriculum and, ultimately, to help others reach and motivate as many children in as many literacies as possible.

One intention of this book is to suggest a model of education for further development of environmental curricula. I challenge educators and architects to work together to expand upon the user guide idea and fully develop an interdisciplinary, K–12 scope and sequence guidebook to learning from the physical environment. As an extension of this idea, several of my architecture students are putting together a model for interdisciplinary design education that draws from state and district educational standards. This study shows how design education can be used to effectively teach traditional standards and benchmarks. The current emphasis on a standards-based curriculum does not preclude project-based design learning.

George Pearl Hall, School of Architecture and Planning, University of New Mexico. Courtyard level. Adjacent outdoor area used for drawing and model critiques. Photograph by Terry Schreck.

Post-occupancy Evaluation and Assessment of the Learning Environment

How do we know if our design intent has succeeded or if the learning facility is indeed being used correctly? The architectural practice of POE is aimed at improving building quality through analysis and feedback after buildings are occupied. While POE is an important issue for follow-up, money is seldom available for such evaluation of school buildings. In light of the need for conversion, renovation, security, greening, and reform of school facilities, POE assumes great importance. I believe it should be funded, especially as it pertains to how a building affects learning. Funding should also include information technology and use of the Internet for sharing information about successful schools.

Appraisal Guides from The Council of Educational Facility Planners International

CEFPI offers instruments for school facility appraisal that can be used as a basis for planning your own assessment checklists. In one such document, authors Hawkins and Lilley (1998) provide a point rating system across six broad categories:

The school site (100 points maximum)

Structural and mechanical features (200 points)

Plant maintainability (100 points)

School building safety and security (200 points)

Educational adequacy (200 points)

Environment for education (200 points)

The authors recommend that evaluators avoid working from memory but instead conduct analysis on-site and carefully review the educational program before beginning the POE.

POE identifies the successes and failures of a building, reveals performance implications of budget cuts, increases the capability for organizational change and growth, considers the entire life cycle of the building in determining costs, and improves the knowledge base for professional practice and future decision-making (Preiser, Rabinowitz, & White, 1988, p. 5). Buildings are assessed for how they affect the occupant/user across technical, functional, and behavioral performance—in short, for the three levels of habitability described earlier: health and safety, functionality, and psychological comfort/aesthetic satisfaction.

In *Post-Occupancy Evaluation*, Preiser et al. (1988) identify and elaborate upon some quantifiable and some qualitative elements of building performance:

Technical: Fire safety, structure, sanitation, ventilation, electrical, exterior walls, roofs, interior finishes, acoustics, illumination, durability, and environmental control systems

Functional: Access and egress, personal security, parking, spatial capacity, utilities, communications, building security, change and growth, circulation, equipment, storage, adjacency, work flow, operational efficiency, and specialized functions of the organization. Also evaluated are human factors, known as anthropometrics or ergonomics.

Behavioral: Proxemics (study of interpersonal distances) and territoriality, privacy and interaction, environmental perception, image and meaning, environmental cognition (mental mapping), and orientation (pp. 40–46)

The three levels of performance form a comprehensive view of a building's overall performance.

In the case of schools, however, high performance as described in this book means that the building not only functions properly but that it also supports the learning process and serves as a safe, aesthetically pleasing, three-dimensional textbook. I am interested in how the building affects student and staff performance as well. More research needs to be developed in this area.

Design Principles for Post-occupancy Evaluation of Schools

Research-based expectations for schools can be used to make observation checklists and surveys that not only measure existing school performance but also suggest the desired performance of schools for the future in terms of both facilities and users, according to architect and educator Jeffery Lackney (1998, as quoted in Sanoff, 2001). At a regional CEFPI conference, Lackney summarized several research-based design principles that are fundamental to developing a school building assessment program. The same principles can be a vital part of programming for schools of the future.

Stimulating environments: Use of color and texture; displays created by students so they have a sense of connection and ownership with the product

Places for group learning: Special places such as break-out spaces, alcoves, table groupings to facilitate social learning and stimulate the social brain; turning break-out spaces into living rooms for conversation

Linking indoor and outdoor places: Encouraging student movement; engaging the motor cortex linked to the cerebral cortex for oxygenation

Public space: Corridors and public places containing symbols of the school community's larger purpose provide coherency and meaning that increases motivation.

Safety: Safe places reduce threat, especially in urban settings.

Spatial variety: Variety of places of different shapes, color, and light, nooks and crannies

Changing displays: Changing and interacting with the environment stimulates brain development.

Resource availability: Provide educational, physical, and other settings in close proximity to encourage rapid development of ideas generated in a learning episode. This is an argument for wet areas/science and computer-rich workspaces to be integrated and not segregated. Multiple functions and cross-fertilization of ideas are main goals.

Flexibility: A common principle in the past continues to be relevant. Many dimensions of flexibility of learning places are reflected in other principles.

Active/passive places: Students need places for reflection and retreat from others for intrapersonal intelligence as well as places for active engagement for interpersonal intelligence.

Personalized space: The concept of "home base" needs to be emphasized more than the metal locker or the desk. Learners should be allowed to express their identity, personalize their special places, and have places to express territorial behaviors.

The community as a learning environment: Utilize all urban and natural environments as the primary learning setting. The school as the fortress of learning needs to be challenged and conceptualized more as a resource-rich learning center that supplements lifelong learning. Technology, distance learning, community and business partnerships, and home-based learning all need to be explored as alternative organizational structures for educational institutions of the present and future.

Post-occupancy Evaluation and Students

Students, architects, and administrators can compile and analyze POE data. During programming, students can help the architect collect data through observation, site analysis, and other techniques (see chapter 10). This research is then applied to follow-up studies during POE. Users on-site who have easy access to the data will best evaluate any design feature that requires constant monitoring and can operate and learn from computer programs and technical performance systems included in the learning facility design.

According to Preiser, Rabinowitz, and White (1998), newer techniques for collecting data include evaluating records and archival material; measuring and monitoring building performance; conducting on-site walk-through evaluations with checklists; photographing building use; interviewing, distributing, and analyzing questionnaires and surveys with ranking scales; reviewing the literature from similar facilities and making comparisons; and applying the POE by reporting findings and making recommendations for future facilities (pp. 75–97). Students can benefit immensely by collecting and compiling such statistics themselves.

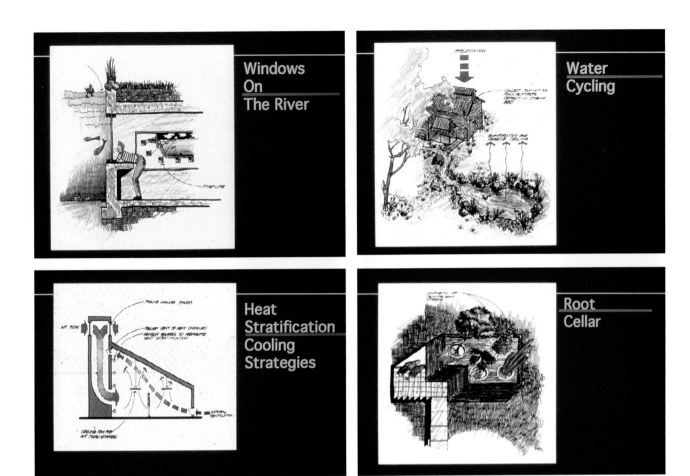

Students Can Develop a User's Guide and POE
Document as a PowerPoint Presentation.
Top left: Windows on the river. **Top right:** Water cycling.
Bottom left: Heat stratification and cooling tower. **Bottom right:** Root cellar.
Illustrations courtesy of Gaylaird Christopher Architect PC.

Post-occupancy Evaluation and Professional Development for Educators

Just as the user's guide can become a teacher professional development tool, so can POE. Many teachers are unaware of the learning potential in their classroom equipment. They have had little or no experience in space planning and designing effective, aesthetically pleasing spaces for learning. This unfortunate observation has not changed much since I first investigated the environment of forty-seven elementary classrooms in the Phoenix area as a pilot study for my dissertation. Results showed that only about one-seventh of the classroom environments showed evidence of concern for art, creativity, and aesthetics and offered a place for the users' self-expression (Taylor, 1971).

To address this lack, I begin my teacher space planning workshops by mapping the classroom and designing changes for more effective learning (for more on reconfiguring classrooms, see chapter 9). POE formats and data collection techniques listed above for students could easily help administrators, school boards, and interested citizens understand, evaluate, and appreciate their schools while forming ideas for improved use in the future. POE workshops can be conducted by experts in the field—interior designers, law enforcement experts, and museum curators as well as architects—to help educators become designers of effective learning spaces.

Post-occupancy Evaluation and Security Issues

School security assessments are available through a variety of expert providers and can be tailored to the needs of specific school districts. According to National School Safety and Security Services, developing an atmosphere of trust and establishing good relations with the community are essential to any security program. The emphasis is on designing planning tools for schools rather than adopting a siegelike mentality. The security services firm helps schools:

▸ Evaluate areas

▸ Prepare for crises

▸ Review security staffing and operations

▸ Review security policies and procedures

▸ Offer security education and training

▸ Link security with prevention and intervention services

▸ Investigate personnel and internal security interests

▸ Examine transportation security

▸ Collaborate with community and establish a sense of ownership, and

▸ Address physical security, including access control, intrusion detection, inventory and key control, perimeter/night security, and physical design (National School Safety and Security Services, 2008).

Summary and Review of the Taylor/ Vlastos Programming and Design Process

Before I move on to part 4 and the learning environment of the future, I'd like to review the programming and design process described in these early chapters. In this chapter's Tools for Thought section, the Architectural Programming as an Educational Process chart provides an overview, including the types of educational support materials that can be generated and distributed by the architect acting as a partner to educators and as a design leader. The chart covers the complete process that should be marketed to the school district and Board of Education before the planning and design process begins. Note that at every step, the design process generates educational materials and potential learning experiences. These materials can be collected to form an interdisciplinary environmental curriculum full of experiences tied directly to the specific learning facility. The programming and design process becomes an organizational tool, a curriculum, and a guideline for evaluating learning environments after buildings are occupied.

Architectural Programming as an Educational Process
Summary of Taylor/Vlastos Programming and Design Process for Educational Facilities

Step	Topics Discussed/ Description of Architectural Process	Supporting Educational Documentation and Active Learning
One: Client Orientation Establishing ties of communication and a common design language	▶ Determine who will participate and the roles of stakeholders. ▶ Engage the greatest possible diversity of stakeholders. ▶ Organize the workshop format. ▶ Set up communication process, schedule, and location. ▶ Introduce programming and design process and steps. ▶ Provide visual/verbal design vocabulary to clients. ▶ Matrix workshop—set up a central site for matrix or storyboard.	▶ Communication formats, including Web sites ▶ Data collection: write surveys, worksheets, etc., about values and goals; compile information ▶ Use treasure cards to tap the potential of the community and build a database of resources (see forum 3 for a sample card that can be digitized). ▶ Design vocabulary exercises, definitions, and examples. ▶ Research on programming methodology ▶ Research about community stakeholders
Two: Preprogramming Beginning with values	▶ Hold informational meetings with community and school board. ▶ Introduce organizing system of context, content, and learning processes ▶ Begin with the learner and developmental rights ▶ Offer a survey of educational best practices and articulate your philosophy. ▶ Master planning input ▶ Universal design/access input ▶ Introduce green architecture, healthy schools concepts, and new sustainable technologies (photovoltaics, building envelope innovations). ▶ Emphasize whole site design; outdoor spaces are integral to academic process.	▶ Handouts about educational practice, theories, developmental rights, organizing system, ecological principles ▶ Summary of master plan, if available ▶ Research on education ▶ Research on local and state content standards ▶ Preliminary site research data collection formats ▶ Research on ecology ▶ Research on architecture for schools/ small schools ▶ Research on community needs/ shared usage ▶ Budgeting exercises/math experiences
Three: Site Analysis Collecting data on physical, biological, cultural, and regulatory aspects of the site	▶ Visit the site, walk the area ▶ Map building footprints, if needed, and major elements of the site. ▶ Use aerial photos and other tools, including geographic information systems (GIS). ▶ Collect data on topography, soils, climate, solar orientation, water, vegetation, wildlife, existing and past structures, local architecture, people and land use, natural history of the site, economics, community setting, zoning codes, planning boards, construction codes, safety/security, crime analysis, utilities, and other regulations.	▶ Students engage in site analysis as a learning experience and provide maps for data collection. ▶ Teach photographic techniques: 360-degree series of photos to show playground or site; use photographs to document the entire process. ▶ Site research documents ▶ Community use surveys ▶ Centralized posting of site maps and Master Plans ▶ Display concepts

Architectural Programming as an Educational Process *(continued)*
Summary of Taylor/Vlastos Programming and Design Process for Educational Facilities

Step	Topics Discussed/ Description of Architectural Process	Supporting Educational Documentation and Active Learning
Four: Programming Examination of context, content, and learning processes for needs assessment, and translating goals into activity settings	▶ Collect data using multiple methods including interviews and research. ▶ Discover/discuss/prioritize philosophies and context. ▶ Uncover multiple use and shared spaces needs. ▶ Discuss/uncover academic concepts that pertain to this project (content). ▶ Link developmental rights to habitability levels. ▶ Define basic needs and link them to habitability levels. ▶ List activity settings. ▶ Make changes to individual activity settings (going beyond basic needs where required). ▶ Write program covering building systems, ambience (including comfort factors and green elements), interior activity settings, exterior activity settings, furniture and equipment, miscellaneous, and get feedback. ▶ Use the expertise of an interior designer consultant.	▶ Data collection, surveys, and interviews about usage/experiential needs of specific activity settings ▶ Preference surveys (ongoing feedback about programming and design) ▶ Formats to translate human needs into architectural needs ▶ Research on ambience, health, ergonomics, etc., for learners ▶ The final written program document has guidelines for design and states the problem to be solved. ▶ Documents include intended academic goals for student performance.
Five: Schematic Design Preliminary design process to uncover important design relationships	▶ Spatial relationships ▶ Adjacencies ▶ Transitional spaces ▶ Siting ▶ Broad, holistic overview ▶ Security through physical design elements ▶ Link to cost estimates ▶ Look at precedents in the studio workplace and alternate applied learning settings. ▶ Get feedback from clients.	▶ Bubble drawings (circles and arrows) ▶ Research on qualities of multiuse, flexible, adaptable, transformable spaces, equipment, and furniture systems ▶ Education and space use data/formats/charts ▶ Research on instructional delivery methods, such as constructivism and hands-on learning
Six: Design Development Translating activity settings into physical design determinants	▶ Determine innovative design solutions for activity requirements. ▶ Include implications for education for each physical element. ▶ Respect "found" manifestations while planning for design enhancements. ▶ The level of detail increases. ▶ Link indoor and outdoor settings.	▶ Formats for translating activity settings into physical design determinants (habitability formats) ▶ Lists of settings and qualities ▶ Narratives about design of new facility and how it can be used ▶ Formats for viewing physical cues or prompts as learning possibilities (early environmental curriculum)

Architectural Programming as an Educational Process *(continued)*
Summary of Taylor/Vlastos Programming and Design Process for Educational Facilities

Step	Topics Discussed/ Description of Architectural Process	Supporting Educational Documentation and Active Learning
Seven: Architectural Conventions, Documents, Models Translating design determinants and needs into final drawings and models	▸ Create plan view, elevations, and perspective drawings. ▸ Translate data into final drawings. ▸ Create models that translate two-dimensional drawings into three-dimensional form. ▸ Obtain approvals/review.	▸ Portfolio of drawings linked to learning potential ▸ Ask: How does this design decision teach? ▸ Map of design innovations keyed to curriculum ▸ Design education research
Eight: Construction Documents Creating large copy documents that contractors can use to build the structure	▸ Providing detailed documents (blueprints, now often digitalized) ▸ Linking to education through signage, openness, legibility ▸ Seeking approvals, review	▸ Materials research (environmental, natural resources, regional influences, properties of matter) ▸ Formats for linking concepts behind construction techniques to designs ▸ Ask engineers, construction workers, etc., for input into how things work.
Nine: Construction Building and equipping the structure	▸ Bidding and contracts ▸ Work on-site. ▸ Recycle or reuse extra materials for project-based learning with children. ▸ Link construction to curriculum. ▸ If renovating, review safety concerns for children on-site, including health issues.	▸ Document the process with photographs and narrative. ▸ Document the process online. ▸ Sort and assemble all user instructions for installed systems into a technical guide.
Ten: User's Guide A book or electronic system that describes the learning potential of the school, based on the ideas uncovered during programming and on school district standards	▸ Put all previous documents into a book, CD, DVD, or Web site for learners. ▸ Collect data on maintenance and stewardship. ▸ Develop the role of the student in the care and stewardship of the building. ▸ Give examples of how the building can teach. ▸ Develop visuals/drawings.	▸ Create a document that translates environmental prompts, cues, or manifestations into learning experiences. ▸ Formats for designing curricula based on environment ▸ Teacher professional development documents ▸ Digital formats shared with community ▸ Signage that explains the school to visitors
Eleven: POE Post-occupancy evaluation can be linked to needs and programming criteria to determine the success of the design as perceived by users (learners) and architects.	▸ Develop systems for self-monitoring and data collection by students. ▸ Walk through site/visit while occupied. ▸ Interview and collect data based on earlier programming lists, values, and documents. ▸ Following through on educational data/test scores of learners, attendance and dropout rates, etc., using the new facility. ▸ Share information for continuous school improvement.	▸ Final report, follow-up documents ▸ Building performance data graphed ▸ Educational performance data formats that can be shared with others and used to design schools of the future ▸ Tools for teacher space planning and evaluation ▸ Student essays about the facility ▸ Open houses, celebrations, press releases to share successes with community

Learning from the Environment at Santa Fe Indian School: Data Collection

Environmental Manifestation   Use this form to explore the potential of the built, natural, and cultural environment

HVAC System

Math	▸ Data collection ▸ Graphing temperature ▸ Costs of operation and energy savings
Science	▸ Physical forces ▸ Laws of motion ▸ Properties of gases ▸ Heat and energy ▸ Scientific investigation and data collection ▸ Ecology ▸ Cycles ▸ Monitoring air quality indoors
Language Arts	▸ Descriptive writing ▸ Advertising analysis and writing ▸ Technical writing ▸ Reading and research on climate ▸ HVAC technology ▸ Ecology ▸ Energy ▸ Labeling and signage ▸ Interviewing skills
Social and Cultural Studies	▸ Systems for temperature control/shelter worldwide ▸ Energy use and politics ▸ Careers in energy ▸ Climate and geography ▸ Natural resources ▸ Civics—regulatory codes and laws
Health/PE	▸ Body systems ▸ Circulation and skin ▸ Health—hydration, heat stroke, hypothermia ▸ Pollution and air quality indoors and out ▸ Healthy lungs
Technology	▸ Use of measurement tools ▸ Internet research ▸ Create informational brochure about system on computer—publishing ▸ Use of digital camera, scanner, etc.
Fine Arts	▸ Museum-quality displays and using visual media ▸ Diagrams and sketches of machines and systems ▸ Speech—presentations, docent ▸ Photography

Community Connection

Students:
▸ Work with local building maintenance personnel to understand and monitor controls
▸ Assume stewardship roles in upkeep of HVAC system
▸ Host tours of HVAC system for visitors
▸ Visit museums to understand possibilities for informational displays
▸ Devise plans for energy savings/alternative energy sources in the community.

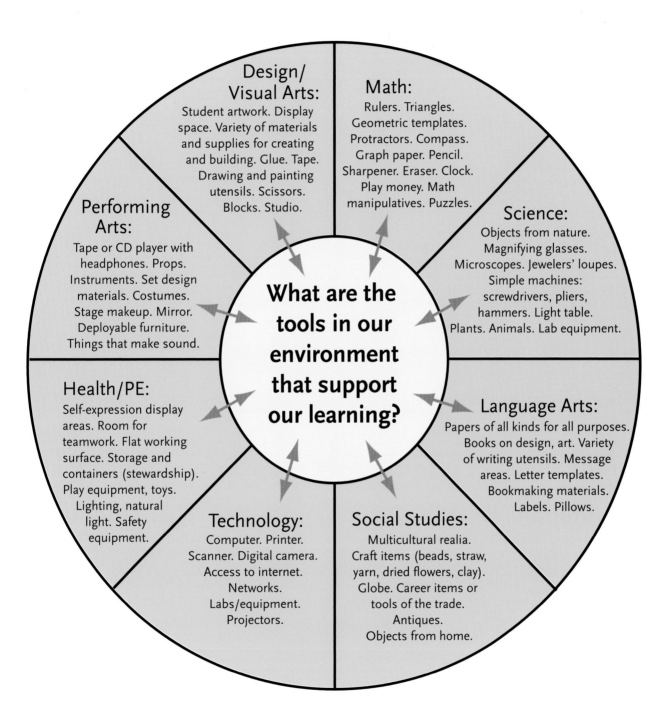

Design/Visual Arts:
Student artwork. Display space. Variety of materials and supplies for creating and building. Glue. Tape. Drawing and painting utensils. Scissors. Blocks. Studio.

Math:
Rulers. Triangles. Geometric templates. Protractors. Compass. Graph paper. Pencil. Sharpener. Eraser. Clock. Play money. Math manipulatives. Puzzles.

Performing Arts:
Tape or CD player with headphones. Props. Instruments. Set design materials. Costumes. Stage makeup. Mirror. Deployable furniture. Things that make sound.

Science:
Objects from nature. Magnifying glasses. Microscopes. Jewelers' loupes. Simple machines: screwdrivers, pliers, hammers. Light table. Plants. Animals. Lab equipment.

What are the tools in our environment that support our learning?

Health/PE:
Self-expression display areas. Room for teamwork. Flat working surface. Storage and containers (stewardship). Play equipment, toys. Lighting, natural light. Safety equipment.

Language Arts:
Papers of all kinds for all purposes. Books on design, art. Variety of writing utensils. Message areas. Letter templates. Bookmaking materials. Labels. Pillows.

Technology:
Computer. Printer. Scanner. Digital camera. Access to internet. Networks. Labs/equipment. Projectors.

Social Studies:
Multicultural realia. Craft items (beads, straw, yarn, dried flowers, clay). Globe. Career items or tools of the trade. Antiques. Objects from home.

Examining a Single Object for Meaning

Name of Object: _____ Reviewer: _____

Location: _____ Date: _____

√ Check each step after you have completed it. Record your responses. Discuss.

☐ What do you notice using all your senses—colors, shapes, sounds, smells, textures, etc.?

☐ List quantitative data here—counting, measuring, classifying, sorting.

☐ Label parts of the object and how they relate to other parts—locational vocabulary.

☐ Relate the object to an event that you remember or to another object.

☐ Do something with or to the object and use verbs to describe the usage of the object.

☐ Ask questions about the object. Wonder about it. Identify problems and potential answers.

☐ Respond personally to the object. Say what you like and don't like about it and why.

© Anne Taylor Associates, 2009.

Learning Environment Assessment (Classrooms)

Assess the learning environment with the following criteria	Body	Mind	Spirit
	Health and safety: Moving within a given space and time	Functional support: Responding to the design with specific activities	Psychological and aesthetic: The comfort and sensory delight experienced
1 Circulation	Easy to "read," move through, about, and in; open sight lines	Easy to see and understand where to go	Self-directive and open with little interference
2 Activity Setting	Safe once the system is installed	Uncluttered and easy to use without confusion; signage	Not intimidating and not disorienting or unwelcoming
3 Structure	Supports the activities designed for children	Perceivable and straight forward and logical—can be used as teaching tool	Complements the scale of the children; is beautiful
4 Surfaces	Easy to clean and work with; smooth	Multipurpose and very useful and accessible; sustainable materials	Mono-textural not to be confusing; calm but interesting, SMART boards, walls, and floors
5 Height	6'6" height maximum for overhead elements	Distributes electricity and overhead structural network with hanging logic	Open and airy and child-related overhead plane, total volume used
6 Components	Easily moved about and lightweight (wheels); ergonomic	Flexible and interchangeable parts	Dynamic and interactive systems understandable to teacher and child
7 Lighting	Existing systems work with new task lighting; day lighting when possible	Flexible task lights can light special activities; some are automatic or on timers	Exposed systems, full-spectrum (light switch visible behind plastic)
8 Electrical System	Safe and has outlets where useful; wireless	Outlets are accessible throughout system; personal controls	Outlets are visible but unobtrusive; some wireless
9 Ambiance	Child-centered, user-friendly; high air quality	Accessible and usable; plants	Contemporary, high-tech, uncluttered, green
10 Color	Brought to the room by users	Basic neutral and light background color	Accent colors: light, bright, minimal applications, not busy
11 Storage	Adult-directed and child-oriented; personal	Accessible, functional, and teacher controlled	Simple and open, not cluttered; for projects
12 Security	Appropriate items and spaces are lockable and protected	Limited locked areas that work with the activities; open views/surveillance	Trusted and accessible with the honor system reinforced
13 Visual Access	Limited obstructed view throughout room	Open and visible; fenestration	Low mass and uncluttered space throughout
14 Adjacency	Interactive	Accessible to all areas everywhere in classroom	Simple, free, and supportive
15 Display	Child-oriented and scaled, framing system	Changeable; easy access and relevant to the lessons taught; art by children; orderly	Supports developmental needs: cultural, geographic, distinctive, imaginative, museum-quality

© Adapted from Vlastos, 2006.

Terry Dunbar's work anticipates chapter 10's discussion of the transformation of school grounds into learning landscapes. A user's guide can be more than a list of manifestations and how they function. Dunbar, acting as science curriculum consultant, teamed with Anne Taylor Associates and architect Charlene Brown to create curricula for use of the playgrounds at several schools in Sanger Unified School District in California, then under the guidance of Superintendent Denise Hexom. A sample learning experience follows this article.

The Schoolyard as Lesson Plan

Terry Dunbar, PhD

Instructional coach, Rio Grande High School, Albuquerque, New Mexico

According to the National Science Education Standards, "Scientific literacy means that a person can ask, find, or determine answers to questions derived from curiosity about everyday experiences" (National Research Council, 1996). We cannot ask much more of our public schools than that students are able to make sense of and use the knowledge and skills they are asked to learn. One would hope that students would be able to relate facts and concepts learned in school to what they see around them on their school campuses and in their neighborhoods.

With the current narrow emphasis on test scores as a primary measure of school success we are in danger of losing sight of the solid educational goals of the teaching standards. Instead of teaching unrelated factoids we should be striving for deeper understanding and higher-level thinking skills. Failure to help students make larger connections, to show the interrelatedness of all knowledge, leads to futility and frustration with the educational process. Students report that they actually lose interest in science as they progress through school. Science as it is taught in public schools still involves bookwork followed by occasional laboratory activity. Field trips are sporadic and not always related to the curriculum in any meaningful way.

Even when teachers have taken science courses, they often have difficulty translating what they have learned from university courses into lesson plans appropriate for their students. A major reason for this difficulty is that textbooks deal primarily in generalities. Universal facts and concepts are stressed, with occasional specific examples and illustrations. To find in a nationally used textbook an example of a fact or concept specifically relevant to any particular school site is rare. Locally produced environmental teaching materials are scarce and not well disseminated.

Yet the natural and built environments are chock-full of learning opportunities that are typically overlooked. The numerous species of weeds growing in cracks in the sidewalk, the behavior of insects, and the pattern of windblown sand offer the content material for lesson plans that are often a direct hit on the required curriculum. Many teachers are not aware of the potential of their school campuses and neighborhoods for generating meaningful and enjoyable learning experiences. Rather than thinking of outdoor activities simply as a physical break from sitting in class or as an add-on to the regular curriculum, teachers should recognize the value of regularly using what is readily at hand to stimulate students' curiosity. Natural objects and existing structures offer a concrete focal point and readily available materials for high-quality lessons in many subject areas (Dunbar, 1994).

With support from the National Science Foundation, I conducted a series of summer institutes during the mid-1990s in New Mexico called Natural History of the School Campus. Elementary school teachers participated in activities that they could in turn use with their own students. To ensure follow-up, their principals worked alongside them during many of the investigations. Teachers identified birds, trapped reptiles, pressed plants, and collected and preserved insects. They developed lesson plans using sow bugs and earthworms. Through gardening and composting activities they developed an understanding of ecosystems. Field trips to areas near their communities helped unravel the geological and ecological history of the region. Physical science activities included using existing walls and varying soils to demonstrate solar energy and temperature change principles.

Science is more than a body of knowledge. It is also a process for producing that knowledge (Rutherford & Ahlgren, 1990). Too much of current science teaching consists of rote memorization of isolated facts. Summer institute participants gained valuable practice in using the science process skills of observing, predicting, measuring, categorizing, designing experiments, and drawing conclusions. The process skills have since been enshrined in the science standards as **scientific inquiry**. The key point is that students do not learn the scientific method by reading about science in textbooks; they become scientific thinkers by doing science. Doing science means asking questions, designing experiments to answer the questions, and making connections to relevant concepts in related fields. Doing science requires manipulation of materials and equipment. It makes sense to use the materials that are available for free near any school.

Learning Landscape Experience

A crack in the asphalt provides a microhabitat for studying the diversity of living things.

Title:
Life on the Asphalt

Theme:
Community

Age groups:
Grades 2–4

Time it takes:
1/2 to one hour

Where it happens:
Any school with cracks in pavement or sidewalks

Objectives:

Students will . . .

Practice inquiry and observation skills

Sketch from real life

Sort and compare information gathered in outdoor study

Gain awareness that living things are found in a great variety of habitats. "Nature abhors a vacuum."

Input/Modeling:

Ask questions about sidewalk habitat before going outside (determine level of students' experience)

Prepare science notebooks or clipboards

Reading the Three-Dimensional Textbook

Learning Landscape Experience

Title: Life on the Asphalt

Materials:
Notebooks or clipboards
Colored pencils and pencils
Magnifying glasses (optional)
Trowel (optional)
Terrarium (optional)
Butcher paper or poster board and markers
      for making a mural (optional)

Resources:
Field guides to insects, plants, and birds may be helpful

Student experiences:

Ask students before going outside: What lives on the sidewalk, parking lot, etc.? Write responses on the board. Take students outside to an area where moss and/or small plants are growing in cracks in the sidewalk. Ask students to observe closely for a few minutes, and then list, describe, and/or draw what they see. Ask them to be attentive to plants, spiders, ants, birds, and anything else they see or believe might use these special microhabitats.

Questions to explore: Is there soil in the cracks? How much soil is necessary for plants or moss to grow? Is the soil damp? How did the plants get there? How can plants survive with so many students and adults walking on them? Is the moss a different color in the fall after a dry summer, compared to after the winter rains come? What are the insects doing? Where do they live and what do their homes look like? Why might a bird land here?

In the classroom, compare observations and drawings to earlier speculation. Students may sort and group life forms found in cracks in the asphalt (insect, spider, flowering plant, moss, bird, etc.), or they might produce a mural of this habitat with labeling.

Variation: Try transplanting some moss from outdoors to a classroom terrarium. See the National Wildlife Federation Web site (http://www.nwf.org/) for some wetlands activities involving runoff and water quality.

Content and performance standards:

▶ Life sciences: the germination, growth, and development of plants can be affected by light, gravity, touch, or environmental stress

▶ Students know examples of diverse life forms in different environments

▶ Ecosystems can be characterized in terms of their living and nonliving components

▶ Children use a variety of artistic media

▶ Language arts: vocabulary development, writing description

Photograph courtesy of Gaylaird
Christopher, architect, A4E.
Cordogan, Clark & Associates, Inc.
Architects and Engineers.

Community and the Learner

INTRODUCTION: SCHOOL AS COMMUNITY, COMMUNITY AS SCHOOL

It is time to dissolve the literal and figurative walls that isolate schools from their communities. The total community is an interdisciplinary environment that can be seen as a treasure chest of learning manifestations and educational resources. Parks and rural areas teach about nature, ecology, stewardship, and science; businesses teach skills and varied content through internships, apprenticeships, and work programs; systems thinking is manifested in local infrastructure; galleries, music halls, theaters, and architecture offices produce artistic inspiration; government buildings teach about law, the justice system, and civics; financial institutions teach math and economics; and health clubs, fitness centers, and sports venues teach physical education.

Schools can reach out to the community and its resources as described above, but school planners also can design inviting schools that encourage parent and community involvement. People in all walks of life, not merely those in academia, remain a tremendous resource for schools. It may be that a new model of education requires nontraditional personnel working in the schools and a change in state and national licensure regulations to include experts in different professions (engineers, musicians, lawyers, nutritionists, etc.) as teachers. Public schools and community exist in a reciprocal relationship that is at the heart of democracy and a free, open society. A democratic spirit of openness that invites the public in and encourages lifelong learning can be reflected in the architecture of our schools, which must resist the temptation toward fortified isolationism. School facilities can honor and reflect local culture, becoming icons for community or centers of community. Schools are a part of, not apart from, community.

Zia Elementary School, Albuquerque, New Mexico.
Top: Several students with visual challenges joined their peers and parents to design and build a walled courtyard that, along with an adjacent family center, would define cultural experiences at Zia Elementary School. Participants planted native plants and helped plan and construct an adobe entrance wall, an *horno* (oven, pictured), a ramada (shade structure), an amphitheater built into a grassy slope, and a mural wall reflecting the region's Hispanic cultural heritage. **Bottom:** View of the courtyard mural created by parents and students at Zia seen through an opening in an adobe wall.
Photographs courtesy of Anne Taylor.

Several themes bring schools and community closer together

Participation: Engage community stakeholders (including students) in school facilities planning and design, research different models for overcoming taxpayer resistance, and achieve meaningful participation including increased willingness to fund projects. An excellent planning resource is *Schools As Center of Community: A Citizen's Guide for Planning and Design* (2003) by Steven Bingler, Linda Quinn, and Kevin Sullivan. It lists six guiding principles for design of better learning environments formulated by a group of educators, architects, planners, government leaders, and other citizens.

Reform of instructional practice: Schools can attract community participation by making learning real and relevant, encouraging lifelong learning, and offering alternate learning environments such as shared, collaborative research centers and vocational, art, or technology schools and curricula. Laws about inclusion and bringing children with disabilities into the regular classroom are changing how special education services are administered and how classrooms should be configured in the future.

Mixed-use benefits: Schools serve and benefit the community through mixed-use facilities, location of facilities (siting for shared use and easy access), and by addressing local health, safety, and security concerns. Schools can also serve as childcare centers, emergency shelters, libraries, and business incubators. Opportunities afforded through master planning and sharing of facilities also reveal advantages in work/study programs, longer hours of use for facilities, language acquisition/learning English, multiple ages served, and relevance of academics to career and life (Nathan & Febey, 2001). Colocation offers expanded learning opportunities and expansion of services for students and their families, allows families to spend more time together, and uses tax funds more efficiently (Nathan & Sheena, 2007).

Small schools: Small schools can create a sense of community within the school. Small schools and schools within schools might offer the best way to lower dropout rates while serving different academic and community needs in rural, urban, and suburban settings. Definitions for what constitutes "small" vary. Researcher Kathleen Cotton suggests 300–400 students for elementary level and 400–800 for secondary schools. (Please see forum contributors Elliot Washor, Dale Lang, and Jeffery Lackney for more on the small school.)

Neighborhood revitalization: Schools can revitalize neighborhoods through retrofitting schools and adaptive reuse of existing community facilities such as historical sites, abandoned strip malls, or warehouses. Schools can have a positive impact on property values through vibrant, well-maintained designs. Planners can use alternate sites for meeting dual goals of learning and cost saving. Renovating and retrofitting existing structures are also ecologically valid uses of school facilities, including recycling and saving on energy costs for new construction materials.

THINK LIKE AN URBANIST

The architecture of civic spaces or public squares can support or frustrate our sense of belonging to a city, according to Mark Childs, author of *Squares: A Public Place Design Guide for Urbanists* (2004). Urban spaces meet our needs for sociability, love of natural landscape, and identification with the townscape or built forms that surround us (pp. 3–5). "Good squares are visually, socially, psychologically, and physically accessible" (p. 147). Understanding how elements of the environment influence human behavior is inherent to the design of urban commons, and I believe this same attention can be applied to schools as urban centers.

Urban design also has direct applications to the design of schools as public spaces. Studying the forms of our cities and urban patterns can help us imagine and design our school facilities and grounds as inviting public squares, centers of democratic discourse, architectural records of our shared history, sites for public art, parks, or civic rooms open to a variety of uses.

TWELVE BRIDGES LEARNING CENTER— A SHARED VISION

In 1996, Steven Bingler of Concordia LLC, Anne Taylor Associates, and other firms began a master planning process called Project Build to encourage California's Western Placer Unified School District to work with the town of Lincoln to develop a community-based vision for educational facilities. As part of this effort, students in the district took an active role in uncovering

Twelve Bridges Learning Center, Sierra Community College, Western Placer Unified School District, Lincoln, California.
Above: Partnerships and collaboration resulted in a lifelong learning campus with a high school, community college, and a full-service civic library sharing common facilities. Plan view courtesy of Jordan Knighton, partner at NTDStichler Architecture. **Inset:** The library functions as a resource center for Sierra Community College, Lincoln High School, and the community of Lincoln, addressing the needs of lifelong learners. Rendering courtesy of Jordan Knighton, partner at NTDStichler Architecture.

Left: With its distinct grade-level academies, Twelve Bridges reflects district and community educational goals of celebrating science, culture, environment, and technology through high-performance building systems and indoor and outdoor interpretive learning areas. Photograph © 2007 Steve Whittaker. Photograph courtesy of Jordan Knighton, partner at NTDStichler Architecture.

hidden community resources by using bilingual "treasure cards." These cards, which can easily be digitalized as an online resource, were used to collect and present data about local resources as part of the planning process for a community center and school (see a sample card at the end of this introduction).

The Project Build framework introduced in 1996 has since evolved and culminated in the Twelve Bridges Learning Center, a joint-venture educational project developed by Western Placer Unified School District, Sierra Community College, and the city of Lincoln, California. Jordan Knighton, AIA, partner with NTDStichler Architecture, writes that a systemic approach utilized community participation and optimized data on the rich resources of the county. Community members, teachers, students, and businesspeople met to examine community resources within the four-point framework of physical resources, learning, governance, and socioeconomic opportunities. From this process the district embarked on a detailed educational programming effort to define elementary, middle school, and high school needs in response to the community's vision. A separate task force explored an intergenerational curriculum between high school and college. The project was developed to address the need for a seamless educational program to train college and high school students for regional careers as well as lifelong learning. The Lincoln community is changing from a homogenous agrarian population to a more diverse community with a rapidly growing technological economy.

The architectural solution weaves contextual and thematic learning as well as joint-use collaborative opportunities throughout the design. A lifelong learning campus evolved with a high school, community college, and civic library sharing common facilities. The design emphasizes high performance and sustainability, multicultural and historic influences, indoor/outdoor relationships, social interaction, natural light, and public art.

Through this entrepreneurial undertaking, the citizens of Lincoln, the schools, and business partners are working together to maximize available state, local, and private funding.

Interactive bronze *Building Bridges* sculpture is part of "the crooked mile" at Twelve Bridges Elementary School, a meandering path connecting outdoor project learning labs for solar technology, physical science, astronomy, weather, and agriculture history. Zoe Alowan, sculptor. Photograph courtesy of Jordan Knighton, partner at NTDStichler Architecture.

WHAT IS BEST FOR THE COMMUNITY?
More on Small Schools and Alternative Learning Settings
A recent cover story in *Time* puts the public high school dropout rate in America at nearly 30 percent. About 67 percent of prison inmates in the United States are high school dropouts, and unemployment rates for sixteen- to twenty-four-year-old dropouts are at about 50 percent (Thornburgh, 2006). Clearly, these rates are of great importance to the quality of life in communities large and small. According to Cotton (2001), "Research over

the past 15 years has convincingly demonstrated that small schools are superior to large ones on many measures and equal to them on the rest" (p. 1). Benefits of small schools range from improved attitude and behavior, to a sense of belonging, to curricular quality and increased student achievement (pp. 13–20). School attendance and graduation rates are higher in small schools (p. 15). As a result of the research, the Bill and Melinda Gates Foundation has generously donated millions of dollars toward the creation of personalized small learning communities (SLCs) in urban areas. It is not feasible or desirable for many urban schools to be forced into the suburban model of large structures surrounded by acres of land.

Unfortunately, a trend away from small schools is occurring in some rural areas. Special problems with the small tax base in rural areas, poverty, and declining enrollment have put pressure on rural schools to close facilities and consolidate and centralize services into large schools. Some acreage requirements and other regulations for school facilities encourage sprawl and limit smart growth by forcing districts to close small schools rather than renovate. Districts are also forced to build large buildings in suburban or outlying areas on isolated parcels far from any local resources. This creates schools that are divorced from community and that require dependence on automobiles.

Small towns that lose their schools often lose the heart of community. Revitalization of towns is also important to rural schools, according to Rachel Thompkins of the Rural School and Community Trust in Arlington, Virginia (Roybal, 2006). Thompkins points out that student achievement gaps depend not just on the schools themselves, but on nutrition, health, housing, language, and economic vitality of the community. The more schools can strive to meet community needs, the more likely they are to be perceived as essential to small towns.

Suburban schools, too, have difficulties supporting dramatic increases in student populations whose first language is not English. These students need small, personal learning environments to do well in school (Cotton, 2001, p. 48).

In 2001 NCEF published a report titled *Smaller, Safer, Saner, Successful Schools.* Authors Joe Nathan and Karen Febey examined case studies to uncover what small schools can provide, and the possibilities that sharing facilities can offer. A quick survey of the case studies reveals benefits of small facilities:

▶ A family environment

▶ Frequent student contact with advisors

▶ Portfolio assessment and more time-consuming diagnostics

▶ More individualized learning and personal workspace

▶ More use of the outdoors

▶ Long-term learning and projects

▶ Mini-businesses (or business incubators for students)

▶ Tutoring/peer tutoring

▶ Better technology ratios

▶ Opportunities for multidisciplinary learning

▶ Independent study

▶ Apprenticeships (Nathan & Febey, 2001)

In light of these advantages, I recommend that no school house more than five hundred students. In addition, teachers have pleaded with me to recommend that there be only thirteen to seventeen pupils per classroom (if individual classrooms remain the rule for teaching).

Charter Schools

Many communities make use of charter schools, which are nonsectarian public schools that offer alternative programs and operate outside traditional regulations while still remaining accountable to the academic and budgetary standards of the school system. According to the Charter School Leadership Council, close to a million students attend approximately 3,400 charter schools in the United States (Vanourek, 2005). On the plus side, charter schools

Amy Biehl Charter High School, Albuquerque, New Mexico. Top: North facade. Gregory Hartman and Richard Deutsch of the Hartman + Majewski Design Group maintained and adapted the Mediterranean Revival style architecture of the former federal building to suit the needs of the high school. Photograph courtesy of the General Services Administration and the City of Albuquerque. **Center:** Curving stairs fallen into disrepair. Photograph courtesy of the General Services Administration and the City of Albuquerque. **Bottom:** Renovated stairs. In addition to winning a national historic preservation award, Amy Biehl Charter High School and its designers received the 2006 New Mexico Heritage Preservation Award for the renovation work on the long-vacant downtown site. Photo courtesy of The Hartman + Majewski Design Group, Albuquerque, New Mexico.

are significantly smaller than public schools, have distinct missions, often take advantage of community participation, and offer many models and choices for students. Unfortunately, many charter schools are located in substandard facilities. Capital outlay funds for charter schools are limited. Charter schools are often underfunded academically, too, receiving smaller per-pupil allocations than traditional schools. Academic performance of charter school students is uneven, and data for assessing performance are absent (Vanourek, 2005, p. 1).

The Amy Biehl Charter High School in Albuquerque is an award-winning example of mutual benefit through cooperation of city and schools. The school, co-founded by teachers Tony Monfiletto and Tom Siegel, recently moved into its new home, a 1908 federal courthouse and post office located in downtown Albuquerque that was renovated by the Hartman + Majewski Design Group. The preservation and reuse of the older structure contributes to the revitalization of the downtown area, while some two hundred students have easy access to the community "classroom." Through its yearlong community service projects and other programs, the charter school recognizes the spirit and dedication of Amy Biehl, who lost her life while working for social justice in South Africa.

After-School Programs

Many children, especially at the elementary school level, are spending more and more time after school in programs that may not be optimally serving their needs. Some programs rely heavily on televisions and video games as entertainment, and others function as study halls or drab extensions of the school day. Perhaps school planners can consider new options, creating spaces or access to spaces such as music practice rooms, media centers, cooking and nutrition labs, and studios for design, art, and dance where students can be active, creative, and productive. Many children would benefit from exercise and fitness programs. Deployable furniture and more storage for materials, equipment, and backpacks in multipurpose rooms, cafeterias, and gymnasiums also allow flexibility and choice for children and after-hours staff. Community members can more easily share their expertise with children when they have access to well-equipped environments specially designed for visitors and extended learning.

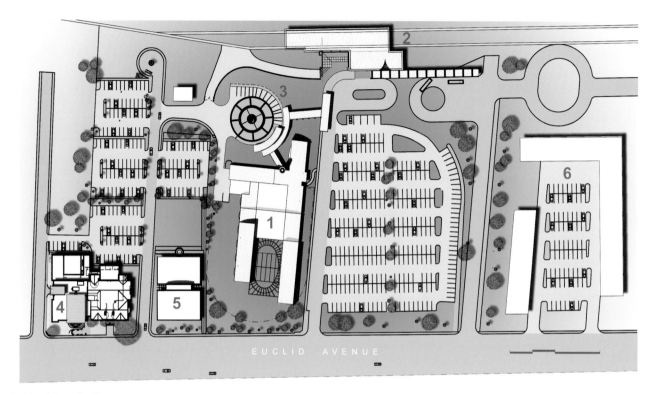

1. Head Start facility
2. Louis B. Stokes Inter-modal station
3. Connecting canopy
4. East Cleveland Public Library
5. Potential development site
6. New retail development

Head Start Facility at Windermere, South Cleveland, Ohio. Canopies link the facility to nearby public transportation, making it easy for parents to drop off children on their way to work. Richard Fleischman + Partners Architects, Inc.

Schools Serving Community

Community needs include health care, libraries, transportation, adult education, senior centers, childcare, recreation, exercise, technology, security, and a variety of social services. School facilities acting as community centers can provide multiuse facilities to address many of these needs (Abramson, 2000).

Benefits of shared facilities include forming partnerships for better learning, maintaining usefulness of school facilities when enrollment declines, avoiding duplication of services, saving costs, using buildings and time efficiently, designing for flexibility and changing needs, and providing aesthetic models of pride for community. Steven Bingler of Concordia LLC describes this last quality as the "noble character of public architecture" (Bingler, Quinn, & Sullivan, 2003, p. 8). I hope to see schools restored to their valued place in community not only through their usefulness, but also through their aesthetic quality.

WHAT TO LOOK FOR IN THE STEWARDSHIP FORUM ON COMMUNITY

Several of our forum contributions in this section are aimed at engaging community in planning of school facilities. In these essays, look for the many ingenious ways architects and planners enlist public support, money, and interest. These leaders are similar to teachers in their methods for motivating and inspiring their "students," the diverse stakeholders who must believe in the project to make it work. Once the community is truly involved and informed, remarkable accomplishments follow. Schools truly can become anchors of community.

Community Resources for Learning

T R E A S U R E   C A R D   english

Recorder _____

Date _____

Treasure _____

Category ☐ Governance Resources ☐ Learning Resources

☐ Physical Resources ☐ Socio-Economic Resources

Source

COMPANY NAME	CONTACT PERSON
ADDRESS	ADDRESS
CITY/STATE/ZIP	CITY/STATE/ZIP
PHONE	PHONE

General Description _____
_____
_____
_____

Mission of Resource _____
_____
_____
_____

How can this resource be used as a learning tool? _____
_____
_____

Curricular subject areas addressed. _____
_____
_____

Age level appropriateness _____

Comments, sketch, or photo.
(attach additional information on a separate sheet)

Servicios de la comunidad para la ensenanza

T R E A S U R E   C A R D   spanish

Registrado por _____

Fecha _____

Bien Comunitario _____

Categoria ☐ Servicio Gubernamental ☐ Servicios de Ensenanza

☐ Servicios Materiales ☐ Servicios Socio-Economicos

Fuente

COMPANIA	PERSONA ENCARGADA
DIRECCION	DIRECCION
CIUDAD/ESTADO/CODIGO POSTAL	CIUDAD/ESTADO/CODIGO POSTAL
TELEFONO	TELEFONO

Descripcion general _____
_____
_____
_____

Metas del servicio _____
_____
_____
_____

¿Como puede usarse este servicio como herramienta de ensenanza? _____
_____
_____

Areas de la materia del curriculo que cubre este servicio. _____
_____

Edades recomendadas de los participantes. _____

Comentarios, bosquejo, o foto.
(Envie cualquier informacion suplementaria en una pagina adjunta)

Finding Community Treasures: The bilingual treasure card used in 1996 for data collection at a California school is now adapted as a Web site for inventorying usable educational community assets. Card reproduced courtesy of Concordia LLC.

Steven Bingler is devoted to the collaborative planning and integrative thinking that can reduce the isolation of schools from community. The name of his architectural firm, Concordia, reflects his interest in harmony, concord, and teamwork. Grassroots reform enables diverse participants, people who share common interests but may not have communicated with each other in the past, to assemble at the local project level. These individuals from all sectors of the community work together to create innovative learning facilities designs—a form of community empowerment akin to old-fashioned barn raising but also serving the participatory aims of the larger democratic society. Concordia LLC's latest work in New Orleans introduces the "community campus" as a replacement for schools. Schools, day care centers, health services, community libraries, and police stations will be housed in separate facilities located on one master-planned site. Advanced facilities would be within walking distance of neighborhood residents, replacing stand-alone school buildings (Concordia LLC, 2008).

Common Ground
Schools as Centers of Community

Steven Bingler
Concordia LLC, New Orleans, Louisiana

A movement toward disintegration and diffusion characterized much of the twentieth century. The design and construction of buildings, a practice that was once accomplished by a master builder and a team of talented journeymen, now involves a legion of architects, engineers, general contractors, construction managers, electricians, plumbers, mechanics, and attorneys, along with a host of support agencies and institutions. In education the delivery of knowledge, which was once conducted in one-room schoolhouses with an educator generalist, now includes multiple specialists in all core subjects as well as early childhood, special education, art, athletics, vocational education, assessment, governance, counseling, administration, and transportation.

Although it is difficult to argue the benefits of exploring and expanding one's field of endeavor, it is also important to recognize the need to understand how this extended kit of parts still fits together as a whole.

THE ETHIC OF INCLUSION AND INTEGRATION
The restructuring of education is responding to counter this trend toward dissipation with theories and best practices that embody an ethic of inclusion and integration, including teamwork and team teaching, assimilation of special needs learners, and interdisciplinary and real-world learning.

As the dialogue about the total learning environment continues to expand, its logical resting place will be in the environment of the total community. Leonard Duhl, the father of the international Healthy Cities movement, has advocated such a focus for more than thirty years. Duhl's point of view is that communities function much like human bodies, where an illness in any vital organ significantly and sometimes radically affects the health and well-being of the whole body system. Because education is a complex, interdependent assemblage that influences and is impacted by all of the community's individual parts, it is here that a healthy and fully functioning system is most crucial for long-term community stability and sustainability.

VISUALIZING THE TOTALLY INTEGRATED LEARNING ENVIRONMENT

Case One: The "academical village" Thomas Jefferson designed for the University of Virginia manifests the philosophy of an integrated learning system that remains applicable to learning environments on every scale. The underlying structure was Socratic and cooperative, with the student and the professor/mentor living around a common quadrangle. There were ten pavilions that housed the professors on the second level and a meeting room or classroom below. Each of the pavilions was designed in a different classical architectural order and served as a kind of architectural laboratory for the students who lived in clusters of rooms between each pavilion, all connected by a single colonnade. Behind each pavilion was a formal garden open to everyone, which also served as a botanical laboratory. At the four corners of the campus Jefferson's plans called for restaurants with food prepared by families from foreign countries, with native décor and native languages spoken in each one. The end result was what noted educator and environmental researcher Anne Taylor would call a "three-dimensional textbook."

Case Two: In Dearborn, Michigan, a partnership including the Ford Motor Company, the Henry Ford Museum, and the Wayne County Regional Educational Service Agency has produced a charter high school located in the Henry Ford Museum. Grade level studios are strategically located throughout the museum environment, which also includes the eighty-acre Greenfield Village with its collection and reconstruction of nearly one hundred historic buildings. This innovative integration of the museum and a formal ninth-through-twelfth-grade educational institution provides students with access to thousands of artifacts of innovation in manufacturing arts and sciences along with mentoring from some of the most experienced museum curators in the nation. Because the formal learning facility was constructed within the existing museum structure, the Henry Ford Academy can offer its exceptional learning programs at a significant reduction in the capital and operating costs than would normally be required for a new facility.

Henry Ford Academy Charter High School, Dearborn, Michigan. Museum railroad cars house some classrooms in the ninth-through-twelfth-grade Henry Ford Academy, a partnership among school, museum, and community. Steven Bingler, Concordia LLC. Image courtesy of the Henry Ford Learning Institute.

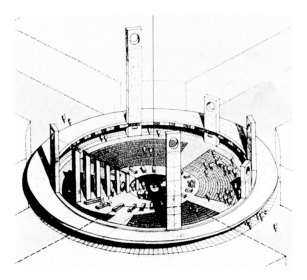

Tishomingo County Learning Center, Mississippi.
A tangible exhibit of math, science, and ecology concepts as a central plaza with sundial. Image courtesy of Steven Bingler, Concordia LLC.

Case Three: The Tishomingo County Learning Center is located in the town of Iuka, Tishomingo County, Mississippi, an area rich in Native American, Appalachian, and Southern heritage, all of which are embodied in the design of the center. Iuka and Tishomingo were both chiefs of the Chickasaw Nation. The cosmology of the Chickasaw tribe, with its ties to the movement of the sun and stars, also forms the inspiration for a major program element of the learning center. A central plaza provides for circulation while illustrating math and science concepts—the summer and winter solstices, sundials and time, compass bearings and cardinal directions—all in a tangible exhibit. A circular covered walkway also collects rainwater from the roofs of adjacent buildings, providing a lesson in hydraulics in motion. An auditorium doubles as a community theater, and the cafeteria is used as a town meeting hall, while the gymnasium also serves as a public fitness center.

These examples of integration and shared efficiency point the way to a new and more sensible approach to the development of facilities for learning. Given the vast resources of information and knowledge developed through the past century's proliferation of individual disciplines, there now exists an unprecedented opportunity for the development of a new wave of inclusive, community-based schools, a common ground that can foster the expansion of the collective human spirit.

Key Exercises during the School Design Process
Bridging Students to Educators to Architects

Atsuko Sakai
International architectural educator, Design Plus LLC

Truly engaging community in design is a primary goal of many architects. I have encountered several techniques that serve to bring architects, educators, and their students together during the planning and design process for schools.

Involve stakeholders in observation and analysis of current conditions
- Photography exercises
- Data collection through space analysis sheets

Involve stakeholders in design charrettes
- A charrette is a collaborative session in which a group of designers drafts a solution to a design problem.
- Demonstrate how to read architectural plans and the use of visual symbolic language.
- After understanding the architectural drawing conventions, move to designing spaces and brainstorming together.
- Follow up with additional charrettes focusing on key issues raised in the first workshop.
- Set up a design center in the school, a place to keep track of ideas as they evolve.

Plan architectural experiences with students
- Introduce the world of architecture and landscape architecture into the classroom.
- Use the new building project or the existing school to show how architects work and to learn about client issues.
- Go on a walking tour, site analysis, or construction tour with students and architects together at different stages of the design process.
- Take visual notes (make sketches) and talk about what you see.
- Ask students and teachers to look at their surroundings with critical eyes, using their five senses as much as possible.
- A visual checklist form can be helpful for gathering data.

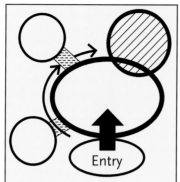

Bubble diagrams to show spatial relationships

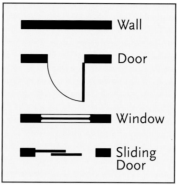

Plan view of architectural conventions

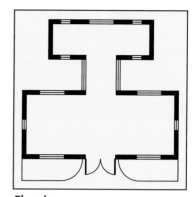

Plan view

Schematic images similar to these are often used in Architecture and Children workshops. Partners in school planning can communicate using the language of design through schematic drawings and architectural symbols to convey spatial information. Schematics by Atsuko Sakai.

Two-point perspective

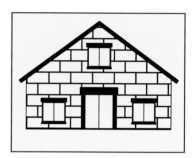

Elevation

Incorporate clients' characteristics into design

▶ Think about how students' work can be incorporated into their spaces through display spaces, murals, or sculptures.

▶ At each stage of the planning and design process, ask "What are the ways to bring community support into the project?"

Seek support from others

▶ If the architectural firm does not have enough architects and time to conduct all the above exercises, try contacting the architecture school at a nearby university for additional support.

▶ The workshops can be made a part of an undergraduate or graduate design studio, which emphasizes aesthetics, or they can form the basis for a research project that analyzes education, spatial relationships, and the learning environment.

▶ Be sure that university students provide learning exercises *before* actual design begins with the architects. That way, clients will already have detailed analyses and programming ideas to share with the design team.

THREE

The next two forum contributors provide a shared dialogue on public school projects for West Aurora School District 129 in Illinois. Sherry Eagle, then superintendent, and Gaylaird Christopher, design architect of Architecture for Education (A4E), brought community stakeholders together, forging new partnerships that led to shared use of facilities.

Designing Learning Environments
A Community Agenda

Sherry Eagle, PhD
Educational consultant and former superintendent of schools

INTRODUCTION: SHARED DIALOGUE

The quality of a learning environment in a school district is best achieved when it aligns with the district's mission and belief about teaching and learning. Facilities are best designed through a process that involves students, staff, administrators, and vested community stakeholders. Everyone with a stake in the school's success needs the opportunity to be a part of a dialogue with an architect who has the ability to capture stakeholders' visions and translate them into concept drawings.

Our district had been fortunate to have steady growth of approximately 250 students per year for the past ten years. We'd had the opportunity to take the time to understand our own values and beliefs as a school community. Even if time had been more of a factor, however, it would have been an error not to engage stakeholders in the process of designing and learning about the value of space. The shared dialogue results in shared vision. Shared dialogue invests the stakeholders and ultimately achieves learning environments created by the community for its children. In this way, true "ownership" of the school is achieved for all who are a part of its creation.

DREAM ABOUT THE FUTURE

The West Aurora School District engaged its community through an invitation to "dream about the future." Members of the business, social service, government, higher education, and local school communities were invited to a "futures conference" to engage in a dialogue about education and the type of environments needed to deliver those educational goals. The process brought the stakeholders together as partners and ultimately afforded us the opportunity to maximize the impact of the school district's construction and programmatic funds. The participants launched the conference by discussing the school community's beliefs about education and the corresponding implication for our learning environments.

Robert L. Herget Middle School, West Aurora, Illinois.

Top: Resources area. The school plan is composed of six learning clusters of 100 students each. Each learning community has a large resource area that opens to a "great hall of learning" shared by the whole school. Individual classrooms access the resource area through fenestrated garage doors.

Center: The school, located adjacent to a nature preserve, reflects the agrarian past of the region through its architecture and use of fieldstone, corrugated metal, standing-seam metal, and brick. I

Bottom: Tiered seating and exposed trusses. Images courtesy of Gaylaird Christopher, architect, A4E. Cordogan, Clark & Associates, Inc. Architects and Engineers. Dr. Sherry Eagle, former superintendent of schools.

PARTNERS: PUBLIC LIBRARY

Members explored how they could work together to partner on space and programs. At this juncture the public library saw an opportunity to design a branch connected to our existing middle school. The branch would include a city technology center that could be used by the school during the day and the community at night and on weekends with all costs for infrastructure and technology acquisition shared.

PARTNERS: UNIVERSITY

In addition, the local university saw an opportunity to provide space on its campus to accommodate a one-grade-level center. This provided space for one hundred district elementary students and a rich learning environment for aspiring elementary educators. Also, it fostered the collaboration with the university on future designs of new schools that would be built in partnership, both in terms of program and infrastructure. Our work together promoted the idea of designing and building an eight-court outdoor tennis facility on the high school campus to benefit both our high school and university tennis teams. This unique collaboration also had the effect of creating a political climate of support and encouragement for our school district. Momentum to further address school needs was developed.

PARTNERS: YMCA

As time passed and one bond ended and another began, other entities in the community saw the benefits of achieving common goals through partnership. The YMCA in partnership with the district garnered significant local and state grants to renovate space at its local facility to accommodate a state-of-the-art young-child center. The district's preschool program and four classes of kindergarten students moved into the facility, increasing the school district's overall student capacity while providing a rich learning environment.

THE PROCESS

In each facility project, joint committees were formed for each partnership. These project committees, composed of vested stakeholders, determined the goals needed for each construction project and the necessary resources to operationalize those goals. The resources included mechanical, lighting, furnishings, room size, and finishes. Given the necessary professional development through bond funds set aside for such purposes, these members became our local experts in their role as educational facility planners.

Once the goals and resources were determined, the designing of the actual buildings, additions, and renovations began. A school principal in collaboration with that school's partners led each project. All meeting agendas and presentations to the Board of Education were given by the principal leader(s) with the partners and architect present. It gave credibility to a project that committee leaders knew the work well enough to present it publicly. It was their project and they accepted ownership. Again, this process also provided growing political support for future bond issues.

The results of our school district projects have been phenomenal. When the schools, libraries, university center, school additions, renovations, and sports complexes were completed, the contribution of the collaborating committee was demonstrated clearly. The hard decisions made as a result of budget constraints were accepted because each was a community member's project, not one owned by someone who did not work at the school or contribute to its support.

ARCHITECTS AS TEACHERS

What our school district found is that a good architect must be a great teacher. The architect must have the knowledge and skill to assist the internal and external school communities in a process that ultimately helps them define what education goals they want to achieve for their students and how the resources within that community will lead to that end. The process of designing facilities for education must involve time, professional development, and shared decision making. If wisely done, the process will be used to build community support for an educational system and encourage all stakeholders to see connections where appropriate. This makes good sense for all concerned and was applauded by our community's patrons and taxpayers. The greatest bonus for the superintendent and board is that the collaborative process engages the community in a positive dialogue about education and the future of its children.

Greenman Elementary School, West Aurora, Illinois.
Top: Exterior. **Center:** Hallway view of classroom cluster resource room. **Bottom:** Main hallway. A playful window arrangement of colored glass creates an expression of music, rhythm, and harmony from the exterior. Photographs courtesy of Gaylaird Christopher, architect, A4E. Cordogan, Clark & Associates, Inc. Architects and Engineers.

When a 107-year-old school no longer met the needs of students, a replacement facility was built on the existing school grounds, thus preserving important connections to the neighborhood.

Architecture for Education

Gaylaird Christopher

Architect, Architecture for Education (A4E)

We've grown to expect certain implicit standards regarding the quality of materials, atmosphere, or ambience in a cathedral, sports arena, convention center, corporate headquarters, or retail shopping center. For public schools the expected standard of quality is much less clear. Certainly there are some glorious public schools in our nation; however, all too often the learning environment is addressed as a mere commodity. Plans are replicated from one community to the next, with portable classrooms being the acceptable norm rather than the exception. My premise is that the quality of a learning environment is at least as important as the other building types listed above. Educational buildings should teach and inspire learners to seek and achieve their highest goals.

Greenman Elementary School in West Aurora, Illinois, is a replacement school project that won the Learning by Design Grand Prize Award in 2005. The architectural design was a result of a community engagement process that included district leaders, the Board of Education, administrators, teachers, staff, students, parents, community members, and business representatives.

The "school within a school" feel at Greenman is created through classroom clusters that overlook outdoor learning courtyards. The clusters contain four classrooms, two technology/resource areas, and a flexible learning corridor. Every classroom contains a learning wall, bay windows for quiet areas, and a private bathroom. Interior fenestration between rooms and hallways allows teachers to monitor groups of students working in adjacent project areas and hallways.

The building's design emphasizes a philosophy that the arts are an integral part of academics. Students learn in a variety of ways, and a commitment to the arts as a part of the curriculum is revealed in the school lobby, which brings together windowed

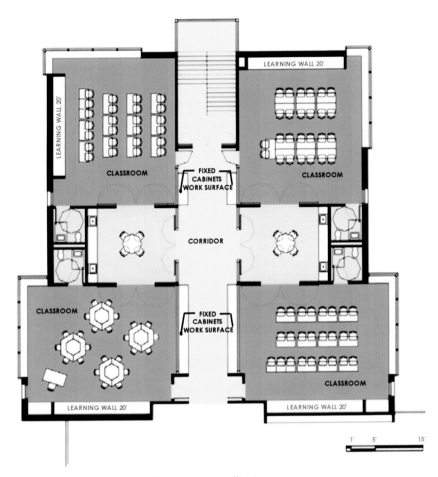

Greenman Elementary School, West Aurora, Illinois.
Plan view of classroom cluster. Note learning walls, which are custom made, flexible, and adaptable millwork that can conform to individual teacher and student needs for shelving, storage, display, whiteboards, filing systems, and data/power. Image courtesy of Gaylaird Christopher, architect, A4E. Cordogan, Clark & Associates, Inc. Architects and Engineers.

Below top: Portholes look into mechanical rooms, inviting children to observe how building systems function at their school.
Below bottom: Gymnasium with stage. Photograph courtesy of Gaylaird Christopher, architect, A4E. Cordogan, Clark & Associates, Inc. Architects and Engineers.

music and art rooms and a performance center. The formal stage is two-sided. One side opens to the gymnasium, which allows for large group gatherings and assemblies. The other side opens into the lobby area, where the grand staircase doubles as small amphitheater seating.

One of the strongest environmental characteristics that research has connected to student achievement is a sense of community. Our goal is that every design decision made during the collaborative planning process inspires learning and positively impacts the community. How wonderful it is when a school pays tribute to the local heritage and yet creates its own sense of place.

Dale Lang reminds us that an egalitarian ideal was the original inspiration for our national public school system. Our nation's founders rejected a European society based on social, political, and economic rights and privileges for just a few. A democratic school system means more than giving our children the skills or knowledge to economically succeed as individuals. It also requires fostering a sense of responsibility to others and to the environment in which we all live. This is difficult to do in today's sprawling, impersonal high school facilities.

Adapted and excerpted from

High School Reform

Opportunities for Improving Academic Outcomes through Small Learning Communities

Dale Lang, PhD

Educational consultant and partner in Educational DESIGN, a planning and research-based learning organization

Two significant philosophies emerged early in the twentieth century that have had a profound yet oddly polarizing effect on the design and culture of our present-day high schools. The first concept involved a reinforcement of original democratic and egalitarian ideals through socialization, attributed to social reformer John Dewey. Dewey advocated a practical and experiential teaching method rather than the prevalent drill-and-recitation pedagogy of his day. Education should not be a means to an end but rather an ongoing discourse (Dewey, 1916).

The second philosophy was quite the opposite, involving an emphasis based on a bureaucratic efficiency of the industrial "factory model." Leading this reform was Stanford dean and professor Ellwood Cubberley. Children were regarded as raw products to be indoctrinated and processed, and teachers were viewed as line workers with little decision-making capability. Students were to be separated according to their abilities. "We should give up the exceedingly democratic idea that all are equal and that our society is devoid of classes. The employee tends to remain an employee; the wage earner tends to remain a wage earner . . . One bright child may easily be worth more to the National Life than thousands of those of low mentality" (Cubberley, 1916).

The Truman Center, Federal Way, Washington.
Symmetrical interior, open activity area. Photograph courtesy of Mahlum Architects.

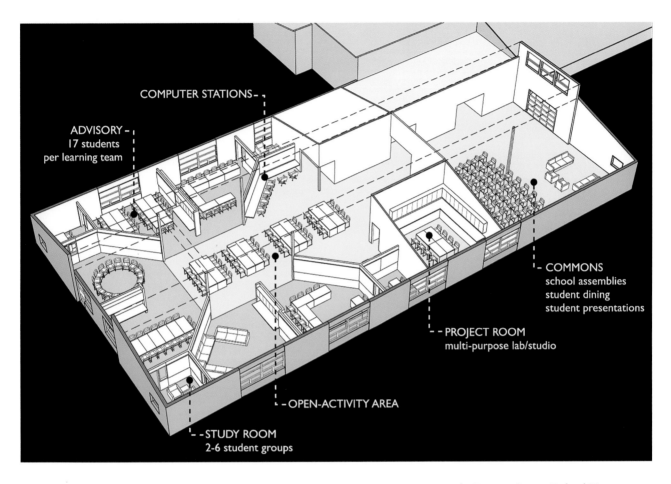

COMPUTER STATIONS

ADVISORY –
17 students
per learning team

COMMONS
school assemblies
student dining
student presentations

PROJECT ROOM
multi-purpose lab/studio

OPEN-ACTIVITY AREA

STUDY ROOM
2-6 student groups

LINGERING IMPLICATIONS OF THE FACTORY MODEL

Many today disdain Cubberley's original approach and its resulting huge, inhuman, factory-like school structures, but somehow the model survives and continues to replicate itself in spite of its terrible tradition and outcomes. Today's high schools exhibit what Michael Engel calls a "market-driven ideology." Born out of a philosophy of efficiency, discourse concentrates mainly on international economic competition, test scores, and school choice. What have been largely neglected are larger issues of civic welfare, democratic values, and a commonly conceived future. A fundamental conflict exists between a market-driven ideology and the desire for democratic ideals, and the two are diametrically opposed (Engel, 2000).

Qualities of democracy must include community participation, a sense of justice, equality and liberty, interpretive skills, willingness to debate and compromise, reflective habits, and multiple perspectives (Wood, 1992). How can we expect these quality student outcomes to emerge from such an uninspiring environment as exhibited in factory-like high schools?

The Truman Center, Federal Way, Washington. Conceptual view of the alternative high school, a stand-alone structure for about 250 students. Image courtesy of Gerald "Butch" Reifert of Mahlum Architects.

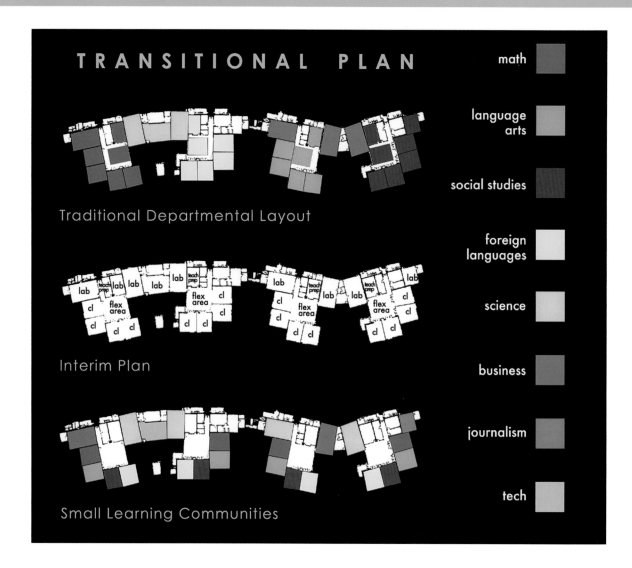

TRANSITIONAL PLAN

Traditional Departmental Layout

Interim Plan

Small Learning Communities

math

language arts

social studies

foreign languages

science

business

journalism

tech

Edmonds-Woodway High School, Edmonds, Washington. Gradual transition of large facility to small learning communities. Image courtesy of Dale Lang and Lorne McConachie of Bassetti Architects.

RENEWED HOPE

The small learning community (SLC) model may be the most expedient and economical solution to counter the factory model or what may be called "Cubberley's disaster." Although the precise definition of "small" varies, the schools must be small enough so that each student is recognized by name by every faculty member and known well enough by more than one adult, and so that families feel welcome (Meier, 1995).

Several different architectural strategies have been employed, from gradual transitions to reorganization of existing structures, to transition to an SLC model in a larger school. As Meier and others point out, however, it is not enough to simply divide existing school environments into four to six subgroups and expect improvements to take place automatically. Here are a few guidelines that are necessary for the success of SLCs. Architects might also use these terms, adapted from Cotton's work (2001), as qualitative program determinants for a more student-centered approach to school design, in addition to facility size and capacity.

Qualities of Small Learning Communities

Self-Determination: The SLC is characterized by autonomy, separateness, and distinctiveness; users have the ability to make internal decisions and to adapt and reform pedagogy as needed.

Identity: Everyone involved should have a common mission or vision that may include a thematic focus. The mission must emphasize student learning and be derived through continuous, detailed planning.

Personalization: Students are well known by as many adults and other students as practical. They are heterogeneously grouped instead of "tracked," and teachers typically stay with students for more than one school year. Parents and community members are more intimately involved.

Healthy Teacher Support: Educator support includes regular professional development, collaboration with peers, work in teams, and access to a large repertoire of instructional strategies or ways of teaching and learning.

Functional Accountability: Valid learning is credible, authentic, and accountable; uses multiple forms of assessment; makes use of SLC support networks; and is fully supported by the public school administration that accredits the school (Cotton, 2001; NREL, 2005).

How does architecture support these desired SLC traits, help maintain a positive school culture, and allow better capacities for learning for a greater number of students? The physical setting of a small school environment requires and enables a different architectural planning strategy from large comprehensive schools. In smaller progressive settings teachers typically take more planning time together, students and teachers also interact more with each other, and parents and community members become more involved. Spaces enable interaction and democratic dialogue.

▸ Physical surroundings may be unconventional, with movable, deployable furniture.

▸ Emphasize the welcoming lobby entrance or foyer with human oversight rather than the security screens of large inner-city schools. Include kiosks.

▸ Planning rooms where teachers may all gather around one table, advisory spaces for smaller groups of students, private (acoustical) conference rooms for discrete meetings, interdisciplinary learning areas, a common gathering-socialization space, and individual student and teacher work areas can all be part of small school settings.

▶ Attention to volume, scale, and shape personalizes the environment. Children have different site lines than do adults, which should be taken into account in design. Sense of scale, choice, independence, and autonomy can be reinforced through furniture systems that adjust to different heights, student access to storage, and student-operable windows and doors.

▶ Ceiling height should be in proportion to room size (generally, larger rooms have higher ceilings). Other materials such as banners or exposed framework can adjust to accommodate children's perceptions of ceiling height.

▶ Activity-based learning takes more space (volume/size per number of students) than traditional, passive modes of learning such as listening or writing.

▶ L-shaped rooms, alcoves, and niches humanize learning spaces, reduce disruption, and allow diverse activities to take place concurrently.

▶ Elements of schools should enable a broad exhibition of student work and reflect community culture.

▶ Schools can display their operation and identity in applied ecological ideals: floor tiles made from recycled plastic bottles, renewable bamboo laminate for wainscoting, light shelves, recycling venues, etc.

▶ Some small learning environments make use of existing community amenities and may choose not to build libraries, gymnasiums, or food service areas. This encourages interaction beyond the physical school setting.

Smaller learning environments are approximately 5 percent more expensive due in part to potentially higher salary costs. It is important to look at student performance outcomes, however, to determine the true value of SLCs. If the total costs expended for all students are divided by the number of students who actually graduate, smaller learning environments are of higher value because a greater number of students graduate. The costs in terms of human lives and value to society far outweigh any initial operating costs.

The small group gaming methods advocated here by Henry Sanoff rely on the power of visual information and graphic symbols as communication tools that bring people together during the community planning process. Sanoff has successfully initiated and implemented these methods for such diverse settings as Nanao, Japan; the Perpich Center for Arts Education in Minnesota; and a family center at Laguna Pueblo in New Mexico.

Methods of Community Participation

Henry Sanoff, PhD

Professor emeritus of architecture, North Carolina State University–Raleigh

INTRODUCTION

The activity of community participation is based on the principle that the environment works better if citizens are active and involved in its creation and management instead of being treated as passive consumers (Sanoff, 2000). Participation is defined as a general concept covering different forms of decision making by a number of involved groups (Wulz, 1986). Studies in small group behavior have produced evidence for the "participation hypothesis." Verba (1961) states that "significant changes in human behavior can be brought about rapidly only if the persons who are expected to change participate in deciding what the change shall be and how it shall be made."

To reveal an individual's knowledge and expertise and to increase awareness of environmental problems, the application of small group theories and gaming simulation form the basis of a new type of participation. Small group design gaming is a participatory approach to problem solving that engages a real-life situation compressed in time so that the essential characteristics of the problem are open to examination. This technique permits learning about the process of change in a dynamic environment requiring periodic decisions. Basically, a complex problem is identified, its essence is abstracted, and the end result is a process referred to as simulation.

The individual makes choices and holds positions and debates them, but the final goal of the exercise is a plan of action

In our increasingly visual society we often communicate through global symbols and graphic information. Photograph courtesy of Anne Taylor.

for an entire group of people—a goal that requires some compromising. Participants in these design groups learn about each other's value differences and use the game props to clarify and reconcile them. The props include objectives and graphic symbols corresponding to spatial activities, and the basic format is people working toward group consensus decisions.

Visual information is powerful. It is evident that nonverbal forms of communication are used to continuously transmit messages to people. For example, graphic symbols are often used as a guidance system in airports or the sites of large international events. People's increased reliance on graphic symbols suggests its possible application to cross-cultural communication and to finding common modes of communication between community members bound by different social norms.

The application of graphic symbols to building and site planning projects allows all people to participate equally, irrespective of their language or reading ability. Through the manipulation of activity symbols, participants directly experience the roles of architects and planners while gaining an appreciation of the consequences of their decisions. Such workshops also have an educational purpose, since participants become acquainted with relationships between human behavior and the environment. The potential value of the design games approach to participation constitutes logical, emotional, technological, and economical benefits.

Top: Teams presented their proposals at a community workshop for the development of a recreation area in Nanao, Japan. Photograph courtesy of Henry Sanoff.
Center: Perpich Center for Arts Education, Golden Valley, Minnesota. An architect team located on campus reviewed forty master plan proposals from 250 students and teachers, submitted as part of the participatory planning gaming process advocated by Henry Sanoff. Photograph courtesy of Henry Sanoff.
Bottom:: Perpich Center for Arts Education, Golden Valley, Minnesota. The completed music building resulted from student, teacher, and parent participation in the design process. Photograph courtesy of Henry Sanoff.

Questions remain about precisely why small learning communities are effective. In this study, Lackney uses the community metaphor of the neighborhood to create a positive school culture that will support learning. This project is from the early phases of a longitudinal research program seeking to define the specific physical conditions—the features, components, and organization—that make small school environments successful.

Involving Students in the Design of a Neighborhood Center within an Existing Large High School

Jeffery Lackney, PhD
American Institute of Architects

The widening gap between low- and high-achieving students motivated James Madison Memorial High School in Madison, Wisconsin, to apply for and successfully obtain a three-year U.S. Department of Education Small Learning Communities Federal Grant starting with the 2000–2001 academic year for initial staffing, remodeling costs, supplies and equipment, and training. The goal of the Memorial High "neighborhoods" was to close the achievement gap through test scores, attendance, grade point averages, and more; to create a collegial school culture; to build student leadership and ownership for the future direction of the school; and to increase student participation in extracurricular activities.

RESTRUCTURING

The project restructured the entire school of two thousand students into a nested organizational structure consisting of backyards, blocks, and neighborhoods. First, one hundred backyard groups of twenty multi-grade-level students and one teacher were formed, each with its own governance structure. Students were assigned randomly at the beginning of the year to a backyard group. Five backyard groups formed a block group of one hundred students, including a block council to plan and coordinate a variety of activities, such as undertaking service-learning projects, or making decisions to share at the neighborhood level. Five block groups combined to form one of the four large neighborhood groups (five hundred students and twenty-five faculty members). Each neighborhood had a "community center" in a newly remodeled space within the school, a "park" (green space immediately adjacent to the center), and an "improvement budget" (discretionary funds). At the neighborhood level, students might form study groups, clubs, or intramural sports teams.

Memorial's physical layout offered very limited common spaces for social interaction. A significant portion of the federal grant for this project was dedicated to the creation of a community center for each neighborhood in newly

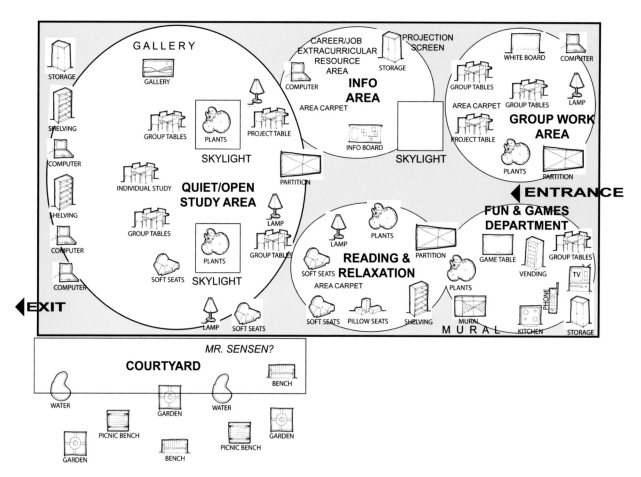

James Madison Memorial High School, Madison, Wisconsin.
Courtyard Neighborhood Center. Vision from a student design workshop. Image courtesy of Jeffery Lackney.

remodeled space at Memorial. Study-hall time was shifted into neighborhood center activities that emphasized achievement and productivity. After the school day, the neighborhood centers offered tutors and mentors an environment that was conducive to study and computers for those students who did not have access at home.

PLANNING NEIGHBORHOOD CENTERS WITH YOUTH

Autonomous neighborhood centers were identified throughout the building in available existing spaces of approximately 1,250 square feet that could accommodate sixty to seventy-five students at one time. These community centers were intended to act as nodes of organized activity. What should these neighborhood centers look like, and how should they be organized and managed over time? In order to practice building capacity in the student body, students were directly involved in having a say as to what they would like to see in the new neighborhood centers.

David Hoffert, former student at James Madison, showed initiative with his own ideas for the future in this computer-generated design inspired by involvement in planning at the high school. Digital image by David Hoffert. Image courtesy of Jeffery Lackney.

A series of design workshops were conducted with more than one hundred high school students from Memorial over a three-month period in determining the program, activities, organization, and layout of each neighborhood center. The first workshop involved the entire volunteer group of students and faculty working in small groups. The next two workshops involved subsets of students assigned to one of the four neighborhood center sites throughout the building. A series of design game exercises was employed in each workshop to facilitate student discussion.

In the final two workshops, students from all the centers were brought together and worked as cross-functional teams identifying furniture, equipment needs, and other components of the centers. The result of the workshops was a series of diagrams outlining the intentions of students.

CONCLUSIONS

Surveys and other research conducted by students revealed mixed results in early reaction to the neighborhood plan. A majority of students felt the restructuring would have some positive social impact and that the administration had listened to student input. Many students, however, remained cynical about the future success of the neighborhoods to bring about desired social and academic changes. The most important outcome was that young people got involved, and a few followed up with their own creative ideas.

PART FOUR

SEEING THE FUTURE OF THE LEARNING ENVIRONMENT WITH THE KNOWING EYE

Kuoppanummi School, Finland. Perko Architects.
Interior design by Architects Meskanen &
Pursiainen. Photograph by Jussi Tiainen.

CHAPTER NINE

Beyond the Existing Classroom

Introduction: How Can We Update Our Millions of Classrooms?

I hesitate to use the word *classroom* because it conjures an old picture that I would like to see replaced with a new multifaceted and flexible image. In *The Language of School Design* (2005), architects Prakash Nair and Randall Fielding ask, "Is the classroom obsolete?" Their answer is yes, but with the caveat that thousands of new classrooms are being added each year, joining the millions that already exist.

Though we are saddled with outdated classrooms, there are steps we can take to make learning and teaching more palatable through remodeling and reconfiguring of interior spaces to form learning studios, design studio workshops, small learning communities, and other optimal collaborative and interdisciplinary spaces. We can open up the classroom through fenestration and semiopen plans so that children can make visual connections between different learning activities and see how their actions impact others, reinforcing personal responsibility and self-reliance. Schools need diverse spaces to support multiple learning styles, to accommodate inclusion practices for specially abled students, and to shift from teacher-centered paradigms in education. We need entirely new furniture to support technology and to increase the flexibility of learning environments.

This book anticipates and recommends extreme change in our educational delivery system and in the architecture that supports it. This shift is reflected in our society today, which is moving from the information age to an inventive, intuitive, flexible, and "right-brain" conceptual age, as Daniel Pink described in *A Whole New Mind*, his book about the thinking processes that will serve us best in the future. The standard classroom or activity setting, today's basic building block or crux of learning for schools, must evolve, as must teaching practices as outlined earlier.

In chapter 9, I discuss how we can move beyond the boxlike conception of the classroom to create interior learning studios with furnishings and graphics that support a project-based, constructivist model for learning and new uses of technology. Chapter 10 completes my vision for the future of the whole school environment by encouraging radical transformation of the school grounds

Learning to read and compose music involves learning another language, in this case with the aid of digital tools. I believe that if everyone engaged in making music, the world would be a more peaceful place. Creative Learning Systems (CLS). Photograph by David Joel. Image courtesy of Matt Dickstein of CLS.

into learning landscapes, which are carefully designed spaces for interdisciplinary outdoor learning. Although presented separately in part 4, I envision a future with innovative school designs that blur distinctions between indoor and outdoor environments, seamlessly blending technology and ecology and transforming buildings from machines into sustainable, organic forms. The building and site will be considered as one entity, an educational park or campus, perhaps including many community services.

Linking People with Technology

Technology looms large in most visions for the future of learning. In *2020 Visions: Transforming Education and Training through Advanced Technologies*, several guest writers describe powerful new technologies that have the potential to transform the learning environment through simulations, visualizations, immersive environments, game playing, virtual tutors and mentors, networks of learners, assistive technologies for handicapped learners, automated archiving and tracking, and more (Neumann & Kyriakakis, 2002). The authors see a new partnership between technology and pedagogy due to broadband Internet capability and new remote immersion technologies. Technology "extends the classroom, opening it up to a vast treasure trove of educational experiences beyond the physical room walls and delivered in specific ways designed and crafted to enhance learning and understanding" p. 2–3). New methods to evaluate divergent creative thought will be generated, instead of relying solely on tests or metrics for convergent thinking. Information management technology will provide automated tracking of students' progress, including statistical models of presentation sequences and paths, providing instant feedback to the student, the instructors, and administrators (p. 2).

Open source technology—online material that goes beyond read-only to read/write through blogs, wikis, and podcasts— can transform how students learn and how educators gather and assemble information. This technology challenges many assumptions we have about the classrooms and textbooks we still rely on today. The world of the Web offers an abundance of knowledge, connections, and primary sources, and yet, as Richardson (2006) points out in *Edutopia*, "we teach in classrooms limited by physical walls, contrived relationships, and mind-numbing assessments" (p. 36). Rubenstein (2006), writing in the same issue of *Edutopia*, interviews educators who believe that open source resources will replace traditional textbooks. Many teachers are already using open source content to

Seeing the Future of the Learning Environment

supplement their primary texts. Educators and their students will assemble modules of information into personally designed courses or textbooks that offer more diverse and current information than is possible with more static textbook publications (p. 39). Young people are already well aware of this new world and educators have yet to tap its full potential.

Wireless technologies also are intriguing when we think of architecture and the configuration of educational spaces. A wireless laptop mobile lab requires far less space, offers more flexibility, and provides more opportunities for sharing equipment than a single room designated expressly for computers. Technology can move with the student and teacher and can be anywhere in a school, including expanding learning to the outdoors and fieldwork. New, increasingly portable devices change how and where we use technology.

Our commitment financially and in terms of teacher professional development is essential to the realization of these visions of technical literacy. Technical training is perceived as part of a trend toward professionalism of the teacher, and some have advocated that licensing standards include technical proficiency. Teachers must not only feel comfortable using technology, but also need to know how to adapt instructional strategies to move beyond computer drills to effective problem solving with technology, thereby aligning computer use with curricular objectives. As computer-assisted instruction evolves from drill, to tutoring, to dialogue, to real time hypermedia exchanges, teachers must learn new roles for acting as a facilitator to these processes.

In addition, we must fund desperately needed technical support staff to upgrade and maintain equipment and software. Technology support is stretched thin if it exists at all in our schools. Technology personnel should be prepared to act as educators for teachers who are reluctant to use technology. More support from community technology maintenance and upgrade experts can help teachers focus on their students while they integrate new technologies into their teaching strategies. The technology we envision for schools has also been used to increase opportunities for distance learning, reaching teachers everywhere in efforts to create a new generation of technologically literate educators.

Other issues that must be addressed when building a philosophy of technology are (1) working to overcome the digital divide by providing access to technology for all, (2) safety on the Internet, and (3) increasing media literacy so students learn how to conduct research online and critically evaluate what they encounter in the highly commercialized virtual world.

Despite the justified enthusiasm for the power of technology, a few words of caution are in order. The more we use cell phones, e-mail, and increasingly sophisticated technology, the more impersonal our relationships with each other seem to become. We must be thoughtful about technology and not forget that it is the love between us that needs to be fostered through social/emotional skills. Sometimes in the push to be constantly in virtual contact with friends or businesses, we neglect the people right in front of us. While reviewing the possibilities for the future in this chapter, I urge us all to keep in mind the necessity of human interaction with prevailing love and consideration for our fellow human beings.

A second observation involves how technology is used in the learning environment during this period of transition to a new model of learning. CEFPI recommends that technology be regarded as a tool for teachers and students, not as an end in itself (Myers & Robertson, 2004). Eileen Clegg of the Institute for the Future suggested in a recent online article about future schools that technology be viewed as an "enabler" rather than a "driver" of curriculum (Clegg, 2005, p. 2). We must integrate technology into the curriculum and, specifically in terms of curriculum reform, "technology works best when used with project-based learning techniques" (Myers & Robertson, 2004, p. 8–10). The technology we use should be aimed at a purpose that guides learning. As we continue to change, we must ask ourselves: What constitutes a well-rounded educated person in our society?

Six Models for Rethinking Classrooms

As a start, I have identified six ways to think about this much-needed architectural revolution based on examples from the research, design, and development work I have done with George Vlastos and other architects. Many of the designs are experimental and many of the concepts behind them overlap. They are variations on a theme of change rather than distinct entities. One day my colleagues and I would like to see these models refined, produced, and further tested as arenas for education. Our primary goal has always been to motivate children by empowering them to take active charge of their environments and their learning. The following examples are ordered loosely by degree of change from traditional models and the ease in which the changes can be made.

Model 1, the evolving remodel: Remodeling, reconfiguring, and updating existing classrooms, often with student help as a learning experience

Model 2, the diversity cluster: Providing diverse spaces for a variety of activities; learning zones, usually organized around a centralized group gathering space

Model 3, the technology studio: Motivational and technology-rich workspaces and plazas for learning, fully equipped and furnished to support technology use and deployability

Model 4, the cultural nexus: Concordia LLC architect Steven Bingler refers to schools as the nexus of community, which includes culture and community resources moving into schools, schools serving community, and preservation of cultural values through participation and design

Model 5, the home family learning center: A family learning environment created through conversion of traditional spaces in the home, also seen as a model for ambient treatment of smaller school spaces

Model 6, the mobile stage set: Deconstructing the classroom with flexible, deployable environments that may make use of traveling classroom kits, possible privatization of facilities, prefabricated environments, and leasing of updated furniture and equipment by school districts from private firms. Modern choices in furniture and flexible infrastructure support the mobile learning environment.

Case studies illustrating the six models follow.

MODEL 1: THE EVOLVING REMODEL

Teachers can involve their students and community members in the renovation or reconfiguration of their present classroom using the furniture and equipment they now have and with little or no expense.

We envisioned student participation in developing a sequence for evolving technology zones in the traditional classroom, a program George Vlastos and I designed for a Regional Educational Technology Assistance project with partners at New Mexico State University in Las Cruces, New Mexico. As classroom configurations evolve, so does the role of the learner from passive to active user of the environment. Older classrooms can be revitalized with the help of a master plan, which can be created with students and used as part of the curriculum to teach math, science, social studies, and language arts as well as the art of space planning and interior design. A summary of steps for creating and implementing a master plan follow.

Taking an Inventory

Students break up into four groups, each focused on one of four categories that compose the support system for learning. Space planning logic for classrooms includes investigating:

Curriculum: How the space is and will be used, what activities occur there

Architecture: Fixed elements such as floor, ceiling, walls, windows

Furnishings: Semifixed or mobile objects, bookshelves, chairs, desks, tables, cabinets, lights, storage, display

Resources: Movable items such as equipment and manipulatives (computers, DVD players, books, maps, toys, tools, etc.)

Student groups list objects, display results, and discuss the inventory.

Reconfiguring the Classroom to Reflect Student Empowerment:
A Series of Steps for Changing the Learning Space

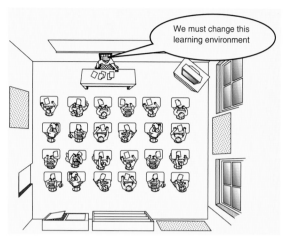

Step 1: Recognize that the typical classroom configuration and the mode of teacher-centered learning are unsatisfactory for twenty-first-century student-centered learning.

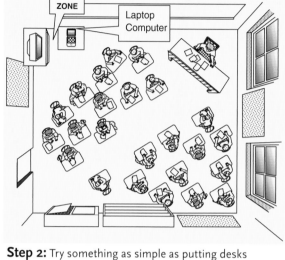

Step 2: Try something as simple as putting desks on a diagonal at a forty-five-degree angle to the walls. Align desks so they are not all facing the teacher as sole provider of information. Define a tech zone.

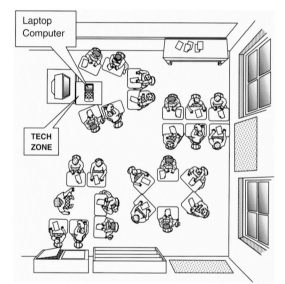

Step 3: Replace the teacher's desk with a side table, which enables the teacher to evolve into a facilitator, moving from small group to small group, with each group focused on its own problem to solve. The "power" has shifted to the student teams.

Step 4: Expand the technology zone. Provide configurations that support the entire learning process: research and experimentation, production, and presentation and reflection. Support individual, small group, and large group learning. The balance of power has shifted to the "gainfully employed" student.

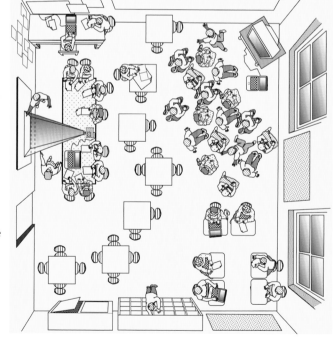

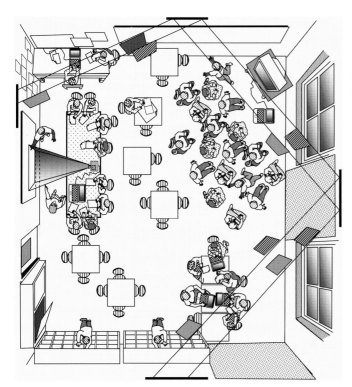

Step 5: Technology use is diffused throughout the learning space while maintaining a tech zone for teamwork and production. Add student work display space such as floor-to-ceiling tackable surfaces, suspended overhead display, storage, and drop-down elements.

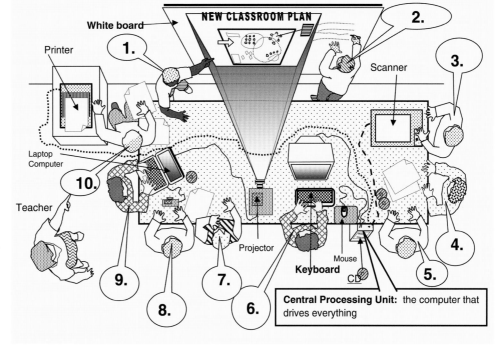

Enlargement of the technology zone. The tech zone is a microcosm of the shift in power. Now the teacher is a "guide on the side" and students are in charge of their own learning. The reconfiguration of spaces not only enables but also *requires* the evolution of teaching and learning strategies and radically alters the teacher's role.

Illustrations by George Vlastos.

1. **Group leader**
2. **Discussion leader**
3. **Scanner operator**
4. **Visual organizer**
5. **Keyboard operator's helper**
6. **Keyboard operator**
7. **Visual and text coordinator**
8. **Digital photographer**
9. **Laptop computer and digital projector operator**
10. **Hard copy editor**

Beyond the Existing Classroom

Drawing a Floor Plan of the Classroom

Groups of three or four students measure the classroom and work together to get correct measurements to scale on a sketch of the floor plan, which can then be finalized and copied for further planning.

Following the Planning Process

Defining the goal: Students define their planning goal. Designers call it "the scope of work."

Data collection: Students use research and interviewing skills to gather information including preferences for the new classroom (see chapter 10 for a child-friendly preference survey).

Design developments: Student groups take different aspects of the classroom and design them in bubble diagram form, using arrows and circles to show spatial relationships.

Presentation of ideas: Students pin up diagrams and present ideas. This fosters communication skills, from speech to video projections and computer graphics. Getting ready for the presentation in a logical and cooperative way helps students organize thoughts.

Implementing and Evaluating

Students, teachers, and parents implement change in the classroom based on their research ideas and evaluate how the project succeeded or did not succeed in realizing their goals. With this process, it is possible to make changes in small increments while reinforcing a sense of belonging and empowerment in students and teachers. As an example, with the help of architecture students and the permission of forward-thinking principal Vita Saavedra, parents and children took everything out of their second grade classroom at Los Ranchos Elementary School in Albuquerque and redesigned the total classroom. The corners of the room had not been used except to accumulate unrelated junk, so the students and volunteers invented a better use for the corners. An artist parent helped build a loft and with the students designed a variation on the Zia sun symbol for the loft area. The corner became a cozy place for children to read and acted as a personal space, something children crave but is not often provided in school.

Los Ranchos Elementary School, Albuquerque, New Mexico. Top: Before: Unrelated stimuli have no exhibit logic and are visually confusing to the student. **Bottom:** After: A redesigned corner space becomes a reading loft including a Zia sun symbol painted by a parent. Photographs courtesy of Anne Taylor.

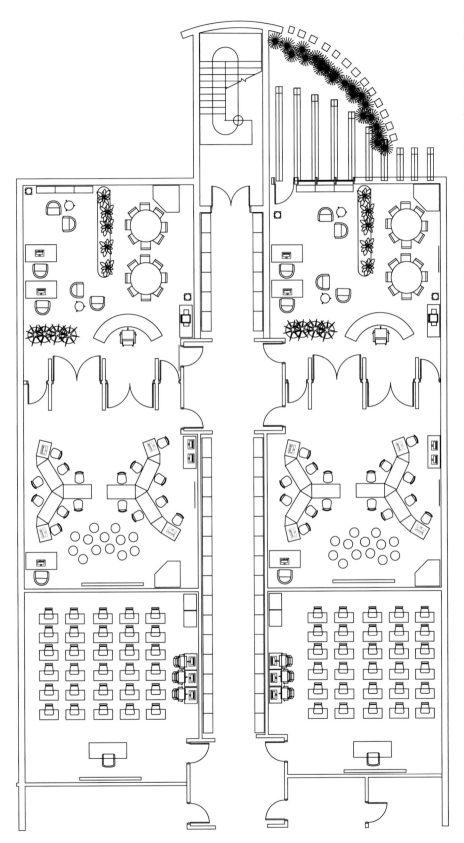

Remodeling can be extensive. In this plan view, we combined two classroom spaces to encourage technology use and independence in learners. At the bottom, classrooms are in the traditional configuration. The proposed combined spaces above allow students to move between activity zones including technological, multimedia, outdoor patio, presentation, a teacher zone, production/supply, library, storage wall, and small group learning settings. Doors between the original rooms could be eliminated. Original middle school concept by Van H. Gilbert Architect PC. Adapted by Robert Peters, architect, Anne Taylor, and Jerod Bosey.

White Sands Missile Range Kindergarten

The White Sands Missile Range Kindergarten gives children mobility and choices for learning experiences as they move through the school's space. The use of developmental needs and curriculum as design criteria has resulted in an innovative set of diverse activity settings, from small *nichos* (niches) or zones to a large open space as a forum and stage for plays, storytelling, and gross motor development.

ZONES OF DIVERSE LEARNING ENVIRONMENTS

An entry from the playground passes through a greenhouse, sand, and water play area with a concrete floor and a drain. One enters a curvilinear gallery-hallway where cubbies house coats and other items that often become clutter in many schools. An expansive gross motor forum of 830 square feet in the center of the space is used for large muscle play. A large stage is used for role-playing and storytelling. Block building, construction, and games occur in this forum.

Mirrored on either side of the large forum, along the perimeter of the two sides of the building, are "learning nichos" for children:

- ▶ Cooking/science zone
- ▶ Art, woodworking zone
- ▶ Library/museum zone
- ▶ Cognitive, literacy, computers, and communication zone

Children move through the environment each day but may spend one week in each learning zone for in-depth project-based learning with a particular theme. The thematic environment puts the child first, empowers the child to devise his or her own learning, and places the teacher in a role as a facilitator. In a POE by the architect, one of the teachers told us that she would quit her job if she ever had to transfer to another school. She loved the design of the learning environment as a workplace, its aesthetic, and the way it functioned and excited children to learn.

White Sands Missile Range Kindergarten, New Mexico.
Courtyard play area.
Van H. Gilbert Architect PC.
Photograph by Robert Reck.

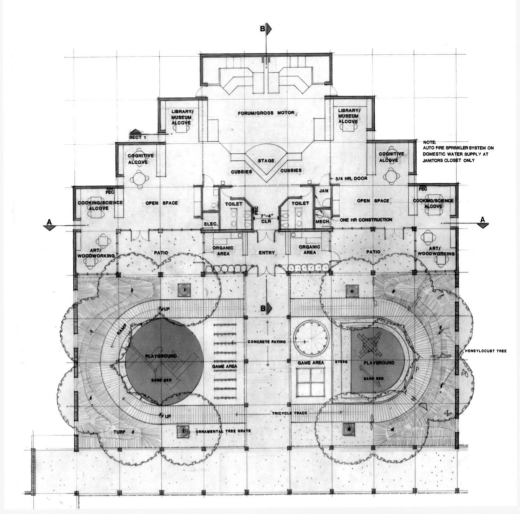

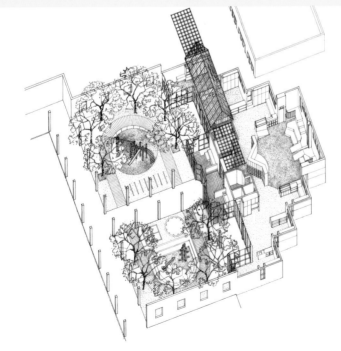

White Sands Missile Range Kindergarten, New Mexico. Above: Learning zones surround a central forum for gross motor play and creative dramatics. **Left:** Isometric view of interior and exterior. Van H. Gilbert Architect PC.

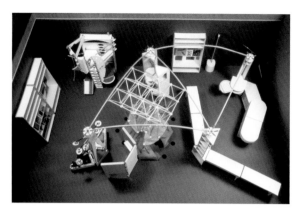

Head Start design model. Deployable elements
create learning zones in classroom space.
Courtesy of Anne Taylor and George Vlastos.

MODEL 2: THE DIVERSITY CLUSTER

Classrooms as Diverse Learning Environments in a School

A single or a few classrooms combined can be transformed into a cluster of spaces or zones where diverse learning experiences take place based on different subject matter areas, themes, and/ or ways of learning (such as multiple intelligences). Students move through the spaces rather than remaining at their desks. Similarly, rows of identical classrooms can be converted into different activity settings staffed by teacher experts, places for music, dance, career learning, solar greenhouses, or nutrition kitchens for cooking food from school gardens. Learning zones are an applicable design concept for all ages. The current replication of identically provisioned classrooms in elementary schools, where one teacher teaches everything, is obsolete and not cost-effective. Complementation replaces duplication with the model of diverse learning environments.

The Taylor/Vlastos Head Start classroom prototype combined the zones model with deployability and flexibility of learning settings (model 6). The values-driven design of portable environments was based on a fulcrum series of columns with electricity delivered overhead through arched pipes. (New wireless technologies could revolutionize this concept.) Foldout tables, which were nested, came out of trylon columns that could be rotated 359 degrees, transforming into deployable learning environment zones. These learning zones could be easily brought in and set up, providing for continuity of quality learning experiences in varied Head Start settings.

Metaphoric names for the zones were

The nest: A nonliteral multisensory soft
environment positioned to be the "heart" or
center of the room from which all events emanate
and return. This idea was derived from the
sacred nature of the Native American plaza.

The garden: A growing zone

The hearth: A nutrition and cooking
environment with an induction cooktop

The design studio: An art and design zone
with drop-down tables and light tables

The frame: A spatial relationship zone

The media center: A media center with
computer, drop-down keyboard with
headphones, and a DVD player

The construction zone: A building system zone

The showcase: A mirrored zone, for drawing and creative dramatics, and

The trash management system: For sorting, classifying, and recycling.

In a two-year experiment for Health and Human Services comparing adjacent prototype and traditional early childhood classrooms, the children preferred the "real" environment of the experimental setting to the "pretend" environment offered in the traditional environment. The design and results of the Head Start study are in the public domain (Taylor & Vlastos, 1993).

MODEL 3: THE TECHNOLOGY STUDIO

What can be done in schools with the technological advances available today? The technology studio often requires starting from ground zero and conceiving an entirely new learning environment, one that is larger and more open, where self-selection and an office or studio-like workspace motivates learners. There are many planes of information, not just one in a textbook, and learning involves using many forms of technology, not just computers. To bring educational facilities into the twenty-first century, architects and educators will have to collaborate with computer programmers, engineers, and equipment specialists to share new information and problem-solving techniques done with smart walls, intelligent paintbrushes, tactile and facial cues, and other biofeedback systems that affect schools' walls, windows, doors, and floors.

The model is an extension of the design studio with horizontal work surfaces, more and larger storage, appropriate and easily accessible tools, lighting controls, and places for problem solving, multimedia work, teamwork, presentation, and gallery display. The ambience is adaptable, autonomous, and free, encouraging self-directed learning. Attendance is taken through technology as students enter the learning environment, which is less disruptive than current methods. Students track their own learning schedules on PalmPilots and laptops and share ideas using interactive SMART Boards. Documentation will occur through student-directed videos, and electronic portfolios will summarize student involvement and accomplishment. The teacher is the coach, facilitator, and "guide on the side."

One technology studio of the future comes from the successful Creative Learning Systems (CLS), of San Diego, California. CLS helps schools design learning settings for the study of integrated and interdisciplinary science, technology, design, and engineering. It also fully provisions its SmartLab to support

Kuoppanummi School, Finland. Curvilinear desks and interior fenestration give a new look and accessibility to computers. Perko Architects. Interior design by Architects Meskanen & Pursiainen. Photograph by Jussi Tiainen.

Top: The CLS Technology Studio is an integrated system of furnishings, equipment, and computers for fostering independence in learning. Students are interested, excited, and challenged by technology, project-based approaches to learning, and creative problem solving. For example, CLS worked collaboratively to install a "smart lab" in Albuquerque's Southwest Secondary Learning Center. In state-mandated tests, Southwest Secondary Learning Center students' test scores now rank among the highest for all Albuquerque schools. In this environment all students are expected to succeed and accountability is paramount. **Bottom:** Students not only create designs, but also record and present their work, learning digital multimedia concepts. Creative Learning Systems. Photographs by David Joel.

eighteen to sixty students, or its Creative Learning Plaza for sixty to 150 students. While the system incorporates an extensive collection of computers and peripherals, it is more than the typical computer lab where machines are lined up against a wall around the perimeter of the room. This studio represents a totally integrated system of furnishings, equipment, and computers configured into an officelike environment. The aim of the CLS studio is to support self-directed learning based on learning theories of constructivism, multiple intelligences, and brain-based learning principles. A case study Creative Learning Systems released in 2005 cites dramatic improvement in standardized test scores after three years of collaboration at a New Mexico charter school. Students at the Southwest Secondary Learning Center used a CLS-developed SmartLab environment as a core element of their education program. Test scores in core subject areas increased by an average of 52 percent (Creative Learning Systems, 2005).

The integrated technology system of CLS acts as a powerful learning platform. The SmartLab provides learners with foundations in each of eight basic systems of technology or "core competencies." Included are some of the following resources for each of the eight learning strands.

Computer Graphics

Photo process manipulation

Animation and special effects

Bitmap graphics (digital painting)

Computer-aided drawing (CAD)

Science and Data Acquisition

Probeware for measuring sound, light, temperature, movement, voltage, rotational speed and acceleration, acidity of fluids, and human psychology

Laser exploration collection

Interactive strength challenger for compression and tensile testing and analysis

Jet Stream 500 Wind Tunnel for study of lift and drag forces

Robotics and Control Technology

Advanced Vex control system with software and interface

Fischertechnik control system

Lego NXT control system with software

The Mid-Pacific Institute
Technology Plaza, Honolulu, Hawaii

The institute is a preschool-through-twelfth-grade community whose campus includes the Mike and Sandy Hartley Math, Science, and Technology Complex, housing the Harry and Jeanette Weinberg Technology Plaza. The plaza, designed by CLS, unites learning zones provisioned with advanced technology not generally available to high school students. According to Mark Hines, technology coordinator, both learners and facilitators become part of the system they study; learners become teachers and teachers continue to pursue the goal of lifelong learning. Civic responsibility and technology are balanced through community service as part of the school program (Hines, 2006).

In addition to the plaza, classrooms in the institute are equipped with SMART Boards (large, interactive, touch-sensitive wall computers); lightning boards (combine functions of chalkboards, whiteboards, movie screens, and magnetic surfaces); video and audio equipment, including cable TV, DVD players, and VCRs; full network connectivity; and movable furniture.

Mid-Pacific Institute, Honolulu, Hawaii.
Top: Rendering of the Technology Studio Plaza.
Center and Bottom: Collaborative learning in a businesslike setting fully supported by technology from CLS. The teacher on the side acts as a facilitator in the new CLS environment. Teachers can also benefit from wireless microphones and headsets to increase their mobility. Images courtesy of the Mid-Pacific Institute and Creative Learning Systems.

Circuitry

Beginning and advanced microelectronic collection

Electricity exploration collection

Pneumatics exploration and silent compressor

Publishing

Music sequence and notation software

Project software or fast-track schedule software

Audio looping and Musicbed creation

Digital cameras

Desktop publishing

Computer Simulation

Car building software

Business simulation software

Flight Simulator and USB flight yoke

Three-dimensional model bridge simulation

SimCity

West Point bridge designer software

Mechanics and Structures

Capsela construction kits

Fischertechnik mechanism

Lego construction kits

Zome tool geodesic structuring and interdisciplinary learning system

Zoob construction system for rapid visualization and prototyping

Multimedia Design

Claymation animation kit

DVD/CD creation and labeling kit

Stop-motion animation software

Professional-quality camcorders

Video postproduction software

Super arm camera clamping systems, tripods, and dolly

Video monitors (Creative Learning Systems, 2008)

The technology labs can be opened on weekends and evenings for parents and the community as part of a plan to use the school building more fully and optimally (Creative Learning Systems, 2008).

Design for Technology Support

Angela Dando, formerly of the CLS organization highlighted here, recently made a few requests to architects preparing schools of the future based on her experiences with planning for installation of technical environments:

▶ In general, the new school learning environment should develop into a series of large spaces to contain the workstations that support group learning, with adjacent storage rooms, break-out rooms, and seminar rooms.

▶ Computers require a head-end room for the servers, data networking of the rooms, and electric power outlets to computers and equipment that is fixed but flexible to the needs of the students.

▶ Direct sunlight can readily bleach out computer monitors, especially when set up, not in rows, but in opposing locations to better support workstations. Light therefore needs to be bright but diffuse and indirect, with the possibility for blacking out certain rooms.

▶ Add a receiving and temporary storage facility with a loading-dock and roll-up door. This much overlooked but badly needed facility is so often missing from new schools. More than ever, the deliveries to schools from vendors of learning materials and computer equipment require that a loading dock and space for the maneuvering of pallets be present. Without such facilities, unloading becomes not only cumbersome, but expensive, when the cost of pallet deliveries by a truck, increased by having to include a pallet jack and a lift-gate on the truck, are passed on to the school district.

▶ Another issue is the positioning of electrical outlets and data cabling. In the school of the future, the ideal is actually a raised "power floor" that can take all cabling for data and electricity, and be more flexible, with more outlets. Furniture and equipment can move around more easily and all connections are then flush at table level (Dando, personal communication, February 14, 2006).

MODEL 4: THE CULTURAL NEXUS

Although technology is part of the cultural environment—as in the cyber café—the emphasis here is on nurturing community and on students as the caretakers of the future. This model is derived from the ideas in stewardship forum 3, which was devoted to community and the learner. The term "nexus" comes from the work of Steven Bingler in New Orleans. Schools are not only central showplaces for community, as students are also encouraged to extend their learning into the community through investigations off campus, service learning programs, and real-life learning. Interior and exterior designs reflect local influences to encourage a sense of ownership in students and the community at large.

Santa Fe Indian School, New Mexico. Left: Interior. Honoring tribal educational goals and preservation of culture at Santa Fe Indian School through use of natural and indigenous materials, local architectural styles such as the kiva fireplace, *latillas* (beams), carved corbels, bancos, and curvilinear forms. Regionally made furniture completes the attention to cultural detail. **Center:** Entry hall with tinwork sconces. **Right:** Kiva interior. Photographs courtesy of Van H. Gilbert Architect PC; ASCG, Inc.; Flintco Construction Solutions.

Bam, Iran. Educating children in participatory architectural design as part of rebuilding efforts following a major earthquake. Girls had the unusual opportunity to critique the boys' work. Image courtesy of René Dierkx.

The Santa Fe Indian School (SFIS) demonstrates the effectiveness of the community model, serving nineteen New Mexico pueblos (Native American villages along the Rio Grande). SFIS is regarded as the "twentieth pueblo" for students who will become caretakers of the culture. The recent upgrade of the middle high and high school campus in Santa Fe is a synthesis of meaningful ideas, beliefs, and spatial experiences indoors and out (see more about the SFIS master plan in chapter 10).

Important work for UNICEF by René Dierkx, an urban and education planner and architect from the Netherlands, represents models for best practices in sustainable design and community-based programming. In 2003, Dierkx worked with citizens of Bam, Iran, to help them rebuild after devastating earthquakes. As part of the project to design new schools, houses, hospitals, playgrounds, public parks, and urban infrastructure such as roads, water, and sanitation, he trained Iranian architects as facilitators and helped conduct urban planning and school design workshops with children in Bam.

Dierkx's goal in this and other programs is embedding the child-friendly school in the city. He sees schools as:

Three-dimensional textbooks for whole learning,

Ecosystems for whole settlement, and

Tools for community development for whole living.

MODEL 5: THE HOME FAMILY LEARNING CENTER

Many parents are choosing to homeschool their children. I have even seen old desks set up in a row for some home schools! Most home learning environments are makeshift, though many homeschooled children are using the potent resources of the community. Interior designers, architects, and home builders should begin to design "learning centers" in the home, or provide and provision spaces that can be converted for multipurpose use.

Home environments also have implications for student comfort levels in schools. In her research on design features that support project-based learning, Susan Wolff found that psychological and physiological factors such as sense of belonging and ownership, access to food and beverages, get away spaces, zones, caves, natural light, and other features contribute to the optimal collaborative project-based learning experience (Wolff, 2002). Many architects know that including some of the comforts of home can humanize schools, making them more attractive to students. And by humanizing schools, I do not mean the worn-out, dirty, torn, and overused couches that are sometimes donated to schools. I am talking about a variety of attractive, well-designed, appropriately scaled, functional places for conducting student work and encouraging social interaction.

Cleveland Public Library, Villa Angela branch, Cleveland, Ohio. Reading area with a vivid red couch. Richard Fleischman + Partners Architects, Inc. Photograph by Eric Hanson.

Fountain Valley School, Colorado Springs, Colorado. A college preparatory, coed, boarding, and day school. What better way to reflect the cultural model than through homelike schools or schools that were once literally homes? **Top:** Penrose East Commons. Fountain Valley's sense of place and distinct aesthetics are part of its seventy-five-year history. **Bottom:** Frautschi Campus Center. Photographs courtesy of Fountain Valley School.

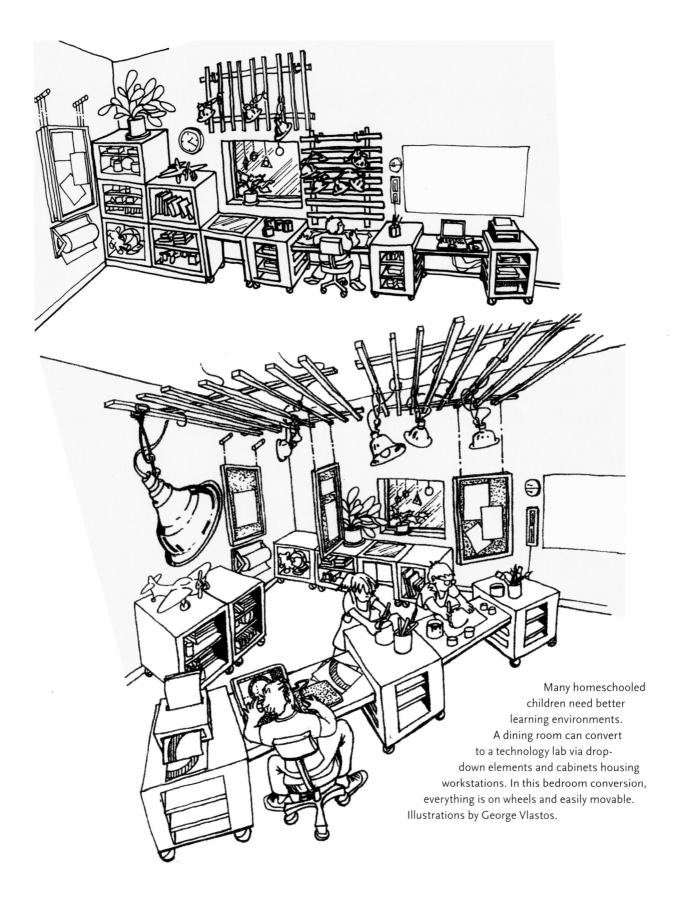

Many homeschooled
children need better
learning environments.
A dining room can convert
to a technology lab via drop-
down elements and cabinets housing
workstations. In this bedroom conversion,
everything is on wheels and easily movable.
Illustrations by George Vlastos.

Seeing the Future of the Learning Environment

MODEL 6: THE MOBILE STAGE SET

The mobile stage set can take many forms. My early research and development of learning environments projected the "classroom in a box" that would unfold as dynamic and ever-changing theatrical set designs on themes of interest to children. The Head Start zones described earlier highlight the idea of flexibility and deployability through design of trylons with drop-down elements. We have envisioned a mobile and deployable Techno Tent that would travel to rural schools and a CyberVillage conceived as deployable learning environments within high-quality portable buildings that could be composed into a school. At the end of this chapter I examine the need for updated versions of school furniture for the twenty-first century. In a sense, modern ideas for deployable, mobile furniture return us full circle to model 1, in which children are involved in reconfiguring their existing classrooms. New types of furniture make the transformation of spaces easier than ever before.

The empowerment of mobility is at the heart of all the design models and should not be underestimated. As Childs (2004, p. 156) writes of seating in public spaces, "A major design factor in providing for social comfort is the movability of the chair. People adjust chairs to form conversation groups, signal civil inattention, . . . watch passers-by, and express an infinity of other body language. In this sense, chairs, like clothes, can be an extension of our bodies." The arrangements we create for our spaces communicate our intentions.

CyberVillage

As part of an exploratory design team, Vlastos and I proposed an offering for middle schools that would empower students to configure their own environments for selected curricular experiences. We conceived the learning environment as a theatrical set design based on a hexagonal system of ceiling geometry and well-designed portable buildings that could be composed into a school. This movable system of buildings has no resemblance to present portable buildings. We not only designed the environments but also developed curriculum scenarios around the environments that helped students envision making studio production spaces, stage sets for plays, galleries for presentations and critiques, cooking environments for outdoor fairs, and other activity settings based on curricular needs. Technology was a great part of this model, including the "village videot" who was the documentarian for events taking place in CyberVillage (School Zone, Inc., 1997).

Techno tent on the move.

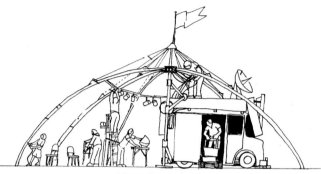

Assembling the techno tent.

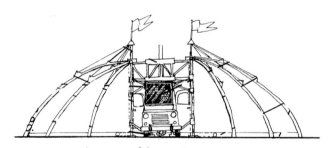

Front elevation of the tent's superstructure.

University of New Mexico, Albuquerque.
The Techno Tent project aimed to teach technology through design education in rural areas of New Mexico. The traveling Techno Tents were to be deployable, contemporary in design, pressurized to ensure cleanliness and ventilation, and staffed with educators who would provide training using the advanced technological equipment contained in the tents. Students and communities also could use the technology as part of the participatory planning process for schools and community facilities (Taylor & Brown, 1998). Image courtesy of Anne Taylor and Charlene Brown.

CyberVillage. This experimental design for a movable building structure with hexagonal ceiling system grid bears no resemblance to typical portables. School Zone Institute. Illustration by George Vlastos.

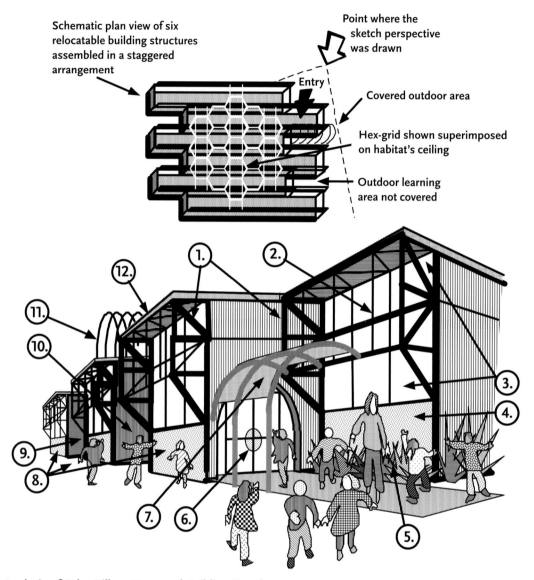

Schematic plan view of six relocatable building structures assembled in a staggered arrangement

Point where the sketch perspective was drawn

Entry

Covered outdoor area

Hex-grid shown superimposed on habitat's ceiling

Outdoor learning area not covered

Analysis of CyberVillage Entry and Building Facade

1. Steel truss extensions.

2. Vertical space frame as part of building's wall structure.

3. Glass windows set behind space frame.

4. Special stuccoed surface at entry for graphics and outdoor entry art (windows above wall can be used in the same way).

5. Seasonally appropriate entry plantings selected and designed by learners.

6. Special entry security system that opens with ID card.

7. Translucent entry canopy scaled for learners.

8. Special stuccoed walls for learners to paint and create supergraphic artwork.

9. Outdoor learning area that works as transition between indoor and outdoor activities.

10. Another outdoor learning area that can change to meet the space required by learners.

11. A structure that covers an outdoor learning area for year-round outdoor activities.

12. Deep overhangs for sun control.

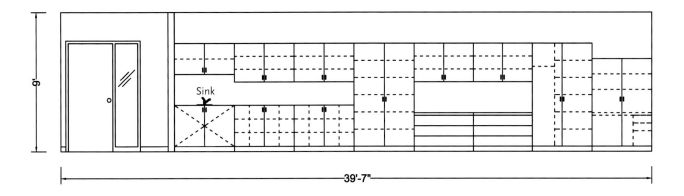

6'

39'-7"

Learning Wall / Stelter Partners

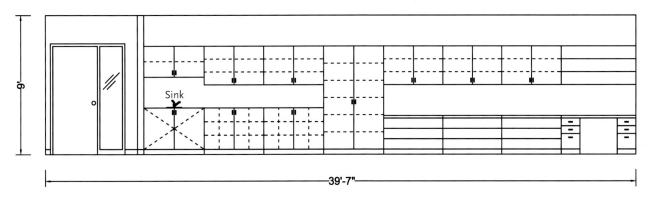

6'

39'-7"

Learning wall. Elevation drawing of built-in casework that supports learning. Customized elements with easily accessed storage for students below and more space above for teacher use could also house drop-down tables. Drawing by Beverly Diddy. Furniture by Stelter Partners.

Business Assistance to Schools

Schools of the future will provide square footage for companies that will keep schools current by installing technological equipment, furniture, and appropriate storage, and servicing the technology to keep it usable. This educational business service will provide a high-tech, high-quality mobile system to be "drop shipped" and installed with all the systems integrated within its architecture, ready to become a vital part of an ever-changing learning environment. The business world already makes use of ready-to-install prewired floors, wall units, and partitions. Imagine classroom-sized kits or labs that come fully equipped with the latest technology has to offer, or specific learning environments based on subject matter disciplines: botany and physics labs, architectural design studios, math manipulative labs, media or filmmaking centers, and more.

This learning environment will include equipment such as printers, digital cameras, LCD projectors, keyboards, scanners, personalized data assistance devices (handheld tablets with styluses), cell phones, iPods, video cameras, and projectors that act as a means to an end for self-expression.

"Surface intelligence" will move us beyond the chalkboard. Smart surfaces (panel systems with embedded media technologies) offer new options for display, communication, and presentation in the form of virtual flipcharts, image capturing systems, front and rear projection screens, interactive whiteboards, and Web-based signs. SmartSlab systems offer higher-resolution images than traditional screens and large format display technology that can be used for walls, floors, billboards, and buildings. This technology is load-bearing, interactive, allows for global simulcasts and remote data transfer, and is no doubt evolving even as you read this.

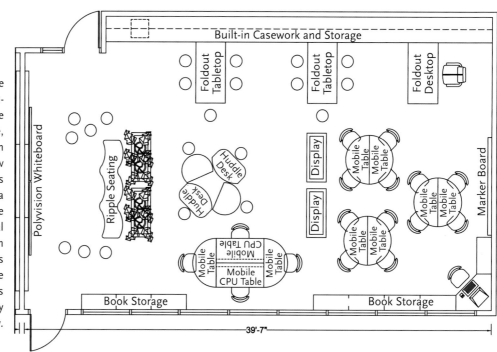

Not only can the whole environment be drop-shipped, but within the learning space, mobile, modular components can be arranged to create new spatial possibilities. This schematic drawing of a learning environment of the future employs individual deployable and drop-down furniture components discussed later in the furniture section of this chapter. Drawings by Beverly Diddy.

Variation 1. Reconfigured environment using flexible, mobile furniture components.

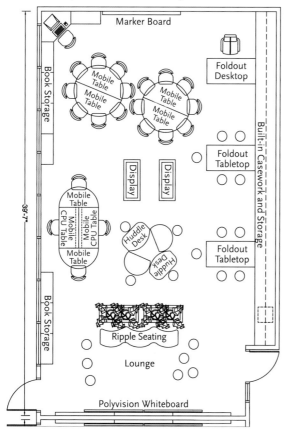

Variation 2. Furniture supports different learning styles and groups through the arrangement of components.

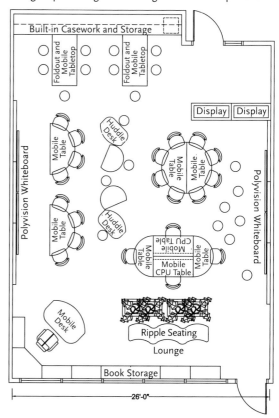

Relocatable Buildings (Portables) and Modular Building

Many environmental quality issues found in regular classrooms are exacerbated in the thousands of portables we find at more than 36 percent of our nation's schools. Some problems that are more frequently found in portables according to a 2004 report from the California Air Resources Board include inadequate ventilation, high classroom noise, poor thermal comfort, inadequate lighting, and toxicity levels from materials used in construction as well as outside pesticides and pollutants. In response, new designs in modular construction address environmental stewardship as well as safety, health, and durability. Los Angeles architect Jennifer Siegal has been working to meet this challenge by creating designs that open up the portable classroom with large windows and higher ceilings. Her designs also call for portables with garden areas maintained by students. Sustainable materials selection, careful siting, and use of color ensure comfort and aesthetic satisfaction while acknowledging the functionality of the portable classroom.

VITETTA, an architecture and engineering corporation, designed a prototypal "Little School House" to be adapted to various sites for full-day pre-kindergarten programs in Pennsylvania. The program consisted of a core element with an entry vestibule, lobby, administrative space, and a multipurpose room. Classroom modules with bathrooms attached to the sides of the core allowed for flexibility specific to the site (VITETTA, 2007).

The Traveling Exhibit

Museums of all kinds are saving money by sharing and renting traveling exhibits. According to an article by Andrew Webb (2006) in the *Albuquerque Journal*, a local exhibit developer has teamed with a major science museum and the publisher of the Eyewitness line of science books for young readers to create durable displays with up-to-date content in a variety of mediums that will appeal to a range of audiences. Similar prepared installations could be a big hit in our schools, drawing in community and giving students a chance to learn curatorial skills.

Autonomous Designs

Students become responsible for their own learning when they "set the stage" themselves, configuring the environment based on their own goals. Architecture and furniture that support this premise are extremely flexible, multipurpose, deployable, and not predetermined but left open to the user. This model employs movable partitions and lighting, furniture on wheels, modular furniture systems, tackable surfaces, and ample storage.

Herman Miller Furniture systems for reconfiguration: This system is based on patterns built on the concept of 120-degree angles. Shown here in plan view is the Delta system for workstations, including poles with screens offered at three heights. Other patterns include the Honey, Zigzag, Shell, Wide Shell, and the Half-Honey. The system demonstrates considerable geometric efficiency and could offer additional versatility to users of school furniture. Image courtesy of Herman Miller Furniture. Resolve System. Designed by Ayse Birsel and the Resolve Team.

The design is a support system that will highlight and augment the work of the student but not dictate what type of experience occurs. If a studio is needed for drawing, painting, or model building, students will create it with large, drop-down horizontal surfaces and the appropriate tools. If a gallery is needed for display or to make presentations and have critiques, students will design and make it. If a technology zone is needed for group work, students will assemble the necessary components and set up communications. Teachers will be coaching on the side, diagnosing and prescribing as architecture professors do when they critique at individual desks in a design studio.

Seeing the Future of the Learning Environment

The Future of Furniture

To conclude my vision for interior environments of the future, I examine furniture as a microcosm of all I have discussed for transforming school classrooms. New and creative uses of furniture have implications for all six design models. Many school districts have relied on the same tired old furniture and lighting ideas for years. The furniture budget is often slighted due to lack of knowledge, poor planning, or cost overruns during other phases of construction. For whatever reason, the penurious mentality of those who provision schools has spawned a whole industry of furniture that may be inexpensive, yet is also unattractive, outdated, and ergonomically incorrect. Lack of storage or the wrong kind of storage remains a huge problem for students and teachers, creating chaos and overstimulation in the learning space and violating fire codes. Our increasing understanding about the importance of indoor air quality also must be taken into account when selecting interior décor (see the Greenguard Environmental Institute for a certification program and criteria). In short, many of us would not think of working with the furniture one finds in school settings, especially when it becomes damaged, neglected, and dirty. Students deserve healthy, safe, and beautiful design—design that is of the future, not the past.

Backpacks and student projects pile up on classroom floors and in corners, adding to the visual confusion. Photograph courtesy of Anne Taylor.

WHO CAN HELP?

I recommend that school officials include architects and interior designers in the decision making about furniture early in the design process. Experts can ensure that the furniture we use for children is ergonomically correct as well as durable. In an article about accessorizing the classroom, Mike Kennedy (2002, June) writes that the fees saved by leaving professionals out of the selection and bidding processes are miniscule compared to the long-term costs of making poor decisions. Furniture and equipment longevity, upkeep, and ease of repair factor heavily into operations and maintenance costs.

Health experts can weigh in with current research on ergonomics and posture and the effects of indoor pollution or new technologies on student populations.

It is also my hope that the furniture industry will step into the school arena with some of its new designs. We have only to look to the business world and "office landscaping" to find inspiration for improved designs for schools, including not just furniture but storage and display systems, smart surfaces, lighting, and elements for spatial configuration such as easily deployed shelving, partitions, and portable post and beam systems. Creative

Two sizes of the mobile laptop lab from Anthro Corporation store twenty or thirty computers in a compact cart with internal outlets for recharging computers built into the cart. The top shelf of the cart can hold a network printer, wireless AirPort hub, and/ or projector. The cabinet has vents for air circulation, heavy-duty casters, and locks. Image courtesy of Anthro Corporation, Technology Furniture.

"Technology walls" placed on tables, housing digital functions. Implied spaces are defined with flexible post and beam structures, which can be enclosed or left open. Steelcase, Inc. PolyVision. Vecta. University of Connecticut, Schoenhardt Architecture and Interior Design. BKM Total Office. Image courtesy of Business Environments, Albuquerque, New Mexico.

University of Connecticut

School of Business Graduate Learning Center
Source: Steelcase, Inc. (2005)

THE INTEGRATION OF ARCHITECTURE, FURNITURE, AND TECHNOLOGY

Planners at the University of Connecticut envisioned a graduate learning center that would be part college, part research lab, and part working business. Renovations of an existing building were put on the fast track: four months of construction were completed for a total of forty thousand square feet on four floors.

To support learning goals, technology had to be easy to install, manage, and change. Some solutions included the following:

▶ Installation of Pathways Low-Profile Floors, three-inch raised floors. Beneath the floor are miles of power and data cabling.

▶ Modular power and cabling systems arrived precut and pretested, ready for plug-in installation.

▶ Pathways Technology Walls, including integrated ports and interchangeable modules provide power, voice, and data for supporting technology.

▶ Steelcase movable walls, which arrive on-site fully assembled and prewired, provide flexible infrastructure and transparency for interior environments where desired.

▶ Creative use of Ellipse furniture, including tiered furniture set at different heights, rather than tiered classrooms, which are more expensive. Furniture has wheels for movement in and out of break-out rooms.

▶ Hallways include café tables and stand-up islands with data connections and wireless service to bring students together in casual groups.

design and use of flexible furniture systems can replace expensive fixed infrastructure costs (see the University of Connecticut case study). Several furniture companies that I have contacted through the years have felt that the school furniture business was not lucrative, but the picture is changing now and some are marketing to schools, especially universities, attempting to change the settings in which our children and adults learn.

Newest designs for offices support my idea that the fixed classroom with fixed products is obsolete. The furniture of the future is on wheels, reconfigurable as break-out spaces, studios, collaboration "coves," and presentation galleries. As mentioned earlier, a mobile laptop lab with a wireless hub can serve many students, while a mobile console with wireless headsets can turn any space into a language lab. Chairs stack, and tables fold down or up or are rolled away to provide more space. Retractable, flexible furniture can be housed in inclusive wall, ceiling, and floor systems. Flip-down computers can be concealed within desks and tables when not in use, and drop-down beds can be used in nurses' offices. Designers at Steelcase, a furniture manufacturing company based in Michigan, remind us that the learning environment is no longer a passive backdrop, but rather an essential tool to support active problem solving and changing technology.

All of the school models for change discussed previously in this chapter can benefit from furniture that is

Orderly	Drop-down
Clean	Deployable
Comfortable	Stackable
Modern	Nesting
Beautiful	Modular
Natural	Portable
Personalized	Clustered
Creative	Configurable
Mobile	Green and produced
Adjustable	with sustainable technologies, and
Ergonomic	
Foldable	Low-emitting (indoor air quality).
Detachable	

Furniture for the Future
These photos and those through page 310 offer just a few examples of the many possibilities for making our school environments contemporary, dynamic, deployable, and supportive of new learning styles.

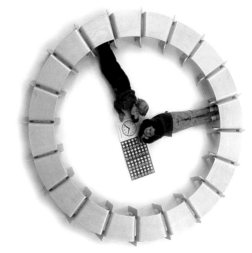

Top: A lobby with post and beam partitions offers choice and flexibility for spaces through different degrees of transparency in selected panel materials. Image courtesy of Business Environments, Albuquerque, New Mexico. Steelcase, Inc.
Bottom: Children can connect stools that support up to five hundred pounds to form circles, zigzags, or snakes. Twelve-inch-high stools can double as lap desks and can easily be carried by a toddler. Kinderlink Educational Furniture, Inc.

Water table. Community Playthings. Used by permission.

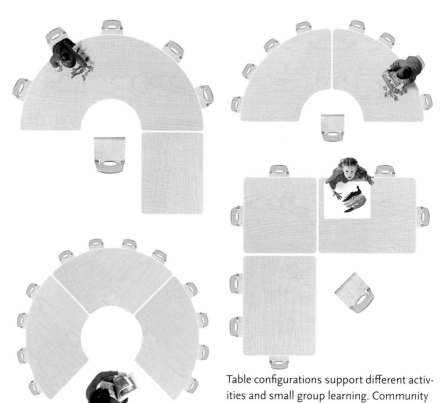

Table configurations support different activities and small group learning. Community Playthings. Used by permission.

Child-scale curvilinear furniture defines play spaces. Community Playthings. Used by permission.

Round, nesting flip-top Au Lait tables designed by Russell Plant and the Vecta Design Team, and Kart stacking chairs designed by 5D Studio. Image courtesy of Business Environments, Albuquerque, New Mexico. Vecta.

Assisa stacking chair on wheels. Vecta increases options for flexibility with its dolly for these stacking chairs. Images courtesy of Business Environments, Albuquerque, New Mexico. Vecta.

Seeing the Future of the Learning Environment

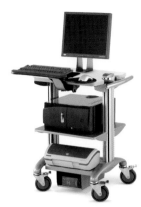

Convoi functional carts on wheels allow users to configure personal mobile workstations. Image courtesy of Anthro Corporation, Technology Furniture.

Computer system desk on wheels for easy deployment. Curved console for video editing and other multimedia work. Image courtesy of Anthro Corporation, Technology Furniture.

The teacher tech center can be hidden from view when not in use. The computer center could be on wheels and reconfigurable as part of a storage wall system or learning wall described earlier. Image courtesy of Business Environments, Albuquerque, New Mexico. Stelter Partners. LearningWorks.

PolyVision's Walk-and-Talk interactive whiteboard transforms the standard classroom from a passive, static space into a unique, creative learning environment. Teachers and students can display and interact with information, as well as revise, save, and print anything written or projected on the board. Image courtesy of PolyVision Corporation.

Hat storage in a Japanese school. Photograph courtesy of Anne Taylor.

Cedar Valley Community School, Lynnwood, Washington. Activity areas near classrooms are defined by casework with display, storage, and deep-sink wet areas for art projects. A continuous clerestory provides daylighting to interior spaces. Mahlum Architects. Gerald "Butch" Reifert, principal architect. Mitchell Kent, AIA, project architect.

Ripple pliable seating can be used as a flattop or wave-top surface and as a space divider. Image courtesy of Brayton International. Design by Laurinda Spear, FAIA.

RoomWizard, a Web-based tool for scheduling rooms and monitoring room availability, usually mounted at the room's entry. Image courtesy of Business Environments, Albuquerque, New Mexico. PolyVision Corporation.

East San José Elementary School, Albuquerque, New Mexico. Personal storage units. Cubbies with curved lines tucked into an alcove rather than taking classroom floor space encourage stewardship of and responsibility for personal possessions. Garrett Smith Ltd.

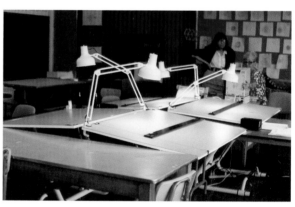

Task lighting and drafting tables are part of a studio design lab. Photograph courtesy of Anne Taylor.

Children's Art Resource Room. Virginia Museum of Art. These drop-down tables and storage units can be used to manage space during classroom or shared space usage and can also be built into large rooms such as cafeterias for conversion to activity centers for after-school or community use. VMDO Architects.

There is a need to reexamine the students and faculty as consumers. Some manufacturers set up showrooms of furniture, providing the opportunity for learners to state choices and preferences for the furniture they will use. For presentations on new ideas for furniture, I have written day-in-the-life scenarios that depict how students can use the furniture to create their own spaces and to support their own project-based learning. These narratives are effective for bringing needed changes to life in the imaginations of those who provision our schools.

Provisioning of Learning Environments

Choice of furniture is just one of many provisioning concerns for schools. Excellence for schools is reflected in the details, including the smallest items we select as learning tools for children of all ages. The logic behind these choices can be made accessible to the teacher as well as students so that every object in the environment becomes an effective part of the environmental curriculum. In work with the Louisiana Children's Museum in New Orleans, Anne Taylor Associates developed an education-based inventory for evaluating every object within each exhibit. Worksheets allowed docents and teachers to examine exhibits in terms of school district standards and key interdisciplinary concepts, and suggested related learning experiences for more in-depth use of the exhibits. For the Keystone Early Learning Center in Alabama, we developed "provision pages" consisting of a database for educational inventory with the ultimate goal of using the environment and the objects within it to maximum capacity. The inventory not only provided purchasing information, but also linked provisions to educational and developmental data across the body, mind, and spirit of the child. The idea was that a teacher could access information based on the prescribed needs of the child, tailoring the environmental curriculum and use of manipulatives to the individual. A sample of a provision page is found at the end of this chapter in Tools for Thought. Its use could easily be expanded to include other age groups, with corresponding provisions and developmental data stored on computers.

Cultural artifacts, works of art, plants, and other aesthetic touches also round out the image of the learning environment of the future as a desired destination and source of inspiration for students and teachers.

| Provisions X | Zone: | ☐ infant | ☐ toddler | X preschool |

Description: Unit Blocks—Preschool Set

Supplier Information:

Community Playthings

Phone:

Fax:

Web site:

Size: Weight:

Catalog #:

Page: Date:

Price:

Quantity:

Location of Provision
☐ Art and Design
☐ Cognitive and Technology
☐ Cooking and Nutrition
☐ Entry and Parent Display
☐ Greenhouse
☐ Music and Dance
☐ Playground
☐ Science and Museum
☐ Storage
X Zone A (Open Area)

Subject Matter
X Art and Design
☐ Dance/Movement
☐ Ecology
☐ Health and Nutrition
☐ Language
X Math
☐ Music
☐ Physical Education
X Science
☐ Social Studies
☐ Technology Integration

Body

Visual Setting
To be able to sort by color, size, shape, use, or other categories.

Visual Comparison
Examines the character of a particular object by color, size, shape, texture, use, etc.

Activities for Fine Motor Development (Examples)
Stack graduated-size objects.
Build a tower with blocks.
Develop precision by manipulating forms and building complex structures.

Keystone Early Learning Center, Montgomery, Alabama. Provision pages, 1998.
At Keystone, designers envisioned a computer database for an educational and developmental inventory system for environment-based learning. This example explores the potential of well-made, well-proportioned, architectonic blocks from

Mind

Experimental and Discovery Concepts

Child experiments with various tools, items, or mediums (including art and music). Child describes why he or she was using the blocks in a particular way. Child explores new ways to use familiar items.

Form and Function Concepts

Child understands that a point becomes a line, a line becomes a shape, then a form, then a building, and many buildings make a city (math concepts).

Position Concepts

Child develops an understanding of placement and of object in reference to another object—up/down, in/out, top/bottom, over/under, near/far, left/right. Move from simple to complex building/structures. Balance, symmetry, asymmetry, and geometry have purpose.

Creative Problem Solving and Hypothesis Testing: Construct and Build

Using blocks, Legos, or other building materials for construction play gives children an opportunity to figure out how they can create a structure from the materials.

Expression/Valuing

Visual Art Communication

Children view and create their own architecture to better appreciate the aesthetic expressions of others and themselves. How can the children express an idea they have in pictures?

Valuing: People/Sharing

To develop a sense of valuing other people, children cooperate with others in group projects, share materials, and help each other finish projects.

Social: Group Pride and Accomplishments

Imagination and Fantasy

Children design their own structures and watch their ideas take on shape and form.
Children incorporate the use of other toys.
Children create stories/themes to accompany their play.

Self-Esteem through Physical Accomplishment

Children develop muscle coordination and increase pride.

Group Expressions and Creativity

Children participate in art projects to allow for group and individual expressions of creativity.

Behaviors to Notice

Body

Child sorts blocks by size, shape, color, etc.

Child demonstrates skill in balancing blocks, stacking blocks, or building a tower or more complex structure.

Child places blocks in a precise manner and demonstrates motor control and muscle coordination.

Child loads, unloads, and maneuvers block storage cart.

Mind

Child demonstrates position concepts using blocks, and uses placement and shape language.

Child builds simple to complex structures and shows creativity.

Child explores and describes math concepts including length, volume, fractions, and geometry.

Child describes what he or she has created, referring to both function and fantasy.

Child compares his or her structures to real buildings/elements of architecture.

Expression

Children work together for an extended time to create a complex structure.

Children create individual and group stories to accompany their designs.

Children act out scenarios based on function of structures in real life.

Children draw, paint, sculpt, or design plans for architecture.

Children show group and individuals in built structures.

Community Playthings for teaching concepts across body, mind, and spirit, and concludes with behaviors to observe for assessment of the child's learning. © Community Playthings, blocks image used by permission. Concordia LLC, Chambless and Brown Architects, and Anne Taylor Associates.

This excerpted article by Bruce Jilk challenges many assertions about programming. Not only are the theories expressed here refreshing and enlightening, but their implementation is also feasible and well within our grasp, as illustrated in the architectural case study that follows this article.

Contingency and Place Making for Learning

Bruce Jilk

Architect and educational planner

INTRODUCTION

Our current approach to learning, measured against what is possible, is like the narrow band of visible light compared to the rest of the electromagnetic spectrum. The possibilities that we cannot see are immense. Imagine expanding the potential for learning and creating more places where learners are engaged, enthusiastic, and motivated.

To do this, we must abandon practically everything we know about today's school facilities. Both the process and the content for school design have been focused on functional efficiency. The functionalist's narrow interpretation of schools is increasingly limiting and is being called into question, resulting in numerous attempts by school planners and users to inject flexibility into old designs. School facilities still remain unsupportive of multiple effective learning strategies.

One new approach is to frame the problem around the idea of contingency. The definition of contingency used here is "that which is dependent on conditions or occurrences not yet established." Actually integrating contingency concepts into learning and the design of learning environments is a necessity.

Economics and public policy are pressuring educators toward changes in their approach to learning while communities expect a long-term return on their investment in schools. To be sustainable we must design simultaneously for greater longevity and increased flexibility of use. This will result in facilities that are not only durable but will also accommodate numerous use patterns, including noneducational use. Schools must not only be designed for their first life, but also for their second, third, and even fourth lives. The following will explore these new strategies as they apply to the classroom, the whole school, and the community.

THE PURPOSE

There are limited resources in society, so the objective of an efficient education (a quantity measure) is certainly valid. But that by itself falls short of the goal of a good education. Education also needs to be effective (a quality measure). Certainly the design of learning environments should be responsive to supporting effective education. Although most people would agree with this, in practice this has not been the case. Our efficiency-driven learning environments become barriers to the creativity of learning.

Creativity is used here in the broadest sense, as an aspect of human behavior that encompasses more than the creativity of an artist or a composer. To form a word as you speak, to imagine an image in your mind, or to recognize the smell of a flower takes a creative action in the mind. To hit a ball is to act creatively. In learning, one formulates thoughts in the mind that did not exist there before. Learning is a creative action.

The purpose is to enable learner creativity. The learning setting needs to engage the learner. This is why the wilderness is such a powerful place. When you are in the wilderness it is out of necessity that you are engaged and thinking creatively in order to take action. Unfortunately, to ensure discipline and behavior control, creativity is designed out of schools, and the environment becomes a barrier to actions not predetermined. The users are told what to do—to take noncreative action. This is often done in the name of safety and security. These concerns are important, but it is possible to achieve them without resorting to a prisonlike, barrier-impregnated atmosphere. The key is for the architect to share the "authority" in the design with the learners and their teachers.

The alternative approach proposed here is to build all major spaces to be permanent but incomplete, sometimes called the "unfinished aesthetic."

THE CONCEPTS
Critical Pedagogy of Place
Today's approach to learning is a hybrid stemming from two learning theories, one focused on culture and the other on ecology. This hybrid has recently been articulated as "critical pedagogy of place." It is the synthesis of "critical pedagogy" and "place-based education." Both are concerned with the space or geography of learning.

Critical pedagogy speaks to learners taking action based on their situation—the social, political, and economic forces surrounding them. It is the cultural dimension. This includes recognizing and dislodging dominant ideas, which is called *decolonization*. It is a process of reading the world by taking it apart.

Place-based education, as the name suggests, is focused on the complexities of the places citizens inhabit. This is the ecological aspect. Learning to live well where you find yourself, which is almost always in a place that has been previously exploited, is called *reinhabitation*. It is a process of understanding and taking action by putting things together.

A critical pedagogy of place suggests learners are creative in addressing not just the spaces but also their relationships. The learning concept of taking it apart and putting it together becomes a metaphor for design.

Authority in Architecture

To become active players in their own learning experiences, learners must also become authors of their environment. Authority becomes shared between the producer (architect) and the consumer (learner). Places are incomplete without the users' involvement. The goal is a design for a setting that requires learner participation. Buildings are not experienced all at once, but rather piece by piece in moments separated by gaps in space, time, and climate. These gaps or relationships become the focus of the design, engaging the learner through a strategy identified as the "montage of gaps."

"Uselessness" and the Architecture of Disjunction

The concept of uselessness in architecture connects directly to the concept of contingency because the space's use is not yet established. Useless space is not tied to predetermined use. The program or use is established, not through numerous meetings prior to design, but rather by the user as appropriate within the interactive place after construction.

An architecture of disjunction concerns spaces, events, and movements and their separation. As a user experiences such fragmented situations, it is the nature of the mind to try to put things together. Therefore, disjunction suggests that users display constructional and conceptual creativity, consistent with the designer's purpose. This also negates the common architectural concept of designing a school as an object in space. The effort in recent decades to raise the meaningfulness of schools through better-looking buildings has not only been a futile exercise; it has also been counterproductive. The shift is from objects in space to place-making space.

THE EXAMPLE

The following example stems from a collaboration in Scotland to redefine learning environments for secondary school students. The groundwork came out of a Design Down workshop in Edinburgh in May 2003, the objective of which was to define an exemplary learning environment in order to inform other projects.

Because this design was not site specific, only a site strategy was applied. Consistent with the Design Down directions, the siting approach considered the school as public space. This is similar to the way churches were perceived in Rome around the eighteenth century. Public space included streets, parks, plazas, courtyards, and churches, as depicted here in a portion of a 1748 map of Rome by Gianbattista Nolli. The shaded area shows all private buildings, and the white space is the public space, including the insides of churches. This is an exemplary case of place making. The round building to the right is the Pantheon, built nearly two thousand years ago. It has had several functions and still serves the community well as a public space. We should be able to say the same thing about the schools we build.

The objective is to make major portions of the school accessible to the public. Other portions of the building would be the exclusive realms of the learners. Because both students and the public share the use of some places, a third, shared zone between the other two is envisioned.

The program is straightforward. Fifty percent of the space is to be "useful space" and the other 50 percent is to be "useless space." With the exception of a lecture room and a theater, each with sloped floors, all other occupied spaces are functionally undefined.

The white boxes represent learning labs (useful space). They are accessible by the public, the students, or both depending on their location. The other white space is support space. The light shaded area is useless public space and the dark shaded area is useless learner space. The textured space represents courtyards.

The useful spaces are supported with an intense infrastructure underneath (hot and cold water, waste systems, compressed air, exhaust, gas, multiple power levels, hardwired and wireless networking, etc.). Furnishings are movable and designed for interactive use. This allows the particular use of the space to be established by the users and the equipment they bring to the box. The possibilities include small or large group discussions, various forms of research, multiple means of production, experimentation, performance, indoor sports, and so forth.

The useless spaces have only minimal support infrastructure (power and networking). Furnishings are available for various forms of social interaction, which allows for the natural formation of communities of practice.

The useful spaces gain meaning through the establishment of activities developed in collaboration with the learning programs. The useless spaces gain meaning through the creative interactions of the learners and the environment.

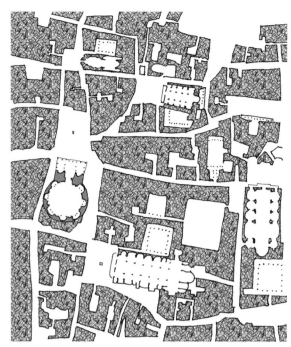

Rome, 1748. Map by Gianbattista Nolli, provided by Bruce Jilk.

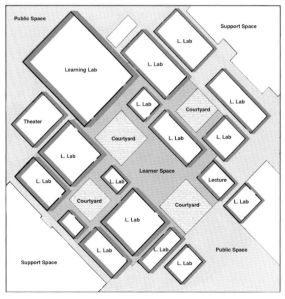

Plan view. Image courtesy of Bruce Jilk.

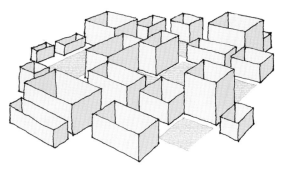

Image of the learning labs (exterior walls, roof, windows, and doors not shown). Image courtesy of Bruce Jilk.

The image of the learning labs begins to suggest the architectural character of the design. To inhabit this space is to experience a montage of gaps, which demands the creative participation of the learner. An environment for critical pedagogy of place is an environment where standardized, "placeless" curriculum cannot survive.

The last image is intended to show how this concept would fit into an urban setting (in this case, historic Rome). The exterior enclosure would take on an appearance in keeping with its surrounding historical context. Daylight would come through a glass roof vaulting over the complex. Like the Pantheon and other churches, the school becomes public space.

The design is also adaptable to suburban or rural locations. The exterior enclosure should reflect the context of the site and not be an end in itself (designed as an object in space). This adaptability illustrates another dimension of how the design fits the concept of contingency. Its location is indeterminate.

SUMMARY

Learning itself is not a passive mode of behavior; rather, it is active and creative. This can be reflected in building learning environments that share authorship, invite learner participation, and belong to the community. The environment is not a "solution," but a setting that needs the learner to establish the full situation.

The ideas presented here are not intended to totally replace the existing system. Rather, like the electromagnetic spectrum, the idea is to reach out into those realms that have not been visible. Based on today's knowledge about learning, the intent is to expand the possibilities.

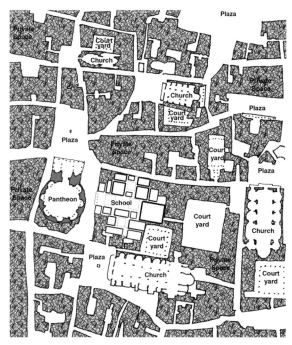

Conjectural siting, Rome. Image courtesy of Bruce Jilk.

Evolution of a Design for Change

Bruce Jilk

Ingunnarskoli in Reykjavik is a new school design model for Iceland constructed at Grafarholti. It is designed for four hundred students in grades one through ten, the standard basic school configuration in Iceland. A Design Down committee—a multistakeholder group of parents, teachers, administrators, students, employers, neighbors, and other concerned citizens—made the decisions during the planning process.

SIGNATURE

Early in the design process the learning signature is developed and becomes the identity of the school. At Grafarholti the Design Down committee defined four themes as its highest priorities: community, nature, spirit, and flow.

The signature for Ingunnarskoli integrates these themes into a graphic image. The circle represents community, green indicates nature, the waves are symbolic of flow, and the image of the child imbedded in the graphic implies the spirit. The signature becomes a major driver of the physical design.

DESIGN CONCEPT

The design concept is a synthesis of the Design Down parameters, the site, the landscape, and historic precedents. To accommodate variations in use, only an armature for learning is built. This basic home base is organized into two components: the fixed service zones (shaded in the plan of the basic home base) and the flexible served space.

> ▶ The service zones include all the structure, pipes, ducts, and conduit. The zone's space supports utilitarian needs.

> ▶ The served space is flexible for numerous use configurations or variations. Flexible walls can be placed as desired. All service spaces have ready access to all utilities. Users determine how the space is applied.

Graphic signature for Ingunnarskoli in Reykjavik, Iceland. Image courtesy of Bruce Jilk.

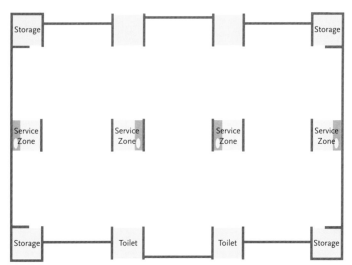

Basic home base layout. Images courtesy of Bruce Jilk.

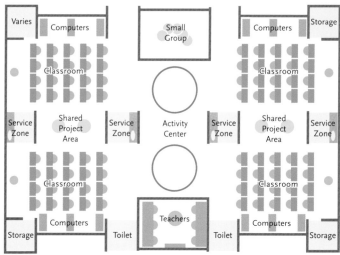

Variation one: traditional layout.

USE VARIATIONS

Three use variations allow users to begin with what is familiar to them and then to grow into the more innovative learning systems. The three variations are on a continuum from the "traditional classroom" to the more personalized "students at their own workstations in small groups" to a future-focused "learner- and teacher-determined" environment. Corresponding space-defining elements include impermanent walls (traditional variation), landscaped partitions (team-based variation), or what the learners develop (learner-determined variation).

> **Variation one:** A traditional classroom layout, this variation features four classroom areas for twenty students, common activity space, small group room, and teacher planning room.

> **Variation two:** A cooperative, individual workstation layout, with four team areas for twenty students each. The common space functions for large group instruction. The work zone is for project work. As in the traditional layout, there is a small group room and a teacher planning room.

> **Variation three:** A creative, user-determined layout. This layout emphasizes that the freedom and

creativity of the users is enhanced (not restricted) by the built environment. Organizing multiple student groups around multiple learning tasks is possible in a moment's notice. The curved, broken black line indicates a flexible, movable space divider as an alternative to fixed partitions.

Predetermining every aspect of children's interaction with their environment limits the range of possible learning experiences, minimizing the development of creativity. The approach to design at Ingunnarskoli has intentional ambiguities to provide a space that allows children the freedom to create their own environments.

HEART OF THE LEARNING COMMUNITY

Uniting the learning units described above is the central forum. All learning places, including the gym, are directly connected to the forum.

This two-story space is filled with daylight, which flows into the adjacent learning units, thereby assuring natural daylight to every learning environment. The forum functions as the heart of the school and includes the activities of dining, library research, and performance.

Seeing the Future of the Learning Environment

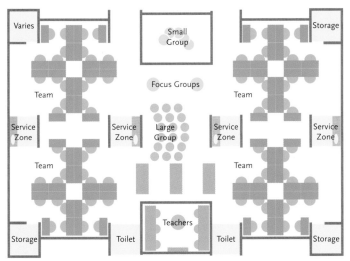

Variation two: cooperative layout.

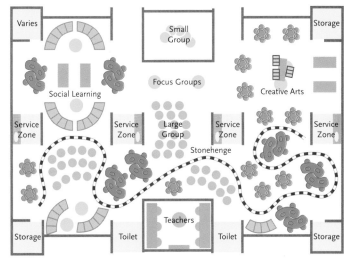

Variation three: creative layout.

**Ingunnarskoli school design model constructed at Grafarholti, Iceland.
Above:** Exterior. **Left:** Forum.
Images courtesy of Bruce Jilk.

West High School, Aurora, Illinois. Gaylaird Christopher, principal architect, A4E. Perkins + Will Architects. Photograph courtesy of Gaylaird Christopher.

CHAPTER TEN

Learning Landscapes

Introduction: Transforming the School Grounds into a Learning Landscape

The school of the future is designed as a whole, with equal design emphasis placed on the geological site as well as the school facility. School grounds as we know them today, however, rarely reflect the importance of place in our lives. Travel across our incredibly varied nation through several life zones and you will see virtually identical playgrounds surrounded by chain link fences. The large acreage of many schools—often the richest piece of real estate in the neighborhood—is lying fallow, untended, and neglected. Other schools rest on pieces of property that have been isolated from community, heavily engineered, stripped clean, paved with too much asphalt, hidden behind security screens, and robbed of character. Sense of place has been erased.

The drive toward environmental quality (greening and sustainability) makes the issue of landscaping for cities and public spaces such as schools more critical than ever before. *Land art* is a beautification tool, a focus of public art, and a soft embrace for the built environment. In a 2005 exhibition at the Museum of Modern Art, the museum recognized the design of constructed landscapes and the spaces between buildings as being as important to the quality of the urban environment as the buildings themselves (Reed, 2005). *Biotecture*, or the greening of cities seen in green roofs, facade gardens, vertical farms, and other applications, reduces the urban heat island effect, cleans the air, helps manage water and runoff, and reduces human stress. Constructing the contemporary landscape requires a new synergism among architects, artists, landscape planners, ecologists, engineers, urban planners, and politicians. All new development should include a certain amount of landscape as part of the design.

Top: Montage of school playground. Forsaken, forlorn, and all too familiar. Photograph courtesy of Anne Taylor. **Above Left: West High School, Aurora, Illinois.** Landscaped school courtyard. Gaylaird Christopher, principal architect, A4E. Perkins + Will Architects. Photograph courtesy of Gaylaird Christopher. **Above right: Instituto Tecnológico y de Estudios Superiores Monterrey Santa Fe High School, Mexico City, 2004.** Large windows allow varying perspectives and a visual connection between indoor and outdoor environments. Photograph by Lourdes Legorreta. Legorreta + Legorreta Architects.

My primary purpose in this chapter is to awaken the minds of architects and educators to the limitless learning potential of the school grounds, and to promote the development of specially designed spaces for outdoor learning experiences through an informed sense of landscape architecture. Our children and our communities need settings that help students participate in creating their own landscape architecture. It is time to transform our underutilized playgrounds and educational campuses into potent, integrated learning landscapes that reflect our culture and our values.

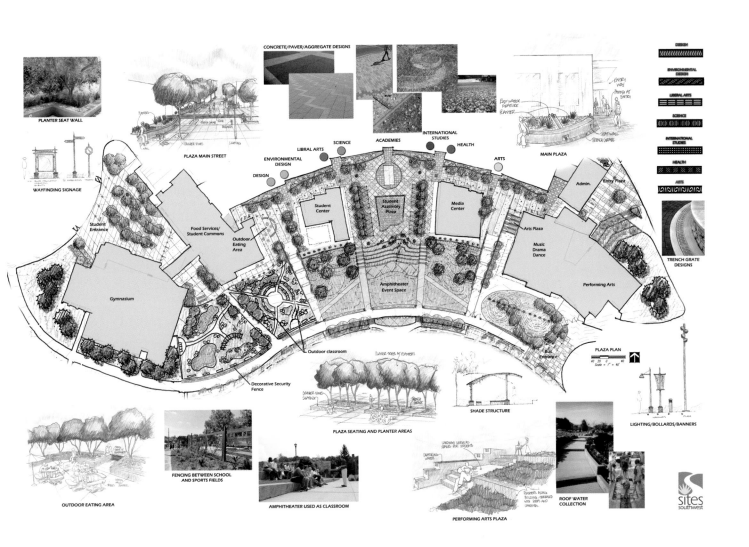

CONCRETE/PAVER/AGGREGATE DESIGNS

PLANTER SEAT WALL

WAYFINDING SIGNAGE

PLAZA MAIN STREET

ENVIRONMENTAL DESIGN

DESIGN

LIBRAL ARTS

SCIENCE

ACADEMIES

INTERNATIONAL STUDIES

HEALTH

ARTS

MAIN PLAZA

DESIGN

ENVIRONMENTAL DESIGN

LIBERAL ARTS

SCIENCE

INTERNATIONAL STUDIES

HEALTH

ARTS

TRENCH GRATE DESIGNS

Student Entrance

Food Services/ Student Commons

Outdoor Eating Area

Student Center

Student Assembly Plaza

Media Center

Admin.

Entry Plaza

Arts Plaza

Music Drama Dance

Gymnasium

Amphitheater Event Space

Performing Arts

Outdoor classroom

Decorative Security Fence

Bus Entrance

PLAZA PLAN
Scale = 1" = 40'

LIGHTING/BOLLARDS/BANNERS

SHADE STRUCTURE

PLAZA SEATING AND PLANTER AREAS

OUTDOOR EATING AREA

FENCING BETWEEN SCHOOL AND SPORTS FIELDS

AMPHITHEATER USED AS CLASSROOM

PERFORMING ARTS PLAZA

ROOF WATER COLLECTION

sites
southwest

V. Sue Cleveland High School, Rio Rancho, New Mexico. Designing for outdoor spaces as well as structures supports learning throughout the whole school environment. Van H. Gilbert Architect PC. George Radnovich, Sites Southwest LLC.

The Nations Park, Lisbon, Portugal. Expo '98 coincided with the five hundredth anniversary of explorer Vasco da Gama's voyage to India and resulted in a makeover of the Nations Park area. This *Vasco da Gama Park Installation* has nonliteral yet intriguing architectonic forms that could double as play equipment. Why don't we enliven school grounds with more public art? Why don't child development specialists collaborate with sculptors to create great playground art? Photograph by Anne Taylor.

What Is a Learning Landscape?

Learning landscapes are thoughtfully designed, attractive school grounds that offer outdoor spaces for learning math, science, history, art, literature, ecology, and stewardship. They are teaching and learning tools that go beyond the undisputed benefits of relaxation, physical exercise, sports, and fresh air to act as organic, three-dimensional textbooks. They are resources for readily accessible, real-life study, and an inspiration for curriculum development as well. Learning landscape architecture may contain

Natural elements: The climate, plants, animals, habitats, soils and rocks, sun and shadows, water, hills/topography, wetlands, and more

Multisensory elements: Variety in textures, colors, patterns, sounds, tastes, and smells

Agricultural elements: Gardens of all kinds, farms, orchards, irrigation systems, land management areas, animal pens

Built elements: Play structures and equipment, exercise equipment, pathways, bermed earth, steps, shade structures, sports venues, pavilions, gazebos, seating, storage, fencing, walls, ground surfacing and graphics, signage, rooftop play areas

Outdoor classroom elements: Weather stations, energy stations (windmills, solar panels), sundials, amphitheaters, musical playscapes of outdoor instruments, nature trails, fitness trails, solar greenhouses, water harvesting systems, science labs

Cultural elements: Indigenous design, entryways, student art, public art, courtyards, plazas, gathering spaces for different-sized groups, architectural styles, local materials, separate access for public use, and

Transitional elements: Ways to bring the outside in and to expand the learning environment, including porches, patios adjacent to classrooms, decks, sunrooms, terraces, openable walls and windows, vistas, skylights, open courtyards, roof gardens/green roofs, vertical wall plantings/green walls, landscape inclusion indoors, intelligent facades and new photovoltaic functions, transparency in design, juxtaposition of formal and naturalistic landscapes (terraced hillsides, cascading drains, lily ponds in courtyard settings).

All of these elements and many more not listed can become teaching and learning manifestations, as discussed in part 3. Students themselves can be instrumental in programming and design of these outdoor spaces for learning. Participation in maintenance and ongoing care of school grounds can encourage sedentary students to get outside and get moving, and upkeep also provides learning experiences in stewardship and pride of place. The hope is that students who understand, use, and feel connected to the natural environment will grow into adults who appreciate and protect its healthy, functional, and aesthetic properties. As a side benefit, perhaps students will become aware of social problems such as hunger in America and the world and help convince adults that school property can be put to better use as an agricultural resource than as an asphalt wasteland.

Years ago, when the idea of student stewardship first emerged, students began to maintain a nature trail at this Hillsboro, California, school. Photograph courtesy of Anne Taylor.

Master Planning and Recognizing the Need for Better Outdoor Design Early in the Planning Process

Because many schools are already built, my emphasis as a consultant has been on redesigning existing sites and making the most of "found" learning on school grounds. For new designs, however, NCEF reports that options for learning landscape architecture are greatest at the earliest stages of facility planning. At the site selection stage, important choices can be made about the learning potential of the site, neighborhood interface, landscaping issues, noise, safety, and proximity to hazardous materials. Site development must be done carefully if schools intend to use school grounds for educational purposes. Building orientation for solar design, plant and wildlife surveys, access, microclimates, and circulation must be thoroughly understood to achieve success in outdoor learning. Similarly, during the design process, infrastructure can be laid specifically to support outdoor learning, including storage, water access, shelter, seating, and other needs (Wagner, 2000).

Master planning is instrumental in effective outdoor designs. The SFIS master plan, for example, shows how designers began with the larger picture of community and landscape so that the newly renovated school truly represents the values of the Pueblo people it serves. The site is an integral part of the academic picture for the school and is informed by the Pueblo connection to the land, the sacred mountains, the sun, and the seasons. The site is oriented on a north-south-east-west axis in order to benefit from passive solar energy and natural lighting, but also to emphasize and celebrate the strong Pueblo reverence for the spiritual nature of the cardinal directions. The master plan conforms to the local topography to minimize the scarring of the Earth. Native design is inseparable from the landscape, as seen in the careful massing and orientation of forms. The style is not only about organic materials, but also about the spaces between buildings.

The master plan provides a bond between the school and the tribal homes not only with architectural form and spatial organization, but also by siting agriculture and water harvesting on school grounds. At school, students learn

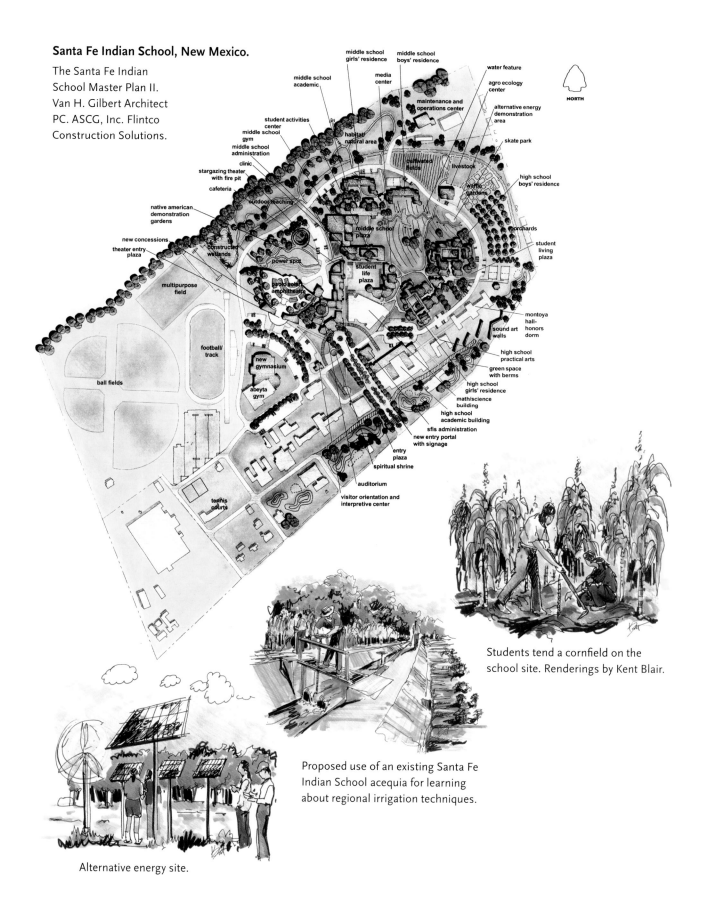

Santa Fe Indian School, New Mexico.

The Santa Fe Indian School Master Plan II. Van H. Gilbert Architect PC. ASCG, Inc. Flintco Construction Solutions.

middle school girls' residence

middle school boys' residence

middle school academic

media center

water feature

agro ecology center

maintenance and operations center

alternative energy demonstration area

NORTH

skate park

student activities center

middle school gym

middle school administration

habitat natural area

cultivated fields

livestock

high school boys' residence

clinic

waffle gardens

stargazing theater with fire pit

cafeteria

outdoor teaching

middle school plaza

orchards

native american demonstration gardens

student living plaza

new concessions

theater entry plaza

constructed wetlands

power spot

student life plaza

multipurpose field

paolo soleri amphitheatre

montoya hall-honors dorm

sound art walls

high school practical arts

football/track

new gymnasium

green space with berms

high school girls' residence

ball fields

abeyta gym

math/science building

high school academic building

sfis administration

new entry portal with signage

entry plaza

spiritual shrine

auditorium

tennis courts

visitor orientation and interpretive center

Students tend a cornfield on the school site. Renderings by Kent Blair.

Proposed use of an existing Santa Fe Indian School acequia for learning about regional irrigation techniques.

Alternative energy site.

about sustainability issues that are of key interest to Pueblo life. Through Community-Based Education (CBE) programs, students regularly visit the pueblos that sponsor the school, becoming familiar with Pueblo concerns and engaging in on-site research. Recently, students working with laptop computers to test soil at the pueblos discovered that one of the earthen dams upstream was causing salinization of the farmland—real-life information that the pueblos could use to improve productivity.

The campus is designed to support the CBE process by incorporating field demonstration and research facilities into the open space of school grounds. Other proposed elements are

- ▶ Main growing space

- ▶ Crop processing room and wet lab

- ▶ Meeting area with teleconferencing and audio/visual capabilities

- ▶ Cool room and root cellar

- ▶ Seed bank

- ▶ Herbarium and clean room

- ▶ Solar barn and workshop, and

- ▶ Exterior landscape with weather station, water cistern, irrigation ditches, composting area, wetlands, shade house nursery, solar oven, solar composting toilet, freshwater pond, fruit orchard, tilling equipment, and more (ASCG, Inc., 2002).

The lesson illustrated by SFIS and careful master planning is that we must familiarize school boards, administrators, parents, architects, and community members with the idea of the learning landscape as an essential part of school and urban design. The Boston Schoolyard Initiative, for example, has redeveloped some sixty playgrounds through a participatory process that considers the schoolyard part of the city's open space as well as a space for experiential learning. A similar learning landscape initiative involved a public-private partnership with the Department of Landscape Architecture at the University of Colorado to transform twenty-two neglected Denver elementary school playgrounds. Designers responded to the culture of the schools' neighborhoods with greening of school grounds, new play equipment, outdoor classrooms, shade structures, and gardens. Other elements included early childhood play spaces, athletic fields, new entries, and parking lot upgrades. Children, community members, and AmeriCorps volunteers helped fund and build the projects. Due to the success of the program, voters passed a bond issue to continue funding for the initiative, adding twenty-five new sites to the list at an average budget of about $450,000 per playground (Children, Youth, and Environments Center for Research and Design, 2008).

With community awareness and appreciation of school grounds, funding becomes possible. Both the man-made and natural environment are crucial to learning and should not isolated from each other or left out of school planning.

Santa Fe Indian School, New Mexico.
Top: Massing of forms in the Pueblo style.
Bottom: Significant pathways. Spaces between buildings focus on sacred directions and mountains.
Photographs courtesy of Van H. Gilbert Architect PC. ASCG, Inc. Flintco Construction Solutions.

Noma Kindergarten

Ito, Noma, Shizuoka, Japan

The Noma project, located in the city center of Ito, Shizuoka, restores an original site that was more than fifty years old while maintaining memory of place through its beautiful lawn garden. The architect's primary concept was to highlight the *engawa* space, which is a corridor running along the boundary of interior and exterior spaces in traditional Japanese architecture. The entire volume of the building is one-sided to the west, and the side facing the garden is cut with a gentle arc, supporting the theme of children living and learning with nature.

The lawn garden is an island of green in the urban setting. © Tadao Ando Architect & Associates. Photograph by Mitsuo Matsuoka.

This smooth, sculptural, organic form allows for exploration without dictating the content of play. © Tadao Ando Architect & Associates. Photograph by Mitsuo Matsuoka.

The recycled wood finish of this *engawa* space (transitional space or outdoor corridor) provides a smooth surface for children walking barefoot. © Tadao Ando Architect & Associates. Photograph by Mitsuo Matsuoka.

The Early Childhood Learning Landscape

A child's play is his or her work, so everything that is built into the early childhood playscape should relate to the child's developmental growth across body, mind, and spirit. My research and project experience indicate that nonliteral play equipment and organic settings are best for children. Architectonic, generic, sculptural, and geometric forms are most educational. The locus of imagination is in the mind of the child, where anything can become anything. A small personal place can become a fort. A bridge can be a castle, a spaceship, or just a bridge with a troll under it. A hillock can give the child a feeling of conquest.

In interviewing and observing young children I have found that they love nature and organic places. For this reason alone, caregivers can make great use of the outdoors as a learning tool for many kinds of development. Plant life, animals, water, earth forms, trees, bushes, flower and vegetable gardens, and multitextured pathways should dominate the landscape, with perhaps a solar greenhouse to transition between indoor and outdoor learning spaces. I regret that safety concerns have dictated that many early childhood playgrounds have only brightly colored plastic slides and jungle gyms set on flat surfaces. Observe children outdoors and you will see that they love running up and down hillsides. We need more contrasting levels in playgrounds, which help young children learn positional concepts, a prerequisite to learning how to read.

To summarize the best features of early childhood playscapes, categories for design include child play, ambient features, biotic and spatial elements, outdoor classrooms, and therapeutic/access areas. In all cases, the designer of the learning landscape should first study the developmental needs of young children and then design to support them.

In 2004, landscape architect Joy Kuebler collaborated with the Buffalo Public Schools to bring this enlightened view of early childhood spaces to an interior courtyard for the Dr. Charles R. Drew Science Magnet school (see next page). While the initial goal was to create a curriculum-based outdoor science space, designers expanded the scope to include math, music, art, geology, and language arts/culture with physical education interwoven throughout. A water channel and a centralized gathering space unified the various "classrooms" while allowing a variety of simultaneous small and large group instruction.

Because the school was located in a harsh urban environment, it was important to the faculty that the students experience a true variety of landscapes and outdoor activities, from growing their own fruits and vegetables to understanding Native American uses for local plants to simply being inspired by a bright yellow daylily. Plant materials were selected to provide the most impact in spring and fall, and a fescue turf selection greatly reduced lawn maintenance. Garden areas ranged from naturalized native plantings to perennial gardens.

Top: For her UNM thesis and landscape design project, Peggy Wright envisioned a daycare landscape that would charm young children with its hillocks and level changes. **Center:** A summer lilac room. **Bottom:** A rock enclosure affords opportunities for climbing, jumping, hiding, and sitting quietly. Concept drawings by Peggy Wright.

Elements in a featured interior courtyard

- ▶ Pergola shade structure
- ▶ Water channel
- ▶ Large gathering space with compass and clock elements
- ▶ Climbing mounds
- ▶ Raised beds and fruit trees
- ▶ Bamboo tepee
- ▶ Sand play area
- ▶ Small group instruction areas for art and music
- ▶ Boulders of native rock

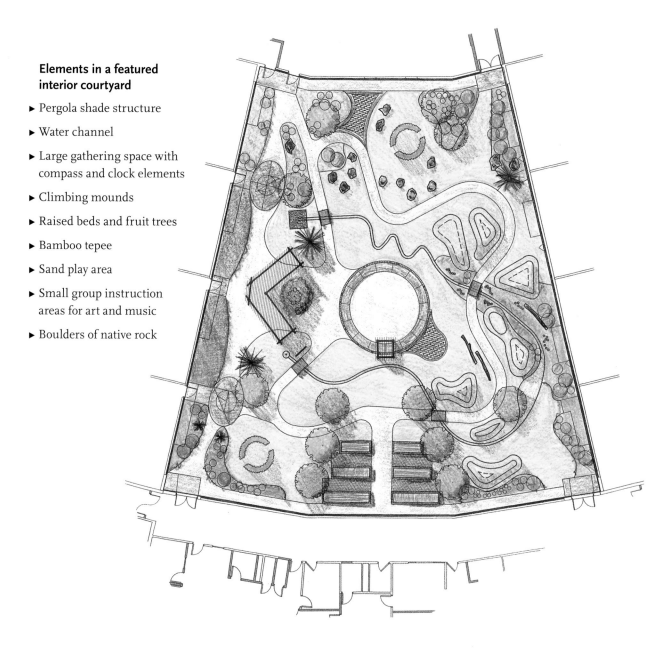

PS 90, Dr. Charles R. Drew Science Magnet, Buffalo, New York.
Interior courtyard. Throughout the courtyard, curriculum activities overlap with play activities, creating an outdoor learning environment that continually stimulates and expands young minds. Joy Kuebler, landscape architect.

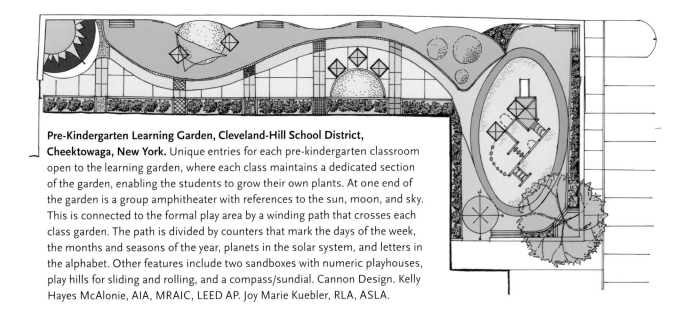

Pre-Kindergarten Learning Garden, Cleveland-Hill School District, Cheektowaga, New York. Unique entries for each pre-kindergarten classroom open to the learning garden, where each class maintains a dedicated section of the garden, enabling the students to grow their own plants. At one end of the garden is a group amphitheater with references to the sun, moon, and sky. This is connected to the formal play area by a winding path that crosses each class garden. The path is divided by counters that mark the days of the week, the months and seasons of the year, planets in the solar system, and letters in the alphabet. Other features include two sandboxes with numeric playhouses, play hills for sliding and rolling, and a compass/sundial. Cannon Design. Kelly Hayes McAlonie, AIA, MRAIC, LEED AP. Joy Marie Kuebler, RLA, ASLA.

The Playground and Beyond

Playgrounds are more important than ever, given current child obesity rates and sedentary lifestyles. Many of our school playgrounds are fenced off from community, and some of the newest playground designs are destinations that have been moved away from neighborhoods into large, self-contained buildings that limit access and spontaneity. How do we keep playgrounds relevant for today's children? Two playground design groups outlined here—Kompan and Leathers & Associates—emphasize going to the source: the children themselves.

The Kompan concept originated about thirty-five years ago when artist Tom Lindhardt Wills created a sculpture for a new housing estate. He noticed that children were more interested in climbing on the sculpture than admiring it from afar, and a business in playground design was born. Helle Burlingame, director of the Kompan Play Institute in North America, uses her experience as an educator, author, and developmental psychologist to examine the interrelationships between environments and children's behavior. In her numerous workshops and presentations she stresses the need for play and playgrounds that balance safety and challenge in an age-appropriate way and are "visually motivating" at the same time.

Leathers & Associates brings relevance through community-built creative playgrounds. The company provides expertise in design, equipment and materials, and fund-raising for playgrounds that are imagined by children and built by community volunteers. The true value of the Leathers playscape is the cohesiveness it brings to the community during design and construction. Leathers & Associates, with community help, has built more than 1,600 playscapes worldwide. Once a design is tailored to community needs, construction begins with company consultants and volunteers of all ages building the playground, usually in the span of five days to two weeks, a process reminiscent of an old-fashioned barn raising.

Projects are built with a combination of structural plastic and plastic composite lumber. The company also builds with arsenic-free, pressure-treated lumber for communities that request wood. Contextual themes change for different regions and life zones, but many of the designs contain pyramidal towers, rocket ships, cargo nets, boats, castle lookout towers, tree houses, plazas, and sometimes cartoon characters or monsters.

School playgrounds should be designed to help children of all abilities develop basic motor skills, relieve stress, and challenge them not just on the physical level,

Top: Kamalani Kai, Kauai, Hawaii. A bridge playground. Image courtesy of Leathers & Associates.

Top row. Left: Museum de Tabasco, Tabasco, Mexico. Kompan elements in white sand, targeting ages two through five. Attributes include curved design, meandering spaces, hand-friendly forms, smooth surfaces, and contrasting colors. Image courtesy of Kompan Playgrounds and the Kompan Play Institute. **Center: Montreal, Canada.** Kompan Supernova is one of several "constellations" that appeal to children of all ages. Image courtesy of Kompan Playgrounds and the Kompan Play Institute. **Right:** The Galaxy Meteor Shower from Kompan presents a challenge to children five through twelve and older. Its transparent design allows it to blend into any setting. Image courtesy of Kompan Playgrounds and the Kompan Play Institute.

Bottom row. Left: Lake Charles, Louisiana. Sound walls. Musical pieces built into Leathers & Associates environment. Image courtesy of Leathers & Associates. **Center: Brevard Zoo, Rockledge, Florida.** Sand dinosaur dig. Leathers & Associates play space. Image courtesy of Leathers & Associates. **Right:** Jon Del Secco, eagle scout (wearing the yellow vest), volunteered as a captain for the Sycamore Park project in Mill Valley, California, leading boy scouts and youth groups to assist with the build. He also camped on-site to serve as the site security during the construction. Image courtesy of Leathers & Associates.

Oñate Elementary School, Albuquerque, New Mexico. The playground is isolated from a city park. Note the contrast in the landscapes. Photograph by Amy Duckert.

but on intellectual, aesthetic, and social levels as well. "Landscape architects should be more engaged in the growing interdisciplinary efforts to create more healthy living environments. . . . The next frontier in children's environmental design will likely focus on school landscapes and neighborhood design" (Dennis, 2008).

Site Analysis as an Interdisciplinary Learning Tool for Multiple Ages

WHAT IS A SITE ANALYSIS?

Before a building can be constructed or a natural area landscaped, the designer has to know the place. Site analysis involves researching every aspect of a given area and defining the context for where one lives, learns, works, and plays. It is the first step in transforming an ordinary playground into a learning landscape. With the help of the architect, laypeople, including students from elementary school to high school and beyond, can conduct their own site investigations as a way to develop an ecohistoric sense of place or a sense of belonging. An analysis brings opportunities to explore several real-life skills and disciplines, in this case right in the school's immediate location. Learners of all ages can observe, sketch, collect data, analyze, compare, classify, measure, and define. Many elementary schools that are concentrating on No Child Left Behind are limiting or eliminating recess and field trips. A learning landscape designed to productively strengthen academics could help students learn core material without depriving them of outdoor learning experiences.

A site analysis can be an informal or formal process. The Private Eye project in Seattle, Washington, makes creative use of jewelers' loupes (magnifiers) to pique the interest of young children as they examine the environment around them. An accompanying text helps children develop literacy and perceptual skills through a circular process of close observation followed by analogous thinking (Reuf, 1992). Other site analysis experiences resemble the more formal process architects go through to prepare for site development and design.

Powell Barnett Park, Seattle, Washington. The Kompan Edge line of products engages children ages five through twelve. This climbing wall is vandalism resistant, offers different levels of challenge, and allows children to circumnavigate the entire structure without touching the ground. Image courtesy of Kompan Playgrounds and the Kompan Play Institute. Photograph by Peter Tammetta.

FACTORS EVALUATED IN A SITE ANALYSIS

Many physical, biological, cultural, and regulatory factors are involved in evaluating an existing site. Physical factors include a wide range of natural and built phenomena. Biological characteristics include plant and animal life. Cultural attributes include history, land use, ownership, and economic value. Zoning codes, requirements of planning boards, safety, and construction codes all apply to the regulatory influences on site analysis. As students collect data and present discoveries, they will address many subject matter disciplines in an integrated way.

The first step in the process of site analysis is to establish an overview of the site, a map of the site's size and primary features. New geographic imaging system tools can be used in site analysis, environmental inventory, and restoration projects. Geospatial information viewers allow students to explore geographic data for the entire world in two and three dimensions. Maps can also be created based on architectural blueprints of the site or aerial photographs. Using a simple site map as a base, students may then develop vocabulary, investigate, sketch, and observe some or all of the following elements of a site, derived from the AIA's site analysis guides:

Physical Aspects
Topography
    Whole site survey map of physical features (including north arrow, boundaries, position of existing structures, school buildings, land forms, and contours)
    Site survey maps, elevations
    Access maps for vehicles, pedestrians, handicapped

Soils
    Soil types, qualities, and mapping
    Rocky areas
    Erosion, drainage

Climate
    Wind patterns, directions
    Solar orientation, shading, and shadow
    Temperature and humidity (microclimates)
    Precipitation

Water
    Bodies of water/wetlands on map (dimensions)
    Drainage and flooding
    Water quality

Biological Aspects
Vegetation
    Grasses/ground cover
    Bushes/shrubs/trees
    Native/nonnative status for the local life zone
    Poisonous plants/safety

Wildlife
    Birds, insects, fish, mammals, reptiles
    Microlife

Cultural Aspects and Ecohistorical Sense of Place
    Existing and past structures, architecture
    People and cultures (spiritual sites, land use,
       agriculture)
    Natural history of site
    Archeology
    Economic value of the land

Regulatory Factors
    Zoning codes
    Public school regulations
    Community input
    Building, fire, and other construction codes
    Safety and security
    Utilities

In addition, some researchers recommend that crime analysis be included in site analysis for schools.

All of the factors listed above have potential not only for data collection by students but also for cross-disciplinary curriculum development.

What Is the Basic Procedure for Developing a Learning Landscape through Site Analysis with Students?

My colleagues and I used a modified version of the AIA recommended guidelines to involve children in site analysis projects at schools in East Haven, Connecticut, and for playgrounds in Sanger and Stockton, California.

1. Explore the site. Walk the site. Find north, then south, east, west. Sketch. Photograph the site using the 360-degree technique shown here. Make notes.

2. Make a map of the site's boundaries and main features. Include the "footprint" of existing buildings, built structures, and natural landforms. (Aerial photographs, architectural plan views, and satellite images available online can help in the creation of the map.) Include a north arrow and introduce the idea of scale. Make several copies and use the map as a basis for further investigations of specific features of the site. Parents can provide valuable help with site maps and small group exploration.

360° Photographic Technique

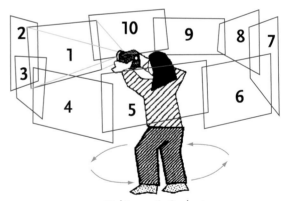

Taking 360° photo

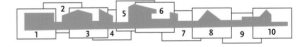

Stand in the center of a site and take several photographs while turning in a circle. Pause to take the photos. Try to make sure the view in your frame overlaps each time.

Line up developed photographs to produce a 360° view of your playground, neighborhood, or community.

Illustration by George Vlastos.

3. Learn and practice schematic drawing techniques for communicating observations and spatial relationships. Techniques include use of arrows, bubble drawings to show adjacencies, sketches, architectural landscape symbols, plan views, and elevations.

4. Collect data about the site. Use multiple disciplines: count, measure, collect, test, interview, research off-site for historical background, and keep photographic records.

5. Make additional maps of the site based on specific characteristics such as wind direction, drainage, location of plant life, animal life, and circulation and use by students.

6. Make maps/graphs/artwork/writings based on the interests of the children as they explore the landscape. Create visual responses to the environment based on personal reactions to the place.

7. Explore past use of the site, historical records, and prior land use. Examine the surrounding community and its cultural attributes for context.

8. Return to the site with an eye toward change, improvement, and preservation. Conduct preference surveys about what should remain and what should go (see Tools for Thought for a sample survey).

9. Use the design process to dream about the future. Create schematic drawings and models and present your work. Submit ideas to a professional landscape architect, who can help draw a final proposal and create a master plan for achieving student goals in small increments over time.

10. Implement your designs in phases, following the long-term master plan (ten years is typical). How can you link your learning landscape to your indoor curriculum? What connections can you make literally in the environment as well as mentally between disciplines? How can your school grounds extend and reflect a sense of community? (Taylor, Dunbar, Hexom, Brown, & Enggass, 2000.)

Los Padillas Elementary School, Albuquerque, New Mexico. Pond studies. Students at Los Padillas learn about the food chain, conduct pond research, and write in their journals as part of interdisciplinary outdoor learning. Photograph courtesy of Sara Keeney, principal.

Seeing the Future of the Learning Environment

Assessment for School Grounds

SAFETY ISSUES

The U.S. Consumer Product Safety Commission (CPSC) has long recognized the potential hazards that accompany public playgrounds and equipment. The majority of emergency room visits that pertain to playgrounds are usually falls to ground surfaces from equipment (see the Morrow and Calhoon designer perspective following chapter 6). Other accidents include entanglement of clothing in equipment, head entrapment in openings, and impact from equipment turnover and protrusions. CPSC publishes the *Handbook for Public Playground Safety*, a resource for assessing equipment safety, which is updated online.

The National Program for Playground Safety (NPPS) provides guidelines for the design of safe playgrounds, safety tips and statistics, information packets, courses for designers, and a downloadable PDF of the NPPS Safety Report Card Form for anyone wishing to assess a playground facility. The report card is a checklist similar to a site analysis for safety. NPPS also offers a lesson geared toward children in which they can evaluate playground safety through four main points that spell out *safe*:

- ▶ Supervision: Adult supervision, visibility of all areas

- ▶ Age-appropriate equipment: Separation of areas by age level and consideration of developmental needs

- ▶ Falls: Cushioning under equipment

- ▶ Equipment maintenance: Items that need fixing

Playground designers must also plan for access for all, including ADA standards for stable pathway surfaces, five-foot-wide paths and platforms for wheelchairs, and a variety of textures or colors to aid in wayfinding (National Program for Playground Safety, 2006).

ASSESSMENT OF QUALITY FOR YOUNG CHILDREN

Beyond important safety issues is the question of the quality of outdoor settings for children of all ages. Few scales exist for measuring the effectiveness of school and child care playgrounds as learning landscapes; however, recognition that outdoor environments should support the developmental needs of young children is growing. A detailed scale for child care settings in *Preschool Outdoor Environment Measurement Scale (POEMS)* rates usage of preschool grounds across five domains: physical environment, interactions, play and learning settings, program (curricular connections), and teacher/caregiver role (DeBord, Hestenes, Moore, Cosco, & McGinnis, 2005).

A Superintendent's Dream of the Ideal Learning Environment

Denise Hexom, EdD

ASSISTANT PROFESSOR AT NATIONAL UNIVERSITY, SACRAMENTO,

AND FORMER TEACHER, PRINCIPAL, AND SUPERINTENDENT

In New Haven, Connecticut, Anne Taylor Associates and I invited all key stakeholders to participate in redesigning school playgrounds. Much to our delight the design groups created imaginative learning landscapes that included serenity gardens, fish ponds, arbors, gazebos, butterfly gardens, special outdoor seating for students, vegetable and flower gardens, and outdoor classrooms. Parent and community groups such as the Parent Teacher Association, Rotary, and teacher organizations helped fund the projects by purchasing benches, trees, plants, and, in some cases, assisting with construction of raised gardens.

Planners also borrowed the idea of a wedding registry and applied it to a local nursery as a "plant wish list" for our schools. Plants were chosen for the wish list based on aesthetics, their attractiveness to birds and pollinators, and for fruit or flower bearing during the school year. This made it easy for community members to purchase the plants for our new learning landscapes.

Wilson School, Sanger, California. Playground schematic. Drawing courtesy of Brown + Wooten Architects. Anne Taylor Associates. Denise Hexom, former superintendent.

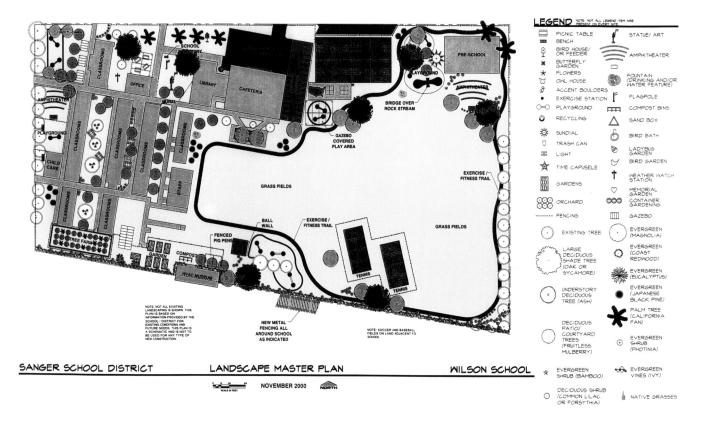

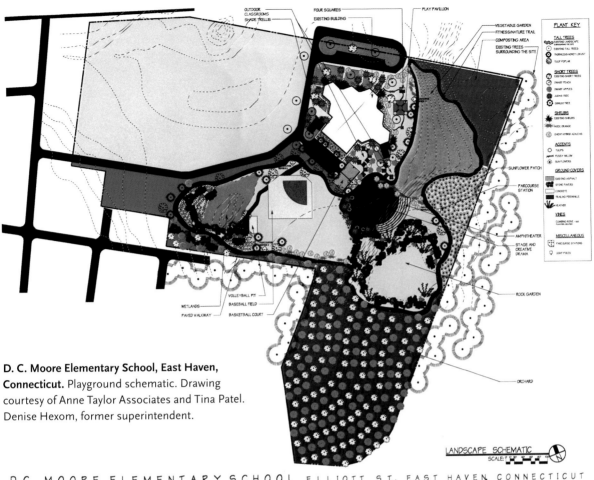

D. C. Moore Elementary School, East Haven, Connecticut. Playground schematic. Drawing courtesy of Anne Taylor Associates and Tina Patel. Denise Hexom, former superintendent.

D. C. MOORE ELEMENTARY SCHOOL ELLIOTT ST., EAST HAVEN, CONNECTICUT

During my position as superintendent in Sanger, California, I once again consulted Anne Taylor Associates about turning our poorly designed playgrounds into learning landscapes and the possibility of opening a charter school using the tenets of the Architecture and Children program as the foundational curriculum. In a short period of time, through the innovative classroom design and outdoor learning landscapes, students learned to monitor the migration patterns of Canadian geese; calculate the arrival of fairy shrimp; build feeders for the more than sixty-five species of birds in the area; complete a site analysis for visual and verbal data collection; propagate and plant vegetables and flowers; design and build a pond; plant one thousand daffodils throughout the community; and use the tools of architects to think, create, design, collaborate, investigate relationships, and understand. The students mastered complex concepts, strategies, and processes through active participation and involvement. They established personal goals, collaborated in teams, designed and executed projects, and developed a sense of esprit de corps.

When students are active participants in learning, they see a purpose to their schooling. When they are outside the classroom investigating the local ecological environment, they understand the web of life; when they are collaborating around the development of a new structure of their own design, they gain confidence in their abilities to make a difference in the world. This is what learning is all about.

Top: Farming encompasses many areas of management that form holistic learning experiences for these young students in Sendai, Japan, who are gathering seeds for a seed bank. Photograph by Hiroko Hosada.
Bottom: Design for animals at school. Children love animals and learn important stewardship skills as they care for living things. A small school zoo can support that aim. Photograph courtesy of Anne Taylor.

Architect and educator Henry Sanoff has also created assessment scales for playscapes that can be used to prioritize improvements in outdoor environments for young children. The analyst identifies and rates eight different categories as inadequate, fair, or adequate:

1. Spatial organization
2. Outdoor/indoor connection
3. Variety of activities
4. Physical design of equipment
5. Zoning activities
6. Circulation path
7. Safety
8. Year-round use

I would add plants and living things to this list (gardens, natural zones, and habitats).

QUALITY FOR MIDDLE SCHOOL AGE AND BEYOND

Most of the designs I have encountered for these age levels focus on sports and do not serve as multifaceted learning landscapes. Even at the university level, I see that college students may appreciate sitting on the grass and relaxing under trees, but they rarely know about or interact with the ecosystem of the campus site. Because the grounds are not viewed as learning landscapes, the corresponding scales for their performance evaluation have not yet been developed.

I believe that the use of school grounds as a teaching/learning tool should be part of POE criteria. We need to move beyond our current view of POE for outdoor sites, which ranges from isolated issues such as parking lot use or access to the overly general, as in "the site is well landscaped." Assessments or POE for learning landscapes for middle and high schools and universities could easily be formulated from criteria for public parks, green architecture with eco-friendly checklists such as the LEED criteria, universal design principles, and/or federal and state regulations for wilderness or wetlands areas.

Until we view the school grounds as holistic learning landscapes, we will continue to waste valuable real estate and squander opportunities for our students of all ages to make the deep connections to the natural world that will sustain us in the future.

Visions of the Learning Landscape as Agricultural Resource

In the upcoming designer perspective, Janet Hawkes brings agriculture to the classroom and school grounds. Programs for growing food are springing up across the country, even in urban settings. For schools that cannot fund or support larger agricultural systems, there are several small-scale options: compact hydroponics systems, aquatic ecosystems, container gardens, mini-greenhouses, and books about setting up your own growing laboratories, according to the National Gardening Association's Web site.

The scale of farming and agricultural projects is easily modified to fit time and budget constraints. For example, a fishery can take the form of a small fish pond or a larger hatchery. A small insect zoo or an aviary can represent the larger concept of a zoological park.

Learning from plant nurseries can expose young people to the newest technologies in agriculture. For example, the Root Production Method (RPM), a natural process of producing trees developed by Forrest Keeling Nursery, combines air pruning of the root system, trademarked soil preparation, and plant husbandry techniques that result in hardy, dense root systems for healthier, faster-growing trees. Applications of the new technology include

- ▶ Restoration
- ▶ Agroforestry
- ▶ Watershed management
- ▶ Bottomland forest
- ▶ Degraded landscapes
- ▶ Wildlife habitats
- ▶ Wetlands
- ▶ Landscaping
- ▶ Water filtration, and
- ▶ Erosion control.

Top: Children build their own greenhouse each year as part of this outdoor learning program in Sendai, Japan. The scale of farming and agricultural projects is easily modified to fit time and budget constraints. Photograph by Hiroko Hosada. **Center:** Students at a school in Hagi, Japan, tending a koi pond not only learn stewardship concepts but could also focus on aquaponics, the symbiosis of fish and plants. Photograph courtesy of Anne Taylor. **Bottom:** Aviary structure in Japan for housing and learning about birds.

I would like to add that RPM and similar programs can be used for improvement of school grounds or as part of student work on community restoration projects.

A recent therapeutic farming project brought to my attention by social worker and therapist Jo Eekhoff reinforced my belief that nature and the outdoors, combined with the cooperative venture of farming, can heal. Casas de Vida Nueva of New Mexico is linked to an organization whose mission is to serve adults with mental health needs in a safe, caring, culturally sensitive, and sustainable therapeutic farm community. Patients receive treatment while they work in peaceful rural settings. This model can offer some restfulness to our educational system as well. Perhaps every school needs to remove some asphalt and include a garden or farm based on sound ecological practices. We and our children are out of touch with natural cycles. We are losing the survival skills, common sense, and practicality that come from working with the land. We need to value the complex systems and hard work that bring local food to the table and learn about our Earth by digging into the soil and planting some seeds for the future.

Make Our Learning Real!
Proposed campus for Lincoln High
School West, Stockton, California.
Top: School as farm. Community input for Lincoln High School West brought together diverse groups in the valuable antecedent thought process. **Center:** Aerial view of a learning environment on the San Joaquin Delta. Students proposed a school farm and environmental study center in Stockton, rather than another ordinary high school. **Bottom:** Students envisioned a rancher's barn converted into learning environments. Students involved in the project insisted, "Make our education real!"
Concept drawings courtesy of Steven Bingler, Concordia LLC.

Bulldozer removing asphalt

Perhaps every school should reduce the asphalt and put
in a garden or farm. Illustration by Pat Lange.

TOOLS FOR THOUGHT

Landscape Architecture in Relation to Other Disciplines

Ecology
Natural history
Geology, topography
Hydrology, climate
Soils
Botany
Zoology
Field ecology

Land-use
Human ecology
Settlement patterns
Land-use history
Land reclamation
Sustainable development
Utilities/transportation
Real estate issues
Environmental policy

Data methods
Surveying and platting
Map-reading
Air-photo and remote imagery
GIS (Geographic Information Systems)
GPS (Global Positioning Systems)
As-built documentation
Scientific literature
Graphic display of numeric data

Horticulture
Agriculture and forestry
Propagation
Plant identification
Arboriculture, tree surgery
Landscape maintenance
Gardening methods
and styles

Social sciences
Culture/multi-culture issues
Anthropology, sociology
Client/user psychology
Spatial perception and behavior
Territoriality and NIMBY
Accessibility and privacy
Security and vandalism
Fad environmentalism
Anti-environmentalism

Design
Architectural and urban context
Vernacular design
Zoning and preservation statutes
Landscape style traditions
Interpretive landscapes
Fine arts/ public art
Meaning and message
Presentation graphics

Landscape Architecture Synthesis

Management
Public participation
Multi-disciplinary teamwork
Liability and compliance
Ethics of practice
Time accounting and record-keeping
Financing, bonds, insurance
Office management and marketing

Construction
Engineering
Safety and code standards
Contract drawings and details
Specification writing
Estimating
Project management and planning
Supervision and inspection
Conflict resolution and claims
Construction law

© Kim Sorvig 1992

The Preference Interview and Frequency Count

Survey students, teachers, and/or community members about their likes, dislikes, dreams for the school, and dreams for the community. Work with students to make a simple full-page chart for recording responses in each category, or use technology to create a database.

Sample (add as many rows as you need):

Like 	Dislike 	Dream for School 	Dream for Community 

Next, make a list of all ideas taken from the surveys. Have children vote on the preferences you have collected. Make a new chart, as in the sample below. Count and record the frequency of numbers for each item, and tally each category as shown below. Then rank your preferences from high to low.

Preference/Item	Do like	Don't like	Tally
Butterfly garden	+18	-6	+12
Compost area	+10	-0	+10

Agriculture in the Classroom

Janet Hawkes

Former director of the Kids Growing Food Program at Cornell University

The phrase "agriculture in the classroom" may conjure visions of hay bales or cornstalks or perhaps a cow grazing contentedly in the middle of the classroom with a tractor parked outside the door. The true intention of agriculture in the classroom, however, is to reconnect students to the natural world through the food they eat, the clothes they wear, and the homes in which they live. Students are surrounded by everyday items that are derived from the Earth and can be used to teach about life experiences. Chains of learning come from investigating food, clothing, and shelter, and the corresponding resources that support production.

Methods for integrating agriculture into the curriculum are as varied as there are classrooms, but there are some common means and many successes:

Animals in the classroom: Principles of husbandry and care are the same whether it is a hamster, lizard, or goat.

Botany in the classroom: Growing plants takes many forms, including windowsill pots, yogurt cups, "torturing" plants in student research projects, hydroponics, and the use of EarthBoxes or other container gardening.

School gardens: These offer multiple experiences in food production, specialty gardens, arts, wildlife, and herbs.

School solar greenhouses: Greenhouses may be connected to the school building as transitional spaces, separate structures, or featured on rooftops.

Nature areas and outdoor living labs: Nature trails, wildlife plantings, study areas, ponds, streams, habitats, and areas for examination of native or invasive species all contribute to an understanding of living things.

Landscaping: Outdoor design requires understanding of agriculture and horticulture.

The school farm: The working farm embodies all elements of agriculture. Specialized land uses, which can be operated with help from other organizations, include tree or plant farms, orchards, animal pens or zoos, forested areas, aquaculture, and fisheries.

PRACTICAL TIPS FOR BRINGING AGRICULTURAL LEARNING TO YOUR SCHOOL

I have assisted many schools in developing nature study areas, outdoor learning labs, and gardens galore. Some considerations for implementation of programs include the following:

▸ Learning areas should be close to the classroom. Nature and agricultural study need to be convenient and part of the everyday flow of instruction. Also, if daily chores are required, children need to be kept close by for supervision, safety, and other logistical reasons.

▸ Design the space for learning first, not for farming or gardening. For example, a regular animal barn would not include a place where students can gather to observe, learn, and partake in demonstrations and practice.

▸ Features need to be added for the safety of students and animals (see the Examples of Design and Facilities Considerations chart).

▸ School gardens need to accommodate many people working at once in short periods of time.

▸ Practicalities of care for living things include school days, overnights, weekends, holidays, and vacations.

▸ Support for learning requires signage, labeling and interpretation, static learning aids, directions, safety rules and regulations, graphics, and other written material.

▸ Transparency and cutaways can be built into the agricultural structures to provide opportunities for teaching what is going on in the background or behind the scenes (utilities, mechanics, etc.).

Kids Growing Food Program, Cornell University, Ithaca, New York.
Top: Recycling through composting. **Bottom:** Irrigation and water systems concepts include hydroponics, indigenous irrigation techniques, chemistry of pollution and filtering systems, ecosystems, and properties of water. School greenhouses also can be freestanding, used as entryways or extensions to the classroom, used as sources of solar power, or located on rooftops. Photographs courtesy of Janet Hawkes.

Kids Growing Food Program, Cornell University, Ithaca, New York. From farm to market, economic principles are explored through vegetable sales. Photograph courtesy of Janet Hawkes.

▶ Consider the design of the garden, farm, or outdoor lab as part of instruction and part of the learning process. Stay flexible for maximum student input.

▶ Access for all is an issue. Consider ADA and other adaptations.

▶ Think about access and proximity to water (a must!) and other utilities.

▶ Plan to work with maintenance and custodial staff and management and their schedules for upkeep, spraying, and more. Cooperation may need to occur at district level, not just school level. At the Enfield School in New York, for example, planners made sure orchard rows were planted far enough apart to accommodate mower deck width.

▶ Designers need to plan spaces and structures for learning outdoors, including places for observation, writing, reflecting, and teaching. Ways of using spaces must also be planned, i.e., keeping garden notebooks and journals, making presentations.

▶ Remember the practicalities of maintaining nature trails and working around ponds, streams, lakes, or forests, and taking children outdoors to learn. This may require special equipment and storage as well as safety measures.

▶ Remember that each situation is different and locally specific issues must be addressed and accommodated before you begin bringing life to the school.

Retrofitting existing space, changing the schoolyard, and designing for new space are all loads of work, but loads of learning, too. The following is a sampling of some common design and facilities considerations for schools engaging in agriculture in the classroom programs.

Examples of Design and Facilities Considerations for Agriculture in the Classroom
By Janet Hawkes

Activities and Features	Facilities and Design Considerations
Animals in the classroom	▶ Easy access to water in the classroom ▶ Appropriate housing for animals with cleanable surfaces and floors ▶ Double entry doors for animal housing to prevent escapes and provide safety for students ▶ Large capacity feeders and water containers (possibly automatic or self-filling) for weekends ▶ Sealed storage for food and bedding ▶ System for storage and disposal of animal waste from classroom ▶ Quarantine area for sick animals ▶ Good ventilation
Plants in the classroom	▶ Easy access to water (water in the classroom) ▶ Access to sunlight or grow lights ▶ Storage for plant food ▶ Leakproof containers for plants and washable floors and surfaces around plants ▶ Area in or near classroom for potting plants ▶ Quarantine area for "sick" or infested plants
Composting facilities (inside and outside)	▶ For vermicomposting (composting using worms), see considerations for "animals in the classroom" above ▶ Composting has been done successfully in containers directly outside the classroom or kitchen door ▶ Well-ventilated composting system required ▶ Waste material, such as cafeteria food waste, in long windrows using wood chips (or other biofilters) will break down over time in a static composting system. ▶ "Active" composting requires turning or other forms of aeration. ▶ Metal composting containers (or an enclosed composting area) may be required where rodents are a problem.
School garden	▶ Best if located close to the classroom (easier to integrate into instruction) ▶ Access to water ▶ Access to sunlight most of the day ▶ Storage on-site for classroom tools and supplies ▶ Wide gates and paths with accessible surfaces ▶ Raised beds or containers work well where soil is limited or poor, or if gardening on rooftop or within playground ▶ Needs to fit with overall schoolyard design and usage and should fit with grounds maintenance plan (e.g., easy to mow around) ▶ Consider access to refrigeration for preserving the quality of harvested fruits and vegetables. ▶ Long rows or garden beds spaced far apart allow many students to work safely with garden tools simultaneously.

Examples of Design and Facilities Considerations for Agriculture in the Classroom *(continued)*
By Janet Hawkes

Activities and Features	Facilities and Design Considerations
Greenhouse	▶ Needs to be close to the classroom and accessible ▶ Access to water necessary ▶ Automatic ventilation and heating systems required for maintaining proper growing conditions ▶ Wide aisles needed for instruction and accessibility ▶ Bench height should be compatible with the size and abilities of students using the facilities.
Nature area and outdoor learning laboratories	▶ May include trails; wildlife plantings; study areas; safe access to ponds, streams, wetlands, or other water features; fitness trail; wildlife blinds (viewing stands); benches; gazebos or pavilions; interpretive signage; and other built or planted features. ▶ If lab highlights native species or specific plantings, consider removing invasive species ▶ Consider access for emergency vehicles. ▶ Needs to be accessible and close to the school
School landscaping for learning	▶ Wildlife plantings, bird feeders, and other landscaping to attract wildlife should be close to windows so students can observe. ▶ Needs to fit with overall schoolyard design and usage and should fit with grounds maintenance plan (e.g., shrubs may require pruning)
Trails	▶ Accessible to persons with physical disabilities ▶ Include areas where a class can gather (e.g., clearing, pavilion, "pull off," etc.). ▶ May include interpretive signage, views, or areas of interest. ▶ Even in a small area the route can include twists and curves for interest. ▶ Should have a destination or be looped ▶ Consider access to trails for emergency vehicles.
School farm	▶ Design for safety and learning. ▶ Close proximity to classroom (within walking distance) ▶ Access to water and power (including backup systems) ▶ Include teaching spaces at the farm. ▶ Double entry latches, double fencing (electric on the inside near the animals), holding areas or pens, observation areas, livestock stanchions and/or shoots increase safety for the animals, students, and public. ▶ Consider a perimeter fence for the whole farm. ▶ Accessibility needs to be addressed. ▶ Consider fire safety and emergency access elements. ▶ Need easy access for deliveries (e.g., bulk feed or bedding) and disposal and/or removal of waste material

Holten-Richmond
Middle School,
Danvers,
Massachusetts.
DiNisco Design
Partnership,
architect.
Photograph by
Peter Vanderwarker.

Ecologically Responsive
Design and the Global Learner

INTRODUCTION

Biophilia means "love of nature." Edward O. Wilson describes biophilia as the instinctive bond between humans and other living systems. Our affiliations with nature are rooted in our biology. According to a 2006 online article on the Building Green Web site, we should care about biophilia in building design for two main reasons:

1. Research has uncovered real, measurable benefits to human productivity, well-being, stress levels, learning, and healing through green environments; and

2. Appreciation of nature leads to greater protection of nature by humans, including the elimination of pollution and maintaining a clean environment.

Earlier in the book, I introduced ecoism or ecological thinking by suggesting that a philosophy of sustainability addresses our most crucial needs for the future. If we want to survive, we must move from dominion over the planet to kinship with it. The global view depends on shifts in thinking from traditional linear thought to the rhythms of life cycles, networks, and dynamic systems. Technology has helped to bring on this shift and the corresponding need for interactive, autonomous student work, but the deepest forms of ecological understanding emerge from nature and patterns that have been evolving since the origin of the universe. As mentioned earlier, Capra's principles of ecology and his description of systems thinking contribute to this holistic worldview, including patterns of life such as the food cycle and its resulting interdependencies, diversity, partnerships, and how the energy driving natural cycles flows from the sun. Teaching the ancient wisdom of ecological knowledge is the most important role of education in this new century (Capra, 1999).

Tarkington School of Excellence, Chicago, Illinois.
Rooftop gardens and green roofs reduce the volume and impact of storm water runoff, mitigate urban heat island effects, reduce cooling costs, provide a habitat for wildlife, increase human connections to nature, and provide an excellent learning tool. OWP/P, design architect. Warman Olsen Warman, architect of record. Image courtesy of SchoolDesigner president Joel K. Sims, AIA. Photograph © 2005 James Steinkamp.

Sustainable design essentially means that meeting our needs today should not compromise the ability of future generations to meet their own needs. Green architecture refers to design and construction practices that significantly reduce or eliminate the negative impact of building on the environment and its occupants. Some add to this definition by stating that green architecture fosters resiliency and regeneration. It is a positive force that can make the world a better place by giving back more to the environment than the architecture takes from it. Principles of green design include

▶ Saved costs through increased energy efficiency and designs for generating power on-site;

▶ Conservation of resources including water harvesting and careful use of construction materials from selection to production methods to transport;

▶ Improved interior environments for people through thoughtful use of ambient systems for daylighting, thermal comfort, acoustics, air quality, use of nonhazardous materials and minimal finishes; and

▶ Minimal negative environmental impact through recycling, use of renewable or salvaged materials, site planning and location, consulting community, and education.

ECONOMICS OF BUILDING GREEN

In his online report on costs and financial benefits of sustainable buildings, Kats (2003) analyzes energy, waste, and water costs, which can be measured with some precision, as well as health and productivity benefits, which are more difficult to assess. These are some of his findings:

▶ Green buildings average a 30 percent reduction in energy use compared with those built to minimum energy code requirements.

▶ Emissions in green buildings average 36 percent lower than in conventional buildings.

▶ Cost-effective practices include life cycle assessment, commissioning (a systems approach to planning and design), integrating building systems, heat island reductions, more maintenance planning, and reduced electrical consumption at peak periods.

▶ Water conservation can be achieved through technology that increases the efficiency of potable water use, capture of gray water for irrigation, on-site storm water capture, and use of recycled, reclaimed water. Tools include automatic rain sensors, water audit programs, leak detectors, efficient appliances, and better distribution systems.

▶ Health and productivity is affected by poor indoor air quality. There is an estimated 2 percent reduction in productivity because of sick building syndrome (Kats, 2003).

Energy Star is a partnership among businesses, the government, and others, which helps organizations recognize and promote the financial value of top-performing energy-efficient products and buildings. According to a 2002 Environmental Protection Agency (EPA) report, Energy Star–designated office buildings generate utility bills that are 40 percent lower than those of the average office building (U.S. Green Building Council, 2000).

Benefits of green schools far outweigh the costs when the gap between capital and operating costs is addressed. A national review of thirty green schools examined the financial benefits of green school design across several categories, from energy use to worker performance. The cost per square foot for green design was $4, while the operating benefits of green design added up to approximately $68 per square foot (Kats, 2005, quoted in Suttell, 2006).

THE IMPORTANCE OF DAYLIGHT

A well-integrated daylighting design has a greater positive impact on a school than any other sustainable design strategy, according to Innovative Design, Inc.'s Web site. Architects and educators can benefit from many guidelines issued recently on the subject of daylighting, including these found at the Innovative Design Web site (2008):

▶ *The Guide for Daylighting Schools* (2004) by Innovative Design for the Daylight Dividends program.

▶ *Energy Design Guidelines for High Performance Schools* (2002) by the U.S. Department of Energy, National Renewable Energy Laboratory. Includes sustainable school design guidelines developed for seven regions throughout the country, written in accessible language with extensive checklists and case studies.

Conceptual sketch of an Innerscape for a thesis that investigated the architectural and structural means used to introduce the sounds and rhythms of nature to interior environments. Ideas from the research included bioscreens and fences, green walls, bioflower towers, parking lot greenhouses, and other installations of greenery. Image courtesy of A. Shafee Jones-Wilson.

Holten-Richmond Middle School, Danvers, Massachusetts. Exterior solar panels on the south facade increase energy efficiency. DiNisco Design Partnership, architect. Photograph courtesy of SchoolDesigner president Joel K. Sims, AIA. Photograph by Peter Vanderwarker.

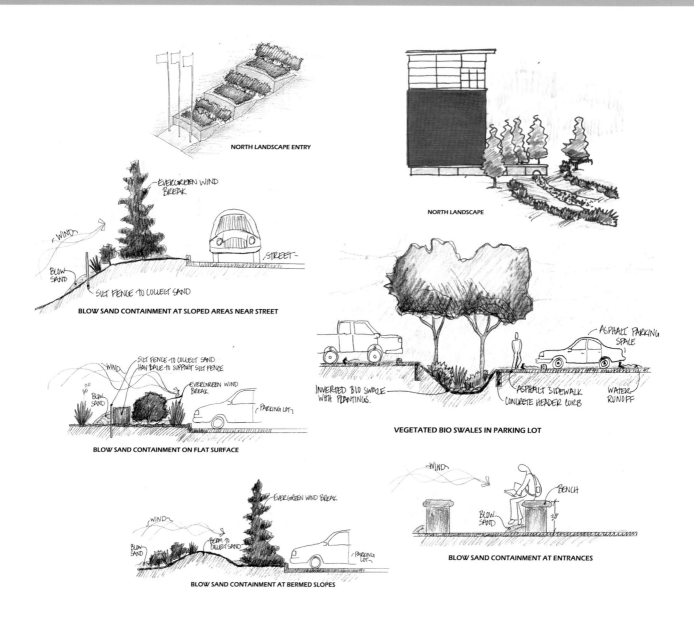

NORTH LANDSCAPE ENTRY

NORTH LANDSCAPE

BLOW SAND CONTAINMENT AT SLOPED AREAS NEAR STREET

BLOW SAND CONTAINMENT ON FLAT SURFACE

VEGETATED BIO SWALES IN PARKING LOT

BLOW SAND CONTAINMENT AT BERMED SLOPES

BLOW SAND CONTAINMENT AT ENTRANCES

V. Sue Cleveland High School, Rio Rancho, New Mexico. Creative, eco-friendly designs address local conditions of blowing sand, parking lot microclimates, and native landscape for a new high school. Van H. Gilbert Architect PC. George Radnovich, Sites Southwest LLC.

LEARNING FROM GREEN DESIGN OF SCHOOLS

Research in the areas of green architecture and ecologically responsive design reveals some basic benefits specifically for schools. Green schools are not only successful buildings in terms of sustainability, but they are also living examples of life choices and systems for the future that can teach children how to live with the new philosophy of ecoism. Many variations in ecological practice can be modified for use in schools.

Preoccupations of green builders and designers are often highly technical, focusing on engineering; mechanical, solar/photovoltaic, monitoring, waste or recycling systems; and the latest environmental technology and materials. When these systems are explained and made highly visible, they can be used to teach science and technology concepts. For example, even the simple concept of a white, reflective roof can be used to teach properties of light, reflection, absorption, and temperature.

Even the school parking lot can be put to educational use. Parking lots and black asphalt create their own climates, which are often harmful to the environment. Students can use parking lots to study ecological issues of runoff, pollution, heat absorption, and nighttime urban warming. Some design solutions that could be incorporated into eco-friendly parking lots include using parking garages, white concrete, and islands of trees and grass to filter runoff and provide shade. A resource for parking lot design is *Parking Spaces: A Design, Implementation, and Use Manual for Architects, Planners, and Engineers* by Mark Childs (1999).

Some technical advances rely heavily on understanding and imitating the beauty and efficiency of natural processes, or *biomimicry*. Many green builders concentrate on creating designs that are not only compatible with nature but that also follow natural laws (how nature works), including creative use of siting, solar energy, natural ventilation systems, daylighting, indigenous materials and design, renewable resources and recycling, and even buildings that can change form, sensing and responding to exterior conditions such as wind, temperature, and light (including tensegrity structures). Greenery is also integrated into the design, including biotecture or greening through green roofs, green facades, green walls, balcony gardens, and plants everywhere.

Permaculture is a design system used to create sustainable habitats by following nature's patterns. Ecological truisms discovered through observation of nature are applied to food production, land use, and sustainable communities through the integration of ecology, landscape, organic gardening, architecture, and agroforestry. School grounds developed using this approach would help students appreciate the efficiency and productivity of natural ecosystems.

The National Wildlife Federation (NWF) provides curriculum and interdisciplinary teaching resources that show learners how to establish and maintain wildlife habitats on school grounds. A side benefit is the enhancement of natural habitats located on school property. NWF is known as a leader in the habitat movement, which recognizes that many of today's children have lost contact with their natural surroundings, in part through urban development and increased use of cars and television. Openness to diversity and a particular sensitivity to climatic conditions and local culture help unveil local rhythms and patterns so children in these environments begin to develop a sense of place.

Building systems and carefully designed outdoor environments can be used to teach the cyclical, dynamic order in the universe such as the changing state of matter or properties of water, biology and the life cycle, Earth science, or other ecological concepts. For example, a green roof demonstrates biology and Earth science concepts associated with the plant life cycle as well as the benefits of plants to environmental air quality and thermal comfort.

Higher education also experiences the impact of increased demand for green design. At the UNM School of Architecture and Planning, my own employer, all courses will be developed around the theme of sustainability. The growing ecodesign movement will require more ecological design degree programs at universities.

Sustainable Design Examples in Schools

▶ Roy Lee Walker Elementary School in Texas, designed by SHW Group in 2000, includes provisions for daylighting, rainwater collection, solar panels, geothermal technology, wind energy, a weather center, sundial, greenhouse, outdoor amphitheater, water habitat, careful materials selection, and computer stations with information about the school's sustainable design (Furger, 2004).

▶ A study by the Capital E group, Lawrence Berkeley Laboratory, and others reveals buildings certified by the LEED program pay for themselves ten times over in a twenty-year period (*School Construction News*, January/February, 2004).

▶ New Mexico Technet is a nonprofit organization that recycles usable computer equipment to be given to schools and other organizations. Health hazards from toxic metals such as lead, mercury, and cadmium exist if computers are not disposed of properly. Young people involved in the program have broken down and properly recycled more than eight hundred computer systems (Moskos, 2004).

▶ Sustainable Technology Center of the San Juan Islands, Washington, is a privately funded research project that provides a visible demonstration of technologies that can be used effectively today. (Schools could do this, too!) The center is largely self-sufficient for its water, sewage, power, and heating needs (Seventh Generation Systems, Inc.).

▶ Larry Shore, an Albuquerque hydrologist, tested his water conservation and reuse ideas at Comanche Elementary School. Shore tested techniques such as hills, hollows, and vegetation to slow water runoff; gravel-filled basins designed for overflow from one to the next, filtering debris and keeping mosquitoes from breeding; a heavily mulched school garden filled with xeric plants; a gravity feed drip irrigation system; and a "water stack" that collects water from roof drains and delivers it to a storage tank (Redman, 2004).

▶ The High-Performance Green Buildings Act of 2006 requires the EPA to develop school site acquisition guidelines. The EPA provides grants to educational agencies for use in addressing environmental issues using EPA assessment tools and for developing state school environmental quality plans.

Other Trends in Green Schools

The long view: Because renovation and design of new schools continues at a high rate, addressing green design at the same time makes sense. Planning based on whole building use and maintenance costs over time (life cycle costs) gives a better idea of a building's true worth, sustainability, and effectiveness than merely considering up-front costs. A recent study written for California's Sustainable Building Task Force concluded that conforming to LEED's Gold Level criteria for green design is very cost-effective for schools. An up-front increase of 2 percent equals life cycle savings of 20 percent of total construction costs (Kats, 2003).

New guides for green schools: Jane Holtz Kay developed criteria for the top ten green schools in the United States for the *Green Guide* (2005). Points include LEED criteria; healthy school lunches (organic, local, composting); schoolwide green initiatives (carpooling, recycling); environmental curricula; school procurement policies (green products); contaminants (pest management, cleaning); and green spaces (student gardens, native plants).

High performance: Schools can be better "high-performance" buildings that equate to better productivity in staff and students, reduced liability, and increased property values. They can also offer opportunities to participate in cost incentive programs for saving energy, and they make good neighbors in the community (U.S. Green Building Council, 2000).

A TANGIBLE MODEL FOR ECOLOGICAL LEARNING:
The Adam Joseph Lewis Environmental
Studies Center at Oberlin College, Ohio

The Environmental Studies Center (ESC) is often cited as a model for maximizing the relationship between a building and its landscape. David Orr, chair of the environmental studies program at Oberlin College and author of *Earth in Mind* and *Ecological Literacy*, worked with students, architect William McDonough + Partners, landscape designers at Andropogon Associates Ltd., landscape architect John Lyle, and many others to develop a building that would:

► Discharge no wastewater

► Generate more electricity than it used

► Use no materials known to be carcinogenic, mutagenic, or endocrine disrupters

► Use energy and materials with great efficiency

Oberlin College, Adam Joseph Lewis Center for Environmental Studies, Oberlin, Ohio.

Right: The campus landscape surrounding the center is a component of the larger energy system and is designed to teach ecological competence in forestry, aquaculture, gardening, biodiversity, and ecological restoration. Andropogon Associates, Ltd., landscape architecture.

Below left: The building itself teaches principles of green architecture and sustainable design, and students monitor many of its operations.

Below right: The Living Machine, a wastewater treatment system, uses living creatures to break down pollutants and purify water. Pictured here are open aerobic tanks located in the building's greenhouse. The tanks are hydroponically planted with rafts of large tropical plants to aid in the purifying process. William McDonough + Partners. Photographs © Barney Taxel.

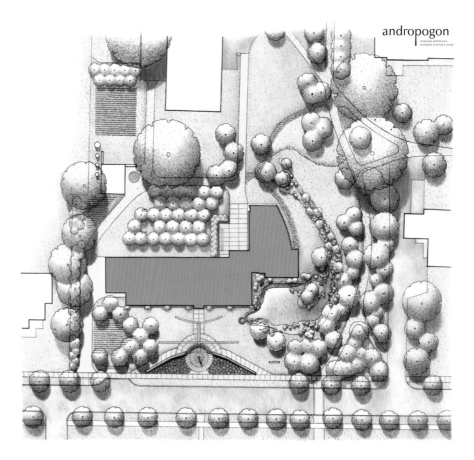

▶ Promote competence with environmental technologies

▶ Use products and materials grown or manufactured sustainably

▶ Be landscaped to promote biological diversity

▶ Promote analytical skill in assessing full costs over the lifetime of the building

▶ Promote ecological competence and mindfulness of place

▶ Become genuinely pedagogical in its design and operations

▶ Meet rigorous requirements for full-cost accounting (Oberlin College, 2008).

The *AIA Journal of Architecture* referred to the measurable success of the Oberlin project in an issue on building performance design. The ESC was selected as one of thirty "milestone buildings in the twentieth century" by the U.S. Department of Energy (Gordon & Stubbs, 2005, p. 15). Student involvement in design and maintenance of systems and outdoor features is essential to that success. The facility features

▶ A large photovoltaic array

▶ A greenhouse/organic wastewater treatment plant

▶ Orchards, gardens, and trees planted and maintained by students

▶ Rainwater collection for gray water storage and for wetlands restoration, and

▶ Low-mow grass in areas that do have turf (pp. 14–15).

Of special interest is a Living Machine wastewater treatment system designed by John Todd that incorporates helpful bacteria, plants, snails, and fish in a series of ecosystems that break down organic pollutants.

THE QUESTION OF BEAUTY

David Orr's writings on sustainability and his work at Oberlin lead us to the question of beauty and the messages we send to young people through current architecture. Orr says that architecture that is wasteful or devoid of local personality teaches us "mindlessness; it teaches that disconnectedness is normal." We need to convert to sustainable technologies, but we also need to incorporate sustainability into a far-reaching definition of aesthetics. Beauty is more than what is right in front of us today. "In the largest sense, what we must do to ensure human tenure on the Earth is to cultivate a new standard that defines beauty as that which causes no ugliness somewhere else or at some later time" (Orr, 1997).

Heerwagen and Hase (2001) argue that buildings are habitats for people. Humans are psychologically adapted to certain landscape features likely to have aided in the early survival of the human race, and the authors suggest a model loosely based on the savannah with its diversity of plant and animal

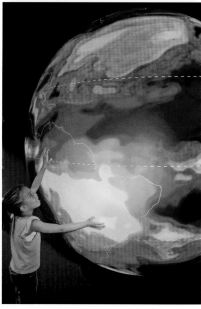

Flint RiverQuarium, Albany, Georgia. Top: Skywater lobby. The RiverQuarium illustrates a complex and collaborative integration of architecture and exhibit design, inspired by the biology, geology, and hydrology of southwest Georgia. Focusing on an axial view to the Flint River, the building wraps and embraces the primary outdoor exhibit, a fifteen-thousand-square-foot naturally landscaped Blue Hole and Cypress Creek. **Bottom:** "World of Water" exhibit. Antoine Predock Architect PC. Robbins Bell Kreher, Inc., executive architect. Photos © Richard T. Bryant. Lyons/Zaremba, exhibit designer.

El Monte Sagrado, Taos, New Mexico.
Top: Tree sculpture with solar collectors provides an alternative energy source at this resort and spa in northern New Mexico. **Bottom:** The Biolarium is a place for quiet contemplation and a living lab illustrating principles of self-sustainability, consisting of water, plants, and rock formations. Photographs by Emily Stout. Living Design Group. Dharma Living Systems.

life, topographic relief, open grassland, bodies of water, and big sky. The more buildings can address this innate sense of beauty, the more they will support our complete satisfaction across body, mind, and spirit (pp. 31–32). As we begin to plan and design school facilities from pre-kindergarten to higher education, we should ask ourselves how nature is integrated into the designs through sensory detail, geometry of nature, diversity, or restfulness. How will the buildings reflect our aesthetic connections to nature? Perhaps the aesthetic quality (spirit connected to nature) of all buildings—schools included—should be considered first in design, with functional quality and health and safety flowing naturally from this aesthetic core.

In *Green Architecture*, James Wines asks why so few architects have used the powers of computer-aided design to move away from the machine age idea of what buildings are. Why have so few architects made the connections between the integrated systems of technology and their ecological parallels in nature to create a new language of mutable, flowing, fluid, responsive, and interactive systems? Wines describes a need for a "visionary 'eco-digital' iconography in architecture" (Wines, 2000, pp. 235–36). Once again, however, he is careful to point out that remedial technology is not the full answer to our history of planetary misuse. Sustainable technologies must be combined with a philosophy of sustainability, a thorough understanding of how important the Earth is to us, resulting finally in a new architecture and a new visual language. The ultimate challenge for our species, Wines concludes, "is not so much trying to understand nature, but re-learning how to intuitively, organically, and cosmologically live on its terms" (p. 236).

THE FORUM: LOOKING AHEAD

As I have said, one of the best ways to educate children and adults for the future is to immerse them in learning environments that are living examples of sustainable design. For inspiration, I recently made a return visit to the Arcosanti project in the Arizona desert. Italian architect Paolo Soleri initiated this experimental city, an alternative to urban sprawl, in 1970. Soleri and his nonprofit Cosanti Foundation promote a new concept of a highly integrated and compact city through the philosophy of *arcology*, a fusion of architecture and ecology. Arcosanti occupies only twenty-five acres of a 4,060-acre land preserve (and uses only 2 percent of the land that similar populations would), has eliminated dependence on automobiles, and works through the interactions of many systems for efficient circulation of people and resources. Arcology offers a "lean alternative" to today's hyperconsumption. Imagine if our schools could emulate the spirit of Arcosanti, adopt a philosophy of sustainability, and become miniaturized, ecologically sound communities surrounded by open, accessible wilderness areas for study outdoors. The following stewardship forum articles reveal how the changeover to a new way of thinking begins with education.

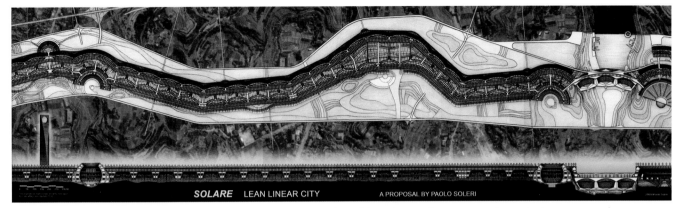

SOLARE LEAN LINEAR CITY   A PROPOSAL BY PAOLO SOLERI

Above: Solare, the lean, linear city. Soleri proposes a continuous urban ribbon designed to intercept the region's wind patterns and to be sensitized to the sun's photovoltaic and greenhouse radiation. A climate-controlled volume constitutes the inner park, which is defined by two main structures of thirty or more stories extending for miles. At the base of the city on the south side are greenhouse aprons, with orchard aprons on the north side. Architect Soleri provides much-needed inspiration for the reformulation of both our attitudes and the structures we build. Paolo Soleri, architect. Image courtesy of the Cosanti Foundation and the Soleri Archives.

Above: Arcosanti, southern exposure. Arcosanti, located seventy miles north of Phoenix, is an experimental project or "urban laboratory" inviting people of all ages to come together to promote an efficient and ecological lifestyle and a rebirth of the concept of cities. Structures include staff housing, a visitors' center, clay bells apse, resident housing, a music center, and more. Paolo Soleri, architect. Image courtesy of the Cosanti Foundation and the Soleri Archives. Photograph by Ken Howie.
Right: Early conceptual sketch of a section of Arcosanti from Paolo Soleri's *Sketchbook #7*, May 1971. Soleri coined the term *arcology*, a fusion of architecture and ecology. Paolo Soleri, architect. Image courtesy of the Cosanti Foundation and the Soleri Archives.

Los Angeles Unified School District Central Region High School #13. Top: Courtyard view. Courtyards between classroom buildings open the visual and pedestrian pathways to the playfields.
Bottom: Aerial view. The high school utilizes a native drought-tolerant landscape pallet and porous paving, while classroom buildings feature outdoor circulation and shading devices to screen direct sun and maximize daylighting. Renderings courtesy of HMC Architects. SchoolDesigner president Joel K. Sims, AIA.

Kuppaswamy Iyengar considers teaching sustainable design to be an ethical imperative for an environmentally stable future. New generations of designers must know how to work with limited energy budgets and resources, respond to regional needs, and effectively use technological advances of green architecture.

Toward a True Ecohistoric Sense of Place

Kuppaswamy Iyengar

Designer, professional engineer, and associate professor at the University of New Mexico School of Architecture and Planning

The concept of sustainable design recognizes that human civilization is an integral part of the natural world, and nature must be preserved and perpetuated if the human community is to survive. Modern technology and methods of construction have degraded our natural resources. Sustainable green architecture declares that this misuse and waste of resources cannot be accepted.

WASTE NOT . . .

The United States has become a wasteful society and, according to Paul Hawken, author of *Natural Capitalism* (2000), the rest of the world is catching up with us. That is a scary thought because the rest of the world has twenty-one times the population of this country. The overall solid waste in the United States exceeds 50 trillion pounds a year. The Fresh Kills Landfill, now closed to further deposits, holds 2.9 billion cubic feet of waste from New York City alone. James Womack, author of *Lean Thinking*, reports that in the United States we are throwing away 88 percent of aluminum, enough to replace an entire commercial aircraft fleet every three months. This kind of waste depletes other resources, ultimately squandering human resources by denying workers the opportunities to be usefully employed.

It appears that we are treating the Earth as if it is in liquidation. Current indicators show that tropical forests are shrinking by 11 million hectares per year; 31 million hectares of forests in industrial countries are damaged by air pollution; underground water tables are failing in parts of Africa, China, India, and North America; fifty types of pesticides contaminate groundwater in thirty-two American states; and the sea level is projected to rise between 4.7 and 7.1 feet by the year 2100.

Under these conditions building a more environmentally stable future requires vision. A wide-ranging analysis and evaluation of the material culture is alerting decision makers and designers in all disciplines to look into reasons to support sustainable design education.

FIVE REASONS

Susannah Hagan in *Harvard Design Magazine* (2003) argues that there are the following reasons to teach sustainability in our schools:

The intellectual: To understand the dynamic and creative operations of nature

The practical: To understand what buildings are doing and effective environmental performance

The technical: To develop software that can test building physics and the complex patterns and interactions between nature and buildings

The economic: To prove that sustainability is economically viable (industrial ecology); and

The pedagogical: To accept the challenge and obligation of training our students for a sustainable future.

All learners should know and be prepared to act on the following principles of sustainability:

1. Support humanity's right to sustainable conditions.

2. Recognize interdependence.

3. Respect the spirit of matter.

4. Accept responsibility for design consequences.

5. Create safe objects of long-term value.

6. Eliminate the concept of waste.

7. Rely on natural energy flows.

8. Understand the limitations of design.

9. Seek constant improvement and share knowledge.

Learners should also be educated in schools that recognize and embody the key elements of sustainable design:

► Energy efficiency

► Building ecology (site transportation impacts)

► Recycle, retrofit, and reuse

► Water efficiency

► Cultural and behavioral issues

THE IMPERATIVE OF GREEN DESIGN

It is impossible to ignore the global environmental crisis: the depletion of the ozone layer, the loss of wildlife habitats, effects of pollution and CO_2 emissions, and changes to the microclimate. Green design not only addresses these energy issues, but it has other advantages, too, including financial savings due to energy efficiency. Daylighting, for example, offers higher architectural quality and improved, long-term life cycle costs. Sometimes less is more *and* less is beautiful.

Sim Van der Ryn defines sustainability as "giving back," a balance between what people take from natural systems and what they return. His "ecomorphic" designs focus on copying the processes in nature rather than merely imitating organic forms, which is the aim of biomorphic design.

Five Broad Principles of Ecological Design

Adapted from Van der Ryn, S., & Cowan, S. (1996).
Ecological Design. *Washington DC: Island Press.*

Sim Van der Ryn

author and president of Van der Ryn Architects.

ONE: SOLUTIONS GROW FROM PLACE

Specific-site conditions and users' values lead to design solutions. Many design opportunities and possibilities are sacrificed to centralization and standardization. If we are sensitive to the nuances of place, we can inhabit without destroying.

TWO: ECOLOGICAL ACCOUNTING INFORMS DESIGN

No design can get by without an economic accounting of cost. We should also provide an ecological accounting of costs, from resource depletion to pollution to habitat destruction. Determine the most ecologically sound design possible.

THREE: DESIGN WITH NATURE

By working with the patterns and processes favored by the living world, we can dramatically reduce the ecological impacts of our designs. By engaging in processes that regenerate rather than deplete, we become more alive.

FOUR: EVERYONE IS A DESIGNER

Distinctions between designer, participant, and user vanish when the solution grows and evolves organically out of a particular situation, process, and pattern of communication. Listen to every voice in the design process.

FIVE: MAKE NATURE VISIBLE

Effective design helps inform us of our place within nature. Our environments are the most powerful teachers we have.

Sim Van der Ryn's *Design for Life* is a look at his life's work designing sustainable architecture. An understanding of living things and natural patterns can address the spirit of green architecture. Source: Van der Ryn, S. (2005). *Design for Life: The Architecture of Sim Van der Ryn*. Layton, UT: Gibbs Smith, Publisher. **Left:** Nautilus cross section. The harmony of the Fibonacci series is present in the shell's curvature (Doczi, 1981). **Center:** Pine cone. Scales grow along the intersections of two sets of helixes, spirals that unfold in three-dimensional space like the DNA molecule (Doczi, 1981). **Right:** Trees adapt a branching pattern to match the demands of their environment. Other branching patterns are seen in erosion, rivers and tributaries, blood vessels, roots, and leaves. Photographs by Michael J. Resudek, Imagic Digital Imaging and Design.

Shannon Horst applies the principles of a holistic worldview to the school as a farm. Her broad vision involves long-term thinking about land use and decision making by students in real time. We are talking about the real-life management questions faced each day in the real world. Our students must learn to ask what constitutes quality of life and how we sustain it.

The School District Farm and Areas of Management Concern

Shannon Horst

Senior director of strategic initiatives, Holistic Management International

A school farm can encourage study of holistic principles and land management. Photograph courtesy of Shannon Horst.

The chief aims of any school wishing to start or augment an existing farm will be to help learners:

▸ Develop a deep and broad understanding of and appreciation for the physical/ biological world around them,

▸ Create a sound process for making decisions about the human impact on the environment based on holistic thinking (consideration of wholes when changing any of the parts),

▸ Adopt an interdisciplinary approach, bringing the world of plants, animals, water, and sunlight into focus with all humanities and sciences,

▸ Experience the flow of curriculum over time (long-term learning) from initial master planning to site analysis, site development, continuing documentation and research to ongoing role-playing, and

▸ Use intergenerational and multicultural processes in their own communities, or, simulating and role-playing the makeup of real communities.

To start, first-year students approach the initial development of farm resource areas as if they were a small community of farmers, ranchers, and conservationists who have just moved onto the land. This requires establishing long-term goals melding social aspects of their lives (relationships, communication), financial concerns, and external environmental realities of place. It is important to ask the following goal-setting questions:

▶ What constitutes quality of life? What is most important?

▶ What will students have to produce or create to reach that quality of life?

▶ How will their resources, products, and creations have to function in order for coming generations to enjoy and maintain a similar quality of life far into the future?

STUDENT-CENTERED LEARNING

The master plan for construction of a new farm should set aside designated areas for agricultural study and nothing further. Students, rather than professional engineers or extension agents, should be required to determine organizational elements such as the proximity of water to pastures and crop areas; location of buildings for materials, equipment, and feed; natural flow of the landscape; and how to encourage wildlife habitats. We do not recommend that planners place temporary structures or purchase in advance any of the equipment to be used. In fact, until the learners decide the types of crops, animals, and farming processes they intend to use, structures and equipment cannot be determined. Students can play a viable role in planning and designing all of the needed spaces and places. The process of determining what, where, how, and why will be invaluable to the first classes of learners. The process of studying how the first learners made their decisions and the critique of outcomes will be invaluable to follow-up generations of learners.

AREAS OF MANAGEMENT CONCERN

Once the site is fully analyzed across multiple disciplines by students and by teachers acting as facilitators, students begin to think about categories of land management and how they can be used to create an all-encompassing learning environment. Six areas of management and some corresponding support systems are described below.

One: Croplands

▶ Based on the decisions made by the students, land plots can be small, diverse, and intensely managed at the human level, or they can be larger monoculture plots. The larger the land acreage, the greater the need to make large management equipment available.

▶ The availability of water is probably the most important issue to address. If a cash crop is to be grown, some type of irrigation needs to be designed: flood, ebb and flow, sprinkler disbursement, or drip irrigation. Irrigation practices should be appropriate for the crop they will be servicing. Water conservation is always an important consideration in any good irrigation design.

▶ Crop specialists should be consulted before any design is implemented.

▶ Regarding equipment, students will need basic tools before the start of any planting. Tillage occurs before planting and allows the wakening of the soil through loosening of soil particles and movement of microbial activity, increasing the success of the crop. Reviewing planting practices and the proper use and purposes of tools is recommended before any activity occurs.

▶ Students must have an understanding of the plant life cycle—from seed to produce-bearing vegetation—before engaging in any crop production. They should understand photosynthesis and its impact on our lives.

▶ Conventional fencing may or may not be necessary, depending on alternatives tested by the students. Any structures that are implemented should be designed and built by the students.

Two: Pasture

▶ These open spaces are used to provide food for livestock, usually cattle, sheep, and horses. Fences or other enclosures are usually required. Again, water availability for the livestock as well as the vegetation must be considered.

▶ Students can be assisted in their decision-making process by role-playing pastoral lifestyles. Through this activity they begin to understand other cultures and the history of various civilizations. Again, students themselves should determine how they would deal with the issues they come across during role-play.

▶ Fencing has implications for local wildlife. Students may need to contact local wildlife societies and agencies to get a better understanding of the regional niche. There are opportunities to investigate new technology for controlling animal movement, such as radio wave technology similar to that used for burglar alarms.

▶ In the event the land is unable to provide adequate forage for a large herd of animals, storage facilities for hay and other mineral supplements (oats, pellets, grain, salt, molasses) will be needed. Other facilities for handling (breeding, branding, weaning, etc.) also may be needed.

▶ Pasture and cropland areas may need to be relatively close to one another so animals can graze crop residue and fertilize the land. Again, these are the types of problems learners will address and test.

Three: Timber

▶ Forested ecological systems provide a wonderful learning atmosphere. The tall stories of tree canopies provide filtering light onto a very active microbial city. The forest floor is filled with decomposing microbes that regenerate energy and minerals back into the soil, providing nutrients for future plants.

▶ At least one area of intense timber should exist for students to study and research forest settings. Smaller timber areas can be scattered throughout the site, however, not only for learning but also for beauty.

▶ Students will want to consider both deciduous and coniferous trees. They should research what was once native to the area and work with these varieties. Nonnative varieties can be tested—carefully—for learning experiences.

Four: Fishery

▶ If there is access to abundant water, a fishery can be established to study aquatic life. The fishery could be an especially valuable tool for studying other cultures because a large percentage of the world eats fish as its only source of protein.

▶ Holding ponds, breeding ponds, the flow of water, etc., could be designed by the learners. Numerous organizations, including many international development agencies (U.S. Peace Corps, Unitarian Universalist Service Committee, Save the Children) can assist with suggestions on design and construction.

▶ Fish, microlife, aquatic plants, birds, and other wildlife attracted to the fishery could be documented and studied.

Five: Wetlands

▶ Students can establish constructed wetlands on the site. Using the wetlands for treating liquid waste gives learners good examples of new technologies for cleaning up the environment. Water, after it has left the wetland, is 99.9999 percent clean. It is not suggested for human consumption but can be used for crop agriculture and for animals.

▶ Wetlands are especially useful to the students' education because they encompass several orders of land management. In any wetlands, the wildlife, vegetation, livestock, and fishery all become an integral part of the success of their sustainability.

Six: Wildlife

▶ Habitat for wildlife can and should be woven throughout the management areas. Once the students have a good understanding of these habitats, they can work to improve habitat qualities and characteristics. The presence of wildlife (or lack thereof) is a valuable indicator of the health of the soil, water, and vegetation.

▶ It may be difficult to encourage wildlife on some sites, given the amount of human activity that will be occurring. Wildlife can often learn to live side by side with human activity as long as the animals feel safe. Birds, insects, and small rodents can usually be found on most sites.

INTERDISCIPLINARY LEARNING FROM AREAS OF MANAGEMENT

Areas of management serve as contexts for learning key concepts and skills from all disciplines. Man's relationship to agriculture provides a history of civilization, from hunter-gatherer to settled farmer. Throughout the centuries, dance, literature, painting, and music have expressed the themes of land, water, sun, plants, and animals. The politics and economics surrounding food and environmental issues represent a major portion of any government's agenda. Agriculture requires care and maintenance of equipment and hands-on mechanical understanding. Technology for agriculture runs the gamut from hybrid seeds to sophisticated watering systems to genetic engineering of animals to conservation and energy technology. Environmental issues can also be used as themes for knowledge acquisition. Students learn that sound resource management must be approached from a holistic base—people, land, and wealth that can be generated from the land forever.

FURTHER SOURCES OF INFORMATION FOR LEARNING FROM AGRICULTURE

There are numerous organizations whose sole mission is to provide information on agriculture and the environment. The Institute for Earth Education based in Illinois offers some wonderful programs for teaching children about the physical Earth. Appropriate Technology Transfer for Rural Areas (ATTRA) is a division of U.S. Fish and Wildlife in the Department of the Interior. ATTRA accepts queries on crops, herbicides, farming techniques, and more; researches issues; and provides answers or further sources of information.

The United States has an unsurpassed network of extension services tied to its land-grant institutions. Their services are provided mostly free of charge to farmers and ranchers. Government agencies such as the U.S. Forest Service, U.S. Fish and Wildlife, U.S. Soil Conservation Service, and various state game and fish departments can provide a wealth of information and advice. Many of these organizations have access to computer software that can map on-screen various alternatives in resource management and can give graphic representations of the effects any change might have on the greater whole. The Environmental Systems Research Institute in Redlands, California, develops most of the very best systems used for these purposes.

A couple of key electronic networks deal with environmental and agricultural issues. These include EcoNet (environmental issues), HandsNet (agricultural and farming-related concerns), and InterNet (the largest multi-issue source, with avenues to other networks, including most of the universities and colleges in the nation). For additional sources, please see the reference list at the end of the book.

This material is excerpted from "Sustainable and Energy-Efficient Schools,"
a report prepared by Becker (2002). Through his work with Albuquerque
Public Schools, Becker was also instrumental in designing Edward Gonzales
Elementary School, known as the Mazria "E" school prototype design.

Sixteen Building Blocks for High-Performance School Buildings

Robert Becker, Architect

Former staff architect for Albuquerque Public Schools in New Mexico

Three key characteristics distinguish high-performance schools from conventional school facilities. They

- ▸ Promote health and productivity through increased attention to ambient elements such as acoustic, thermal, and visual comfort

- ▸ Are cost-effective because they use energy analysis tools and life cycle cost analysis, and

- ▸ Are sustainable because they use energy conservation techniques.

Sixteen building blocks incorporate a whole building design approach to ensure a high-performance school.

1. ACOUSTIC COMFORT

Solutions that increase acoustic comfort in classrooms include configuring rooms and walls to dampen rather than magnify sound reverberation (bounce); specifying sound-absorbing materials; avoiding the location of mechanical rooms adjacent to classrooms; using larger mechanical ductwork with lower air flow speeds; and providing earth berms at property lines to reduce street noise.

2. COMMISSIONING

This systematic process provides a checklist for all phases of the project from programming to POE to ensure that building systems (mechanical, electrical, and controls) deliver the proper results for the end user. Proper initial installation of building systems is extremely important. Construction documents must therefore include any costs associated with additional time spent on inspections, testing, and monitoring equipment. The end product will be a written comprehensive commissioning plan with a final report that should contain documentation of design intent and operating protocols; testing and measurement of in-place systems; preparation of operation and maintenance manuals; and equipment used with a logging process to monitor performance.

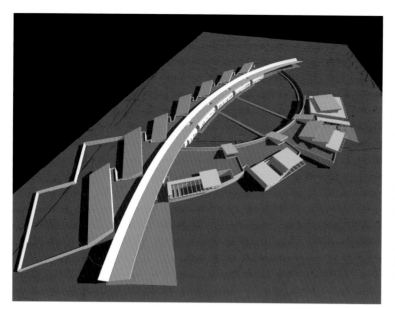

Edward Gonzales Elementary School, Albuquerque, New Mexico. Gonzales Elementary is an energy-efficient elementary school, or e-school, a prototype sustainable school located in a rapidly growing area of southwest Albuquerque. Santa Fe solar energy architect Edward Mazria, author of *The Passive Solar Energy Book*, included many eco-friendly elements. **Top:** This aerial conceptual model shows the pinwheel design with angled wings extending from a central curved axis, getting the most out of the New Mexico sun. **Bottom:** The roof collects and funnels rainwater runoff into a cistern. Buildings shelter the playground from prevalent westerly winds. Images courtesy of Mazria Inc. Odems Dzurec. Edward Mazria, architect. Robert Becker, architect formerly with Albuquerque Public Schools.

3. DAYLIGHTING

One concept uses internal and external light shelves located high to reduce internal glare and not obstruct view, in concert with large expanses of exterior glass and interior partition openings. Other features of daylighting use skylights and roof monitors, clerestory windows, and the concept of introducing light from two sides to eliminate glare. Daylighting can be maximized if the footprint of a structure is laid out on an elongated east-west axis on the building site. Because of our country's location in the northern hemisphere, an abundance of south-facing glass should be used. Solar gain can be regulated throughout the year by using predetermined overhangs for maximum winter solar gain and elimination of any sunlight on glass in the summer. The light element is controlled by using interior shades, louvers, blinds, and exterior overhangs and trees. The introduction of controlled light into the building saves on energy costs by allowing the building's electric light fixtures to be turned off.

4. ENERGY ANALYSIS TOOLS

Different whole building models can be analyzed with computer programs to determine annual energy consumption with accurate cost estimates to see which models are most efficient and meet the owner's budget. Two commonly used programs are Energy-10, developed by the National Renewable Energy Laboratory's Center for Building and Thermal Systems, and Building Design Advisor, offered by the Lawrence Berkeley National Laboratory.

5. ENERGY-EFFICIENT BUILDING SHELL

The term "building shell" is used to describe components that compose the exterior skin of a structure, including the walls, roof, floors, and windows. Three items to consider are high-performance glazing, shading devices, and light-colored surfaces. These techniques are easy for students to understand and for instructors to use as teaching tools. Depending on the specific application and climatic factors, designers must consider the best combinations of insulating value (R-value), daylight transmittance, and solar heat gain coefficient when evaluating glazing components. Designers must also consider thermal mass and air leakage control. Thermal mass materials such as concrete and brick store heat but do not transmit it quickly. On hot days it can slow heat penetration into the building until nighttime, when ventilation can cool it down. Air leakage control techniques include caulking dissimilar material joints and weather-stripping doors and windows.

6. ENVIRONMENTALLY PREFERABLE MATERIALS AND PRODUCTS

Construct a facility with durable, nontoxic materials that contain a majority of recycled content and can easily be recycled after their latest use. Avoid materials that release volatile organic compounds (VOCs). The harvest and manufacture of products must not pollute our air and water, destroy animal and plant habitats, or deplete our natural resources. When manufacturing products, try to use a single, well-integrated operation at one site with local raw materials to cut down on distance transportation.

7. ENVIRONMENTALLY RESPONSIVE SITE PLANNING

Sensitive site planning theories include leaving as much undisturbed natural landscaping as possible, restoring damaged areas, minimizing storm water runoff, and controlling erosion. One technique to minimize storm water runoff and control erosion is to reduce the number and size of hard surface areas, known as "heat islands." The more moisture that can be immediately absorbed into the ground without flowing across impervious surfaces the better. Plan for on-site storm water retention ponds to keep moisture from leaving the site too quickly.

8. HIGH-PERFORMANCE HEATING, VENTILATING, AND AIR-CONDITIONING

A building's HVAC system should use high-efficiency equipment, be sized properly for the estimated demands of the facility, and have controls that boost the system's performance. A properly sized system will cost less to install, take up less space, use less energy, and run more efficiently over time.

9. HIGH-PERFORMANCE ELECTRIC LIGHTING

Save energy and provide visual comfort for school occupants by installing pendant-type fixtures with up-shining indirect lighting features that allow the illumination in a room to reflect off light-colored ceilings and not glare directly on work surfaces. For exterior area lighting, keep light poles away from neighboring property lines. The fixture itself can be designed with top shields to keep nighttime light pollution to a minimum.

10. LIFE CYCLE COST ANALYSIS

Enlightened owners consider the total cost of the facility over time. Not only do they evaluate the initial cost of design and construction, but they also look at operating cost factors like utilities and maintenance, repair, and replacement expenses. A sustainable school will often have higher initial costs for some items. The energy savings and fewer maintenance requirements over time, however, will often pay for the item in a short period of time.

11. RENEWABLE ENERGY

Renewable energy can be defined as a free source of power that can be harnessed. The most common renewable energy sources are solar, wind, and geothermal. Wind turbines or propellers convert the kinetic energy present in wind into mechanical power and electricity. Photovoltaic panels are being integrated into building components more frequently, and stand-alone systems are often used to power caution lights in school zones or remote security lighting. Geothermal heat pumps are used to pump water in and out of the ground at great depths in a closed-pipe system to heat and cool a building.

12. SAFETY AND SECURITY

Increase opportunities for physical surveillance, reinforce a sense of territory, and control access to buildings and grounds. Outside areas such as parking lots, playgrounds, and drop-off points should be well-lit and easily observable from inside the building. Consider providing view ports in doors and windows from classrooms to observe corridors. Open up stairwells for easy monitoring. Features such as decorative fencing and paving treatments help reinforce the sense of territory in aesthetically pleasing ways. Less institutional-looking spaces and smaller, personal-scale spaces make a learning environment feel more like home. Use graffiti-resistant materials and finishes. Limiting the number of entries to the building and grounds helps control access, and providing good visual surveillance of entries is a good practice. Some parts of a facility need to be "locked down" when the community uses other parts after hours or in the event of an intrusion. All of these suggested design features can be enhanced by using security technologies such as surveillance cameras, high-security locks, metal detectors, or fingerprint identification.

13. SUPERIOR INDOOR AIR QUALITY

Controlling the sources of building contamination, providing adequate ventilation, preventing unwanted moisture accumulation, and implementing effective operations and maintenance procedures will help provide superior indoor air quality.

14. THERMAL COMFORT

"Thermal comfort" means how hot or cold the building's occupants are. The variations between temperature and humidity can be devastating if they are disproportionate and do not remain within a tolerable comfort zone. Hot and stuffy or cold and drafty conditions, especially between seasonal climate changes, can be improved by providing manually operated windows for fine tuning ventilation or configuring rooms and operable windows to take advantage of cross ventilation.

15. VISUAL COMFORT

A good mix of design elements should provide a properly lit visual environment using daylighting effectively while reducing the need for artificial lighting. Consider using automatic dimming controls to adjust artificial lighting levels or shut lighting off completely. An important principle in lighting theory is to design for uniformity with flexibility.

16. WATER EFFICIENCY

School districts and individual schools can implement their own water conservancy programs to save water while offering instructional tools for students to learn about ecology and the environment. Schools can save costs by using water reduction techniques in landscaping (xeriscaping, using native vegetation and drip irrigation); conservation during construction; water-conserving fixtures (shower heads that restrict flow, aerators at sink faucets, electronic water regulation of plumbing fixtures, waterless urinals); plus rainwater and gray water reuse management (water harvesting).

CONCLUSION

A reoccurring theme throughout all the research in this field is the concept of using many of the energy-saving techniques as teaching tools for our students and future leaders. An approach as simple as exposing structural and mechanical systems not only saves the construction cost of a ceiling, but also allows the students a view into the material makeup of their facility. Recycling programs, weather stations tied to local television stations, and water habitat projects are all ways to involve community access in schools. Attracting outside professionals and experts to schools is equivalent to having more teachers in the classroom.

Daylighting and the Environmentally Responsive School

Stephen Dent

*Associate professor and former associate dean
of the School of Architecture and Planning
at the University of New Mexico*

The primary purpose of a school facility is to create a physical setting that enables, perhaps even ennobles, the learning process. Creating a school that is highly energy efficient and that minimizes its impact on natural resources is a worthy part of this goal. Environmentally responsive buildings can contribute to the learning process by their very nature and have much lower operating costs, both critical factors in a time when our schools and educational systems are being attacked for numerous perceived failures and in which budgets are always strained.

LIGHT AND LEARNING

Architects traditionally believed that light was crucial to understanding and amplifying the design intent of their buildings, but many architects lost the skill to design with light when tight budgets, security concerns, and poor understanding of energy conservation led to a generation of buildings with few windows and the cheapest light fixtures possible.

For several decades we have known that the controlled introduction of daylight into larger buildings could dramatically reduce electricity use for lighting and the cooling needed to remove the heat generated by overused electric lights. The Heschong Mahone Group, Inc. has published several reports that document the benefits of natural daylight to the learner in the classroom as well (Heschong, Wright, & Okura, 2002). In one dramatic example from the Capistrano Unified School District in California, researchers determined that classrooms with excellent daylighting were associated with students' standard test score improvements of 15 to 23 percent over a one-year period when compared with the classrooms with poor or no daylighting! The jury is still out on the interpretation of this study and its widespread applicability, but at the very least it reinforces the commonly expressed preference for daylight over electric lighting. It is my hope that such research may hasten the day that all schools are designed with integrated daylighting systems.

Architecture students use models outdoors to test actual solar conditions for their designs. Photograph courtesy of Stephen Dent.

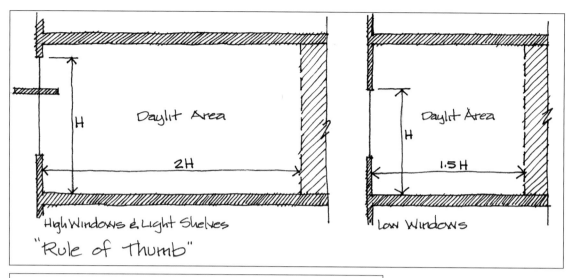

Top: Rule of thumb for daylit areas.
Section drawing by Stephen Dent.

Center: Light shelf diagram.
Section drawing by Stephen Dent.

Bottom: High-performance building
section. Drawing by Stephen Dent.

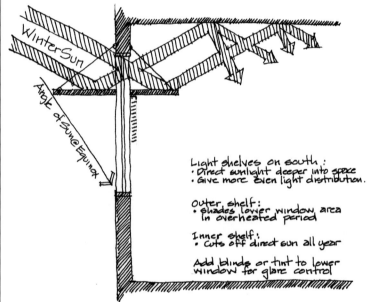

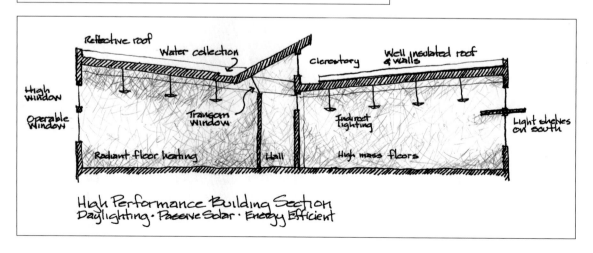

I personally believe that, of all the natural forces and environmental factors that influence learning environments, daylight is the most critical in shaping the architectural response. There are, however, some broad caveats to the use of daylight:

▸ Avoid the direct beam of sunlight on the visual task; widely distributed diffuse light is less likely to cause glare and visual discomfort. Installing skylights and clerestories with baffles and windows with light shelves can accomplish this goal.

▸ Avoid overheating the space with too much direct light and its associated solar heat through the judicious use of shading devices such as overhangs, louvers, fins, screens, and landscaping.

▸ Use daylight models ($3/8$" = 1'0" or larger scale) of critical spaces to evaluate the design, light quality, and light levels. Light has no scale itself, so models that are correct in their spatial geometry and finish characteristics (reflectivity, absorption, and transmission) are accurate representations of the final design.

▸ Use to your advantage the visual variability and drama of sunlight in entries, corridors, and other spaces without critical visual tasks.

▸ Coordinate the daylight design with the electric lighting system in order to maximize energy and cost savings through automated control and dimming systems. Make the daylighting system seamless with the electric lighting and integral to the building design. This helps prevent elements from being "value engineered" out of the project.

▸ Coordinate the daylight design with the need for views and ventilation.

RELATED ISSUES

Daylighting and solar design relate to thermal comfort, which is also critical for learning. Good windows using insulated glazing and low-emissivity (low-e) or spectrally selective technology greatly reduce heat loss and permit the optimization of daylight. Take advantage of the potential for passive solar heating. Collect solar heat without uncomfortable glare in sufficient thermal mass, and thus prevent losing what you gain with generous insulation. Consider the issue of shade. Remember that spring and fall are characterized by large climatic fluctuations and uncontrollable solar gain on a warm day can lead to great discomfort. Shading is the key to managing solar gain and it works even better if it is adjustable or augmented with deciduous vegetation that naturally follows the climate. New double-curtain wall systems may be used to shade and to create thermal buffer zones that moderate solar gain and daylighting while allowing natural ventilation to do much of the cooling.

Look for synergies in application of technologies such as cogeneration with on-site power generation. For a more dramatic effect, use transparent photovoltaic panels to moderate the daylighting while generating power to create oxygen for accelerating the waste treatment process and hydrogen for powering a fuel cell. Sophisticated computerized control systems for optimizing the operation and energy use of mechanical systems, lighting, security, and fire safety systems are usually a great investment.

USING THE BUILDING

The built environment can always offer lessons and settings for learning, but when this attitude begins with the design process, the possibilities expand exponentially. Exposing and expressing construction such as ductwork, trusses, or welded exposed steel joints shows how the building was erected. Built-in sensors and monitors that track energy use and compare it with daylighting and other energy design goals and similar buildings' usage allow for intelligent modifications that continually improve performance.

Special spaces such as solar greenhouses can serve as "classrooms" for biology and ecology as well as provide essential functions. Marking sun paths throughout a day or year from a sundial in a plaza connects us to the continuing variation in our natural environmental systems. Designing adjustable shading and daylight control systems, for example, would allow students to test various hypotheses that involve solar geometry, climate conditions, interior comfort, and energy use. In general, a malleable building offers more opportunity for exploration and learning possibilities than a fixed one.

SAMPLE LEARNING EXPERIENCES

Solar races: Simplified building models that can be modified with more or less insulation, thermal storage mass, window areas, ventilation openings, and shading can be "raced" outside against each other to test and compare these variables in actual climate conditions. Which modifications produce the warmest or coolest results?

Daylight models: Models can predict actual conditions in building designs. Students can determine if the daylighting in their classroom can perform better as they learn and apply solar geometry and the principles of reflection, absorption, transmission, and diffusion of light.

Ice cube melting or water boiling competitions (using solar radiation): These exercises develop knowledge of the properties of materials; measurement and recording of observations; the basics of heat transfer through conduction, convection, and radiation; and phase changes from solid to liquid to steam.

I've heard that we will be building and remodeling more schools in the next ten years than we have in the last forty years. Shouldn't they be the most exciting learning places that we can create and serve as models of environmental responsibility for the next generation as well?

George Pearl Hall at the University of New Mexico School of Architecture and Planning, Albuquerque. Studio. Exposed trusses and ductwork help architecture students understand building systems. Antoine Predock, Architect PC. Photograph by Brad Pullium.

How do we accommodate the educational process for all children on every continent? Perhaps planners need to examine the feasibility of children and communities designing and building their own sustainable schools, following the example of Dierkx and others seeking to make the world a better place.

Dierkx (2003) outlines the benefits of community school models:
- ▸ *Using local materials in a new way*
- ▸ *Creating multiple opportunities for learning*
- ▸ *Integrating architecture, landscape, and climate*
- ▸ *Encouraging full control and participation of communities*
- ▸ *Integrating water and sanitation systems with the environment*
- ▸ *Using architecture as a tool for learning*
- ▸ *Modeling the potential for other school designs*

The following text is adapted from the project summary and proposal Dierkx wrote (2003) for community-based sustainable schools in Sierra Leone, Africa. It serves as a statement of values for the cultural model for schools of the future.

Project Summary

Sierra Leone, Africa

René Dierkx, PhD

Architect and urban planner

Broad improvements in children's welfare will not occur unless children receive wider access to affordable, better quality services in health, education, water, sanitation, and electricity. Without such improvements, freedom from illness, illiteracy, and poverty will remain elusive to many. In *The State of the World's Children 2003* (UNICEF, 2003), one finds that such services often fail children and that authorities, parents, and children can do better. Community-based participation is key in determining the quality and quantity of the services people receive.

The overall aim of this project is to develop a new paradigm, a child-centered methodology for community-based architectural programming, planning, and development of primary schools in sub-Saharan Africa, in which the school building will be used as a tool for learning sustainability principles. This is combined with the development of models for cost-effective, sustainable, and child-friendly schools.

Education is a basic right. Child-friendly, sustainable design in Sierra Leone uses community participation and local labor and materials. Image courtesy of René Dierkx.

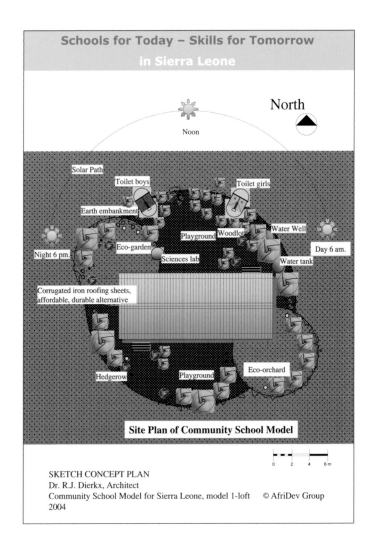

The first objective is to develop a community-based participatory school planning approach to enable communities to plan schools that are affordable, sustainable, inclusive, and conducive to lifelong learning and teaching.

The second objective is to develop a policy framework and strategy work program to support school development that will be incorporated into the United Nations and World Bank education policies, strategies, and technical assistance programs.

The third objective is to develop cost-effective primary school models to achieve the global campaign goal of Education for All by 2015, as this requires an unprecedented number of new classrooms. Currently, 50 million children in sub-Saharan Africa do not attend school. The cost of excluding so many from education and chances for a sustainable economic livelihood is rising sharply, threatening societal stability. Education and schools are basic children's rights and the keys to sustained and equitable growth needed to escape poverty.

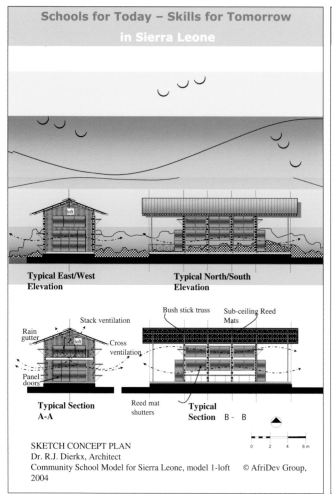

Schools for Today – Skills for Tomorrow
in Sierra Leone

Typical East/West Elevation

Typical North/South Elevation

Stack ventilation
Bush stick truss   Sub-ceiling Reed Mats
Rain gutter
Cross ventilation
Panel doors

Typical Section A-A

Reed mat shutters

Typical Section B - B

SKETCH CONCEPT PLAN
Dr. R.J. Dierkx, Architect
Community School Model for Sierra Leone, model 1-loft   © AfriDev Group, 2004

0   2   4   6m

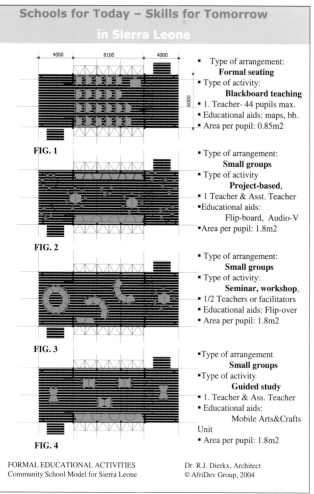

Schools for Today – Skills for Tomorrow
in Sierra Leone

- Type of arrangement: **Formal seating**
- Type of activity: **Blackboard teaching**
- 1. Teacher- 44 pupils max.
- Educational aids: maps, bb.
- Area per pupil: 0.85m2

FIG. 1

- Type of arrangement: **Small groups**
- Type of activity **Project-based,**
- 1 Teacher & Asst. Teacher
- Educational aids: Flip-board, Audio-V
- Area per pupil: 1.8m2

FIG. 2

- Type of arrangement: **Small groups**
- Type of activity: **Seminar, workshop,**
- 1/2 Teachers or facilitators
- Educational aids: Flip-over
- Area per pupil: 1.8m2

FIG. 3

- Type of arrangement **Small groups**
- Type of activity **Guided study**
- 1. Teacher & Ass. Teacher
- Educational aids: Mobile Arts&Crafts Unit
- Area per pupil: 1.8m2

FIG. 4

FORMAL EDUCATIONAL ACTIVITIES
Community School Model for Sierra Leone

Dr. R.J. Dierkx, Architect
© AfriDev Group, 2004

Community school model for Sierra Leone.
Facing page: Site plan of community school model, Sierra Leone. Sketch concept plan by René Dierkx, architect. AfriDev Group, 2004.
This page left: Elevation and section drawings. Sketch concept plan by René Dierkx, architect. AfriDev Group, 2004.
This page right: Plan views of configurations for different learning activities and varying group sizes for the community school model, Sierra Leone. Schematic drawing by René Dierkx, architect. AfriDev Group, 2004.

Glacier View School (K–12), Sutton, Alaska.
Top: A moose visits the school near the overhang porches. Glacier View won the 1997 Lighthouse Award from CEFPI. **Bottom:** It is hard to believe the school's original design turned its back on this view. The Glacier View project consisted of a complete remodeling and addition to the small rural school. Architects Alaska. © Tom Arnot, Ripple Photography.

Making the Most of Site
Remodeling (and Rethinking) a Small Rural School

Glacier View School in Matanuska-Susitna Borough, Sutton, Alaska
Architects Alaska

John Crittenden, project architect
Stuart Smith, project director

The predominant feature of the site of Glacier View School is its location in the Matanuska River Valley, surrounded by mountains, with a view across the valley to the Matanuska glacier. The site itself is a geologic classroom and yet, ironically, the original school building turned its back on the fabulous views and natural scenes. The original facility had been designed in the 1980s during the energy crunch and had called for a 5,800-square-foot earth-sheltered structure with minimal daylight and exterior walls. The original design reveals the flaw in following the fancy of the times without regard to specific circumstances.

Early on in the programming and design process the architects worked with parents, teachers, and students, one-on-one and in open meetings, to identify concepts and features particular to their needs. The architects learned much from the senior high students who had grown up in the school. It was clear from the beginning that the concept of the older, inward-facing, earth-sheltered building did not work from both the design and technology perspectives. The design used as much or more fuel per square foot than other comparable schools in the district. This could have been a result of the extreme lack of windows, which would have admitted solar radiation. Buildings require most of their fuel to heat ventilation air, and the solar radiation can compensate for heat lost through exterior walls. The energy formula for the old building had not been worked out through the complete cycle of school occupancy. In addition, the lack of windows made the space claustrophobic and did not encourage planting or other sun-oriented educational activities.

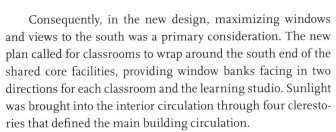

Consequently, in the new design, maximizing windows and views to the south was a primary consideration. The new plan called for classrooms to wrap around the south end of the shared core facilities, providing window banks facing in two directions for each classroom and the learning studio. Sunlight was brought into the interior circulation through four clerestories that defined the main building circulation.

The new design did not entirely reject the earth-sheltered idea of the old building. The height of the berms around the existing building was lowered from fourteen feet to four feet. The building uses a flat membrane roof for the higher central components, surrounded by the lower spaces, which are covered with a standing-seam metal roof. The building has deep overhangs to protect the facade from the wind and snow. Outside the classrooms the roof overhangs are extended to provide covered exterior activity areas. The building is faced with full brick veneer, a material determined to be the best overall value for the long term. The entry wall incorporates a brick mural of a herd of migrating caribou. The building has low, clean lines and good scale for students of all ages.

Glacier View School (K–12), Sutton, Alaska.
Top left: Maximizing windows adds views to the south.
Top right: Berming and roof overhang protect students from searing winds. **Bottom:** Exterior brick mural of a herd of migrating caribou.
Photographs courtesy of Architects Alaska,
© Tom Arnot, Ripple Photography..

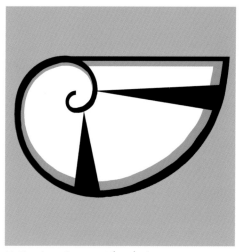

Native American nautilus design.

Thomas Vliet based his project on four environmentally responsive concepts:

- ▶ *Blending children's scale and the local terrain and translating them into different heights of the building*
- ▶ *Retaining water on the site and minimizing the building's environmental footprint*
- ▶ *Using environmentally friendly materials and methods in construction, and*
- ▶ *Using solar power to heat and provide electricity for the building where possible.*

The initial design originated with the Native American nautilus shape, as shown at left.

Laguna Family Center

Pueblo of Laguna, Laguna, New Mexico

Thomas Vliet

Excerpted from Vliet's master's thesis (2004) for the University of New Mexico School of Architecture and Planning

All images courtesy of Thomas Vliet

LIST OF PICTURES

1. Birds Eye: Aerial view of the Laguna Family Center. North is up; the main entrance is from the east and the south entrance links to the middle school. The "toddler village" is located on the southeast corner of the school. At the center is the administration, and the teacher's offices are on the second floor. The center of the building features an opening to the sky. To the north are the preschool playground and preschool classrooms. At the southwest corner is the six-thousand-square-foot multipurpose room with complete banquet-style kitchen.

2. Directional Window: The center window in the preschool playground shows a geometric depiction of the school's floor plan. Geometry, mapping, and wayfinding are featured in the design.

3. Interior Axonometric: On the exterior, the cutaway render shows a green roof and water collection into a sand and water play pond. Clerestory windows provide natural light and photovoltaic panels supply the electricity. The interior has small group areas surrounding a large interior plaza for game playing and gathering. The two classrooms share a central hub of kitchen, toilet, and teachers' offices with a private bathroom.

4. Corner Window: The corner window looks into the preschool playground. Scale and proportion are featured in the design of the interior banco, the ground-level windows, and geometry shapes. Light, color, and time are accented by the stained-glass windows as the colors move across the room during the day.

Ventana Vista Elementary School, Tucson, Arizona.
Antoine Predock Architect PC, in association with Burns
and Wald-Hopkins Architects, executive architect.
Photographs © Tim Hursley.

Conclusion

To paraphrase an old saying, the architectural "skins" we create—the new learning environments—must be filled with new "wine" or models of learning. New facilities are not enough without new ideas and strategies for learning. The core narrative of this book presents a model or process for thinking deeply about the future of education, the rights and delights of children, and the qualities of environments that support learning. It is intended to be compatible with a variety of philosophies, concerns, interests, and viewpoints that all share the common goals of stewardship and individual responsibility toward the greater public good. Every sidebar, case study, fact, image, and quote included in these pages poses an idea intended to stimulate thought and creativity and to encourage readers to make connections to their own experiences. The book provides individuals and communities with a process for fully engaging in cooperative efforts to design and build schools according to a new, hopeful, sustainable vision that exemplifies the knowing eye.

I find myself returning again to the larger themes of interdependence and stewardship that connect my many projects over the years and to educators, entrepreneurs, architects, and students who offer inspiration by looking forward. Among these futurists is Courtney Ross, who founded the Ross School based on her own daughter's home school, and later joined with New York University to create a public charter academy located in the New York City historic Tweed Courthouse. Both schools cultivate a global cultural perspective and embrace technology with small classes for students. Bill and Melinda Gates have supported smaller high schools, hoping to stem the rising dropout rate among our youth. Oprah Winfrey has contributed generously to open the Leadership Academy for Girls in South Africa, and more schools are planned. Taliesin West, a residence and school founded by Frank Lloyd Wright in the 1930s, is still serving as a model for project-based learning for students who design, build, and live in the diverse houses they create as they study architecture and the environment. These influential leaders are showing through their actions that education matters.

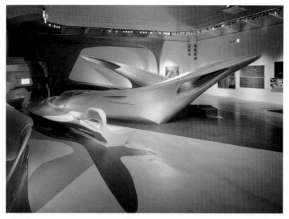

Architects as artists also speak to us about the interconnect-edness of all things through the interdisciplinarity of their profession. Zaha Hadid, winner of the 2004 Pritzker Architecture Prize, pushes the boundaries of architecture and urban design through her many built works, educational projects, paintings, computer renderings, and exhibition work. The influence of new design media allows for playful experimentation. According to Hadid, protoarchitecture needs exhibitions as testing grounds, since the final meaning of architecture requires an audience. In her exhibit work, Hadid seeks to expand the repertoire of spatial ordering to move beyond linear exhibits to a new complexity of anticipation, cross-referencing, and overlapping with visual/spatial links and shortcuts.

Architect Antoine Predock, Fellow of the American Institute of Architects (FAIA) and gold medalist at the 2006 AIA Honor Awards, has an architectural vocabulary all his own, a place-inspired yet deeply personal vision that has received universal acclaim. During his acceptance speech for the gold medal, Predock named influences to his work, from Frank Lloyd Wright to Native American cultures and the landscape of the Southwest. Through his designs, Predock reminds us that we cannot ignore the natural history—the geologic and cultural strata—of the unique site.

Top: The MAK Exhibition Hall, Vienna, Austria. "A Zaha Hadid Retrospective," 2003. New approaches to the spatialization of knowledge. © Zaha Hadid Architects. Zaha Hadid and Patrik Schumacher, designers. Photograph © Helene Binet.
Center: "25 Years of Deutsche Bank Art," 2005. Exhibit space is part of the artistry, not just a passive backdrop. This design has implications for school hallway exhibitions. Zaha Hadid Architects. © Deutsche Guggenheim, Berlin. Photograph by M. Schormann.
Bottom: Discovery Canyon Campus, Colorado Springs, Colorado. View alignments to Pikes Peak punctuate the learning experiences at the Discovery Canyon campus, which is conceived as a receptor observatory, or a "science menu" for all participants. The canyon campus is embedded with references to ancient cultures and the origins and principles of science and math. Fibonacci spirals, logarithmic segmentation, golden section geometry, and solstice alignments organize space in the elementary school's neighborhood, giving way to the cellular nature of the middle school, which then overlaps with the high school, eventually culminating in a monumental public amphitheater and grass court. Antoine Predock Architect PC, in association with MOA Architectural Partnership, executive architect.

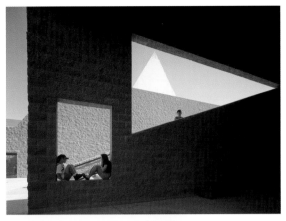

Ventana Vista Elementary School, Tucson, Arizona.
The Ventana Vista project relates a narrative through architecture. Like an ancient ruin, this sunken city does not compete with the desert landscape; it becomes the landscape, with a single "nomadic" tent or sunshade at its hub. Each student belongs to his or her own community and resides in a specifically demarcated village.
Above left: Geometric forms. **Above right:** Framed views. **Left:** Playful peepholes for solstice study. Antoine Predock Architect PC, in association with Burns and Wald-Hopkins Architects, executive architect. Photographs © Tim Hursley.

Indian Community School, Franklin, Wisconsin.
Clockwise from above: The classroom wing seamlessly integrates interior and exterior spaces. Drum theater concept. Conceptual digital drawing of classroom space at the Indian Community School, housing grades PK–8 and community center functions. Antoine Predock Architect PC, in association with Eppstein Uhen Architects, executive architect.

Pin River: Columbia (detail) depicts the Columbia River using fifteen thousand straight pins stuck in a wall. Maya Lin's recent work brings together design concepts of living places and cultures, landscape aesthetics, technology, and principles of ecology. Her artistic vision can help us imagine the future of our schools as a "confluence" of education, architecture, and sustainability. Maya Lin, artist. University of Washington's Henry Art Gallery, 2006. Photograph by Colleen Chartier.

Maya Lin, known for her design of the Vietnam Veterans Memorial, is now exploring sculptural forms that reflect technological views of our world, bridging art and architecture. Her large-scale traveling "Systematic Landscapes" exhibition, which opened at the University of Washington, builds on pixilation, topographic models, and computer diagrams of contours as motifs to explore massive landforms and aerial views of our planet (Sokol, 2006).

Maya Lin's *Pin River: Columbia* delineates the path of the Columbia River using fifteen thousand straight pins. The work, which appeared in 2006 at the University of Washington's Henry Art Gallery, complements another large undertaking, the "Confluence Project," a series of seven art installations planned along the Columbia River basin. The connected yet distinct artworks reinterpret points of encounter between Native Americans and the Lewis and Clark expedition, merging built structures, landscape, and sculpture. As part of the project, Lin collaborated with representatives of Pacific Northwest Native American tribes, civic groups, artists, and landscape architects. Area schools, students, artists, and communities are also creating public art designed to reinforce the "Confluence Project" concepts of civic engagement, multicultural perspectives, and America's complex history.

Confluence—a coming or flowing together, the joining of two or more streams—is an apt and beautiful metaphor for the future we envision for our schools and for our children.

Revisiting the Philosophical Framework

The philosophical framework introduced in chapter 1 organizes and summarizes the views presented in this book. Five key points support a process-oriented methodology for linking architecture and education in the planning and design of successful learning environments and school facilities. I have underscored these five key points below with statements of the book's main themes. In the afterword, I offer a sampling of what these points indicate for our future actions as caring members of society.

A Philosophical Framework for Linking Architecture and Education in Five Points

POINT ONE:
BEGIN WITH AESTHETICS AND A
PHILOSOPHICAL FRAME OF REFERENCE

- ▶ The order in the universe is holistic, or in educational terms, interdisciplinary. Humans are a part of, not apart from, their environment and as such must operate within the context of ecological sustainability.

- ▶ Research shows that the quality of the physical environment affects the quality of learning.

- ▶ Architects are educators who use the designed environment, aesthetics, and creativity as a palette for learning. Educators are designers of the mind. With the proper professional development, we all have the potential to be both educators and designers.

POINT TWO:
DEVELOP AND USE A CURRICULAR ORGANIZING
SYSTEM TO GOVERN THE SCHOOL FACILITY
PLANNING AND DEVELOPMENT PROCESS

- ▶ Best educational practices and contemporary learning theory take priority as design criteria for planning and programming educational facilities.

- ▶ Context, content, and learning processes form a system of thought for the parallel development of educational curricula and architectural programming for design.

- ▶ Students have developmental rights across body, mind, and spirit that must be translated into corresponding levels of architectural habitability for schools across (1) health and safety (codes), (2) functional support, and (3) psychological comfort and aesthetic satisfaction.

POINT THREE:
DESIGN AND LEARN FROM THE ENVIRONMENT
AS A THREE-DIMENSIONAL TEXTBOOK

- ▶ The objects we encounter in the built, natural, and cultural environment represent concepts (ideas) across subject matter disciplines.

- ▶ Architects can design and build these ideas into the school environment as manifestations for learning. A manifestation is the material object that represents the ideas, laws, and principles that govern our universe.

▶ Developing the knowing eye means knowing how to "read" or interpret the physical environment for meaning at increasing levels of understanding throughout a lifetime of learning, aiming for wisdom and stewardship of our world and compassion for each other.

POINT FOUR:

AIM FOR THE FUTURE

▶ The architectural design studio provides a model that can be used in school settings to deconstruct the outdated, repetitive, passive classroom while supporting applied, project-based learning with themes for learning based on student interests. The teacher becomes a coach or facilitator for today's learner, placing responsibility for learning on and giving power to students. Teachers will need a new model of professional development and colleges of education must include specialists in newer courses such as space planning, ecoliteracy, project management, and uses of various technologies.

▶ Learning environments of the future stress flexibility, deployable furniture, custodial order and storage, support systems for a variety of ages and group sizes, communications technology, and more diversity of activity settings for real-life, hands-on learning.

▶ School grounds must be included as part of the whole school program and designed commensurate with the building as learning landscapes, which are outdoor spaces for kinesthetic, academic, and ecological learning.

POINT FIVE:

FOSTER ECOLOGICAL STEWARDSHIP BY NURTURING THE INDIVIDUAL, THE COMMUNITY, AND THE WORLD

▶ Learning environments support the client/learner of today as a powerful, autonomous, active problem solver at the center of learning.

▶ Schools do not operate in isolation but are important tools in maintaining the democratic ideals of participation, equality, and multiculturalism. Schools can serve as community centers, and communities can serve as real-life learning environments.

▶ Ecologically responsive school design (green architecture) is essential to developing a sense of place and stewardship for future generations. All buildings and landscapes should serve as working examples of sustainable design, contributing to a new ecology-based philosophical framework for our lives as global citizens.

Afterword

As I near the end of the writing process, I have felt a moral imperative to articulate the implications of my work in broader terms. Linking architecture and education is a microcosm for thinking in a more integrated, interdisciplinary, cooperative way in all the ventures we undertake. There is a greater message behind the spaces that we inhabit and use. Our behavior is modulated by our environment, and the places we create say something about our humanity.

In America, we live in a pluralistic democracy. It is our duty not only to fight intolerance, but also to encourage participation in our democratic society. We need a more diverse real-life curriculum that better uses our collective mind power and people resources. We need to bring into the educational system more points of view and more expertise from individuals outside the fields of architecture and education as we plan and build the future of our schools. To do this, we must design enduring systems that bring different civic groups and diverse individuals together long after charismatic leaders move on. Beginning with children, we must strengthen our capability for shared research, teamwork, mediation, compromise, flexibility, and consensus building versus pure competition and putting the self first.

We need to cultivate a sense of pride and stewardship for our schools. Think of the constant collective upkeep of a ship by its crew, including painting, sanding, repairing, washing, and polishing. If we did this with our schools, they would be beautiful places in which to learn.

This idea of building, maintaining, and polishing a shared vision—so essential to a well-functioning democracy—returns me to the concept of the knowing eye.

At its simplest level, the knowing eye is a metaphor for visual literacy, for the informed perception that architects espouse in terms of keen observation and spatial understanding. Educators demonstrate the knowing eye when they understand and respond to the needs of the learner. The knowing eye, however, is also the mind's inner eye, and there are many avenues that lead to a deeper personal understanding of our universe. Whatever your route to wisdom, it is important to embark on the journey and to aim high, to be an educated, creative force versus a destructive one, and to become a creative lifelong learner.

Follow the Lead of Your Creative Child.
Top: Musical intelligence. Photograph courtesy of Anne Taylor.
Bottom: Art outdoors. Photograph courtesy of Janet Fancher.
Facing page: Children as designers. Photograph courtesy of Anne Taylor.

Starting Points for Action

We all know what to do; we just need to do it. Though I have advocated an extensive reformation for education and the architecture that houses it, I am aware that the small, positive steps ordinary people take to improve their world can gain a collective power over time to make a huge difference. For example, something as simple as changing a light bulb can change the world. Compact fluorescent light bulbs (CFL) use 66 percent less energy than traditional bulbs and are cool to the touch. If every household in the United States were to replace one light bulb with a CFL, it would prevent enough pollution to equal removing one million cars from the road (see more from EnergyStar at http://www.energystar. gov/). Imagine if we were to get schools on board!

Create something beautiful for yourself, your school, and your community.

▸ Plant daffodil bulbs around a school campus.

▸ Pick up litter every day.

▸ Sweep the sidewalks.

▸ Organize a fund drive for a school sculpture or other work of art.

▸ Build a bench or an arbor for a school.

▸ Insist on and support funding for the reinstatement of all music, drama, design, computer graphics, and visual arts programs in your schools.

▸ Replace your SUV with an energy-efficient model. With the savings in gas money, buy a piano and learn to play it. Sing!

▸ Subscribe to a publication that is outside your usual realm of practice.

▸ Organize a design competition for fixing an area of your school or for soliciting student art.

▸ Pipe in classical music. A good sound system should be a part of schools' environmental designs.

▸ Purchase a copy of *The New Drawing on the Right Side of the Brain* by Betty Edwards, and try the exercises in the book.

▸ Write a letter to the editor describing a success at your school.

▸ Build a database of community "treasures" and use it.

▸ Spend at least one full day per year at a school—preferably more—observing, volunteering, helping, tutoring, or sharing your area of expertise or cultural background with students.

▸ Go outside and walk the perimeter of your school grounds with children. Listen to what they say. Get off the beaten track and see what you can find. Do the same for your neighborhood and city.

▸ Purchase a magnifying glass. Stop and look.

- ▶ Pick a place. Imagine the place as a school. What would you teach there? How would you teach it?

- ▶ If you're a computer whiz, write software that frees up teacher time by scoring, tracking, and compiling data on student work.

- ▶ Reverse roles. Students can teach the teacher to become technologically literate.

- ▶ If you're an architect, become a school superintendent.

- ▶ If you're a janitor or groundskeeper, teach stewardship.

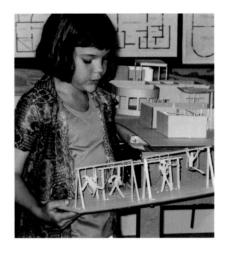

- ▶ If you are a designer, artist, museum director, social services employee, environmentalist, or urban planner, get elected to your local school board.

- ▶ If you are a school principal, photograph and evaluate your school's classroom environments with an eye toward order and cleanliness.

- ▶ Support public schools financially. How you spend your money is a political decision that reveals your moral stance and reflects your attitudes toward other people.

- ▶ Business owners can support public education, volunteerism, and families through matching programs, time off, or whatever is needed to make time spent with children possible.

- ▶ Practice your manners. Get to know the manners and customs of another country. Ideally, travel outside the United States.

- ▶ Change the school cafeteria. Take charge of planning nutritional menus for children. Family-style eating at round tables can promote conversational literacy, social skills, bilingualism, knowledge of customs and manners worldwide, and nutritional knowledge.

- ▶ Fight obesity by getting rid of school desks and sedentary learning. Set up workstations instead. Get outside.

- ▶ Post a world map in your kitchen at home.

- ▶ Walk or ride a bike to school. Start a mileage club for walkers. Purchase a pedometer and see how far you walk in a week.

- ▶ Buy a measuring tape and give it to a child to measure everything and learn math from the environment.

- ▶ Be positive. Be compassionate.

Please remember this: A great nation deserves a great educational system supported by great school design.

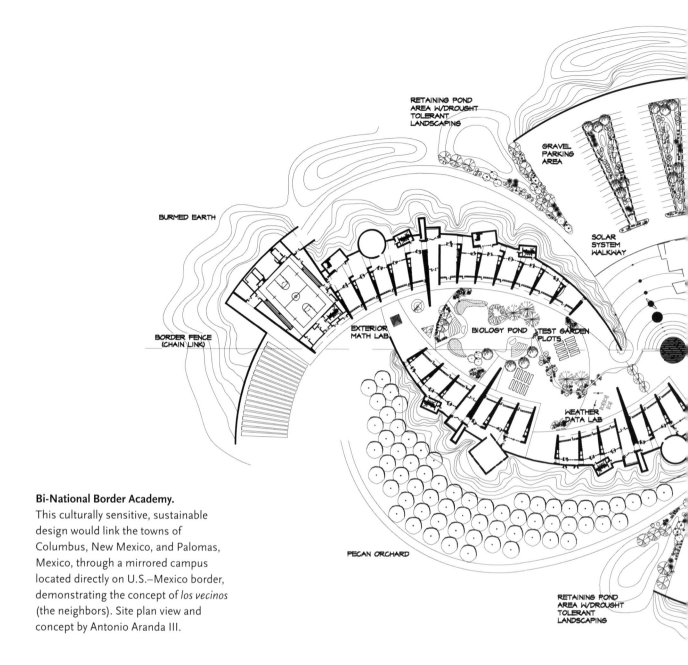

Bi-National Border Academy.
This culturally sensitive, sustainable design would link the towns of Columbus, New Mexico, and Palomas, Mexico, through a mirrored campus located directly on U.S.–Mexico border, demonstrating the concept of *los vecinos* (the neighbors). Site plan view and concept by Antonio Aranda III.

RETAINING POND AREA W/DROUGHT TOLERANT LANDSCAPING

GRAVEL PARKING AREA

SOLAR SYSTEM WALKWAY

BURMED EARTH

BORDER FENCE (CHAIN LINK)

EXTERIOR MATH LAB

BIOLOGY POND

TEST GARDEN PLOTS

WEATHER DATA LAB

PECAN ORCHARD

RETAINING POND AREA W/DROUGHT TOLERANT LANDSCAPING

Leaving on a High Note

One final uplifting design solution comes from Tony Aranda, a postgraduate student from the School of Architecture and Planning at the University of New Mexico. He used his background of living on the Mexican border in Columbus, New Mexico, to design a proposed bilingual, bicultural, and binational K–12 school right on the border that would be open to children from both the United States and Mexico. Environmentally responsive elements include a wind farm, orchards, gardens, retaining ponds, drought-tolerant

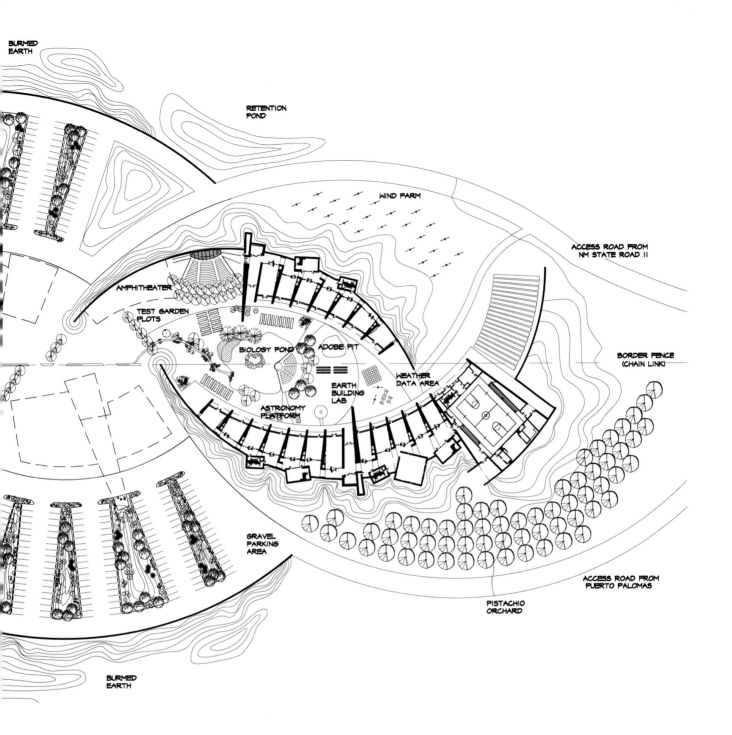

BURMED
EARTH

RETENTION
POND

WIND FARM

ACCESS ROAD FROM
NM STATE ROAD II

AMPHITHEATER

TEST GARDEN
PLOTS

BORDER FENCE
(CHAIN LINK)

BIOLOGY POND

ADOBE PIT

WEATHER
DATA AREA

EARTH
BUILDING
LAB

ASTRONOMY
PLATFORM

GRAVEL
PARKING
AREA

ACCESS ROAD FROM
PUERTO PALOMAS

PISTACHIO
ORCHARD

BURMED
EARTH

landscaping, and emphasis on natural lighting. The program includes a visitors' center, a performing arts center/gallery, middle school, high school, library, health clinic, athletic facilities, and flexible, open academic learning studios. This is an inspiring, hopeful, and cooperative alternative to the expensive and wasteful wall being built between our two countries that not only isolates people but also hampers migration of wild animals. While this border school

proposal is only an idea at present, its design could be implemented and could grow into a mutually cooperative and very beneficial wave of border schools for the future, fostering the educational health of both the United States and Mexico. Breaking down the boundaries that keep us apart will result in designs that transcend our differences and celebrate our similarities while creating a new whole that is greater than the sum of its parts.

Acknowledgments

No person works alone on this planet. This book includes not only my ideas and experiences but is closely woven into the larger efforts of professionals who have spent their lives working for the betterment of architecture, education, and mankind, especially children. I am indeed indebted to many people for their support and help in my life work and in particular, this book.

I am especially grateful to

Katie Enggass for her dedicated editing, organization, and months of collaboration to bring this book to fruition. Katie was incredibly facile at understanding all the intricacies of the emerging model of learning expressed in this book.

Sandee Jensen, an environmental designer who worked tirelessly to support all the projects that emanated from the small office of Anne Taylor Associates.

George Vlastos, architect, for the many hours we shared across the large drafting table in my Corrales farm studio. He and I taught each other about design thinking for education and from this dialogue wrote integrated curricula that ultimately formed a new discipline merging architecture and education. Our enjoyable and informative dialogue became the basis of this book.

George Anselevicius (1923–2008), dean emeritus of the UNM School of Architecture and Planning, for his encouragement and support through the years.

If your name or organization appears within these pages as a contributor—whether it be through photography, written contributions, case studies, or illustrations—please know how much I value your generosity and sharing spirit. Thank you, too, to all the administrative assistants, secretaries, and archivists who worked behind the scenes to help me track, sort, and identify images for this book. Special mention goes to artists who gave us many ideas for visually organizing the book: Atsuko Sakai, George Vlastos, Keith Vlastos, and Peter Wrona. Thanks to Kim Jew, photographer.

I am also indebted to longtime friends and supporters of both the School Zone Institute and the Architecture and Children program, and participants in the many projects generated over the years: to the school administrators open to new ideas, the workshop participants of all ages, to the branches of the Architecture and Children Network in Japan, Seattle, and Anchorage. Specifically, I'd like to thank colleagues Charlene Brown, architect; Fritjof Capra, physical systems theorist and author; George Carver, Steelcase representative; Lucian Cassetta (deceased), architect; Milton Chen, executive director, George Lucas Educational Foundation; Ed Crittenden, architect; Lori Gee of Herman Miller Furniture; Susan Gooding of Antoine Predock Architect; Robert Gorrell, director of the New Mexico Public School Facilities Authority; Hiroko Hosodo, architect; Takeshi Inaba, architect and educator; Jim Jonassen, principal at NBBJ Architects, Seattle; Manny Juarez, architect; Olga Kimball; Edward E. Kirkbride, National Council of Architectural Registration Boards, Recognized Educational Facility Professional; Alice Jean Lewis; Dan Lewis of Business Environments; Myrna Marquez, architect and environmentalist; Alison Marshall, arts educator; Erin MacInnes and Julia Bland, for our work at the Louisiana Children's Museum; Robert McIntosh, technology educator; Dwight Miller of Sandia National Laboratories; Gary Nelson, president of Creative Learning Systems; Joan Norris; Lynne Olson of Antoine Predock Architect; Tina Patel, architect; Ifan Payne, architect and educator; Robert Peters, FAIA, architect; Baji Rankin, educator; Michael J. Resudek of Imagic Digital Imaging and Design; Joe Rice, educator; Roger Schluntz, dean of the UNM School of Architecture and Planning; Julie Stoffler, art educator; and Mark Unverzagt, physician.

Thank you to the many forward-thinking architects with whom I have collaborated on a variety of educational design projects, including Steven Bingler, Lucian Cassetta (deceased), Gaylaird Christopher, Ed Crittenden, Van Gilbert, Takeshi Inaba, and Jim Jonassen.

I would like to thank my manuscript readers, including George Anselevicius, Eleni Bastea, Kathy Feek, Denise Hexom, Kuppaswamy Iyengar, Catherine Loughlin, and Sharon Wolfe, for their time and insights at different stages during the development of this book.

I am grateful to the University of New Mexico for funding projects and research over the years, and for its support of the Institute for Environmental Education in the School of Architecture and Planning. My many colleagues there have been an inspiration, including Andy Pressman, who encouraged me to write this book; UNM Press, Luther Wilson and Kathy Sparkes, book designer extraodinaire; Doug Bell, a technology expert who has kept my computer running; Jerod Bosey, an architect who helped with research and miscellaneous tasks throughout the process; and Jesse Giordano, my graduate assistant from 2006 to 2008. I am deeply grateful to all my students at UNM. Our ongoing dialogue enlightens us all.

To my wonderful family and daughters Meredith, Susan, and Kimberly, thank you for maintaining the bonds of support from early childhood to the present. Interacting with my grandchildren has allowed me not only great pleasure, but also new insight into the ever-increasing influence of technology on all of us, as well as the corresponding digital literacy that seems to come so naturally to young learners today.

Appendix A

Design Education Portfolio Rubric

Two- and Three-Dimensional
Design Process and Product Evaluation

I wrote the attached assessment instrument to evaluate visual thinking and design work of children. There are five parts to this instrument by which designed products such as drawings and models are evaluated. The parts are listed and defined according to the following criteria:

Fluency and clarity of communication

Imagination, innovation, and creativity

Understanding the process

Detail and overall aesthetics

Technical competence

When evaluating many products at one time, the products should be numbered and evaluators should be trained using the "inter-rater reliability index." Gestalt judgments are accepted using a rating scale of one as low and five as high. This instrument is useful for completing a trend analysis on students over time in which each student acts as his or her own control. Averages for a total class can be computed, but that is not the primary purpose of this tool.

Design Education Portfolio Assessment

TWO- AND THREE-DIMENSIONAL DESIGN PROCESS AND PRODUCTS EVALUATION CRITERIA DEFINED

One, several, or all of the descriptions may apply to the assessment.

1. Fluency and Clarity of Communication

- ► The ability to demonstrate control in the rendering of an idea or product
- ► The ability to transmit an idea clearly through graphic visual means

2. Imagination, Innovation, and Creativity

- ► The ability to demonstrate an understanding of the creative process (evidence of the creative cycle—an impulse for creation; exploration; incubation; illumination; revision)
- ► Evidence of experimentation
- ► The ability to see things from multiple perspectives
- ► The ability to consider a variety of approaches
- ► The ability to overcome resistance, to free the eyes and the mind from stereotypes and taboos and see one's surroundings in new ways, make connections between unlikely elements, and sketch, tinker, and imagine until ideas emerge
- ► The ability to accommodate change due to the emergence of an unexpected influence (flexibility)

3. Understanding the Process

- ► The ability to narrate or visualize the stages of development of an idea or product
- ► Evidence of the translation of process into a product or idea (overlays of trace paper)

- ► The ability to present, judge, reject, appraise, criticize, and justify
- ► The ability to recognize patterns and the relationship between patterns
- ► The ability to sequentially develop ideas or products
- ► Use of principles and concepts from math, science, or technology

4. Detail and Overall Aesthetics

- ► Evidence of elaboration
- ► Evidence of understanding of functional versus decorative
- ► Evidence of development of compositional style, design, color, rhythms, repetition, etc.
- ► Evidence of refined sense of expression
- ► Evidence of high overall aesthetic quality

5. Technical Competence

- ► The ability to identify the unique characteristics of materials, their limitations and extensions
- ► The ability to draw schematics, plans, elevations, and perspectives (shade and shadow where appropriate)
- ► The ability to construct in three dimensions in either process or product

Design Education Portfolio Assessment
VISUAL PORTFOLIO ASSESSMENT RATING SCALES
Key to Rating Scale in Each Category

Level 1
- Rendering is erratic and inconsistent.
- Structure and expression is not evident.

Level 2
- Control is apparent through steady or consistent repetition.
- Management of material or technique is a priority.
- Technical expression is demonstrated.
- General impression is impulsive, unplanned, and lacking structural coherence.

Level 3
- Articulation and interpretation is understandable.
- Conventional expression
- Tidy
- Attempts at structural organization

Level 4
- Imaginative touches appear in the expression.
- Deliberate use of variety and contrast to generate structural interest
- Sense of style
- Technical, expressive, and structural control are demonstrated consistently.

Level 5
- Technical mastery totally serves communication.
- Expression, style, and structural detail are refined.
- Form and expression are fused into a coherent and personal statement.
- Imaginative solutions are demonstrated.

Design Education Portfolio Assessment
Scale   1 = Low   2 = Fair   3 = Good   4 = Very Good   5 = High

No.	Projects	1. Fluency and Clarity of Communication	2. Imagination, Innovation, and Creativity	3. Understanding the Process	4. Detail and Overall Aesthetics	5. Technical Competence
1.						
2.						
3.						
4.						
5.						
6.						
7.						
8.						
9.						
10.						

Reviewer

Appendix B

Ideas for Future Research

1. Develop and write new curricula based on environmental learning for all ages and tied to existing standards and the latest educational theory. Use and test the curricula in different demographic regions.

2. Develop and test a pilot or charter school based on the Architecture and Children program and the design studio workshop supported by design of physical spaces that encourages hands-on learning.

3. Explore the impacts of universal design and design for inclusion on teaching strategies and learning. Do negative attitudes toward inclusion improve when supported by spaces designed for inclusion?

4. Design prototype professional educational learning environments that teach educators about using the environment as a three-dimensional textbook (including use of technology and multimedia resources, outdoor learning, community service, design, display techniques, and how to develop the knowing eye). Conduct follow-up studies to see how teachers facilitate learning in their classrooms after training.

5. Program, design, and measure iconic elements of school designs over time. Compare manifestations at different sites and determine which have the greatest potential for learning and why.

6. Collect data on which school designs last (physically, functionally, and aesthetically) and analyze why. Establish Web sites and systems for communication of this and similar information.

7. Design environments that empower students to make their own educational choices and measure performance results using multiple assessment tools including traditional testing, portfolio work, and rubrics.

8. Design programs that involve students in school design and finish with assessments of student involvement and attitudes toward schools following the design process.

9. Research, design, produce, and field-test new furniture suited to children and education.

10. Conduct and publish more qualitative research on the human response across body, mind, and spirit to school facilities, or how buildings teach through the design of windows, doors, floors, and other typical building elements.

11. Design and operate a full-school participatory community service program for a public school. Write a dissertation on the results, including community attitudes toward school funding before and after the service program.

12. Conduct behavioral response/psychological studies on children in academic and/or ambient settings designed to test and support developmental needs, constructivist theory, or other educational values.

13. Implement and test the ATA Taxonomy in classroom settings for all ages. Design a model curriculum that extends vertically through the age levels, or that builds in a spiral fashion based on the six steps for experiential learning. Compare to traditional models.

14. Research and develop a list of one hundred interdisciplinary concepts that could be used to build an entire environmental curriculum and/or translated into design. Test the curriculum in schools.

15. Develop POE documents and surveys that measure students' academic performance within schools based on learning from the environment and how the environment is used as a teaching tool.

16. Develop a system (supported by formats, surveys, checklists, etc.) that integrates school performance from initial programming through design and post-occupancy use.

17. Develop a higher education program for credit enabling crossover between disciplines, including opportunities to team teach in our public schools. Devise a simple licensure and professional development program for nontraditional educators (architects, engineers, lawyers, doctors, nutritionists, ecologists) to teach in the schools.

18. Continue research on green architecture and its many emerging shifts in thinking, and apply its concepts to schools. Measure student understanding of green design when they occupy such schools, as compared to children attending traditional schools.

19. Design a school that is a test facility for ecological design and document the process. Develop an ecological curriculum to accompany the design.

20. Replicate some suggested models of classrooms for the future (chapter 9), and test student performance and satisfaction using the models.

21. Work with children to design and build learning landscapes (chapter 10), and measure student learning from outdoor environments.

22. Develop fitness and exercise areas for schools and test student health as compared to traditional gym programs. Add nutritional education and compare again.

23. Test and compare approaches to security in schools, e.g., systemic and cultural versus policing, and the attendant architecture that supports each approach. What works?

24. Design a school run and maintained by children with corresponding stewardship curricula, and collect long-term data on future citizenship roles of students who attend the school. Do students raised in this tradition expand their learning into a global worldview?

25. In schools, investigate and test principles of implied architectural space, and how signals in the environment suggest its use (moving beyond the initial failure of the open classroom to a more integrated model that encourages autonomy while providing some spatial cues).

Appendix C

Sample User's Manual
from Edward Mazria

Mazria Inc. Odems Dzurec Architecture/Planning of Santa Fe, New Mexico, designed the Edward Gonzales Elementary School as a prototypical solar school for Albuquerque Public Schools. To educate the building's users about daylighting and passive solar design features, Mazria's firm wrote a brief user's manual.

EDWARD GONZALES ELEMENTARY SCHOOL
User Manual

MAZRIA INC.
ODEMS
DZUREC

ARCHITECTURE/PLANNING

607 CERRILLOS ROAD, SUITE G
SANTA FE, NEW MEXICO 87505
505.988.5309 FAX 505.983.9526
WWW.MAZRIA.COM

The Edward Gonzales Elementary School is designed as a new prototype for Albuquerque Public Schools. It is a forward looking design that acknowledges the impact that buildings have on the environment. The school incorporates daylighting and passive solar design features that will result in a 50% reduction in energy usage.

Facts:

- Buildings consume roughly 50% of the energy and are responsible for almost ½ of the greenhouse gas emissions in the United States.

- Most of the electricity in New Mexico is produced by coal fired power plants. These plants emit pollution that causes respiratory illness and cancer. Coal fired power plants are major producers of carbon dioxide and other greenhouse gases.

- The accumulation of greenhouse gases in the atmosphere is contributing to global warming. Global warming is causing a climate change that will affect the entire planet. Some of the possible outcomes of this climate change are: a rise in sea level corresponding with a loss of property and land, an increase in frequency and intensity of hurricanes, catastrophic floods, droughts and wildfires, the extinction of millions of species of plants and animals.

- Recent studies show that children in classrooms with exposure to daylight and views in do better on standardized tests.

- About 80% of the total lifetime cost of a building is spent on operation, maintenance and energy.

The Bottom Line: A school that saves energy helps the environment, helps children learn better and saves APS money.

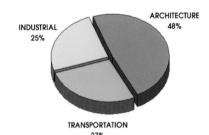

U.S. ENERGY CONSUMPTION

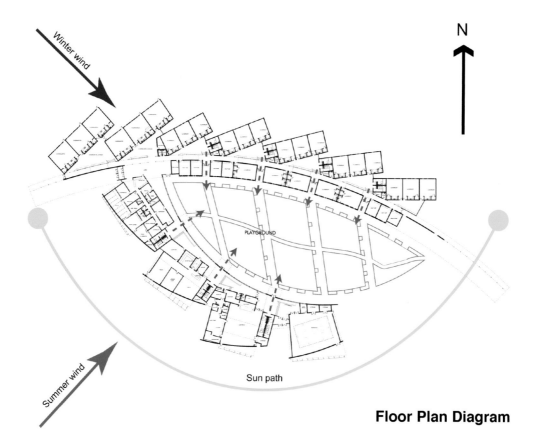

Floor Plan Diagram

Design Features:

- The school is designed in response to the rhythms and forces of nature.

- All the major spaces in the school are daylit. Rarely will lights be needed during the day for these spaces.

- Classrooms and other gathering spaces are primarily heated by the sun through passive solar design principles.

- The building is designed around the play ground. The two wings of the school embrace the children at play and shelter them from westerly winds.

- There are abundant views to the playground from hallways and many doors providing a connection to this central courtyard. These aspects reinforce the playground as the center for the school.

- The heating, cooling, ventilation and lighting systems of the school provide a high level of control for the occupants.

How your classroom works:

The environment is the first source for light, heat and ventilation:

- "Light shelves" bounce natural light into the classroom.

- Window blinds can be used to control the amount of light entering a space.

- In the winter, the sun provides heat. Direct sunlight is allowed into the room and heats up the space.

- In the summer, overhangs block direct sun from entering the space.

- Concrete block walls and concrete floor slabs provide "thermal mass" in the classrooms. This thermal mass moderates temperature swings and keeps the space at a more constant temperature.

- Operable windows can provide ventilation and cooling during temperate days.

Basis of Mechanical system operation:

- Controls - Computer based Energy Management and Control System (EMCS) turns building system on and off based on an occupancy schedule. Room sensor controls can adjust room set point +/- 2 deg F.

- Ventilation - Fresh air ventilation unit introduces outside fresh air for ventilation. Device is an air-to-air heat exchanger that brings in air on one side of the heat exchanger and then relieves the air out the other thereby recovering energy (heat) from the air leaving the room. This device is always running except when the evaporative cooler is running.

- Heating - Hot water convectors that have a valve which modulates to meet the heating need of the room. Window should be shut when heating.

- Cooling - Evaporative cooler with 2 speed control. A window must open for relief. Unit brings 100 % fresh air in to room and cools it via the evaporative cooling process. Just like your swamp coolers at home.

Basis of Electrical System operation:

- Lighting consumes the highest percent of energy on an annual basis than any other system. (i.e. heating, cooling etc).

- With shades up, sufficient light levels should be available from daylight. Motorized shades can be controlled via a switch. Shades should only be down if room needs to be darkened for video presentation. Overhangs in the building design only allow indirect light in the summer and not direct heat. Therefore more energy is saved by having lights off with shades up.

- Occasionally lights will be required. There are several control options to help save energy: 1 tube, 2 tubes or all 3 tubes. Use the option that provides *adequate* lighting.

- A control sweep turns off lights at regular intervals during the day in case lights have been left on. *This is a reminder to keep the lights turned off.*

North Side Classroom

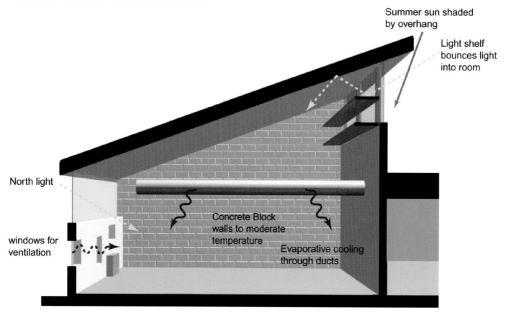

Summer sun shaded by overhang

Light shelf bounces light into room

North light

windows for ventilation

Concrete Block walls to moderate temperature

Evaporative cooling through ducts

Summer

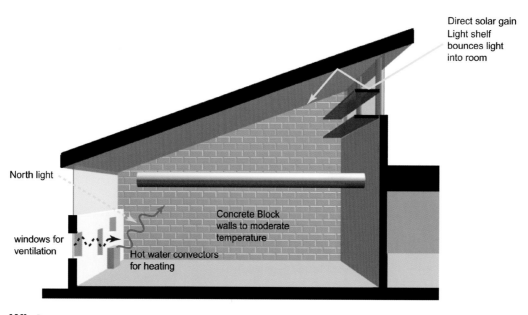

Direct solar gain Light shelf bounces light into room

North light

windows for ventilation

Concrete Block walls to moderate temperature

Hot water convectors for heating

Winter

South Side Classroom

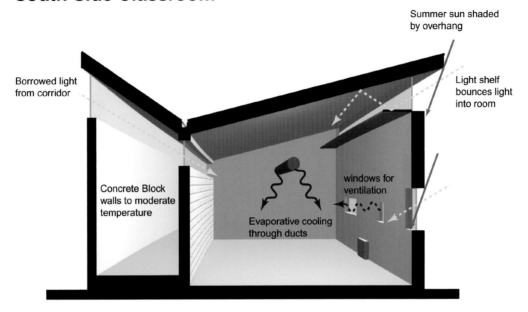

Summer sun shaded by overhang

Borrowed light from corridor

Light shelf bounces light into room

Concrete Block walls to moderate temperature

windows for ventilation

Evaporative cooling through ducts

Summer

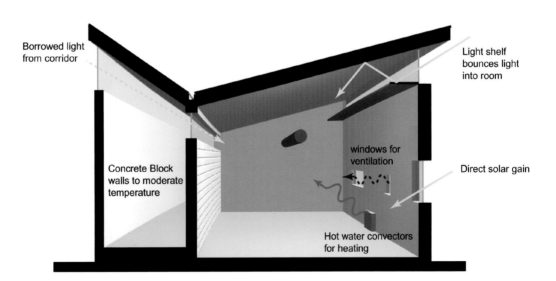

Borrowed light from corridor

Light shelf bounces light into room

Concrete Block walls to moderate temperature

windows for ventilation

Direct solar gain

Hot water convectors for heating

Winter

Glossary of Key Terms and Phrases

activity zone. A space designed with a certain activity in mind. Students usually move from zone to zone around a central gathering space.

agriculture in the classroom. Reconnecting students to the natural world through food, clothing, and shelter.

Architecture and Children program. A curriculum and design education program that uses the design studio model to teach children and adults the visual language of architecture and design.

arcology. Paolo Soleri's term for the fusion of architecture and ecology.

autonomous design. Movable, modular systems on wheels that are configured by the learners themselves.

axiology. The philosophical study of what is moral or good (ethics), or of what is beautiful (aesthetics).

Basic Needs chart. A programming tool that compiles architecture needs for spaces and elements, reducing redundancy in planning documents.

berm. A man-made hill.

biomimicry. To mimic nature and natural systems in design and architecture.

biotecture. Architecture created from living things (green walls, roofs made of plants).

body systems. Digestive, neurological, skeletal, circulatory, and dermal.

building systems. Plumbing, electrical, HVAC, structural, and skin (building envelope).

carrying capacity. The estimate of total population times resource use that an ecosystem can maintain.

charrette. Originally a cart that was pushed through the École des Beaux-Artes to collect students' architectural drawings. Now it means an intense participatory design workshop.

charter school. A nonsectarian, public yet alternate school.

concept or schematic sketch. An illustration of an idea.

context. The entire setting for learning; the built, natural, and cultural environment.

cultural nexus model. A type of learning environment model that serves community and culture and acts as a center.

curricular organizing system. The articulation of an educational philosophy that can be used to plan schools. The Taylor system includes context, content, and learning processes. If used for planning, the resultant environment becomes a learning and teaching tool.

daylighting. The use of natural light in design.

deconstructivist architecture. An architectural approach that follows no precedent and dismantles traditional design. Exemplified by Frank Gehry's works.

developmental rights of students. The developmental needs of children across body, mind, and spirit. These are called *rights* to emphasize how design serves the true client, the student/child or student/adult.

diversity cluster model. An idea for the learning environment of the future that includes diverse spaces or zones organized around a central gathering space.

ecoism. The philosophical framework for ecological thinking.

ecodesign. Design with ecology in mind (siting, solar, water efficiency, recycling, energy saving).

ecohistoric sense of place. The ecological and historical characteristics of a given location.

ecoism. Ecological activism; changing attitudes toward food, transport, etc., to create an eco-friendly and sustainable world.

ecosophy. Ecologically responsive philosophy.

environment. The physical world and the objects within it. Environment can be built, natural, and cultural.

epistemology. The philosophical branch that examines what is true.

ergodynamic. Ergonomically correct and movable. Furniture that moves with and adjusts to the user.

ergonomic. Designed with human factors in mind; supports health, well-being, and performance through design.

evolving remodel. A learning space model or way of reconfiguring and updating existing classrooms to support students as active learners with teachers as facilitators. The power for learning is given to the learner.

experimentalism. The philosophy of human experience, problem solving and constructed meaning.

existentialism. The philosophy of self, choice, and taking responsibility for the consequences of one's actions.

factory or assembly line model. The outdated design for schools requiring identical classroom boxes lining corridors and students' desks arranged in rows all facing a teacher.

gaming. A method of community participation in design used to reach consensus (see Sanoff, 2001).

Golden Mean. The long-revered, harmonious proportional relationship in which the small part stands in the same proportion to the large part as the large part to the whole.

green architecture. Sustainable, ecologically friendly architecture.

green roof/roof garden. Plantings on a roof.

habitability. An occupant's satisfaction with a building or place in terms of safety, functionality, and psychological/aesthetic appeal.

high-performance school. A green, energy conservative, sustainable school.

holism/holistic. The idea that all natural things function in wholes and processes.

home learning center model. The Taylor model for converting traditional spaces in the home to support learning.

idealism. The philosophy of the mind; the world of symbolic thought and great ideas.

the knowing eye. Visual literacy and more. Once we learn to "read" the physical environment and the objects within it, we become open to the wisdom and order in the universe and thus develop the knowing eye. The knowing eye (and in turn the mind) turns the physical world of things into thoughts and ideas.

land use/areas of management concern. These potential uses for school farms include cropland, pasture, timber, fishery, wetlands, and wildlife.

Leadership in Energy and Environmental Design (LEED). A certification and rating program for sustainable building design.

learning environment. Where learning occurs. This could be anywhere!

learning landscape. School grounds transformed into outdoor learning spaces for all subject matter disciplines.

learning process. How we learn, and the skills we need to do so.

life cycle costs for buildings. Looking at the long term from construction to operation and maintenance over the entire life of the building; a new accounting that supports the value of sustainable design.

light shelf. A horizontal reflective shelf positioned outside or inside above eye level in a window to redirect light deeper into a space, reduce sky glare, and produce shading effects.

literacy. Understanding the language, terms, and basic principles in any field (i.e., health literacy means understanding the terminology of nutrition, fitness, and so forth, and what it takes to be healthy).

Living Machine. A natural, organic wastewater treatment system.

manifestations. The physical objects in the built, natural, and cultural environment to be used as cues for learning.

manipulatives. Small items in the environment for children to manipulate while learning fine and gross motor skills.

mobile stage set model. A futuristic learning environment conceived as a deployable, flexible, modular theatrical set design for active learning.

morphology. The study of form and structure.

multiple intelligences. Howard Gardner theory that examines multiple modes of intelligence used in learning such as verbal/linguistic, visual/spatial, mathematical, kinesthetic, musical, interpersonal, intrapersonal, and naturalistic.

multisensory design. Architecture that considers all the senses: smell, taste, hearing, sight, and touch.

multiuse spaces. Places where use is not predetermined but left open to the user.

ontology. The examination of what is real.

orchestrated immersion. Providing rich opportunities for students to make connections between new information and what is already known; constructivist learning (Caine & Caine, 1991).

order of the universe. The interconnectedness of all things, holism. The idea that people are a part of, not apart from, the environment.

participatory design. A process in which architects seek design input from all stakeholders, including children.

plaza. Central area.

post-occupancy evaluation (POE). Determining the success of the building design after completion; for schools the assessment should include how well the setting supports learning, not just building performance.

programming. Architectural planning for a facility; determining needs before design.

project-based. Learning that is hands-on; involves planning, data collection, designing, and presenting projects; and is more concerned with process than uniform results.

realia. Objects or activities used to relate teaching to real life.

realism. The world of matter; natural law.

rubric. A format or system for assessing student performance. Usually a chart or table.

scale. The proportion between two sets of dimensions (as between the architectural model of a home and the actual home).

silent curriculum. The environment of a classroom that has an underlying impact on learning; not always explicitly understood by school facilities' users.

site analysis. The process of examining all the site's features before design: physical, biological, cultural, geographical, and regulatory.

small learning community (SLC). A term for a small school; the antidote to today's large schools.

stewardship. Managing and caring for the Earth and each other.

studio/workshop. A work space conceived for problem solving with large horizontal work surfaces, plenty of storage, display, and places for collaboration.

surface intelligence. New smart technologies for interactive communication; includes walls, floors, and boards.

sustainable school. An energy-, material-, and resource-efficient school that optimizes student health and productivity.

symbology. In architecture, a philosophy in which a building (church, temple, etc.) serves as a metaphor or medium for the transfer of messages and ideas.

systems thinking. A shift from linear modes to networks, cycles, and other nonlinear approaches.

task lighting. Lighting that can be maneuvered to aid a task.

taxonomy. A process of classification. In the ATA Taxonomy, this means classifying levels of students' environmental understanding from concrete to abstract across six levels from observation to stewardship.

technology studio model. A fully equipped and furnished environment for technology learning and creative problem solving; goes beyond the computer lab.

tensegrity structure. A structure that uses continuous tensile members incorporating short compression members to create large structural spaces; sometimes executed with fabric.

three-dimensional textbook. The physical environment and the real-world objects within it that can be utilized as teaching and learning tools for understanding phenomena now studied from textbooks.

transitional spaces. Designs that connect indoor and outdoor spaces (patios, courtyards, decks, greenhouses).

transparency. Negative spaces such as windows that provide vistas indoors and out; open design that counters the opacity of some school designs that are shut off from views and natural light.

treasure card. A data collection method (from Bingler) that can be digitalized. Used to collect and present resources in a community that can be used as assets for school-community system for learning.

universal design. Architecture with access for people of all ages and abilities.

user's guide. Guidelines, manuals, visual dictionaries, and maps of manifestations that demonstrate how to use the school environment as a teaching and learning tool.

visual note-taking. Recording information through sketches and/or photography.

visual/spatial thinking. Architects' and designers' ability to translate concepts into functional objects and buildings; imagery.

References and Resources

Abramson, P. (2000, November). Can schools serve their communities? *School Planning & Management*, 72.

Ahrentzen, S., & Evans, G. W. (1984). Distraction, privacy, and classroom design. *Environment and Behavior, 16*(4), 437–54.

American Institute of Architects. (2004, February). *Best practices*. (BP 21.03.06).

American Institute of Architects. (2004, May). *Best practices*. (BP 18.03.09).

American Lung Association. (2007, December). *Asthma in children*. Retrieved April 17, 2008, from http://www. lungusa.org/asthma

American Society of Civil Engineers. (2004). *Report card for America's infrastructure*. Retrieved April 14, 2008, from http://www.asce.org/reportcard/

Anderson, L. W., & Krathwohl, D. R. (Eds.). (2001). *A taxonomy for learning, teaching, and assessing: A revision of Bloom's taxonomy of educational objectives*. New York: Addison Wesley Longman, Inc.

Angeles, P. A., & Ehrlich, E. (1992). *The HarperCollins dictionary of philosophy* (2nd ed.). New York: HarperCollins Publishers.

Architects Council of Europe. (1999). *A green Vitruvius: Sustainable architectural design*. London: Earthscan Publications, Ltd.

Armstrong, T. (2000). *Multiple intelligences in the classroom*. (2nd ed.). Alexandria, VA: Association for Supervision and Curriculum Development.

ASCG, Inc., Van H. Gilbert Architect, & Flintco Construction Solutions. (2001, May). *Proposal for a new replacement campus for Santa Fe Indian School*. Unpublished document.

ASCG, Inc., Van H. Gilbert Architect, & Flintco Construction Solutions. (2002, February 7). *Draft interoffice memorandum*. Unpublished document proposal for the Santa Fe Indian School.

Ball, A. (2003, Fall). Electrifying music: Band goes digital in Bay Shore. *Edutopia*, 12–13.

Barnett, C. L. (2004). *ABC's of healthy schools*. Retrieved from http://www.besafenet.com/Schools.htm

Beatley, T., & Manning, K. (1997). *The ecology of place: Planning for environment, economy, and community*. Washington DC: Island Press.

Becker, R. (2002, Spring). *High-performance school buildings*. Unpublished master's degree coursework for the Architecture and the Design of School Facilities class at the University of New Mexico.

Bingler, S., Quinn, L., & Sullivan, K. (2003). *Schools as centers of community: A citizen's guide for planning and design*. Washington DC: National Clearinghouse for Educational Facilities.

Biophilia in practice: Buildings that connect people with nature. (2006, July). *Environmental Building News, 15*(7). Retrieved August 13, 2006, from http://www. buildinggreen.com/auth/article.cfm/2006/7/9/ Biophilia-in-Practice-Buildings-that-Connect-People-with-Nature/

Bloom, B. S., et al. (1956). *Taxonomy of educational objectives handbook I: Cognitive domain.* New York: Addison Wesley Longman, Inc.

Bond, M. (2004, March 20). Natural designs [interview of William McDonough]. *New Scientist,* 46–48.

Boese, S. (2005, November). *New York State school facilities and student health, achievement, and attendance: A data analysis report.* Retrieved April 17, 2008, from http://www.healthyschools.org/documents/NYS_SchoolFacilityData.pdf

Boyer, E. L., & Mitgang, L. D. (1996). *Building community: A new future for architecture education and practice.* Ewing, NJ: The Carnegie Foundation for the Advancement of Teaching.

Brandt, R. S. (Ed.). (2000). *Education in a new era: ASCD 2000 yearbook.* Alexandria, VA: Association for Supervision and Curriculum Development.

Brooks, J. G., & Brooks, M. G. (1993). *In search of understanding: The case for constructivist classrooms.* Alexandria, VA: Association for Supervision and Curriculum Development.

Brown, G. Z., & DeKay, M. (2001). *Sun, wind and light: Architectural design strategies.* New York: John Wiley & Sons, Inc.

Brubaker, C. W. (1997). *Planning and designing schools.* New York: McGraw-Hill.

Burke, C., & Grosvenor, I. (2004). *Schools our kids would build.* Excerpted from *The school I'd like.* Retrieved November 22, 2004, from http://www.architectureweek.com/2004/1117/culture_1-1.html

Butcher, D. R. (2006, September 16). *Shape-shifting structures adapt to environment.* Retrieved October 27, 2006, from http://news.thomasnet.com/IMT/archives/2006/09/shapeshifting_responsive_smart_buildings_architecture_adapt_environment.html

Caine, R. N., & Caine, G. (1991). *Making connections: Teaching and the human brain.* Alexandria, VA: Association for Supervision and Curriculum Development.

Callison, D. (2004, Winter). The learning laboratory. *Threshold, 1*(2), 16–17.

Capra, F. (1996). *The web of life: A new understanding of living systems.* New York: Doubleday.

Capra, F. (1999, March 20). *Ecoliteracy: The challenge for education in the next century.* Liverpool Schumacher Lectures. Berkeley, CA: Center for Ecoliteracy. (Available from the Center for Ecoliteracy, 2522 San Pablo Ave., Berkeley, CA 94702)

Capra, F. (2002). *The hidden connections: Integrating the biological, cognitive, and social dimensions of life into a science of sustainability.* New York: Random House.

Capra, F. (2004). *Ecoliteracy: The challenge for education in the next century.* Retrieved November 3, 2004, from http://www.ecoliteracy.org/pages/fritjofcapra.html

Cavanaugh, K. (2003, June 23). Pollution worse in portables. *Los Angeles Daily News.* Retrieved April 11, 2008, from http://www.ewg.org/node/15523

Ceppi, G., & Zini, M. (Eds.). (1999). *Children, spaces, relations: Metaproject for an environment for young children.* Reggio Emilia, Italy: Reggio Children and Domus Academy. Second printing by Grafiche Rebecchi Ceccarelli.

Chan, S. (2008, April 22). The highest per pupil spending in the U.S. *New York Times.*

Chaney, M., Lockman, C. D., & Flurkey, D. G. (1991, Summer). Environmental influence on stimulus screening in the classroom. *Contemporary Education, 62*(4), 318–23.

Cherry, E. (1998). *Programming for design: From theory to practice.* New York: John Wiley & Sons, Inc.

Children, Youth, and Environments Center for Research and Design. (2008). *Learning landscape initiative.* Retrieved May 7, 2008, from http://thunder1.cudenver.edu/cye/lla/index.htm

Childs, M. C. (1999). *Parking spaces: A design, implementation, and use manual for architects, planners, and engineers.* New York: McGraw-Hill.

Childs, M. C. (2004). *Squares: A public place design guide for urbanists.* Albuquerque: University of New Mexico Press.

Cholo, A. B. (2004, May 12). *New school gets green thumbs up.* Retrieved from http://www.chicagotribune.com/archives

Christopher, G. (n.d.). *The effect of architecture on education.* Unpublished document following a study by the American Institute of Architects, Committee on Architecture for Education.

Christopher, G. (2004, April 28). *Design for learning.* Unpublished document faxed to the author, p. 1.

Clark, R. H., & Pause, M. (1985). *Precedents in architecture.* New York: Van Nostrand Reinhold.

Clegg, E. (2005). Future schools: Seamless? Timeless? Themeless? *PT3 Vision Quest.* Retrieved May 11, 2005, from http://www.pt3.org/VQ/html/clegg.html

Community Oversight Committee. (2004, December 13). *2004 summary report to Albuquerque Public Schools,* 4.

Concordia LLC. (1999). *Basic guide to the Concordia early learning environment: Creative interaction and communication through perception, knowledge and imagination.* Unpublished programming document for the Keystone Early Learning Center, Montgomery, Alabama.

Concordia LLC. (2008). *Our hope for New Orleans.* Retrieved April 20, 2008, from http://www.concordia.com/home/article/31/Our_Hope_for_New_Orleans

Cotton, K. (2001, December). *New small learning communities: Findings from recent literature.* (Available from the Northwest Regional Educational Laboratory, 101 SW Main St., Suite 500, Portland, OR 97204, or http://www3.scasd.org/small_schools/nlsc.pdf)

Council of Educational Facility Planners International. (2004). *The Educational Facility Planner, 39*(3).

Creative Learning Systems. (2002). *Self-directed learning, curriculum design and the creative learning environment.* (Document available from CLS, 2065 Escondido Blvd., Ste. 108, Escondido, CA 92025, or http://www.creativelearningsystems.com/)

Creative Learning Systems. (2005, October 18). *Case study: Southwest Secondary Learning Center.* Retrieved April 14, 2008, from http://www.creativelearningsystems.com/news/SSLC_case_study.pdf

Creative Learning Systems. (2008). *Resources and systems of technology: How they come together in a SmartLab.* Retrieved April 8, 2008, from http://www.creativelearningsystems.com. Also available from (800) 458-2880.

Cubberley, E. (1916). *Public school administration.* Boston: Houghton Mifflin Co.

Daniels, K. (1994). *The technology of ecological building: Basic principles and measures, examples and ideas.* Europe: Meyers Neues Lexikon.

Darling-Hammond, L. (1997). *The right to learn: A blueprint for creating schools that work.* San Francisco: Jossey-Bass, Inc.

Davis, M., Hawley, P., McMullan, B., & Spilka, G. (1997). *Design as a catalyst for learning.* Alexandria, VA: Association for Supervision and Curriculum Development.

DeBord, K., Hestenes, L. L., Moore, R. C., Cosco, N. G., & McGinnis, J. R. (2005). *Preschool outdoor environment measurement scale (POEMS).* Lewisville, NC: Kaplan Early Learning Co. (Available from http://www.kaplanco.com)

Dede, C. (1995, September/October). The evolution of constructivist learning environments: Immersion in distributed, virtual worlds. *Educational Technology, 35*(5), 46–52.

Dennis, F. F. (2008, January). Where it's safe to get dirty. *Landscape Architecture, 98*(1), 26–37.

Department of the Interior, Bureau of Education. (1918). *Cardinal principles of secondary education.* (N.p.).

Dewey, J. (1916/1944). *Democracy and education: An introduction to the philosophy of education.* New York: Free Press.

Dewey, J. (2001). *The school and society.* Mineola, NY: Dover Publications.

Dierkx, R. J. (2002). *Cool schools for hot suburbs: Models for affordable and environmentally responsive schools in Nairobi, Kenya.* Doctoral dissertation, Eindhoven University of Technology, Eindhoven, Netherlands.

Doczi, G. (1981). *The power of limits: Proportional harmonies in nature, art, and architecture.* Boston: Shambhala Publications, Inc.

Duckert, A. (2008, May 16). Cultivating ecoliteracy: Edible school garden design for Albuquerque, New Mexico. Unpublished master's design project, Landscape Architecture Program, University of New Mexico School of Architecture and Planning.

Dudek, M. (2000). *The architecture of schools and the new learning environments.* Oxford and Woburn, MA: Architectural Press.

Duke, D. (1998, February 18). *Does it matter where our children learn?* Paper commissioned by the National Research Council of the National Academy of Sciences and the National Academy of Engineering for an invitational meeting in Washington DC.

Dunbar, T. F. (1994, June–September). Acting locally: On site science. *Green Teacher,* 18–19.

Dunne, D. W. (2006). New standards should help children in noisy classrooms. Retrieved September 29, 2008, from http://www.educationworld.com/a_issues/issues073.shtml

Earthman, G. I. (2002). *School facility conditions and student academic achievement.* Retrieved April 16, 2008, from http://www.idea.gseis.ucla.edu/publications/williams/reports/pdfs/wws08-Earthman.pdf

Easton, L. B. (2002, April 10). Lessons from learners. *Education Week.* Retrieved May 21, 2004, from http://www.edweek.org/

EcoSchool Design. (2004). *School and community participation in the design, construction, and stewardship of green school grounds.* Retrieved April 16, 2008, from www.ecoschools.com/Participation/Partic_wSidebar.html

Eberhard, J. P. (2002, August). Giving "delight" its scientific due: Interdisciplinary study will match environmental factors with physiological responses in the workplace. *AIArchitect.* Retrieved April 30, 2008, from http://www.aia.org/

Edwards, B. (1999). *The new drawing on the right side of the brain: A course in enhancing creativity and artistic confidence.* Los Angeles: Jeremy P. Tarcher, Inc.

Edwards, B. (2003). *Green buildings pay* (2nd ed.). New York: Spon Press.

Engel, M. (2000). *The struggle for control of public education: Market ideology vs. democratic values.* Philadelphia: Temple University Press.

Engelbrecht, K. (2003, June 18). *The impact of color on learning.* Retrieved April 11, 2008, from the NCEF archives at http://www.edfacilities.org/

Erickson, H. L. (2001). *Stirring the head, heart, and soul: Redefining curriculum and instruction* (2nd ed.). Thousand Oaks, CA: Corwin Press.

Eriksen, A. (1985). *Playground design.* New York: Van Nostrand Reinhold.

Evans, R. (2001). *The human side of school change.* San Francisco: Jossey-Bass, Inc.

Fedrizzi, S. R. (2006, November 15–17). *Opening plenary remarks at Greenbuild Conference, Denver.* Retrieved April 6, 2008, from http://usgbc.org/Docs/News/openplenaryrick.pdf

Fiell, C., & Fiell, P. (2005). *1000 Chairs.* Köln: Taschen.

Fleming, W. (2003, Fall). Volunteer watershed health monitoring by local stakeholders: New Mexico watershed watch. *Journal of Environmental Education, 35*(1), 27–32.

Friedberg, M. P., & Berkeley, E. P. (1970). *Play and interplay: A manifesto for new design in urban recreational environments.* New York: Macmillan.

Furger, R. (2004, September/October). Green scene: Students appreciate sustainable, eco-friendly building design. *Edutopia.* Retrieved April 14, 2008, from http://www.edutopia.org/green-scene

Gardner, H. (1983). *Frames of mind: The theory of multiple intelligences.* New York: Basic Books.

Gardner, H. (1990). *Art education and human development.* Los Angeles: J. Paul Getty Trust.

Gardner, H. (1999). *The disciplined mind: Beyond facts and standardized tests, the K–12 education that every child deserves.* New York: Penguin Books.

Gardner, H. (1999). *Intelligence reframed: Multiple intelligences for the 21st century.* New York: Basic Books.

Gardner, H. (2003, September 7). The real head start. *The Boston Globe,* p. D1. Retrieved April 20, 2008, from http://www.boston.com/news/globe/ideas/articles/2003/09/07/the_real_head_start?mode=PF

General Accounting Office. (1995). *School facilities: Condition of America's schools.* Washington DC: Health, Education, and Human Services Division.

George Lucas Educational Foundation. (1997). *Learn & live.* Documentary video available through GLEF, PO Box 3494, San Rafael, CA 94912. A production of State of the Art, Inc., Washington DC. Produced and directed by Gerardine Wurzburg.

Gilbert, V. H. (2003). *Santa Fe Indian School.* Unpublished planning document.

Glancey, J. (2000). *The story of architecture.* New York: Dorling Kindersley.

Global Green USA. (2005). *Green schools initiative, Santa Monica, California.* Retrieved April 17, 2008, from http://globalgreen.org/media/greenbuilding/ Academic_Performance.pdf

Global Green USA. (2008). Healthier, wealthier, wiser: A report on national green schools. Retrieved September 22, 2008, from http://www.globalgreen.org/docs/ publication-72-1.pdf

Gonzales, C. (2004, April 19). Built on education. *UNM Campus News.*

Gordon, D. E., & Stubbs, S. (2005, October). Four shades of green. *The AIA Journal of Architecture, 1*(5). New York: The American Institute of Architects.

Gore, A. (2006). *An inconvenient truth: The planetary emergency of global warming and what we can do about it.* New York: Rodale.

Greenspan, S. I., & Benderly, B. L. (1997). *The growth of the mind: And the endangered origins of intelligence.* Cambridge, MA: Da Capo Press.

Greenwald, J. (2004, July/August). Happy land. *Yoga Journal, 182,* 96–101, 144–51.

Gruenewald, D. A. (2003, May). The best of both worlds: A critical pedagogy of place. *Educational Researcher, 32*(4).

Hagan, S. (2003, Spring/Summer). Five reasons to adopt environmental design. *Harvard Design Magazine, 18.* Retrieved April 11, 2008, from http://www.gsd.harvard. edu/research/publications/hdm

Hammond, G. S., & Schwandner, S. H. (1997). *The schoolhouse of quality: How one voice built a better school.* New York: McGraw-Hill.

Harris, C. W., and Dines, N. T. (1997). *Time-saver standards for landscape architecture: Design and construction data.* New York: McGraw-Hill.

Hawken, P., Lovins, A., & Lovins, L. H. (2000). *Natural capitalism: Creating the next industrial revolution.* New York: Back Bay Books.

Hawkins, H. L., & Lilley, H. E. (1998). *Guide for school facility appraisal: Instrument for middle school appraisal.* Scottsdale, AZ: The Council of Educational Facility Planners International. (Available through http://www.cefpi.org/)

Hedges, M. (2006, April 29). Cost of putting each fighter in war zone at record high. *Houston Chronicle.*

Heerwagen, J., & Hase, B. (2001, March/April). Building biophilia: Connecting people to nature. *Environmental Design & Construction,* 30–34.

Hershberger, R. G. (1999). *Architectural programming and predesign manager.* New York: McGraw-Hill.

Heschong, L., Wright, R. L., & Okura, S. (2002, Summer). Daylighting impacts on human performance in school. *Journal of the Illuminating Engineering Society,* 101–14.

Heschong Mahone Group. (2002, February 12). *Re-analysis report: Daylighting in schools, additional analysis.* Retrieved May 7, 2008, from http://www.cashnet.org/ resource-center/resourcefiles/128.pdf

Higgins, S., Hall, E., Wall, K., Woolner, P., & McCaughey, C. (2005, February 18). *The impact of school environments: A literature review.* Prepared by the University of Newcastle upon Tyne and sponsored by CfBT Research and Development. Retrieved April 16, 2008, from http://www.designcouncil.org/uk/en/ Design-Council/Files/Systems-Files/Download

Hill, J. (2003). *Actions of architecture.* New York: Routledge.

Hines, M. (2006). *A vision of tomorrow's curriculum today.* Mid-Pacific Institute. Retrieved October 11, 2006, from http://www.midpac.edu/

Hiss, T. (1990). *The experience of place: A new way of looking at and dealing with our radically changing cities and countryside.* New York: Knopf.

Hoody, L., & Lieberman, G. (1998). *Closing the achievement gap: Using the environment as an integrating context for learning.* State Education and Environment Roundtable. (Available with additional information at http://www.seer.org/)

Hopkins, G. (1997). *Have you heard? Noise can affect learning!* Retrieved from http://www.education-world.com/a curr/curr011.shtml

Horst, S. (2006). From *The school district farm and areas of management concern*, submitted to the author for this publication.

Hunt, J., & Carroll, T. (2003). *No dream denied: A pledge to America's children.* National Commission on Teaching and America's Future. Retrieved April 11, 2008, from http://www.nctaf.org/documents/no-dream-denied_summary_report.pdf

Jensen, E. (2000). *Brain-based learning.* San Diego: The Brain Store Publishing.

Jilk, B., & Copa, G. (1997). The design-down process. *Council of Educational Facility Planners International IssueTrak, 6.*

Jodidio, P. (2003). Santiago Calatrava. Köln: Taschen.

Johnson, K. (2007, September 17). In the Southwest, fixing the fence never ends. *USA Today*, A1–2.

K–12 schools: Lessons learned from three neighborhood schools. (2006, April). *Architectural Record Review.* [A supplement to *Architectural Record*]. New York: McGraw-Hill.

Kagan, S. (1992). *Cooperative learning.* San Clemente, CA: Resources for Teachers, Inc.

Kaplan, S. N., & Gould, B. (1996). *Systems: A thematic interdisciplinary unit.* Calabasas, CA: Educator to Educator Books.

Kats, G., et al. (2003, October). *The costs and financial benefits of green buildings: A report to California's Sustainable Building Task Force.* Retrieved September 24, 2006, from http://www.cap-e.com/publications/default/cfm

Kats, G. (2006, October). *Greening America's schools: Costs and benefits.* Retrieved October 30, 2008, from www.usgbc.org/ShowFile.aspx?DocumentID=2908

Kay, A. (1991, September). Computers, networks and education. *Scientific American*, 138–48.

Kay, J. H. (2005, July/August). The top 10 green schools in the U.S.: 2005. *The Green Guide.* Retrieved April 11, 2008, from http://www.greenguide.com/

Kennedy, M. (2002, June). Accessorizing the classroom. *American School & University, 74*(10), 36.

Kennedy, M. (2002, January). *By design.* Retrieved April 11, 2008, from http://asumag.com/

Kessler, R. (2000). *The soul of education: Helping students find connection, compassion, and character at school.* Alexandria, VA: Association for Supervision and Curriculum Development.

Koerner, B. I. (2006, February). Geeks in toyland. *Wired*, 104–12, 150.

Kozol, J. (2005). *The shame of the nation: The restoration of apartheid schooling in America.* New York: Crown Publishers.

Kozol, J. (2005). *Education: The shame of the nation.* (Tapes and transcripts of this speech are available from Alternative Radio, PO Box 551, Boulder, CO 80306; (800) 444-1977; or http://www.alternativeradio.org)

KRQE News 13. (2008, April 24). *Barker probe speeds up school fire inspections.* Retrieved April 29, 2008, from http://www.krqe.com/Global/story.asp?S=8225201&nav=menu588_2_7

Kuller, R., & Lindsten, C. (1992). Health and behavior of children in classrooms with and without windows. *Journal of Environmental Psychology, 12*, 305–17.

Lackney, J. (1998). School building design principles for an assessment program. In Henry Sanoff (2001), *School building assessment methods.* (N.p.). Note: The project was conducted at the School of Architecture, College of Design, North Carolina State University–Raleigh. Funding came from the College of Design and in part from the National Clearinghouse for Educational Facilities.

Lackney, J. (2003, February). *33 principles for school facilities design.* Retrieved April 14, 2008, from http://schoolstudio.engr.wisc.edu/33principles.html

Lackney, J. (2005). *Educational Commissioning: Educating educators to optimize their school facility for teaching and learning.* Retrieved April 14, 2008, from http://www.designshare.com/index.php/articles/educational-commissioning/

Laeser, K., Maxwell, L., & Hedge, A. (1998, Winter). The effect of computer workstation design on student posture. *Journal of Research on Computing in Education, 31*(2), 173–88.

Lang, D. C. (2004, February). *Seattle design guidelines: Progressive educational reform via building design guidelines.* Retrieved October 8, 2006, from http://www.designshare.com/Research/Lang/SeattleDesignGuidelines.asp

Lantos, J. (2006, October 6). Teaching's about connections. *Albuquerque Journal, Rio Rancho West,* p. A13.

Lawrence, B. K. (2002). *Lowering the overhead by raising the roof: . . . And other rural trust strategies to reduce the costs of your small school.* A Report from the Rural School and Community Trust. (Available through http://www.ruraledu.org/)

Leary, K. (2003). The educational advantages of green: Saving, teaching, learning. *Educational Facility Planner, 38*(2), 35–36.

LEED for Schools. (2007). *A ratings certification system.* Retrieved April 16, 2008, from http://www.usgbc.org/DisplayPage.aspx?CMSPageID=1586

Lerner, M. (2006). *The left hand of God: Taking back our country from the religious right.* New York: HarperCollins Publishers.

Lewis, R. K. (2001). *Architect? A candid guide to the profession* (Rev. ed.). Cambridge, MA: The MIT Press.

Locker, F. M., & Olson, S. (2004). *Flexible school facilities.* Retrieved November 3, 2004, from http://www.designshare.com/Research/Locker/FlexibleSchools.asp

Long, P. D., and Ehrmann, S. C. (2005). Future of the learning space: Breaking out of the box. *Educause Review, 40*(4), 42–58.

Loughlin, C. E., & Martin, M. D. (1987). *Supporting literacy: Developing effective learning environments.* New York: Teachers College, Columbia University.

Lowenfeld, V., and Brittain, W. L. (1970). *Creative and mental growth* (5th ed.). New York: Macmillan.

Lyle, J. T. (1996). *Regenerative design for sustainable development.* New York: John Wiley & Sons, Inc.

Lynch, K. (1993). *The image of the city.* Cambridge, MA: The MIT Press.

Lyons, J. B. (2001, November). Do school facilities really impact a child's education? *IssueTrak, 6*(6). Retrieved May 7, 2008, from http://www.cefpi.org/pdf/issue14.pdf

Macaulay, D. (1988). *The way things work.* Boston: Houghton Mifflin/Walter Lorraine Books.

Malaguzzi, L. (1993, June). *Your image of the child: Where teaching begins.* Comments translated and adapted from a seminar presented in Reggio Emilia, Italy. (B. Rankin, L. Morrow, & L. Gandini, Trans.). (Available from the Child Care Information Exchange, PO Box 2890, Redmond, WA 98073; or (800) 221-2864)

Maslow, A. H. (1943). A theory of human motivation. *Psychology Review, 50,* 370–96.

Maslow, A. H. (1954). *Motivation and personality.* New York: Harper.

Maslow, A. H. (1968). *Toward a psychology of being* (2nd ed.). New York: Van Nostrand Reinhold.

Mau, B. (2004). *Massive change.* London: Phaidon Press.

Mazria, E. (1980). *The passive solar energy book.* New York: Rodale.

Mazria, E. (2003, October). Turning down the global thermostat. *Metropolis,* 102–7.

Mazria, E. (2004, March 11). Building design affects energy use. *Albuquerque Journal,* p. A15.

Mazria, E. (2005). Design to survive. *Architecture Week.* Retrieved September 19, 2006, from http://www.architectureweek.com/

Mazria Inc. Odems Dzurec Architecture/Planning. (2005). *Edward Gonzales Elementary School user's manual.* Self-published document given to school personnel at a new solar school prototype for Albuquerque Public Schools.

McConachie, L., & Lang, D. (2003, January). The Center School: Opportunities and challenges in planning and building a small urban high school. CEFPI's *Educational Facility Planner, 38*(4).

McDonnell, P. (2006, July/August). Preserving Buffalo's schools. *Buffalo Spree Magazine,* 143–44.

McDonough, W. (2002). *Cradle to cradle.* New York: North Point Press.

McSporran, E. (1997). Towards better listening and learning in the classroom. *Educational Review, 49*(1), 13–20.

McVey, G. F. (1994). In search of equitable learning environments: The acoustics of classrooms used in "mainstreaming" hearing-disadvantaged students. *Educational Facility Planner, 32*(3), 16–23.

Meier, D. (1995). *The power of their ideas: Lessons for America from a small school in Harlem.* Boston: Beacon Press.

Moore, G. T., & Lackney, J. (1992, June). *School buildings and school performance.* Keynote talk given at the Wingspread/Prairie School National Conference on Architecture and Education, Racine, Wisconsin. Contact the School of Architecture and Urban Planning, University of Wisconsin–Milwaukee, PO Box 413, Milwaukee, WI 53201-0413; or (414) 229-4014.

Moore, R. C. (1993). *Plants for play: A plant selection guide for children's outdoor environments.* Berkeley, CA: MIG Communications.

Morris, V. C. (1961). *Philosophy and the American school: An introduction to the philosophy of education.* Boston: Houghton Mifflin Co.

Morrow, B. H. (1997). *A dictionary of landscape architecture.* Albuquerque: University of New Mexico Press.

Moskos, H. (2004, April 4). Teens take the poison out of trashed computers. *Albuquerque Journal,* pp. C1, C4.

Murphy, P. (1993). *By nature's design: An Exploratorium book.* San Francisco: Chronicle Books.

Mutlow, J. V. (Ed.). (1997). *Ricardo Legorreta Architects.* New York: Rizzoli International Publications, Inc.

Myers, N., & Robertson, S. (2004). *Creating connections: The CEFPI guide for educational facility planning.* Scottsdale, AZ: The Council of Educational Facility Planners International.

Nair, P., & Fielding, R. (2005). *The language of school design: Design patterns for 21st century schools.* Minneapolis, MN: DesignShare, Inc. (Available from http://www.designshare.com/)

Nathan, J., & Febey, K. (2001). *Smaller, safer, saner, successful schools.* Washington DC: National Clearinghouse for Educational Facilities, Center for School Change, and the Humphrey Institute of the University of Minnesota–Minneapolis.

Nathan, J., Thao, S. (2007). *Smaller, safer, saner, successful schools.* Washington DC: National Clearinghouse for Educational Facilities, Center for School Change, and the Humphrey Institute of the University of Minnesota–Minneapolis. (Available through http://www.edfacilities.org/pubs/saneschools.pdf)

National Center for Education Statistics. (2000, June). *Condition of America's public school facilities: 1999.* U.S. Department of Education, Office of Educational Research and Improvement. Retrieved April 14, 2008, from http://nces.ed.gov/pubsearch/pubsinfo.asp?pubid=2000032

National Center on Education and the Economy, & the University of Pittsburgh. (1997). *Performance standards: English language arts, mathematics, science, applied learning.* Washington DC: New Standards.

National Clearinghouse for Educational Facilities. (2008). *Condition of schools in America: Resource list.* Retrieved April 14, 2008, from http://www.edfacilities.org/rl/conditions.cfm

National Clearinghouse for Educational Facilities. (2008). *School size/small schools.* Available at http://www.edfacilities.org/rl/size.cfm

National Clearinghouse for Educational Facilities News. (2006, June 8). A junior high tells LA Unified: Don't fence us in. [Online news abstract of the *Los Angeles Times* article by Banks, S.]

National Playground Safety Institute. (2003). *Certification course for playground safety inspectors manual.* National Recreation and Park Association. (Available through http://www.nrpa.org/)

National Program for Playground Safety. (2006). *Age-appropriate design guidelines for playgrounds.* Retrieved January 31, 2006, from http://www.uni.edu/playground

National Renewable Energy Laboratory, U.S. Department of Energy. (2002, January). *Energy design guidelines for high performance schools—hot and dry climates.* (Also includes guidelines for other climates.)

National Renewable Energy Laboratory, U.S. Department of Energy. (2002, February). *How parents and teachers are helping to create better environments for learning: Energy-smart building choices.* Brochure. Retrieved April 17, 2008, from http://www.nrel.gov/docs/fy01osti/30557.pdf

National Research Council. (1996). *National science education standards.* Washington DC: National Academy Press.

National Research Council. (2000). *How people learn: Brain, mind, experience, and school.* Washington DC: National Academy Press.

National School Safety and Security Services. (2008, September). School safety services include [Homepage]. Retrieved September 22, 2008, from http://www.schoolsecurity.org/

Nelson, G. (2003). *How to see: A guide to reading our man-made environment.* Oakland, CA: Design Within Reach.

Neumann, U., & Kyriakakis, C. (2002). 2020 classroom. In *2020 visions: Transforming education and training through advanced technologies.* Washington DC: Technology Administration Publications, U.S. Department of Commerce. (Available through http://www.technology.gov/reports/techpolicy/2020visions.pdf

New Economics Foundation. (2008). *Happy planet index: An index of human well-being and environmental impact.* Retrieved April 14, 2008, from http://www.neweconomics.org/gen/z_sys_publicationdetail.aspx?pid=225

North Central Regional Educational Laboratory, & Metiri Group. (2003). *EnGauge 21st century skills: Literacy in the digital age.* Retrieved from http://www.ncrel.org/engauge/skills/engauge21st.pdf

Northwest Regional Educational Laboratory. (N.d.). *Small learning communities: Key elements of small learning communities.* Retrieved October 30, 2008, from http://www.nwrel.org/scpd/sslc

Oberlin College. (2008). *Information on the Environmental Studies Center.* Retrieved April 11, 2008, from http://www.oberlin.edu

O'Gorman, J. F. (1998). *ABC of architecture.* Philadelphia: University of Pennsylvania Press.

Ohrenschall, M. (2008, April). *Building for the earth . . . not against it.* Retrieved May 8, 2008, from http://www.newsdata.com/enernet/conweb/conweb4.html

Olson, S., & Kellum, S. (2003, November 25). *The impact of sustainable buildings in K–12 schools.* Retrieved April 16, 2008, from http://www.cleanerandgreener.org/

Open Window. (1994). Preschools and infant-toddler centers: Istituzione of the municipality of Reggio Emilia, Italy. Published by Reggio Children, Via Bligny 1/a—C.P. 91 Succursale 2, 42100 Reggio Emilia, Italia.

Orelove, F. P., & Hanley, C. D. (1979). Modifying school buildings for the severely handicapped: A school accessibility survey. *American Association for the Education of the Severely/Profoundly Handicapped Review, 4*(3), 219–36.

Ornstein, A. C., & Levine, D. U. (2003). *Foundations of education* (8th ed.). New York: Houghton Mifflin Co.

Orr, D. (1992). *Ecological literacy: Education and the transition to a postmodern world.* Albany: State University of New York Press.

Orr, D. (1994). *Earth in mind.* Washington DC: Island Press.

Orr, D. (1997). Architecture as pedagogy: Part II. *Conservation Biology* (1997, June), *11*(3), 597–600. Arlington, VA: Blackwell Science, Inc.

Ott, J. N. (2000). *Health and light: The effects of natural and artificial light on man and other living things.* Atlanta: Ariel Press.

Pearson, C. A. (2006, June). Antoine Predock rides high with the gold medal. *Architectural Record, 194*(6), 212–23.

Peña, W., & Parshall, S. A. (2001). *Problem seeking: An architectural programming primer* (4th ed.). New York: John Wiley & Sons, Inc.

Peña, W., Parshall, S. A., & Kelly, K. (1987). *Problem seeking: An architectural programming primer* (3rd ed.). Washington DC: AIA Press.

Perkins, B. (2001). *Building type basics for elementary and secondary schools.* New York: John Wiley & Sons, Inc.

Peters, R. (2005). *Mapping the constructed landscape as art: A report from New York.* Unpublished document.

Petronis, J. P. (1993). Strategic asset management: An expanded role for facility programmers. In W. F. E. Preiser (Ed.), *Professional practice in facility programming*. New York: Van Nostrand Reinhold.

Phillips, L. E. (1996). *Parks: Design and management*. New York: McGraw-Hill.

Picard, M., & Bradley, J. S. (1997). *Revisiting speech interference by noise in classrooms and considering some possible solutions*. Paper presented at the 133rd meeting of the Acoustical Society of America. Retrieved April 12, 2008, from http://www.acoustics.org/press/133rd/2paaa3.html

Piaget, J. (1950). *The psychology of intelligence*. New York: Routledge.

Pink, D. H. (2005). *A whole new mind: Why right-brainers will rule the future*. New York: Riverhead Books.

Polynesian Cultural Center. (2006). Information from center's catalogue and Anne Taylor's personal visit.

Poplin, M., & Weeres, J. (1992). *Voices from the inside: A report on schooling from inside the classroom*. The Institute for Education in Transformation at the Claremont Graduate School, California.

Preiser, W. F. E. (Ed.). (1993). *Professional practice in facilities programming*. New York: Van Nostrand Reinhold.

Preiser, W. F. E. (2003). *Improving building performance*. Washington DC: National Council of Architectural Registration Boards.

Preiser, W. F. E., & Ostroff, E. (Eds.). (2001). *Universal design handbook*. New York: McGraw-Hill.

Preiser, W. F. E., Rabinowitz, H. Z., & White, E. T. (1988). *Post-occupancy evaluation*. New York: Van Nostrand Reinhold.

Preiser, W. F. E., & Taylor, A. (1983, Summer). Effects of space on behavior. *Exceptional Education Quarterly*, 4(2).

Pressman, A. (2001). *Architectural design portable handbook: A guide to excellent practices*. New York: McGraw-Hill.

Ramsey, C. G., Sleeper, H. R., & Hoke, J. R. (2000). *Architectural graphic standards* (10th ed.). New York: John Wiley & Sons, Inc.

Redman, D. (2004, April 30). Water wise: Hydrogeologist uses elementary school to test his theories. *Albuquerque Journal, Rio Rancho West*, p. 5.

Reed, P. (2005). *Ground swell: Constructing the contemporary landscape*. Exhibition and catalogue. New York: Museum of Modern Art.

Reuf, K. (1992). *The private eye: Looking/thinking by analogy*. Seattle: The Private Eye Project.

Richardson, W. (2006, October). The new face of learning. *Edutopia*. Retrieved April 12, 2008, from http://www.edutopia.org/new-face-learning

Rivlin, L. G., & Weinstein, C. S. (1984). Educational issues, school settings, and environmental psychology. *Journal of Environmental Psychology*, 4, 347–64.

Ross, Z. A., & Walker, B. (1999). *Reading, writing and risk: Air pollution inside California's portable classrooms*. Retrieved April 12, 2008, from http://www.ewg.org/reports/readingwritingrisk

Rouard, M., & Simon, J. (1977). *Children's play spaces: From sandbox to adventure playground*. New York: The Overlook Press.

Roybal, D. (2006, July 11). Spread the wealth for the sake of rural education. *Albuquerque Journal*, p. A5.

Rubenstein, G. (2006, October). *Toss the traditional textbook: Revamping a curriculum*. Retrieved April 12, 2008, from http://www.edutopia.org/toss-traditional-textbook

Rusch, C. W. (1974). MOBOC: A mobile learning environment. In G. J. Coates (Ed.), *Alternative learning environments* (pp. 132–49). Stroudsburg, PA: Dowden, Hutchinson and Ross, Inc.

Rutherford, F. J., & Ahlgren, A. (1990). *Science for all Americans*. New York: Oxford University Press.

Rybczynski, W. (1992). *Looking around: A journey through architecture*. New York: Penguin Books.

Rybczynski, W. (2001). *The look of architecture*. New York: Oxford University Press.

Sanoff, H. (2000). *Community participation methods in design and planning*. New York: John Wiley & Sons, Inc.

Sanoff, H. (1995). *Creating environments for young children*. Workbook based on a project conducted at the Department of Architecture, School of Design, North Carolina State University–Raleigh, supported in part by a grant from the National Endowment for the Arts.

Sarkis, H. (2001). *Le Corbusier Venice Hospital and the mat building revival.* New York: Harvard Design School/Prestel.

Savory, A., & Butterfield, J. (1999). *Holistic management: A new framework for decision-making* (2nd ed.). Washington DC: Island Press.

Schneider, M. (2002, November). *Do school facilities affect academic outcomes?* Retrieved April 12, 2008, from http://www.edfacilities.org/pubs/outcomes.pdf

Schneider, M. (2002, November). *Public school facilities and teaching: Washington DC and Chicago.* Retrieved April 12, 2008, from http://www.21csf.org/csf-home/Documents/Teacher_Survey/SCHOOL_FACS_AND_TEACHING.pdf

Schneider, M. (2003, August). *Linking school facility conditions to teacher satisfaction and success.* Retrieved May 7, 2008, from http://www.edfacilities.org/pubs/teachersurvey.pdf

Schneider, M. S. (1995). *A beginner's guide to constructing the universe: The mathematical archetypes of nature, art, and science.* New York: Harper Perennial. (For more information e-mail geoman@pb.net or visit http://www.constructingtheuniverse.com)

Schoellkopf, A. (2004, January 27). Montaño Bridge artwork depicts life in the bosque. *Albuquerque Journal, Rio Rancho West,* pp. 1, 2.

Schweke, W. (2004). *Smart money: Education and economic development.* Washington DC: The Economic Policy Institute. (More information on this book is available at http://www.epi.org)

The Second National Invitational Conference on Architecture and Education. (1992, May 15–17). *The design for a new generation of American schools* [Summary report]. Racine, WI: The Prairie School and Wingspread.

Shaw, L. (2002, March 3). Major force directs T. T. Minor Elementary's rise. *The Seattle Times,* p. A1.

Shinsky, J. (2000). *Students with special needs: A resource guide for teachers.* (Available from Shinsky Seminars, Inc., 3101 N. Cambridge Rd., Lansing, MI 48911)

SHW Group. (1998, Fall). Environmentally sensitive design: Texas leads the way in sustainable school development. *Concepts, Texas Edition.*

Simkins, M. (1999). Designing great rubrics. *Technology and Learning, 20*(1), 23–30.

Smith, M. (2002, May 25). *The acoustic environment.* Doctoral paper presented to the School Design and Planning Laboratory Seminar on Acoustics in the Classroom, University of Georgia. Retrieved April 16, 2008, from http://www.eric.ed.gov:80/ERICDocs/data/ericdocs2sql/content_storage_01/0000019b/80/1b/31/51.pdf (Also available through http://www.edfacilities.org/rl/acoustics.cfm)

Sokol, D. (2006, September). Higher ground. *Architectural Record, 194*(9), pp. 86–92.

Spector, S. (2003, August). *Creating schools and strengthening communities through adaptive reuse.* Retrieved April 12, 2008, from http://www.edfacilities.org/pubs/adaptiveuse.pdf

State of New Mexio Legislative Finance Committee. Corrections department review of facility planning efforts and oversight to private prisons and health programs. (2007, May 23). Report #07–04. Retrieved October 30, 2008, from http://legis.state.nm.us/lcs/lfc/lfcdocs/perfaudit/correctionsfacilities0507.pdf

Sternberg, R. J. (1985). *Beyond IQ: A triarchic theory of human intelligence.* New York: Cambridge University Press.

Sternberg, R. J. (1998). Principles of teaching for successful intelligence. *Educational Psychologist, 33*(2/3), 65–73.

Story, M. F. (2001). Principles of universal design. In Preiser, W. F. E., & Ostroff, E. (Eds.), *Universal design handbook* (chapter 10). New York: McGraw-Hill.

Suttell, R. (2006, April). The true costs of building green. *Buildings, 100*(4), 47.

Sustainable Buildings Industry Council. (2001). *High-performance school buildings: Resource and strategy guide.* (2nd ed.). (Note: The new 2008 3rd ed. is available from http://sbicouncil.org/)

Sweet, K. (2003, December 22). Schools change focus of PE classes. *Albuquerque Journal,* p. C2.

Swentzell, R. (1976). *An architectural history of Santa Clara Pueblo.* Master's thesis, University of New Mexico, Albuquerque.

Takahashi, N. (1999). *Educational landscapes: Developing school grounds as learning places.* Charlottesville, VA: Thomas Jefferson Center for Educational Design.

Tapscott, D. (1998). *Growing up digital: The rise of the net generation.* New York: McGraw-Hill.

Tarr, P. (2001). *Aesthetic codes in early childhood classrooms: What art educators can learn from Reggio Emilia.* Retrieved April 12, 2008, from http://www.designshare.com/research/Tarr/Aesthetic_codes_1.htm

Taylor, A. (1971). *The effects of selected stimuli on the art products, concept formation and aesthetic judgmental decisions of four and five year old children.* Unpublished doctoral dissertation, Arizona State University.

Taylor, A. (2001, September 28). *Santa Fe Indian School cultural symposium: Implications for architectural design and construction.* Unpublished report available from the author.

Taylor, A., & Brown, C. (1998). Traveling techno tents: Teaching technology through design education for rural New Mexico. Unpublished planning article written for the Institute for Environmental Education, University of New Mexico School of Architecture and Planning.

Taylor, A., Dunbar, T., Hexom, D., Brown, C., & Enggass, K. (2000). *Developing learning landscapes for elementary schools.* Unpublished planning document. © Sanger Unified School District and School Zone Institute.

Taylor, A., & Gilbert, V. (2001). *Bilingual Early Childhood Center (BECC): An architectural program for design of a unique learning environment.* Unpublished programming document.

Taylor, A., Hexom, D., Dunbar, T., Enggass, K., & Brown, C. (2000). *Developing learning landscapes for elementary schools: Sanger Unified School District.* Unpublished document © Sanger Unified School District and School Zone Institute.

Taylor, A., Hexom, D., & Enggass, K. (2000). *New Explorers' Curriculum.* Unpublished document for Sanger Unified School District.

Taylor, A., Martin, P., Class, K., & Enggass, K. (2000). *Developing an eco-historical sense of place: A self-organizing system for environmental learning on school sites.* Unpublished document funded by the Center for Ecoliteracy for the Lincoln Unified School District, California.

Taylor, A., & Sherk, B. (1994). *Manifestations: A framework for understanding the environment as a learning tool, the ecology of phenomena and its application as curriculum and instruction at Lincoln High School West, CA* (Rev. ed.). Unpublished document.

Taylor, A., Sherk, B., Wolff/Lang/Christopher Architects Inc., & Concordia LLC. (1994). *User's guide: West Campus Lincoln High School.* Unpublished document.

Taylor, A. P., & Vlastos, G. (1983). *School zone: Learning environments for children.* Corrales, NM: School Zone, Inc.

Taylor, A., & Vlastos, G. (1993). *Head start classroom of the future.* HHSS Grant No. 90-CD-0725. Albuquerque: University of New Mexico.

Taylor, A., & Vlastos, G. (1997). *CyberVillage.* Unpublished research document and curriculum for a School Zone, Inc., project.

Taylor, A., & Vlastos, G. (1998). *Program for design of CyberVillage.* Unpublished programming document.

Taylor, A., Vlastos, G., & Marshall, A. (1991). *Architecture and children: Teachers' guide.* Seattle: Architecture and Children Institute. © School Zone Institute.

Thayer, B. M. (1995, November/December). A daylit school in North Carolina, *Solar Today.*

Thompson, J. W., & Sorvig, K. (2000). *Sustainable landscape construction: A guide to green building outdoors.* Washington DC: Island Press.

Thornburg, D. (2002). *The new basics: Education and the future of work in the telematic age.* Alexandria, VA: Association for Supervision and Curriculum Development.

Thornburgh, N. (2006, April 17). Dropout nation. *Time.*

Tilley, A. R., & Richard Dreyfuss Associates (2001). *The measure of man and woman: Human factors in design.* New York: John Wiley & Sons, Inc.

Toch, T. (2003). *High schools on a human scale: How small schools can transform American education.* Boston: Beacon Press.

UNICEF. (2003). *The state of the world's children 2003.* New York: UNICEF.

U.S. Department of Commerce. (2002). *2020 visions: Transforming education and training through advanced technologies.* Washington DC: Technology Administration, Office of Public Affairs. (Available at http://www.ta.doc.gov/OTPolicy)

U.S. Department of Education. (2000). *E-Learning: Putting a world-class education at the fingertips of all children.* The National Educational Technology Plan. (Available at http://www.ed.gov/about/offices/list/os/technology/reports/e-learning.pdf)

U.S. Department of Education. (2000). *Schools as centers of community: A citizens' guide for planning and design.* Washington DC: U.S. Department of Education.

U.S. Green Building Council (2000, April). *Making the business case for high performance green buildings.* Document based on an April 2000 roundtable. Washington DC: USGBC, with the Real Estate Roundtable and the Urban Land Institute. Retrieved April 30, 2008, from http://www.usgbc.org/DisplayPage.aspx?CMSPageID=106

U.S. Green Building Council. (2001, June). *LEED rating system version 2.0.* (Available from the U.S. Green Building Council, 1800 Massachusetts Ave. NW, Washington DC 20036 or at http://www.usgbc.org/Docs/LEEDdocs/3.4xLEEDRatingSystemJune01.pdf)

Van der Ryn, S. (2005). *Design for life: The architecture of Sim Van der Ryn.* Layton, UT: Gibbs Smith, Publisher.

Van der Ryn, S., & Cowan, S. (1996). *Ecological design.* Washington DC: Island Press.

Vanourek, G. (2005, May). *State of the charter movement 2005: Trends, issues, and indicators.* Retrieved February 24, 2006, from http://www.cslc.us

Verba, S. (1961). *Small groups and political behavior: A study of leadership.* Princeton, NJ: Princeton University Press.

Verstegen, D. A. (2002, October). The new finance. *American School Board Journal* archive. Retrieved April 5, 2006, from http://www.asbj.com

VITETTA. (2007). *Little school houses.* Retrieved April 10, 2008, from http://www.vitetta.com/education/_litschool.html

Von Glaserfeld, E. (1984). An introduction to radical constructivism. In P. Watzlawick (Ed.), *The invented reality.* New York: Norton.

VS America, Inc. (2007). *The dynamic school.* Retrieved April 9, 2008, from http://www.vs-moebel.de

Vygotsky, L. (1978). *Mind in society: Development of higher psychological processes.* Cambridge, MA: Harvard University Press.

Wagner, C. (2000, May). *Planning school grounds for outdoor learning.* National Clearinghouse for Educational Facilities. Retrieved April 12, 2008, from http://www.edfacilities.org

Walling, L. L. (1992, Summer). Granting each equal access. *School Library Media Quarterly,* 216–22.

Webb, A. (2006, August 21). Sightworks will rent out knowledge that fascinates. *Albuquerque Journal* (Business Outlook), pp. 1, 7.

Wellington, Y. (1998, May 1). *Assistive technology success stories.* Retrieved April 12, 2008, from http://www.edutopia.org/assistive-technology-success-stories

Wells College. (2007–2008). *Wells College Community Handbook.* Aurora, New York: Wells College.

Wheeler, S. M. (2004). *Planning for sustainability.* New York: Routledge.

Wheeler, S. M., & Beatley, T. (Eds.). (2004). *The sustainable urban development reader.* New York: Routledge.

White, S. A., Nair, K. S., & Ashcroft, J. (1994). *Participatory communication: Working for change and development.* Thousand Oaks, CA: Sage Publications.

Whittle, C. (2005, August 29). Let's have a student uprising. *Time,* 47–48. Magazine excerpt adapted from *Crash course: Imagining a better future for public education.* New York: Riverhead Books.

Wiggins, G., & McTighe, J. (1998). *Understanding by design.* Alexandria, VA: Association for Supervision and Curriculum Development.

Wikipedia. (2008, February 21). *Tensegrity.* Retrieved April 12, 2008, from http://en.wikipedia.org/wiki/Tensegrity

Wilson, E. O. (2002). *The future of life*. New York: Alfred A. Knopf.

Wines, J. (2000). *Green architecture*. Köln: Taschen.

Winter & Company. (2007). *Special needs studio*. Retrieved April 9, 2008, from http://www. winterandcompany.net

Wolfe, P. (2001). *Brain matters: Translating research into classroom practice*. Alexandria, VA: Association for Supervision and Curriculum Development.

Wolff, S. J. (2002, February). *Design features for project-based learning*. Condensed version of doctoral research study, Oregon State University. (Available at http://www.designshare.com/Research/Wolff/Project_Learning.htm)

Wood, G. H. (1992). *Schools that work: America's most innovative public education programs*. New York: Dutton Books.

Wulz, F. (1986). The concept of participation. *Design Studies*, 7(3), 153–62.

Yee, R. (2005). *Educational environments, Vol. 2*. New York: Visual Reference Publications, Inc.

Zander, R. S., & Zander, B. (2002). *The art of possibility: Transforming professional and personal life*. New York: Penguin Books.

ARCHITECTURE AND DESIGN BOOKS FOR CHILDREN

Billings, H. (1996). *Bridges*. New York: Viking Press.

Ceserani, G. P. (1983). *Grand constructions*. New York: G. P. Putnam's Sons.

Corbett, S. (1978). *Bridges*. New York: Macmillan.

D'Alelio, J. (1989). *I know that building! Discovering architecture with activities and games*. Washington DC: Preservation Press.

Forsyth, A. (1989). *The architecture of animals: The Equinox guide to wildlife structures*. Ontario: Camden House.

Giblin, J. C. (1981). *The skyscraper book*. New York: Thomas Crowell.

Hernandez, X., Comes, P., & Ballonga, J. (1990). *Barmi: A Mediterranean city through the ages*. Boston: Houghton Mifflin Co.

Isaacson, P. (1988). *Round buildings, square buildings, and buildings that wiggle like a fish*. New York: Knopf.

Macaulay, D. (1981). *Cathedral: The story of its construction*. Boston: Houghton Mifflin/Walter Lorraine Books.

Macaulay, D. (1982). *Castle*. Boston: Houghton Mifflin/Walter Lorraine Books.

Macaulay, D. (1982). *Pyramid*. Boston: Houghton Mifflin/Walter Lorraine Books.

Macaulay, D. (1983). *Underground*. Boston: Houghton Mifflin/Walter Lorraine Books.

Macaulay, D. (1988). *The way things work*. Boston: Houghton Mifflin/Walter Lorraine Books.

MacGregor, A., & MacGregor, S. (1980). *Skyscrapers: A project book for young people*. New York: Lothrop, Lee and Shepard Books.

MacGregor, A., & MacGregor, S. (1981). *Bridges: A project book*. New York: Lothrop, Lee and Shepard Books.

Sandak, C. (1984). *Skyscrapers: An easy-read modern wonders book*. New York: Franklin Watts.

Silverberg, R. (1966). *Bridges*. Philadelphia: Macrae Smith.

Sullivan, G. (1979). *Understanding architecture*. New York: Thomas Crowell.

Walker, L., & Hogrogian, N. (2007). *Housebuilding for children: Step-by-step plans for houses children can build themselves*. Woodstock, NY: Overlook Press.

Weiss, H. (1992). *Model buildings and how to make them*. New York: Thomas Crowell.

Wilson, F. (1995). *What it feels like to be a building*. New York: John Wiley & Sons, Inc.

Young, C., & King, C. (1991). *Castles, pyramids and palaces*. London: Osbourne Publishing, Ltd.

ORGANIZATIONS AND WEB SITES

The Academy of Neuroscience for Architecture (ANFA)
The mission of ANFA is to build intellectual bridges between brain, mind, and consciousness research and those who design spaces and places for human use.
http://www.anfarch.org/

American Academy of Environmental Medicine
http://www.aaemonline.org/

American Architectural Foundation
    1799 New York Ave. NW
    Washington DC 20006
    (202) 626-7318
    http://www.archfoundation.org/

American Association of
School Administrators (AASA)
    801 N. Quincy St., Ste. 700
    Arlington, VA 22203-1730
    (703) 528-0700
    http://www.aasa.org/

American Association for State and Local History
    1717 Church St.
    Nashville, TN 37203
    (615) 320-3203
    http://www.aaslh.org/

American Horticulture Society
    http://www.ahs.org/

The American Institute of Architects (AIA)
    1735 New York Ave. NW
    Washington DC 20006
    (800) 242-3837
    http://www.aia.org/

The American Institute of Architects
Committee on Architecture for Education
    http://www.aia.org/cae_default

American Planning Association
    1776 Massachusetts Ave. NW, Ste. 400
    Washington DC 20036-1904
    (202) 872-0611
    http://www.planning.org/

American Psychological Association
    750 First St. NE
    Washington DC 20002-4242
    (800) 374-2721
    http://www.apa.org/

American Society of Heating, Refrigerating, and
Air-Conditioning Engineers
    http://www.ashrae.org/

American Society of Interior Designers
    608 Massachusetts Ave. NE
    Washington DC 20002-6006
    (202) 546-3480
    http://www.asid.org/

American Society of Landscape Architects
    636 Eye St. NW
    Washington DC 20001-3736
    (888) 898-1185
    http://www.asla.org/

Amy Biehl Foundation
    http://www.amybiehl.org/

Architecture 2030
A nonprofit organization founded by Edward Mazria to
reduce the building sector's ecological footprint
    http://www.architecture2030.org/home.html

ArcNews
    Published quarterly at ESRI
    380 New York St.
    Redlands, CA 92373-8100
    http://www.esri.com/arcnews
    Also visit ArcGIS Explorer at http://www.esri.
        com/software/arcgis/explorer/index.html

Arcosanti Project
    HC74 Box 4136
    Mayer, AZ 86333
    http://www.arcosanti.org/

Art in the School, Inc.
    A nonprofit organization that provides visual
        arts education to children through parent
        volunteers, professional development
        for teachers, and lesson guides.
    PO Box 3416
    Albuquerque, NM 87190
    (505) 277-6495
    http://www.artintheschool.org/

Association for Supervision and
Curriculum Development
Publishes *Educational Leadership Magazine*
1703 N. Beauregard St.
Alexandria, VA 22311-1714
(800) 933-2723
http://www.ascd.org/

Be Safe
Coordinated by the Center for Health,
Environment, and Justice
PO Box 6806
Falls Church, VA 22040
(518) 732-4538
http://www.besafenet.com/
Click on "healthy schools" for an
environmental checklist for schools.

Bioneers ("Biological pioneers")
http://www.bioneers.org/

Building Design Advisor
Lawrence Berkeley National Laboratory
http://gundog.lbl.gov/

Building Green, Inc.
122 Birge St., Ste. 30
Brattleboro, VT 05301
(802) 257-7300
http://www.buildinggreen.com/

Campus Safety Magazine
http://www.campussafetymagazine.com/

Canadian Network for Environmental
Education and Communication
http://www.eecom.org/
Also visit http://www.green-street.ca

Casas de Vida Nueva
http://www.cvnfarm.org/

Center for Ecoliteracy
2528 San Pablo Ave.
Berkeley, CA 94702
http://www.ecoliteracy.org/

The Center for Holistic Resource Management
1010 Tijeras Ave. NW
Albuquerque, NM 87102
(505) 842-5252

The Ceres Network
A communications network for nontoxic agriculture
15 West Groves Ave.
Alexandria, VA 22305
(703) 739-0006

Child Proofing Our Communities
http://www.childproofing.org/

Children, Youth, and Environments
Center for Research and Design
E-mail: cye@colorado.edu
Visit http://thunder1/cudenver.edu/
cye/lla/index.htm for
Learning Landscape Initiative information.

Classroom Acoustics
http://www.classroomacoustics.com/

The Collaborative for High Performance Schools
http://www.chps.net/

Community Playthings
http://www.communityplaythings.com/

Computer Crime and Intellectual Property Section,
U.S. Department of Justice
http://www.cybercrime.gov/

Concordia LLC
http://www.concordia.com/

Co-op America
National Green Pages Directory
http://www.coopamerica.org/pubs/greenpages/

The Council of Educational Facility Planners
International (CEFPI)
9180 E. Desert Cove, Ste. 104
Scottsdale, AZ 85260
(480) 391-0840
http://www.cefpi.org/

Design-Build Institute of America
1100 H St. NW, Ste. 500
Washington DC 20005-5476
(202) 682-0110
http://www.dbia.org/

DesignShare Awards Program
http://www.designshare.com/index.php/awards

DesignShare Online Journal
http://www.designshare.com

Earth Share
A network of nonprofit environmental
and conservation organizations
7735 Old Georgetown Rd., Ste. 900
Bethesda, MD 20814
(800) 875-3863
http://www.earthshare.org/

Ecological by Design
PO Box 842
Prescott, AZ 86302
(928) 778-9598
E-mail: ecodesign@earthlink.net

Ecological Footprint Quiz
Take this quiz to see how many Earths it would
take to support everyone with your lifestyle.
http://www.earthday.net/footprint/index.asp

EcoNet
18 De Boom St.
San Francisco, CA 94107
(415) 442-0220
E-mail: econet@igc.apc.org

Edible Schoolyard Project
http://www.edibleschoolyard.org/

Edutopia
Publication of the George Lucas
Educational Foundation
http://www.glef.org/

E Magazine
http://www.emagazine.com/

Energy Star
http://www.energystar.gov/

Environmental Design Research Association
PO Box 7146
Edmond, OK 73083-7146
(405) 330-4863
http://www.edra.org/

Environmental Working Group
http://www.ewg.org/

FBI Kids (Internet Safety Tips)
http://www.fbi.gov/kids/k5th/safety2.htm

*The Funders' Network for Smart
Growth and Livable Communities*
http://www.fundersnetwork.org/

Global Green USA
http://www.globalgreen.org/index.html

Global Universal Design Educators Online News
http://www.universaldesign.net/gudeo_news.htm

Green Building News
http://www.greenbuildingnews.com/

Greenguard Environmental Institute
http://www.greenguard.org/

Green Teacher Magazine
http://www.greenteacher.com/

HandsNet
Focuses on rural environmental,
social, and economic issues
PO Box 90477
San Jose, CA 95109
http://www.handsnet.org/

Henry A. Wallace Institute for Alternative Agriculture
9200 Edmonston Rd., Ste. 117
Greenbelt, MD 20770-1551
(301) 441-8777

Herman Miller, Inc.
Furniture
http://www.hermanmiller.com/

Holistic Management International
http://www.holisticmanagement.org/

Human Ecology Magazine
http://www.human.cornell.edu/che/Alumni/
Insider-News/HE-Magazine-PDFs.cfm

Innovative Design (on daylighting)
http://www.innovativedesign.net/guidelines

The Institute for Earth Education
(304) 832-6404
http://www.eartheducation.org/

Interior Design Society
164 S. Main St., 8th Floor
High Point, NC 27260
(888) 884-4469
http://www.interiordesignsociety.org/

Kompan Playgrounds
http://www.kompan.com/

Landscape Architecture
Magazine of the American Society
of Landscape Architects
http://www.asla.org

Landscape Architecture Foundation
818 18th St. NW, Ste. 810
Washington DC 20006
(202) 331-7070
http://www.lafoundation.org/

*Leadership in Energy and
Environmental Design (LEED)*
The LEED rating system is available from
the U.S. Green Building Council
1015 18th St. NW, Ste. 805
Washington DC 20036
http://www.usgbc.org/

LearningWorks
Furniture from StelterPartners
http://www.stelterpartners.com/

Leathers & Associates
Community-built playgrounds
http://www.leathersassociates.com/

Living Library
http://www.alivinglibrary.org/

Living Machine
Wastewater treatment and purification technology
http://www.livingmachines.com/

The Math Forum at Drexel University
Links to many sites for teaching math
through architecture, including patterns,
geometry, shapes, and the Golden Mean
http://mathforum.org/library/topics/architecture

National Center for Education Statistics (NCES)
http://www.nces.ed.gov/fastfacts

National Center for Policy Analysis
http://www.ncpa.org/

*The National Clearinghouse for
Educational Facilities (NCEF)*
1090 Vermont Ave. NW, Ste. 700
Washington DC 20005
(888) 552-0624
http://www.edfacilities.org/
High-performance green schools: http://www.
edfacilities.org/rl/high_performance.cfm
Click on "Resource Lists" for nearly one
hundred articles and links to many of
the sites listed here. Click on "Conditions
of America's Schools" and "Data and
Statistics" for the most current data.

National Educational Technology Plan
http://www.ed.gov/technology/plan

National Gardening Association
Gardening for children
http://www.kidsgardening.com/

National Institute of Building Sciences
    http://www.nibs.org/

National Priorities Project
    http://www.nationalpriorities.org/
    Visit http://www.nationalpriorities.org/costofwar_
        home to see the running tab of the Iraq war.

National Renewable Energy Laboratory
    A U.S. Department of Energy
        research organization
    http://www.nrel.gov/
    To access publications, visit http://
        www.nrel.gov/publications/

National School Boards Association
    1680 Duke St.
    Alexandria, VA 22314
    (703) 838-6722
    http://www.nsba.org/

National School Safety and Security Services
    A Cleveland, Ohio, consulting company
        specializing in school security
    http://www.schoolsecurity.org/

National Sustainable
Agriculture Information Service
    Appropriate Technology Transfer
        for Rural Areas (ATTRA)
    PO Box 3657
    Fayetteville, AR 72702
    (800) 342-9140
    http://attra.ncat.org/

National Trust for Historic Preservation
    Center for Preservation Leadership
    1785 Massachusetts Ave. NW
    Washington DC 20036-2117
    (800) 944-6847
    http://www.preservationnation.org/

National Wildlife Federation (NWF)
    Contact the NWF for packets and information
        on setting up schoolyard habitats.
    http://www.nwf.org/schoolyard/

New Economics Foundation (NEF)
    3 Jonathan St.
    London, SE 11 5NH
    Phone: 020 7820 6300
    http://www.neweconomics.org/

The New England Asthma Regional Council
    http://www.asthmaregionalcouncil.org/

New Scientist Magazine
    http://www.newscientist.com/home.ns

No Child Left Behind
    http://www.ed.gov/nclb/landing.jhtml

Noise Pollution Clearinghouse
    http://www.nonoise.org/

North American Association for
Environmental Education
    http://www.naaee.org/

Oikos
    Information on sustainable design and an
        extensive green product directory
    http://www.oikos.com

PLAYCE: The International
Association of Architecture Education
    An international association of architecture
        and education professionals founded
        after workshops were held at the Alvar
        Aalto Academy in Finland. The group
        raises awareness of spaces and places
        through international workshops,
        projects, articles, and more.
    http://www.playce.org/

PolyVision Corporation
    Office provisioning, interactive whiteboards,
        and scheduling technology
    http://www.polyvision.com/

Project Wild
Council for Environmental Education
5555 Morningside Dr., Ste. 212
Houston, TX 77005
(713) 520-1936
E-mail: info@projectwild.org
http://www.projectwild.org/

Ready America
http://www.ready.gov/

Reggio Children and Reggio Emilia Schools
http://www.reggiochildren.it

Regional Educational Technology Assistance (RETA)
College of Extended Learning, New
Mexico State University
http://reta.nmsu.edu/

Root Production Method (RPM)
Forrest Keeling Nursery
http://www.fknursery.com/

Ross Global Academy
http://www.rossglobalacademy.org/

The Rural School and Community Trust
http://www.ruraledu.org/

School Construction News
http://www.schoolconstructionnews.com/

SchoolDesigner
A resource created to elevate the level of
school design. Visit the site to read
its free monthly newsletter.
http://www.schooldesigner.com/

School Design Research Studio
http://schoolstudio.engr.wisc.edu/
smalllearningcom.html

SchoolDesigns
http://www.schooldesigns.com/

Security on Campus, Inc.
http://www.campussafety.com/

Seventh Generation Systems, Inc.
Jim Sackett, project developer
650 Mullis St., Ste. 201
Friday Harbor, WA 98250
http://www.sevengensys.com

SmartSlab
http://www.smartslab.co.uk/

Society for Environmental Graphic Design
http://www.segd.org/

Solar Living Institute
13771 S. Hwy. 101
PO Box 836
Hopland, CA 95449
(707) 744-2107
http://www.solarliving.org/

SoundPlay
Makers of musical landscapes
http://www.soundplay.com/

Steelcase, Inc.
Furniture and office systems
http://www.steelcase.com/na/

Sustainable Building Industry Council (SBIC)
http://www.sbicouncil.org/

Taliesin West, The Frank Lloyd Wright School of Architecture
http://www.taliesin.edu/

Tensegrity
http://tensegrity.com/

Thomas Jefferson Center for Educational Design, University of Virginia
http://www.virginia.edu/

TimberForm and PipeLine
Playground equipment and
outdoor fitness systems
E-mail: info@timberform.com
http://www.timberform.com/

*Union Internationale des Architectes
(International Union of Architects)*
A global network dedicated to the architectural profession
http://www.uia-architectes.org/

U.S. Consumer Product Safety Commission
http://www.cpsc.gov
Handbook for Public Playground Safety: http://www.
cpsc.gov/CPSCPUB/PUBS/325.pdf

U.S. Department of Justice
http://www.usdoj.gov/

U.S. Environmental Protection Agency
http://www.epa.gov/

U.S. General Accounting Office
http://www.gao.gov/

U.S. Green Building Council (USGBC)
http://www.usgbc.org/

VS America, Inc.
Adjustable, adaptable furniture that promotes movement
E-mail: info@vs-furniture.com
http://www.vs-moebel.de/56.0.html?&L=1&FL=9

Whole Building Design Guide
This is a great resource for sustainable design information.
http://www.wbdg.org/

Winter & Company
Ergonomic furniture and special needs studio
http://www.winterandcompany.net

Index

The letter *c* following a page number indicates a chart on that page. Page numbers in *italic* type indicate illustrations.